GLOBAL IPV6 STRATEGIES:
FROM BUSINESS ANALYSIS TO OPERATIONAL PLANNING

Patrick Grossetete
Ciprian Popoviciu
Fred Wettling

Cisco Press

800 East 96th Street
Indianapolis, Indiana 46240 USA

Global IPv6 Strategies:

From Business Analysis to Operational Planning

Patrick Grossetete, Ciprian Popoviciu, Fred Wettling

Copyright© 2008 Cisco Systems, Inc.

Published by:

Cisco Press

800 East 96th Street

Indianapolis, IN 46240 USA

Printed in the United States of America

First Printing May 2008

Library of Congress Cataloging-in-Publication Data:

Grossetete, Patrick.

  Global IPV6 strategies : from business analysis to operational

planning / Patrick Grossetete, Ciprian Popoviciu, Fred Wettling.

       p. cm.

  ISBN 978-1-58705-343-6 (pbk.)

  1. TCP/IP (Computer network protocol) 2. Computer networks--Planning.

  3. Computer networks--Management--Case studies. I. Popoviciu, Ciprian.

  II. Wettling, Fred. III. Title.

  TK5105.585.G76 2008

  004.6'2--dc22

2008015715

ISBN-13: 978-1-58705-343-6

ISBN-10: 1-58705-343-8

Warning and Disclaimer

This book is designed to provide information about IPv6 from a market perspective and to describe adoption trends and strategies, not to cover the technology itself. Every effort has been made to make this book as complete and as accurate as possible, but no warranty or fitness is implied.

The information is provided on an "as is" basis. The authors, Cisco Press, and Cisco Systems, Inc. shall have neither liability nor responsibility to any person or entity with respect to any loss or damages arising from the information contained in this book or from the use of the discs or programs that may accompany it.

The opinions expressed in this book belong to the authors and are not necessarily those of Cisco Systems, Inc.

Trademark Acknowledgments

All terms mentioned in this book that are known to be trademarks or service marks have been appropriately capitalized. Cisco Press or Cisco Systems, Inc., cannot attest to the accuracy of this information. Use of a term in this book should not be regarded as affecting the validity of any trademark or service mark.

Corporate and Government Sales

The publisher offers excellent discounts on this book when ordered in quantity for bulk purchases or special sales, which may include electronic versions and/or custom covers and content particular to your business, training goals, marketing focus, and branding interests. For more information, please contact:

U.S. Corporate and Government Sales 1-800-382-3419 corpsales@pearsontechgroup.com

For sales outside the United States please contact:

International Sales international@pearsoned.com

Feedback Information

At Cisco Press, our goal is to create in-depth technical books of the highest quality and value. Each book is crafted with care and precision, undergoing rigorous development that involves the unique expertise of members from the professional technical community.

Readers' feedback is a natural continuation of this process. If you have any comments regarding how we could improve the quality of this book, or otherwise alter it to better suit your needs, you can contact us through e-mail at feedback@ciscopress.com. Please make sure to include the book title and ISBN in your message.

We greatly appreciate your assistance.

Publisher   Paul Boger   **Associate Publisher**   David Dusthimer

Cisco Press Program Manager   Jeff Brady   **Managing Editor**   Patrick Kanouse

Development Editor   Deadline Driven Publishing   **Project Editor**   Mandie Frank

Copy Editor   Bill McManus

Editorial Assistant   Vanessa Evans

Technical Editors   Larry Boucher, Anthony Tull, Dave West

Book and Cover Designer   Louisa Adair

Composition   Octal Publishing, Inc.

Indexer   WordWise Publishing Services, LLC

Proofreader   Leslie Joseph

Americas Headquarters	Asia Pacific Headquarters	Europe Headquarters
Cisco Systems, Inc.	Cisco Systems, Inc.	Cisco Systems International BV
170 West Tasman Drive	168 Robinson Road	Haarlerbergpark
San Jose, CA 95134-1706	#28-01 Capital Tower	Haarlerbergweg 13-19
USA	Singapore 068912	1101 CH Amsterdam
www.cisco.com	www.cisco.com	The Netherlands
Tel: 408 526-4000	Tel: +65 6317 7777	www-europe.cisco.com
800 553-NETS (6387)	Fax: +65 6317 7799	Tel: +31 0 800 020 0791
Fax: 408 527-0883		Fax: +31 0 20 357 1100

Cisco has more than 200 offices worldwide. Addresses, phone numbers, and fax numbers are listed on the Cisco Website at **www.cisco.com/go/offices.**

©2007 Cisco Systems, Inc. All rights reserved. CCVP, the Cisco logo, and the Cisco Square Bridge logo are trademarks of Cisco Systems, Inc.; Changing the Way We Work, Live, Play, and Learn is a service mark of Cisco Systems, Inc.; and Access Registrar, Aironet, BPX, Catalyst, CCDA, CCDP, CCIE, CCIP, CCNA, CCNP, CCSP, Cisco, the Cisco Certified Internetwork Expert logo, Cisco IOS, Cisco Press, Cisco Systems, Cisco Systems Capital, the Cisco Systems logo, Cisco Unity, Enterprise/Solver, EtherChannel, EtherFast, EtherSwitch, Fast Step, Follow Me Browsing, FormShare, GigaDrive, GigaStack, HomeLink, Internet Quotient, IOS, IP/TV, iQ Expertise, the iQ logo, iQ Net Readiness Scorecard, iQuick Study, LightStream, Linksys, MeetingPlace, MGX, Networking Academy, Network Registrar, Packet, PIX, ProConnect, RateMUX, ScriptShare, SlideCast, SMARTnet, StackWise, The Fastest Way to Increase Your Internet Quotient, and TransPath are registered trademarks of Cisco Systems, Inc. and/or its affiliates in the United States and certain other countries.

All other trademarks mentioned in this document or Website are the property of their respective owners. The use of the word partner does not imply a partnership relationship between Cisco and any other company. (0609R)

About the Authors

Patrick Grossetete, manager of product management at Cisco, is responsible for a suite of Cisco IOS software technologies, including IPv6 and IP Mobility. He manages Cisco participation in the IPv6 Forum and is a regular speaker at conferences and industry events. Patrick is coauthor of *Deploying IPv6 Networks* (Cisco Press). In June 2003, he received the "IPv6 Forum Internet Pioneer Award" at the San Diego summit. Patrick joined Cisco in 1994 as a consulting engineer. Before joining Cisco, Patrick worked at Digital Equipment Corporation as a consulting engineer and was involved with network design and deployment. He received a degree in computer science from the Control Data Institute, Paris, France.

Ciprian Popoviciu, PhD, CCIE No. 4499, is a technical leader at Cisco Systems with more than ten years of experience in data and Voice over IP communications technologies. As part of the Cisco Network Solution Integration Test Engineering (NSITE) organization, he focuses on the architecture, design, and validation of large IPv6 network deployments in direct collaboration with service providers and enterprises worldwide. Ciprian is a regular speaker or chair at conferences and industry events and contributes to various technology publications. He is an active contributor to the IETF standards, a senior member of IEEE, a member of several academic advisory boards, and a coauthor of *Deploying IPv6 Networks* (Cisco Press). Ciprian holds a BS from Babes-Bolyai University, Romania, and an MS and Ph.D. from the University of Miami.

Fred Wettling manages architecture and strategic planning for Bechtel Corporation, one of the world's premier engineering, construction, and project management companies. Fred is one of 20 Bechtel Fellows out of a population of 40,000. He has extensive experience in project and office startups, major technology transitions, innovations, and technology operations at 20+ Bechtel projects and offices. Fred is active within and outside of Bechtel promoting standards-based technology interoperability that supports global enterprise business needs. Fred is a member of the IEEE, North American IPv6 Task Force, and IPv6 Forum, and is executive director of the IPv6 Business Council. He served as the Network Applications Consortium (NAC) chairman for five years. Fred was selected as one of the 50 most powerful people in networking by *Network World* from 2003 to 2006. He is a senior member of the Cisco Enterprise and Federal Technical Advisory Boards and served on the President's National Security Telecommunications Advisory Committee (NSTAC) Next Generation Network Task Force as a subject matter expert.

About the Technical Reviewers

Larry Boucher is founder, president, and chief executive officer of Alacritech. His technical and business accomplishments include establishing and building three successful start-up companies and authoring an industry-standard technical specification. He is a recognized leader in the areas of server adapter, storage, and networking technologies. Larry received his MS in electrical engineering from the University of California, Berkeley, and his BS in business administration and his MBA from San Jose State University. Larry lives in Silicon Valley with his wife of over 40 years and has two daughters.

Anthony Tull is the information technology director for the City of Granbury, Texas. Prior to working for the city, he was the manger of consulting for SysTech Consultants for 7 years and specialized in large ERP implementations. Anthony spent 13 years with the Bechtel Corporation working on numerous engineering and technology projects. Anthony has been featured in the *Wall Street Journal*, *Washington Post*, and Muniwireless.com for his groundbreaking work in the municipal wireless field. His department owns and manages one of the first successful municipal wireless systems in the United States. Anthony holds certifications from Microsoft, Oracle, PeopleSoft, ADP, BMC, and Computer Associates and is also a certified firefighter/EMT.

Dave West oversees the Cisco Federal Center of Excellence, which is responsible for delivering Commercial Off-the-Shelf (COTS) products and solutions tailored to meet federal requirements. In this role, Dave identifies technical and competitive trends and then works across several functions to develop and execute strategic initiatives that deliver the right architectures and solutions to the market. In addition, Dave chairs the Cisco IPv6 Global Task Force, focusing on product and service readiness, solution integration, and transition tools.

Previously, Dave was senior manager, Systems Engineering, for the Cisco Department of Defense (DoD) Operation. He was responsible for DoD systems engineers and managers worldwide who provide presales engineering support to both partners and customers.

Dave has held a variety of other positions at Cisco, including senior manager, Advanced Technologies, responsible for voice, security, optical, and wireless engineering and presales support for federal customers and partners worldwide; senior manager, Systems Engineering, in support of National Programs and Intelligence; and systems engineering manager, worldwide support for the Navy and Marine Corps. An eight-year Cisco employee, Dave is a former marine officer and is a graduate of the Virginia Military Institute. He holds an MS in information systems from the Naval Postgraduate School.

Dedications

Patrick dedicates this book to Veronique.
Ciprian dedicates this book and the big hill to Nicole and Simon.
Fred dedicates this book to Susan.

Acknowledgments

The authors would like to acknowledge the invaluable contribution to this book of those who helped shape the case studies: Roland Acra, Alain Durand, Wesley George, Lionel Hoffmann, Craig Huegen, Dimitrios Kalogeras, Tammy Kapec, Robert LeBlanc, Anne-Marie Legoff, Athanassios Liakopoulos, Shin Miyakawa, Yves Poppe, Raju Ragahavan, Yurie Rich, Tim Schmidt, Kevin Shatzkamer, and Wen Wang. Together with their respective teams they diligently worked with us to provide a business and technical perspective about their IPv6 vision and experience.

We want to thank our reviewers, Larry Boucher, Tony Tull, and Dave West, for their insightful comments and valuable suggestions.

A big "thank you" goes out to the publishing team for this book. David Dusthimer, Chuck Toporek, Ginny Munroe, Dayna Isley, Romny French, and Bill McManus have been incredibly professional and a pleasure to work with.

Last, but not least, the authors acknowledge the great support received from their respective organizations and teams and from the IPv6 community at large. Enthusiasm and passion leads to great accomplishments.

This Book Is Safari Enabled

The Safari® Enabled icon on the cover of your favorite technology book means the book is available through Safari Bookshelf. When you buy this book, you get free access to the online edition for 45 days.

Safari Bookshelf is an electronic reference library that lets you easily search thousands of technical books, find code samples, download chapters, and access technical information whenever and wherever you need it.

To gain 45-day Safari Enabled access to this book:

- Go to http://www.ciscopress.com/safarienabled.
- Complete the brief registration form.
- Enter the coupon code JPBI-FJYB-9REK-2CBD-Z65I.

If you have difficulty registering on Safari Bookshelf or accessing the online edition, please e-mail customer-service@safaribooksonline.com.

Contents at a Glance

Contents

Foreword

Thirty years ago, when the original team of engineers started to design the Internet technology, none of them could have imagined that this technology eventually would be widely used not only in universities and laboratories but also in enterprises and residences all over the world.

IPv6—Internet Protocol version 6—is the key word. Remarkably, without knowing that the Internet would become so ubiquitous, these engineers designed IPv4, the first widely deployed version of the TCP/IP network layer, in such a way that it has been able to support the tremendous growth of the Internet to date. However, public IPv4 address space is becoming increasingly scarce as heavily populated countries such as India and China and market places such as the cellular phone market converge to IP. The solution is IPv6.

IPv6 adoption represents the necessary step to prepare for the future Internet, addressing the gap between increasing resource needs and available technology to meet the demand. A useful analogy is the transition from old local analog telephone systems and dialing plans to the international telephone numbering system used today. More digits were added and communications infrastructures were overhauled over time resulting in improved global access and new telephony markets based on common standards. The basic protocols used for Internet communications are going through a similar transformation that will have a much more significant impact on the ways the world communicates.

IPv6 offers a larger address space that can handle the spectacular growth in the adoption of the Internet and Internet-based technologies worldwide. If you are not convinced that IPv6 represents the future of the Internet, consider that recent versions of computer operating systems such as Apple Mac OS 10.5 Leopard, Microsoft Windows Vista, and Windows Server 2008 have IPv6 set up as the default. These operating systems are ready for the next generation, IPv6-enabled Internet.

NOTE   It is important to consider the Internet in its globality. The continued rapid evolution of the Internet and products and services connected it is creating challenges of the largest update ever attempted to a business infrastructure.

Many books about IPv6 technology have already been published, but this is the first that is intended specifically for people like you who determine the future IT strategies of organizations. Although you may not need to understand every detail of computer and communication technologies to make your decisions, you do need to understand the impact of technologies that are important for the future of your organization, one of which is IPv6.

The authors of this book have been friends of mine for many years, especially Patrick. We at NTT are the most advanced IPv6 adopters in the world; Patrick has been working with us to develop our network worldwide. Therefore, I'm confident that this is the best author team not only to explain the details of this technology, but also to make other people understand why this technology is so important.

We look forward to seeing many "decision makers" read this book and ask their IT partners (ISPs, vendors, and system integrators) to install this new key technology, IPv6, in their network environments. I believe that will help the organization grow more toward the future.

Shin Miyakawa, PhD
Director, IPv6 Team, Network Project
Innovative IP Architecture Center
NTT Communications Corporation

Introduction

The continued evolution and operation of the Internet as a truly global asset faces multiple challenges: impending exhaustion of the global IPv4 address space, new operating systems and applications, next generation infrastructures, and demand for always-on connectivity for a growing variety of devices. The requirements of a new Internet, the pressure generated by the lack of resources for the existing one, and government mandates are just a few drivers for the soaring interest in IPv6 and the demand for information related to the protocol. The technological aspects of the next generation Internet protocol have been diligently covered through a wide range of publications. Considering, the potential implications of early versus late IPv6 adoption, there is significant interest in information related to adoption strategies, to business perspectives on IPv6 use, and to concrete experiences.

The global impact of a technology or a set of technologies on the larger population and the society as a whole can truly be evaluated years after its creation when enough data has been accumulated for a proper analysis. As an example, the unprecedented, wide range of advances made in all domains of life (arts, education, politics, philosophy, literature, and science) during the Renaissance period, one of the most prolific periods in human history, can be traced to the adoption of one technology: printing. Gutenberg's invention increased the amount of documented knowledge and information by reducing the costs of capturing it. More importantly, printing dramatically increased accessibility to knowledge and information by reducing the replication costs. One technology enabled human civilization to build its knowledge base and to tap into a significantly larger pool of talent. These scaled-up resources were the information and communication infrastructure that enabled innovations in all aspects of human life.

In itself, the "moveable type" technology, as Gutenberg called it, was not the prize but just the enabler. Gutenberg's enterprise defaulted shortly after a promising start but it enabled an information revolution that was the catalyst of many other revolutions. The often drawn parallel between the discovery and history of printing and that of the Internet highlights the same characteristic. The Internet represents the enabler of today's information revolution, changing the way we live, play, learn, and work.

A close evaluation of the two information revolutions highlights a very important difference. The printing-based revolution was to a certain extent asymmetric—it somewhat reduced the cost of producing content while it vastly reduced the cost of accessing content. This paradigm was further supported and expanded in scope through other media means such as radio and television. Although in its initial implementation stages the Internet appeared to do the same thing, as it matured, it enabled a more symmetric information revolution by dramatically decreasing the costs of producing content. The Internet is reducing the costs of producing and consuming information, and bringing together enough users to create an audience for any niche content. In addition, the Internet is providing its users with ubiquitous global access to information, removing the distance and time barriers faced in the past. The Internet has laid the foundation for a new and different information revolution. While traditional media such as newspaper, radio, and television cater to the mainstream, the Internet addresses new audiences and enables new means of communications and new business models.

It is important to make a clear distinction between the Internet and the applications that run over it. These applications are apparent to most of its users and are the true measure of the economic and societal impact of the Internet. With the exception of technologists, however, the terms Internet (infrastructure) and World Wide Web (application) are for most people interchangeable. While like many other technologies such as railroads, automobiles, and radio, the Internet inspired its own economic bubble, it survives, continues to grow, and provides the environment for truly valuable applications and services. This infrastructure and its evolution is the focus of this book despite the necessary references to its uses.

From its initial deployment as a research network to its current state, the Internet as an infrastructure has seen the functionality of the devices, applications, and services deployed on it grow in direct relation to its capabilities, capacity, and scale:

- **Higher speeds:** The Internet is leveraging newer technologies providing wired or wireless access with ever-increasing bandwidths and lower costs.

- **Larger footprint:** The "network of networks," as the Internet is known, continues to expand its geographical coverage and to include more and more businesses and people.
- **Including more device types:** The Internet evolved from interconnecting large mainframes with dumb terminals to connecting personal computers, mobile phones, and sensors.
- **Always-on connectivity:** Ubiquitous in nature, the Internet enables its users to communicate continuously regardless of their point of attachment.

To support Web 2.0, which encompasses the latest set of Internet-based applications and services, the infrastructure continues to evolve through the so-called Next Generation Networks. Web 2.0 is finally taking advantage of the Internet's true potential and distances by its immediate "people-to-people" collaborative environment from the technologies that expanded the information revolution started by printing. Web 2.0 is starting the next information revolution, and for that it requires an ever-increasing user base, individually addressable users, and symmetric (similar upstream and downstream bandwidth), always-on, mobile connections. Will the technology be able to cope with these demands?

Although today nobody could envisage a world without Internet connectivity, the original design of the Internet Protocol, the foundation of this infrastructure, did not foresee this level of adoption. IP simply does not have the resources to connect today's earth population let alone to support its growth over the coming years. Moreover, in an attempt to conserve resources, the Internet today lost the symmetry of its original brilliant design. This is why the time is high for a new version of the Internet Protocol, known as IPv6, a necessary evolution for this mature technology.

As is the case with any foundational, infrastructure technology, the importance and economic impact of this evolution might be difficult to measure. Although the upgrade is an inevitable process, misunderstanding its importance and delaying its planning and adoption can have a significant impact at micro- and macroeconomic levels. This is particularly the case with infrastructure technologies that benefit from very little attention from a market driven mostly by short-term delivery. The right perspective on the evolution of the infrastructure needs to be bootstrapped by strategic, global, and visionary thinking. On January

16, 2003, the National Infrastructure Advisory Council (NIAC) was presented an IPv6 strawman proposal by John Chambers, who at the time was one of its members. In his letter to the council, Chambers stated:

> We believe the United States needs a migration strategy built on a solid investigation of the issues surrounding IPv6 adoption, and therefore propose that the United States National Infrastructure Advisory Council (NIAC) recommend that the President establish a Task Force on IPv6 to develop a national policy on its adoption. Such a policy should cover the U.S. Federal government and the critical infrastructure industry sectors.

Despite weak market interest in IPv6 at that time, NIAC's catalytic initiative was followed by coordinated government efforts, highlighted by the 2003 DoD and the 2005 Office of Management and Budget (OMB) IPv6 mandates. These efforts led to increased IPv6 interest within the United States and helped reverse its falling behind other nations in terms of understanding and adopting the new protocol.

The goal of this book is to provide a global overview of the strategies that developed around the IPv6 adoption and the perspectives taken on it within various markets. Although several sections briefly cover some technical aspects of the protocol, the objective of the book is to complement the technological viewpoint offered by a growing number of publications in the market with a business perspective. IPv6 adoption drivers and trends are reviewed at international, national, and business levels and some of the practical lessons learned are shared through concrete case studies. It turns out that a smooth and optimal integration of IPv6 depends as much on a good adoption strategy as it depends on understanding the technology.

Goals and Methods

This book intends to provide a business perspective on IPv6 and its adoption, complementing the many technical IPv6 titles available today. It also intends to provide the readers with some of the "whys" and the "whens" applied to IPv6 strategies and some of the "hows" discovered through implementation experience by various organizations, countries, and market segments around the world. If the clamor of IPv6 has reached your desk and you simply want to understand what the big deal is, this book will bring you up to speed.

To that end, the book will present you information that answers the following questions:

- In a nutshell, what are the real technical benefits of IPv6?
- What are some of the business and technical opportunities presented by IPv6?
- What IPv6 adoption strategies have emerged in various markets and throughout the world?
- What did other organizations do to adopt IPv6?
- How do I prepare my organization for IPv6?

The book combines market analysis and case study methods to provide the current state of IPv6 adoption. It also provides practical guidelines based on the extensive IPv6 planning and deployment experience of the authors.

Who Should Read This Book?

In the experience of the authors, the big questions of "Why IPv6?" "When IPv6?" and "How IPv6?" are, in various forms and at various levels of intensity, on the minds of all people who are connected with the IT-related aspects of their organizations. These questions still bother the (by now IPv6 savvy) networking specialist as well as the CIOs who start to see IPv6 sneak in among the usual hot topics of VoIP and security. Regardless of their level of familiarity with the protocol, technical and business professionals alike want to understand what drives the IPv6 adoption and to see concrete examples of IPv6 strategies.

This book should be read by IT professionals, by IT department managers, by senior managers, and by executives of all organizations leveraging an IP infrastructure. It should also be of interest to people in academia and to government officials who work on IT-related, government initiatives.

How This Book Is Organized

The structure of the book was developed to start with the larger context of the economic and business importance of IP communications and to gradually focus on the various aspects of the IP upgrade. One chapter is dedicated to debunking some of the common IPv6 technology myths in order to set a realistic baseline for the discussion. The review of perspectives on IPv6 is paired with examples of developed and implemented adoption strategies. The final chapter provides IPv6 integration planning tips gleaned from the lessons learned by organizations that went through the process.

The six chapters of this book cover the following topics:

- **Chapter 1, "The Business and Economic Importance of IP Communications:"** This chapter reviews the importance of the Internet in today's economy. It explains why the Internet infrastructure became a strategic asset for nations, enterprises, and service providers. It also reviews the market trends toward an IP convergence that leads to rapid growth of the overall Internet infrastructure and drives the need for an evolution of the Internet protocol.

- **Chapter 2, "IPv4 or IPv6—Myths and Realities:"** This chapter discusses the original case for developing IPv6 as presented by the Internet Engineering Task Force (IETF). It provides additional arguments in support of developing a new version of IP based on protocol adoption trends and statistics such as the growing world population. The discussion focuses on some technical aspects of the protocol by reviewing the most popular and notorious IPv4-IPv6 myths that you may encounter regularly in the press and open forums.

- **Chapter 3, "The Economy of an IP Evolution:"** This chapter takes a closer look at the constraints presented by an IPv4 infrastructure to national economies and individual businesses. By eliminating these constraints, an IP upgrade opens a set of new opportunities that are less apparent drivers for IPv6 adoption. This chapter presents a more realistic perspective on adoption drivers, a perspective that takes into consideration the foundational nature of the technology considered and departs from the simplistic ROI-based approach.

- **Chapter 4, "IPv6 Adoption Strategies:"** This chapter maps some of the adoption drivers analyzed in Chapter 3 to IPv6 adoption strategies that emerged at the beginning of the 21st century. Both "national" and "business" strategies are analyzed independently in a structure that matches that of Chapter 3. Along with the descriptions of strategies, this chapter presents some of the adoption challenges faced by the industry.

- **Chapter 5, "Analysis of Business Cases for IPv6: Case Studies:"** This chapter is the core of this book, emphasizing its focus on providing practical information that can be applied in developing IPv6 adoption strategies. The chapter builds on the analysis offered in Chapter 4 by offering concrete, real-life examples of IPv6 strategies developed by various organizations in various markets. The case studies highlight the profile of the organizations in order to help the reader to put the strategies in the proper context and to be able to relate to the environments described. The case studies present the perspective that these organizations have on IPv6 and the drivers they identified for developing the IPv6 strategy. Planning and implementation suggestions and challenges are also discussed.

- **Chapter 6, "Planning Your IPv6 Migration:"** As a corollary to the case studies, this final chapter reviews key aspects related to IPv6 planning. It steers away from technology discussions, a topic covered extensively in other books, and focuses on mandatory steps an organization has to take toward a successful and cost-effective deployment of IPv6. There is a lot more to consider in building an IPv6 strategy than the technology itself. This chapter summarizes the experiences gained to date with respect to this process.

Where to Go from Here

Although the industry has reached consensus regarding the inevitability of an IP upgrade, the time to start on that path is largely dependent on the market an organization belongs to, on its long-term vision, and on the national and international environment in which it operates. The timing of an IPv6 adoption is ultimately similar to that of adopting other technologies. It is the result of balancing the benefits and expenses of being an early adopter with the risks of being a late adopter. The important thing in the case of IPv6 is to realize that it is a foundational technology and the benefits or risks of adoption, although potentially significant, might be less apparent. This aspect of IPv6 and its adoption has been made clear by the complex market perception of and approach to the topic.

At the end of this book, if you feel better positioned to confidently define an IPv6 strategy for your organization or you are better informed to understand the reasoning behind IPv6-focused policies enforced within your organization, then this book has achieved its goals. The authors intend to bridge the gap between the technology and the business dimensions of IPv6 to shed some light on a technological evolution with potentially revolutionary business outcomes.

So what's next? A reader with a taste for technology can follow up with books focused on the protocol and its deployment such as *Deploying IPv6 Networks* by Cisco Press. Most importantly, you can analyze your organization's IPv6 requirements and apply some of the lessons learned here to the development of an IPv6 strategy that ensures its efficient, cost effective, and timely integration in the existing or next generation IP infrastructure.

CHAPTER 1

The Business and Economic Importance of IP Communications

If there is one concept that embodies today's idea of the most complete information, the quickest access to the source of that information, and the movement of information, it is without a doubt the Internet. Its attraction to people of all ages, all social backgrounds, and from all parts of the world resides in its ability to be everything for everyone. The Internet's heterogeneous structure enables it to be a source of information, a source of entertainment, and a tool for business enhancement, growth, and development. Children and grandparents, workers, and CEOs are familiar with this concept and they all draw value from it in their own ways.

It is impossible to ignore the Internet's importance in our lives; at one level or another, and given its influence, it is impossible not to sense its business and economic impact. But, to capture all the things we often involuntarily wrap inside the single term "Internet," to get a better sense of its full value, we need to talk about its foundation, the Internet Protocol (IP) and IP communications in general.

The Internet has become the global fabric of business and personal communications. It has spawned new paradigms in the ways that people, devices, and information are connected and interact. So we thought it was worth taking the time to briefly review IP's multifaceted presence in our lives and its business and economic values.

As a decision maker, you are probably fully aware of IP's value to your business and your personal life, so you will relate closely to some of the examples presented throughout the book. Hopefully, the other examples will help you put IP into a larger perspective, help you see new opportunities for your organization, and help you better understand the need to continue to sustain IP's adoption and growth. A lot depends on IP networks and a lot can still be achieved through them.

The Internet Today

In 2005, a team of ten climbers were sitting in Plaza de Argentina, one of Mount Aconcagua's base camps, trying to come up with a good team name before the climb. The team consisted of a mixed group of people with various backgrounds and interests, yet all seemed to refer to "googling this" and "googling that," so the name of the expedition ended up being "Google, where everyone finds what they are looking for." The name captured the essence of the group and the essence of the times we live in, where the Internet and the services it enables provides a foundation for communication. If we are to be precise, we must highlight the fact that the Internet cannot, however, be equated to one of its search engines alone; this is just another minor misnomer, typical in the case of popular technologies. The Internet is much more than a search engine, and even in the middle of nowhere, the Internet and its various manifestations are a major element in our thoughts and our vocabulary.

Originally, the Internet was just a set of interconnected networks operated and used by specialists in Birkenstocks. But the technicalities have become less relevant as the Internet has evolved into a ubiquitous mainstream infrastructure. So the concept was generalized to the point where the Internet is an environment that enables us to exchange pictures, release research papers, sell and buy products, trade stocks, speak over the phone, download our favorite music, watch last night's missed episode of a favorite TV show, or lead a fantasy life in a virtual world.

A 2006 PEW Internet Report on the U.S. market (find it at http://www.pewinternet.org/pdfs/PIP_Internet_Impact.pdf) states that "Internet penetration has now reached 73 percent for all American adults. Internet users note big improvements in their ability to shop and the way they pursue hobbies and personal interests online." The report shows a few examples of how the Internet has been greatly improving many aspects of life for a growing number of people:

- **Shopping online:** Between 2001 and 2006, the share of Americans who say the Internet has greatly improved their ability to shop has doubled from 16 to 32 percent.

- **Pursuing hobbies:** Between 2001 and 2006, the share of Americans who say the Internet has greatly improved the way they pursue hobbies and interests has grown from 20 to 33 percent.

- **Working better:** Between 2001 and 2006, the share of Americans who say the Internet has greatly improved the ability to do their jobs has grown from 24 to 35 percent.

- **Obtaining health-care information:** Between 2001 and 2006, the share of online Americans who say the Internet has greatly improved the way they get information about healthcare has grown from 17 to 20 percent.

Alignment of several characteristics makes the Internet what it is today and what it will become in the future. These characteristics include:

- **Value through distributed innovation:** New ideas, products, and services have spawned rapid growth ever since the Internet first started gaining popularity. Almost-instant global communications enable new ideas to be shared and exploited. The rapidity of network-centric "additive innovation" has been enabled by the Internet. The fuel for innovation will continue to grow as the number of network-connected people, devices, services, and information increases. This compound growth is changing how, where, and why the global economy operates.

- **Needs-based technology evolution:** The evolution of the Internet Protocol specifications has become a broad-based and global collaborative effort. The Internet continues to mature as changes are introduced in response to implementation problems and as obstacles for deploying new innovations are removed. Diversity of participants in the standards process has contributed to the infusion of new ideas and the global adoptability of the standards.

NOTE   The original TCP/IP Internet specifications developed in the mid-1970s were basically sound, but incomplete. From the late 1970s through the mid 1980s, the stewardship of the Internet specifications moved from the Internet Control and Configuration Board (ICCB) to the Internet Research Task Force (IRTF), Internet Research Steering Group (IRSG), and Internet Engineering Task Force (IETF). In January 1992, the Internet Society (ISOC) was formed with a charter of providing an institutional home for the IETF and the Internet standards process. More information about the history of the governance of the Internet and related standards can be found at the following websites:

- http://www.isoc.org/internet/history/brief.shtml

- http://www.garykessler.net/library/ietf_hx.html

- **Transcendent nature:** Few innovations have had the broad impact across markets that the Internet has had. Commercialization to television has found a primary consumer based in the home. Midrange and high-end computers have been primarily business commodities. However, the Internet spans all major economic market sectors and has been a catalyst for explosive cross-market growth. The Internet is not dependent on a particular vendor's product, but allows the interoperability of products and services from multiple suppliers.

- **The Internet "magnet":** In the past, communication protocols were developed to efficiently serve the specific needs of the types of devices they connected, such as telephones, disk arrays, computers, industrial sensors, actuators, cameras, televisions, and alarm systems. The use of multiple protocols has made the integration of different system types and networks a challenge, requiring protocol translators, bridging devices, and parallel network security systems. IP has become a communications magnet, attracting new services and becoming the "go-to" protocol as legacy non-IP networks evolve. IP is not the most efficient protocol for all network traffic, but it does provide a solid platform for communication unification, making new levels of convergence and simplification possible. Growing ubiquity of IP-based communications is attracting new communication opportunities, such as YouTube. Voice and video over IP are now common. IP-based storage products are on the market, and industrial control networks such as PROcess FIeldBUS (PROFIBUS) are moving to IP. Wired and wireless broadband are moving to IP for converged voice, data, video, and mobility services, thereby simplifying services delivery and enabling them to offer new services. The current communications mentality is "put it in the Net."

To build on the previous point about the Internet magnet, the main characteristic of the Internet is its adaptability, its flexibility to integrate new services, new modes, and new means of communication, despite the fact that the Internet is not a perfectly polished engineering marvel. In fact, it displaced along the way many highly (one might even say overly) engineered technologies. Instead, its beauty and power come from a great capability to evolve through distributed innovation and progressive collaborative development of the Internet standards. They might not be the cleanest or the definitive solutions, but they get the job done. After all, perfectly engineered solutions take too much time to satisfy pressing, heterogeneous demands, and their wide spectrum of beneficiaries will likely not appreciate the sophistication of such solutions.

A melting pot of users is best served by a melting pot of environments. The Internet today is a mixed bag of networks built to address specific needs such as data exchange within businesses, collaboration and communications, industrial processes, and telephony services. These networks are connected in a global infrastructure that provides the general population with access to sources of information, content, and applications. The one thing that ties all these evolving parts together is the Internet Protocol.

If you stop for a moment and think of all the services offered to you by the Internet today, of all its services that you depend on and could not imagine your daily life without, you probably do not want to contemplate too long the fact that IP is a best-effort protocol or that, unlike the old mechanical telephony switches designed to operate even if a bullet was shot through them, many of the devices that switch IP traffic today would break if dropped to the floor? Scary, isn't it?

In reality, part of IP's strength comes from its intrinsic design to operate in less than perfect conditions. IP-based infrastructures make it easy to multiplex services at the transport level, leaving the reliability concerns to upper layers for those applications that demand it. The distributed nature of IP networks enables them to better withstand incidents. During the tragic events of September 11, 2001, the collapse of the World Trade Center towers destroyed an entire central office (CO) switching infrastructure, taking down telephony service in the area. The telephony equipment hosted by the CO is expensive and takes a long time to replace. In contrast to the circuit-based infrastructure of traditional telephony, Voice over IP (VoIP) service operates over IP networks, which, due to their best-effort nature, can be built quickly and inexpensively.

High resiliency in the IP world is reserved for the high-end core network routers, while most routers are less hardware resilient but also significantly less expensive. IP networks, however, collectively adapt to failures due to the multiple paths available in the system; availability and survivability can be provided through proper network design. This is a powerful characteristic of IP environments. Moreover, by being less expensive, IP networks can be quickly rebuilt should they be affected by a large-scale disaster. Cisco service teams were able to quickly install a VoIP infrastructure in the affected areas of New York to restore communication service for emergency teams. These types of events lend tremendous support to the Department of Defense (DOD) plans to deploy decentralized and mobile IP communications infrastructures that withstand large-scale attacks.

Internet users tend to forget, if they ever knew, that this environment that shapes our lives is becoming rather fragile. As we depend more and more on the Internet, its somewhat hodgepodge structure might become unsettling. In fact, there is an entire school of thought that believes it irrational the Internet in its current architecture works, and it believes in the need for a more formal and structured Internet to support e-commerce and business operations. One way or another, though, the Internet works and it works well. It has seen phenomenal growth over the past decades and it promises to offer more and more to its users in the years ahead.

The Internet today is more than the infrastructure it operates over, and it is more than the services it offers and the content it hosts. The Internet changed the way we live, work, learn, play, and interact with each other. It has given us a new social environment. This social environment is the great opportunity that you, the business or public service decision maker, should see in the Internet today.

IP Infrastructure: Strategic Assets

With IP networks taking on more and more responsibilities by supporting more services, it is only natural that these networks be recognized as strategic resources. This characteristic of today's IP network is independent of its scope or purpose as it has edged into all aspects of our lives. Let's look at "what-if" scenarios for a dramatic assessment of our dependence on the Internet:

- **Home:** What if your home loses IP connectivity to the Internet? Your VoIP telephones will not operate, you will not be able to check your e-mail through your PC, you will not be able to pay your bills online or order a product that just went on sale, and your child will not be able to complete research on a report due tomorrow.

- **Business:** What if your company's intranet becomes impaired or is no longer operational? The consequences depend on the type of business and can range anywhere from an employee being unable to do his job because he cannot access necessary data, to entire batches of products being lost due to lack of industrial process monitoring, to millions being lost every minute because the stock market is not functioning. The loss of online customers or of customer confidence is damaging to business. The implications are not only financial, but they can be life threatening.

NOTE   A study by Infonetics Research shows that network outages cost large U.S. enterprises an average 3.6 percent of their revenue per year; medium-sized businesses lose 1 percent of their yearly revenue due to network outages. The vertical market analysis shows the following losses in percentage of yearly revenue due to network outages: finance, 16 percent; healthcare, 4 percent; transportation/logistics, 2 percent; manufacturing, 9 percent; and retail, 5 percent. For more information on this study, read "The Costs of Enterprise Downtime: North American Vertical Markets 2005," by Rob Dearborn, Rick Napolitan, Laura Whitcomb, and Jeff Wilson. [http://www.calltower.com/pdfbin/42.pdf]

- **Internet:** What if Internet connectivity is impaired or lost? The branches of a retail store may be unable to process credit cards. You would not have connectivity for your PDA. Businesses such as Cisco and Dell that depend on the Internet for order processing will lose revenue. Businesses that depend exclusively on the Internet, such as eBay, Amazon, and Vonage, will be completely incapacitated.

NOTE   On June 9, 2005, Amazon's website was down for 41 minutes. Based on its March 31 earnings report, this time indicates an $8.8 million per hour revenue loss; the outage cost Amazon $6 million and at least 1 million upset customers.

- **National:** What if the IP infrastructure of a country is not operating or it is isolated from the rest of the world? A piece of each of the previous scenarios would be instantiated in this case. The losses to the national economy would be significant, particularly in the context of a global market. Public service would be significantly affected.

NOTE   In the study "Costs to the U.S. Economy of Information Infrastructure Failure" [http://www.usnews.com/usnews/biztech/articles/060828/28internet.htm?s_cid=rss:site1], authors M. Eric Johnson, Scott Dynes, and Eva Andrijcic estimate that the impact of a ten-day Internet outage on the automobile industry would be losses of $65.6 million, whereas a similar outage impacting the Supervisory Control and Data Acquisition (SCADA) system in oil refineries would generate losses in the range $404.76 million. The cost of one hour of stock exchange downtime is estimated to be in the $6–7 million range.

The strategic importance of the IP environments is reflected in the effort and investments put into protecting them. Home users prefer broadband access not only for its higher bandwidth but also for its "always on" characteristic. Businesses build highly redundant, highly reliable intranets. As an example, the New York Stock Exchange has parallel networks to protect against failures.

Many companies have moved from private line and Frame Relay wide-area network (WAN) services to Internet-based Virtual Private Networks (VPN). In the process, they have realized significant economic savings, have been able to increase network capacity, and have experienced improved network performance. A significant contribution to business comes from the contracts that cover the maintenance of those companies' global infrastructure. The United States continues to maintain control of the Domain Name System (DNS) infrastructure, which, in effect, implies administrative control over the global Internet. Some governments manage all gateways to the Internet in order to have full control over the information that enters or leaves the country. All these examples highlight the value placed on IP infrastructures in homes and businesses and at the national level.

If the minor service interruptions that might only annoy us temporarily are not sufficient to remind us of how critical IP infrastructures and IP devices are to us, we get from time to time more sobering reminders in the form of security threats or incidents. Such events place a clear price tag on the importance of IP in today's economy. The Infonetics Research study "The Costs of Network Security Attacks: North America 2007" [http://www.infonetics.com/cgp/login.asp?ID=27] indicates that large U.S. companies will lose 2.2 percent of their annual revenue due to IP infrastructure downtime caused by security attacks. Small and medium-sized businesses stand to lose 1 percent of their annual revenue due to the same causes.

Security threats also highlight the importance of IP networks to the well being of people. On May 3, 2004, an extortionist hacker compromised the life support systems of the National Science Foundation's Amundsen-Scott South Pole Station, threatening the lives of its residents. A possibly tragic turn of events was averted by a rapid and successful effort by the law enforcement agencies of several countries. It is not surprising that in many countries, crimes against the IP infrastructure and IP services are prosecuted by dedicated national and international law enforcement resources and are severely punished.

There is, however, much more to the strategic characteristic of the IP networks than these defensive aspects. The IP infrastructures are an essential part of all long-term plans. They support and facilitate the implementation of organizational- and national-level strategies. Businesses build IP infrastructures that enable them to

- **Converge and consolidate services:** Enterprises converge voice, video, and data services on the same infrastructure, while service providers pursue the convergence of fixed and mobile services.

- **Integrate new services:** Flexible environments enable businesses to turn on new services quickly, easily, and in a cost-effective way.

- **Expand:** Well-built networks enable businesses to easily acquire other businesses, to enter new markets, and to increase their customer base nationally and globally.

- **Acquire data:** Acquisition of plant, process, and building information facilitates the automation of industrial processes. The acquisition of medical data facilitates real-time remote diagnostics and medical services.

Governments support the development of IP infrastructures because they lead to

- **A more productive population:** Under inclement weather conditions (icy or heavy snow conditions) or under bad health conditions (epidemics), people can work from home and thus reduce the number of traffic accidents or hospital visits. Special messages can be sent to specific groups of people in quarantined areas, providing for a better response to an incident.

- **Support for environmental policies:** High-speed Internet access enables people to work from home, reducing pollution caused by commuting. IP-enabled and instrumented environments such as facilities, manufacturing plants, and transportation operate more efficiently and with lower energy consumption and pollution.

- **A better-educated population:** Schools can have better access to educational information and local or international specialists, enabling individuals to further their education through remote courses.

- **Improved health services:** Remote villages and small cities with limited resources can benefit from better medical assistance through remote consultations and rapid analysis of tests.

- **Local economic growth:** A good national IP infrastructure enables businesses to communicate better and to develop new services and business models to support them. For example, local tourism industry can grow by leveraging the Internet to advertise its offering.

- **Increased global economic presence:** National businesses get access to foreign markets to sell their products and to leverage local labor and natural resources.

Individual governments recognize the value and importance of the Internet. With this recognition comes the realization that there are challenges in managing this global and strategic resource. Nations are now working under the United Nations auspices on the future governing framework for the Internet. As described in Chapter 3," The Economy of an IP Evolution" the social, legal, and political aspects of the Internet make its governance a unique and complex task, yet its perceived importance seems to justify the resources invested in it.

Whether we look at protecting existing operational models or long-term growth, the strategic importance of IP communications and the infrastructures supporting them is undeniable. This understanding must go in all expansion, consolidation, and security plans related to this asset. In fact, one of the common trends in the IT world today is the planning and deployment of Next Generation Networks (NGN). The networks of many organizations grew in an ad hoc nature over several years, resulting in a fragmented infrastructure with unnecessary complexities. Businesses are now enabling integrated services by transitioning their IP infrastructures to reliable, high-bandwidth networks that consolidate next generation services and provide for a converged backbone. These transitions provide tremendous flexibility by virtualizing services throughout the network and providing access to IP-enabled devices that will interact with the network to extend services to consumers and businesses.

The Economies of Scale and the Growth of IP Infrastructures

Despite its incredible growth, the Internet and the many networks it comprises has yet to take full advantage of the economies of scale for the services we are familiar with at home, on the road, and at our desks in the office. The adoption of IP continues at an accelerated rate, and drives the need for an ever-increasing infrastructure that supports a large, growing user base. More interesting, however, is the fact that this growth is not capped by the world population. In fact, over the past several years, we have discovered more and more uses for IP, including new services and capabilities that are only in the initial phases of market adoption. These new services use independent, dedicated IP devices. Today, many people carry a cell phone, a laptop, and a PDA in the execution of their jobs. At home, IP has also become pervasive. We use modems for dial-up; set-top boxes to interact with digital television programming; PCs and wireless IP tablets to send e-mail, chat, or use Voice over IP to make calls across the network. Consider less apparent devices such as the Nabaztag (http://www.nabaztag.com), a Wi-Fi enabled electronic device that needs its own IP address. Overall, the number of IP devices per person is growing and it requires additional infrastructure support.

To take full advantage of the economies of scale applied to each of these service overlays, it is important to provide unfettered, simple IP connectivity to all of them. Because each device requires its own unique IP address in its original definition, IP runs into problems. IP addresses are a limited resource, a resource that did not account for the Internet's incredible success. Various solutions were developed to deal with the address space limitations, such as Network Address Translation (NAT); however, they came at a cost. Flexibility in communication symmetry (peer-to-peer services) was traded to extend the life of IPv4. With this trade-off, the deployment of innovative peer-to-peer services and applications became more complex and costly.

The IP address needs are quantitatively analyzed, based on today's view of present and future IP services, in Chapter 2, "IPv4 or IPv6—Myths and Realities." Addressing constraints in IPv4 networks threaten not only the adoption process of IP, but also its continued development. As a strategic asset to business, global governments, and consumers, IP networks must be designed for growth and innovation, which most likely means that something more than IPv4 is needed.

What Comes Next for IP Communications?

IP by itself is only the network layer that enables applications and services to communicate. Its real value is tied to the evolution of other technologies, such as:

- **Physical and network connections:** Examples include wireless technologies such as Wi-Fi (wireless fidelity), WiMAX (Worldwide Interoperability for Microwave Access), IEEE 802.15.4, 3G/4G, and 802.11p; high-speed technologies such as Packet over SONET, Gigabit Ethernet, and 10 Gigabit (and 40 and 100 Gigabit in the future) Ethernet;

and broadband access technologies such as cable (DOCSIS 3.0), FTTH (fiber to the home), VDSL (very-high-data-rate digital subscriber line), and Power Line Communications (PLC).

- **Applications:** Examples include Web 2.0, VoIP, IPTV (IP television), peer-to-peer applications, and distributed computing or GRID.

In turn, the successes of these application technologies depend on the availability of IP infrastructures and the scale of the user base. Together with IP, these technologies support the services and applications we use today.

Despite all the developments of the past decades, with today's deployments, we have barely scratched the surface of possibilities offered by IP. So let's go through the "what if" exercise again, but this time focus on the possibilities offered by the IP infrastructure and not our dependence on it. Let us call this an "imagine if" exercise and see how it plays out in the same scopes defined in our earlier discussion:

- **Home:** Imagine if your family doctor could monitor a serious health condition while you are at home and mobile. Imagine if your home and cars could be maintained, monitored, and secured over IP. Imagine if all your home appliances could be networked and remotely serviced by the manufacturer.

- **Business:** Imagine if you could open a new project site by deploying a significant number of sensors to improve security, optimize energy consumption, and optimize tracking assets. Imagine if all your field assets were unique IP hosts that could communicate between themselves directly or with the corporate resources. Imagine if you could use sensors in all your corporate buildings to reduce energy costs by at least 30 percent as presented at APRICOT 2005 workshop (http://www.apricot.net/apricot2005/slides/C3-6_1.pdf) and align your organization with progressive environmental policies. Imagine if threat or weather conditions were to stop your employees from going to the office but you could have the infrastructure to support them working from home. Imagine if you could use small IP devices to track products through the production, storage, delivery, and sale process. Imagine if you could offer converged mobile and fixed services. Imagine if the integration of the IT infrastructure of your next acquisition were just a matter of establishing connectivity between the two networks.

- **Internet:** Imagine if the $100 laptops developed by MIT could be handed out to children around the world and could be connected to sources of educational content and to remote educators. Imagine if peer-to-peer video telephony were available between homes and businesses. Imagine if telepresence were available to individuals to communicate with friends and family and not just available to businesses. Imagine if users could become more empowered as content contributors. Imagine if the Internet could accommodate all people in the world.

- **National:** Imagine if the resource and communication assets of emergency management resources could be integrated in a common and efficient framework that provided for seamless interoperability. Imagine if the use of sensors could allow us to operate our living or work environments with less energy and track and monitor pollution of natural resources. Imagine if a modern military could be made more efficient by the extensive use of sensors to track biohazards, receive and send imagery from different sources, and more seamlessly communicate and collaborate between services and coalitions to achieve peacekeeping missions. Imagine if citizens could vote and express positions on policies securely from home and government agencies could better communicate with them remotely.

You may certainly add to this list all the countless possibilities in your own environments. Most importantly, all these services and capabilities could be implemented with today's technologies if IP had enough addresses. IP's limited resources are the only obstacle in achieving its full potential. The efficient and cost-effective implementation of the scenarios imagined above requires significantly more address space than what is available in IPv4 today. An evolution of the protocol is necessary to support its tremendous adoption rate, to support the services it can offer. Chapter 2 makes a quantitative case for the next generation of IP called IP version 6 (IPv6). IPv6 offers enough addressing resources to meet the needs of the most ambitious projects, the most extensive services, and the largest infrastructures. IPv6 is a mature protocol and its integration is under way.

Summary

This chapter reminds us, if not reveals some new aspects, of IP's importance in our lives and our organizations. It presents the many aspects of IP communications that subconsciously or unknowingly we include in the now ubiquitous term "Internet." It highlights how much our business and our economy depends on reliable IP communications and how this dependence will continue to increase over time. Through a few simple examples, the IP infrastructure clearly comes across as a strategic asset that a business uses to support existent services and processes, to build new ones, to differentiate itself from competition, and to compete and operate in the global market.

In our daily lives, failures of the IP infrastructure or restrictions on its capabilities to support the worldwide economy are not any more acceptable. And we must be able to leverage IP infrastructures further to provide for more productive services. Although we are past the times when IT had to prove its costs, we still have yet to invest enough in it to leverage the economies of scale on most existent services. And then there are all those services, feasible with today's technology, that just wait for the infrastructure to support them. The demand for IP services is evident, so the only ingredient required for its growth and success is the business or economic model developed by the decision makers.

As more and more decision makers think about new business-enhancing services in the context of an IP converged world, their ideas, and the development of IP Next Generation Networks (NGN's), will demand additional resources from IP. These new ideas will stretch the capabilities of the hardware and software development community, and IP as we know it today. Some visionaries have already started to realize, as have many decision makers, that to achieve their business visions, a new version of IP, one with more address resources, is required. This chapter's review of the significant business and personal dependence on IP-based communications in our lives and economy positions us for exploring the business and economic implications of continued IP evolution.

CHAPTER 2

IPv4 or IPv6—
Myths and
Realities

The year is 1977. Earth's population has not yet reached 4.5 billion. One hundred and eleven interconnected computing machines make up the ARPANET, a research network.

Thirty years later, in 2008, Earth's population peaks at 6.6 billion and the Internet, with a population of 1.3 billion, has yet to reach 22 percent penetration rate, the threshold that qualifies it as a massively adopted technology. While arguing about the lifetime scope of the available IPv4 address space, the Internet community aggressively pursues a massive convergence of communication technologies (audio, data, video, and voice) over IP. The community is still debating the urgency of an upgrade to IPv6.

In the year 2030, Earth's population is expected to be over 8 billion, adding nearly 75 million people every year, or twice the population of the state of California. The Internet is an integral part of the worldwide economy and everybody's life. The old IPv4 versus IPv6 debate is now history.

NOTE   For more information on the history of the Internet, visit http://www.isoc.org/internet/history/brief.shtml.

Statistics related to the Earth's population and Internet adoption were collected from, respectively:

- http://www.census.gov/ipc/www/idb/worldpopinfo.html

- http://www.internetworldstats.com/stats.htm

The Business Case for IPv6

To a large degree, mass adoption of new technology is fueled by a person's vision of "What's in it for me?" Can the new technology improve my business operations? Can I use it to provide a new profitable service? Is adoption needed to stay competitive? Will the new technology enrich my personal life?

At the end of the '70s, few of the IP designers envisioned the rapid and widespread adoption of IP; IP became *the* convergence layer for communication services in many industry segments such as home, mobile wireless, transportation, media, and many others. This convergence, along with a plethora of new Internet-enabled devices, provides a fertile and unexpected foundation for innovation that far exceeds the original design constructs. Information movement is now the game, and content is king.

So is an Internet upgrade necessary to sustain the growth of the future and to interconnect all the devices of the new global economy? Will IPv6 provide the fire to fuel the growth?

Before debating the pros and cons of the new IP version, let's look at the historical perspective of IPv6 and its development.

A Brief History of IPv6 Standardization

At the end of the '80s, the Internet Engineering Task Force (IETF) began to evaluate the consequences of the Internet's growth on the protocol, with particular emphasis on addressing. The organization evaluated:

- **Address space exhaustion:** The original IPv4 addressing plan was mathematically limited to 65,536 Class B networks for the entire Internet. The assignment rate of the former Class B networks (blocks of 65,536 contiguous addresses) would lead to the exhaustion of IPv4 addresses sometime close to 1994.

- **Expanding routing tables:** The allocation of Class C (blocks of 256 contiguous IPv4 addresses) networks instead of Class B networks would lead to an alarming expansion of the routing tables in the Internet backbone routers—typically Cisco AGS+ or 7000 series.

NOTE   Readers who want to learn more about the IPv6 history should refer to IETF Request For Comments (RFC) 1752, *The Recommendation for the IP Next Generation Protocol*, http://tools.ietf.org/html/rfc1752.

In November 1991, the IETF formed the Routing and Addressing (ROAD) working group (WG) to analyze and deliver guidelines to address these issues. In March 1992, the WG provided its recommendations in two categories:

- **Immediate:** Adopt the Classless Interdomain Routing (CIDR) route aggregation to control the growth rate of routing tables and allow finer-grained allocations than previous 8-bit boundaries defined as Class A, B, and C.

IPv4 Class	CIDR Notation	IP Addresses
A	256	16,777,216
B	65,536	65,536
C	16,777,216	256

- **Long term:** Initiate a call for proposals "to form working groups to explore separate approaches for bigger Internet addresses."

At the beginning of the '90s, the use of the Open Systems Interconnection (OSI) reference model's network and transport layers was heavily promoted through the U.S. and UK Government Open Systems Interconnect Profile (GOSIP). In the end, it failed to get widely deployed due to the lack of applications running over OSI. Nevertheless, by mid-1992, the Internet Advisory Board (IAB) proposed, as an immediate solution, the use of Connectionless Network Protocol (CLNP), which would be the basis for a next generation IP, naming it IP version 7. This proposal was highly debated because OSI was not viewed favorably at the IETF. The IAB recommendation was rejected by the IETF, which called for a number of working groups to work on candidate proposals. In 1993, an IETF IP Next Generation Decision Process (ipdecide) Birds of a Feather (BoF) session set the criteria that would drive the definition of the new protocol. The end result was the creation of an Internet Protocol Next Generation (IPng) directorate that was tasked to

- Define the scope of the IPng effort, keeping in mind the time constraints

- Develop a clear and concise set of technical requirements and operational criteria for IPng

- Recommend which of the current IPng protocol candidates to accept, if any

> **NOTE** RFC 1550, *IP: Next Generation (IPng) White Paper Solicitation*, can be reviewed on the IETF website at http://tools.ietf.org/html/rfc1550.

Four parallel projects began exploring ways to address the identified consequences of the rapidly growing Internet:

- **CNAT:** Tivoli's Comprehensive Network Address Translator.
- **IP Encaps:** The proposal evolved to become IP Address Encapsulation (IPAE) and then merged with the SIP proposal.
- **Nimrod:** A proposal viewed as a research project by the Internet Engineering Steering Group (IESG).
- **Simple CLNP:** The proposal later became TCP and UDP with Bigger Addresses (TUBA).

Three additional proposals were later brought into the discussion:
- **The P Internet Protocol (PIP):** The proposal merged later with SIP and the resulting working group called itself Simple Internet Protocol Plus (SIPP).
- **Simple Internet Protocol (SIP):** The proposal evolved to become IP Address Encapsulation (IPAE) and later merged with the SIP proposal.
- **TP/IX:** The proposal was later renamed Common Architecture for the Internet (CATNIP).

> **NOTE** Projects that were fully documented received an IP version number from IANA. This explains the current allocation shown in the table on the following page.[1]

continues

---

1. Internet Assigned Number Authority (IANA), an operating unit of the Internet Corporation for Assigned Names and Numbers (ICANN), http://www.iana.org/assignments/version-numbers.

continued

Decimal	Keyword	Version	References
0–1		Reserved	[JBP] [RFC4828]
2–3		Unassigned	[JBP]
4	IP	Internet Protocol	[RFC791] [JBP]
5	ST	ST Datagram Mode	[RFC1190] [JWF]
6	IPv6	Internet Protocol version 6	[RFC1752]
7	TP/IX	TP/IX: The Next Internet	[RFC1475]
8	PIP	The P Internet Protocol	[RFC1621]
9	TUBA	TUBA	[RFC1347]
10–14		Unassigned	[JBP]
15		Reserved	[JBP]

The table answers a commonly asked question: Why IP version 6 and not 5 or 7? The table also clarifies the internationally accepted use of IPv9. This version of IP was temporarily used, without IANA approval, for a Chinese research project that intended to expand the IP address from the 32-bit IPv4 standard to 256 bits. While widely publicized as a next generation Internet, the project was shown to be limited in scope.[2]

All the work that went into these projects and the resulting mergers was finally evaluated by the IPng. Three proposals were retained: CATNIP, SIPP, and TUBA. As documented in RFC 1752:

> None of these proposals were wrong nor were others right. All of the proposals would work in some ways providing a path to overcome the obstacles we face as the Internet expands. The task of the IPng Area was to ensure that the IETF understand the offered proposals, learn from the proposals and provide a recommendation on what path best resolves the basic issues while providing the best foundation upon which to build for the future.

2. For more information, see http://www.theregister.com/2004/07/06/ipv9_hype_dismissed.

After countless discussions and reviews of the strengths and weaknesses of updated versions of the submitted proposal, the consensus of the IPng Directorate was to recommend that the protocol described in the SIPP specification, which began as 64 bits and evolved to 128 bits, addressing should be adopted as the basis for IPng, that it should be the next generation of IP, and that is should be named IP version 6. The recommendation for IPng was approved by the IESG and became a proposed standard on November 17, 1994, as RFC 1752. This new version of IP can be considered an evolutionary step rather than a revolutionary step in the development of IP. Some of the principles that guided the changes are to

- Keep all aspects and features of IPv4 that were proven to work and continued to make sense
- Remove or make optional all features of IPv4 that were infrequently used or shown to be problematic
- Add new solutions to fix existent problems or add new features that enable the protocol to address new needs

The core set of IPv6 protocols was made an IETF Draft Standard on August 10, 1998, an event that represented the green light for vendors to develop their implementations and submit their code for interoperability testing. From 1996 to 2006, the experimental 6bone (http://go6.net/ipv6-6bone/) overlay IPv6 infrastructure offered the infrastructure framework for wide interoperability tests. In 2001, IPv6 started to be integrated on commercial products such as Sun Solaris 8, Cisco IOS Release 12.2(2)T, and Juniper JUNOS 5.1. The indication that IPv6 is technologically ready was the IETF intent to close or recharter the IPv6 WG in December 2006.

Is IPv6 ready for deployment in your business? Why should the world care about IPv6 today?

Looking at the Numbers

Initially, one of the main objectives of the IPng effort was to identify ways to cope with the explosive growth of the Internet. Today, this growth continues at a faster rate, reaffirming the premise of the IPng work. Making a business case for the new protocol comes down to a review of the numbers. From a global perspective, these numbers were already described by one of the authors in the "e-Nations, The Internet for All" paper, which was endorsed by the United Nations.[3]

The Internet—an ever growing and widely popular environment for communication, information sharing, and collaboration—could simply not be promoted as a mass-market technology. In addition, the foundation of the worldwide economy would not work if the Internet's base protocol (IP) did not offer the necessary address space resources to equitably connect the population of every country around the world.

The expansion of the Internet is also tied to the rapid development and market penetration of enabling technologies such as high-speed broadband and wireless access. Many enterprises have shifted from point-to-point, ATM, and Frame Relay infrastructures to IP-based local- and wide-area networks (LAN and WAN) for basic business operations. Traditional voice carriers are migrating their voice network to IP-based transport to reduce or eliminate future capital expenditure (CAPEX) and operational expenditure (OPEX) related to redundant parallel network infrastructures. These IP-based technologies modify an application's landscape by changing the use of the Internet from a client/server model to a more distributed model or peer-to-peer model. Very rapid and successful adoption of distributed applications such as Voice over Internet (VoIP), instant messaging, content sharing, and Internet gaming leads people with "always-on" and "always-best" access to the Internet to be content producers as well as consumers. An expanded IP address space is necessary to support this paradigm change in the way the Internet is used.

Lack of IP resources can lead to an increasing digital divide between information and communications technology (ICT) rich and ICT poor countries. So let's have a look at those "numbers" that make IPv6 a "must."

Earth Population Versus Internet Users

By the end of 2007, world population reached over 6.6 billion humans[4] and a United Nations report forecasts an increase to over 8 billion by 2030. Although the

---

3. http://www.unicttaskforce.org/perl/documents.pl?id=1314.

4. Source: *The World Factbook*, Central Intelligence Agency (ISSN 1553-8133), https://www.cia.gov/library/publications/the-world-factbook/geos/xx.html#People.

Internet is deeply embedded in the worldwide economy, it reaches only one-sixth of today's population with 1.3 billion users, as shown in Figure 2-1.

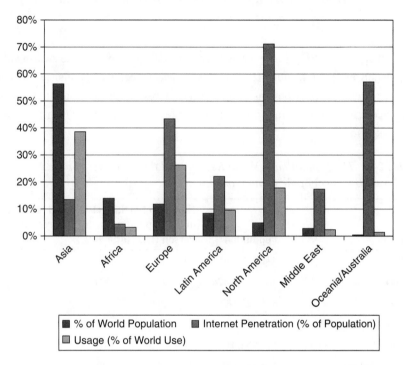

Figure 2-1 *Worldwide Internet Adoption and Population Statistics[5]*

Internet usage has seen accelerated growth across the world, particularly in emerging markets. For example, Africa, the region with the least Internet penetration, has seen the usage grow over 880 percent between 2000 and 2007. To provide equal opportunities worldwide, the Internet architecture must cope with rapid growth in consumer interest and usage. The forecast for growth leads to a new perspective on the demand for IP address space. Even without taking into consideration expected address allocation inefficiencies, IPv4's 32-bit address space is inadequate to support a plethora of connected devices owned by one-third of Earth's population.

5. http://www.internetworldstats.com.

NOTE	"The efficiency of address space use" is measured through the Host-Density (HD) ratio defined in RFC 3194 and RFC 1715.

When accounting for expected growth, 50 percent of the worldwide population ends up without IPv4 address space to connect appliances to the Internet. Table 2-1 provides an analysis of the address space necessary to achieve 20 percent Internet penetration in each world region (expected growth has been accounted for).

Table 2-1   *The Population of World Regions and the IP Address Space Needed to Cover 20 Percent of the Population*

Region	Population	Number of /8 Subnets Needed for 20% of the Population with 1 Address per Person (HD Ratio 90%)
Africa	941,249,130	93
Asia	3,733,783,474	431
Europe	801,821,187	78
Latin America/Caribbean	569,133,474	53
Middle East	192,755,045	16
North America	334,659,631	30
Oceania/Australia	33,569,718	2
World	6,606,971,659	808

NOTE	An HD ratio of 90 percent implies a very good utilization of the addressing resources.

As Table 2-1 indicates, as of February 2008, the world requires 808 IPv4 /8 subnets, more than twice the possible 256 /8 subnets, for the Internet to be considered a massively adopted technology. The IPv4 address space clearly cannot sustain the Internet's penetration worldwide.

NOTE	The number of /8 networks needed to allocate public IPv4 addresses for 20 percent adoption by the worldwide population as a whole is 808. The sum of the /8 networks needed by the individual regions to reach 20 percent adoption is 703. Regardless of the number used in the analysis, the IPv4 address space does not have sufficient resources to meet these needs.

The analysis in Table 2-1 assumes that each Internet user owns a public address. While this becomes a necessity for the latest usage patterns and the new peer-to-peer applications, it was quite common to have multiple Internet users sharing a global IPv4 address when dial-up was the main technology to connect to the Internet.

Highlighting the developing digital divide, it should be noted that as of June 2007, the population of the top 22 countries in Internet penetration represents 10 percent of the world's population.[6] The Internet reached mass-adoption levels in only 99 (40 percent) of the world's 245 countries.

Mobile Phone Market Segment

For the past 15 years, Global System for Mobile (GSM) communications, along with other cellular technologies, has dramatically transformed daily life for billions of people. From Q2 CY07, the number of GSM connections, as shown in Table 2-2, has grown to pass the 3 billion mark in April 2008 globally, as announced by the GSMA, the global trade group for the mobile industry[7]

Table 2-2 *Number of GSM Connections Per Region*[a]

Market	Connections in Q2 2007
World	2,377,790,703 (out of 2,831,345,390 wireless subscribers)
Africa	220,734,625
Americas	252,371,017
Asia Pacific	917,356,568

continues

6. http://www.internetworldstats.com/top25.htm.

7. http://www.gsmworld.com/news/press_2008/press08_31.shtml

Table 2-2   *Number of GSM Connections Per Region^a (Continued)*

Market	Connections in Q2 2007
Europe Eastern	359,637,084
Europe Western	387,248,744
Middle East	146,458,459
USA/Canada	93,984,206

a. http://www.gsmworld.com/technology/what.shtml.

Internet applications and services are not only possible via the public Wi-Fi and upcoming WiMAX infrastructures; they are also fully integrated, including IPv6 support, in the third and fourth generation telephony through the IP Multimedia Subsystem (IMS). The new generation of wireless devices comes with an embedded dual IP stack and multimedia applications, including VoIP. The fierce competition between content providers seeking new revenues and increased market shares is leading to the delivery of new content and services over IP that will rely on always-on connectivity and end-to-end reachability. The combination of wireless and new broadband technologies such as DOCSIS 3.0 for cable or fiber to the home (FTTH) is leading to more and more independence of the service offering from the type or point of access and drives the market toward the convergence of fixed-mobile services.

NOTE	Popular operating systems running on mobile phones are already offering dual-stack IPv4/IPv6 support, including the Symbian, Microsoft Windows Mobile 5 and 6, and Linux operating systems.

If just 50 percent of worldwide subscribers transition to those new technologies and services, they will require an additional 66 /8 networks for always-on connectivity. This example does not take into account the forecasted increase in the number of subscribers and the addresses required by the infrastructure supporting all these users.

Consumer Devices

The digital revolution that marked the end of the previous millennium brought a wide variety of devices into our lives. Although they entered the market as "gadgets," many of these devices quickly became indispensable to many people. Gaming consoles (more than 150 million, including more than 44 million Sony PS3 and PSP), multimedia players, digital video recorders, digital cameras, and Global Positioning System (GPS) consoles are just a few examples of the many devices that are no longer a novelty.

The power of these new devices does not reside in their standalone operation but rather in the services they can offer when connected to other devices. The integration of IP over Ethernet and wireless technologies provides an environment where consumer devices can easily access resources and services. In order to communicate, these connected devices each use at least an IP address. Moreover, for full service and business model flexibility, these devices require public IP addresses. Their rapid adoption represents yet another source of pressure on the IPv4 address space.

Connected homes and public wireless LAN services represent perfect infrastructures to proliferate IP-enabled consumer devices. Although it is difficult to track such a diverse set of products, it is estimated that in 2006 there were 492 million connected consumer devices such as phones, computers, game consoles, and media centers. By 2010 that number is expected to reach 2.8 billion units.[8] At one address per device and an HD ratio of 90 percent, these connected devices require 271 /8 prefixes (surpassing the total IPv4 address pool) and would need 1871 /8 prefixes by 2010. Many of these consumer devices could reuse private IPv4 addresses but this would limit the type of services available and the flexibility to adopt new business models while also increasing the cost of the applications supported.

The number of consumer devices, their need for global reachability, and their expected mobility outside of the home require a significantly larger address space than what IPv4 can offer. Unfettered growth and large-scale adoption are essential in this market space as it stimulates new service concepts and product innovation based on consumer requests. IPv6, with its large address space, is the natural answer to this market's IP address needs. At the same time, IPv6 offers specific features, such as stateless autoconfiguration, that can reduce product costs, a great asset in a low-margin market.

8. http://dhdeans.blogspot.com/2007/01/key-growth-statistics-on-connected.html.

Transportation

A significant part of our day depends to a certain extent on one form of transportation or another. Public or private transportation takes us to and from our place of work; transportation provides the logistics that support our global economy; or perhaps transportation is the very scope of our business. Transportation can also make vacations possible or frustrating. In summary, we depend on various forms of transportation in our daily lives and the means by which we travel have us as a captive audience for a significant part of our day. The combination of wireless access and IP connectivity can provide significant business and increased revenue opportunities in the transportation market. Following are some opportunities for revenue:

- **Telematics:** Sensors distributed in a vehicle can monitor and manage its operation, providing new services to the vehicle owner, including the data for improved maintenance and troubleshooting. In late 2007, BMW's Research and Technology division unveiled its iDrive pilot program, which integrates the large number of control systems and entertainment systems through an integrated IP-based network. BMW's goal is to use a standards-based platform for future anticipated needs, simplify development and manufacturing, and reduce long-term costs. Rail systems are using telematics to manage spacing between trains to maximize passenger loads and improve safety.

- **Vehicle to vehicle:** Along with the development of telematic applications, communications between vehicles could be developed in conjunction with road infrastructures that work together to improve safety and prevent accidents. This type of environment integrates a wide range of wireless/wireline communications and control technologies in a framework developed by the Intelligent Transport Systems (ITS) standards (ISO TC 204).

- **Fleet connectivity:** Transportation companies can leverage municipal Wi-Fi LANs and cellular broadband to connect their assets back to the central office. It is an effective and cost-saving mechanism to coordinate activities, synchronize inventory, and update routes. E-ticketing, real-time information for passengers, and video surveillance are typical applications that benefit from the availability of Internet access on public transportation. The cost of deployment can be covered by additional services such as local advertisements and news contracts negotiated with appropriate channels.

- **Internet access "on the road or in flight":** Inside their own cars, on public transportation, in airplanes, or aboard cruise ships, people represent a trapped audience that will pay a premium for access to content whether it is for work or entertainment.

- **First responders fleet:** This is another market segment that could benefit from bidirectional communications for applications such as video and database access. There is great interest in the integration of all assets that need to be leveraged in case of emergency. Recent press highlighted innovative communities deploying metro wireless infrastructures that could be used by the emergency responders. These new infrastructures lead to radio frequencies traditionally used for those communications to be freed up for other usage. Two notable initiatives are working on the future communications infrastructures for first responders: U-2010 (http://www.u2010.eu/) and MetroNet6 (http://www.metronet6.org/).

- **Cargo monitoring:** Tracking goods in transit is becoming more and more important to provide proper environmental conditions (maintaining temperature levels for perishable foods) and to constantly monitor valuable goods.

Cars, ships, trains, and airplanes have long-lasting power sources and have no major constraints related to the size of the communications devices they can be fitted with. This makes them ideal environments for mobile communications services. It is expected that vehicles will support multiple IP-connected devices, so they will require entire IP subnets to support them. They must also be able to connect seamlessly to various access network types such as wireless services. It should not be expected that a single access media type or access provider can cover all countries or regions or cities. The need for this type of flexibility also makes the case for the use of IP mobility.

It is rather difficult to evaluate the volume of addresses that would be used by networked vehicles but a recent study about the European market forecasts the numbers to be in the millions range. Table 2-3 provides a summary profile of the European road-based transportation.

Table 2-3 *European Market Size for Road Transportation*[a]

Vehicle Category	Vehicle Type	Number of Vehicles	New Vehicles per Year	Vehicle Lifetime (Years)
Public				
Pro Vehicle	Police	200,000	40,000	5
Pro Vehicle	Ambulance Taxi	15,000	3,000	5
High End Vehicle	Bus	175,000	35,000	5
High End Vehicle	Fire (>16t)	32,000	7,000	5
High End Vehicle	Full Ambulance	20,000	4,000	5
Large Vehicle	Metro	20,000	700	30
Large Vehicle	Reg&Sub Rail	55,000	2,000	30
Large Vehicle	Light Rail	25,000	1,000	30
Private				
Pro Vehicle	Car	220,000,000	17,000,000	10+
Pro Vehicle	Goods Vehicles	20,000,000	4,000,000	5

a. Source: Internal Cisco Systems, Inc.

The 2006 data presented in Table 2-3 indicates that if an IPv4 /24 subnet is used per vehicle to interconnect its various sensors and communications devices, a deployment target of 5 percent of the European transportation market alone will require 183 /8 subnets.

The transportation market space is full of opportunities for new communications services. Cruise ships are fully networked and use services such as VoIP internally. Airplanes provide Internet access services, and multiple automakers are piloting networked cars. Table 2-3 indicates that the life cycle of a vehicle is generally long, between 5 and 30 years. Older OEM vehicles may never be updated. Others will be retrofitted with newer in-transit systems where there is business value such as safety, security, or attracting customers.

Industrial Sensors and Control Systems

Industrial networks (building, plant, and process automation networks) are migrating from legacy techniques to reliance on IP-based services, as shown in Figure 2-2. The drivers for change are economics, interoperability, simplification, and common cross-network security enforcement.

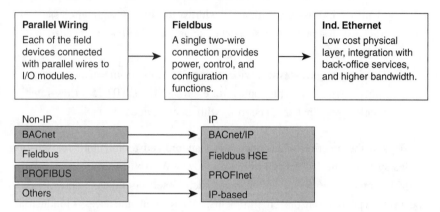

Figure 2-2 *Evolution of Industrial Network Technology*

The more sensors that are used in the manufacturing process and in tracking a product's path through the distribution chain, the more optimizations can be identified and applied to each step of the process, as shown by the European Reconfigurable Ubiquitous Networked Embedded Systems (RUNES) project (http://www.ist-runes.org). Interconnecting sensors into a consolidated product management framework leads to significant productivity increases and cost reductions. They can also enhance security and management of fixed assets. Sensors can be deployed internally by enterprises, but we expect their footprint to grow with more and more sensors deployed in public domains, modes of transportation, and homes.

The migration of industrial sensors and control systems to an IP-based architecture is once again the result of several technologies:

- **Back-end and front-end control systems:** Applications running on computers and exchanging data through an IP network

- **Industrial sensors:** Span a wide range, from passive radio-frequency identification (RFID) with no IP address to Motes (small wireless transceiver attached to a sensor) or smart cards with an embedded IP stack

- **Readers or gateways:** Devices that collect data from sensors over specific wireless technologies; for example: IEEE 802.15.4 (low-rate wireless personal area network) with an embedded IP stack

To help the creation of an open and standardized architecture for sensor-enabled systems, the IETF IPv6 over Low power WPAN (6LOWPAN) working group[9] leveraged IPv6 to solve challenges such as self-configuring networks, an aspect very typical to sensors' environments. Management and access of industrial sensors will be done both within the LAN and over the public domain, driving the need for IPv6 capabilities such as address space, "plug-and-play" autoconfiguration, communities of Interest, and so forth.

As shown in Figure 2-3, an estimated 127 million wireless sensors are expected to be deployed by 2010.[10]

At least 12 /8 prefixes are required to connect these devices. Wireless access facilitates the deployment of sensors and thus helps accelerate their adoption, which in turn increases the demand for IP addresses. IPv6 is perfectly suited for this market space. It has the necessary address space to cover a large number of devices and has the tools necessary to provide for simple provisioning of this type of devices, which generally have little processing power.

---

9. Source: IEEE 802.15 Task Group 4, http://www.ietf.org/html.charters/6lowpan-charter.html.

10. http://onworld.com/research/industrialwsn/vip/.

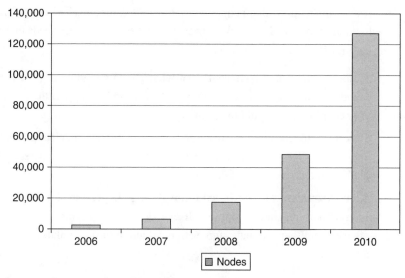

Source: http://onworld.com/research/industrialwsn/vip/

Figure 2-3 *Number of Deployed Nodes (in Thousands)*

Common Observations When Looking at the Numbers

Interestingly, as soon as the depletion process of the IPv4 address space was slowed down through various conservation and management mechanisms, the immediate interest in its successor diminished. For the years that followed, the search for a reason to invest in an IP upgrade to IPv6 focused mainly on the application layer. The thorough scrubbing of IPv6-specific features and the brainstorms of IPv6 enthusiasts have yet to produce a killer application that would trigger market adoption. But, did we really make the most out of the last killer app we came up with, the Internet? The true potential of the Internet and of IP has yet to be unleashed, and this cannot happen in the context of its initial definition.

This chapter intends to show the technical arguments related to the new protocol. By looking at just a few statistics, we highlight the basic resource requirements for the continued growth of current markets. Some of the estimates presented here are backed by formal reports of address shortages. For example, the large cable providers in the United States reported running out of private IPv4 addresses in 2005.

Innovative applications that people will later call "killer apps" will certainly come with the IPv6 protocol. For now, however, just the basic market needs make a strong case for IPv6, which provides:

- **Resources to scale up current networks:** The larger address space is mandatory to meet current numbers of devices and to support the expected Internet population growth.

- **Resources to simplify network and service architecture:** Network and service design constraints due to address shortage can be eliminated, leading to reduced costs of operation.

- **An environment for continued innovation:** A larger and simpler Internet that integrates ever more diverse devices represents an environment that stimulates innovation, which in turn stimulates adoption.

IP: Today's Constraints and Tomorrow's Solutions

Despite 15 years' worth of efforts to develop, implement, and deploy a new version of IP, "IPv6 lovers" and "IPv6 haters" still argue about what IPv6 can do and cannot do. This debate has resulted in many myths and rumors, which often are contradicted by facts and papers, such as "The Case for IPv6," which was published as a draft RFC in 1999 (draft-ietf-iab-case-for-ipv6-06.txt). To offer a realistic and honest perspective on the benefits and challenges of the new protocol, this section addresses some of the common questions related to IPv6's capabilities. The IPv6 myths must be debunked and its true strengths must be reiterated. This is a necessary step in understanding where the strengths and weaknesses of the technology stand.

Is IPv4 Running Out of Addresses?

One of the most intense debates related to IPv6 focuses on the prediction of the Internet's doomsday, the day when we run out of IPv4 addresses. For the most part, the networking community is in agreement that the IPv4 address space will be depleted. The question left unanswered is: When will this event occur?

NOTE   Free IPv4 addresses will likely become extinct in an asymptotic fashion, so the criteria for total depletion will be more pragmatic in nature: When will the Regional Internet Registries (RIR) become incapable to service all address requests?

Much has been written about this question, but forecasts are not easy to make. By 2006, the two main predictions that emerged rely exclusively on different approaches to extrapolating historical IPv4 address allocation data:

Exhaustion of addresses by 2010: This prediction is based on an analysis by Tony Hain.[11]

Exhaustion of addresses by 2012: This prediction is based on an analysis by Geoff Huston.[12]

NOTE   Neither of these predictions took into consideration a very likely "last chance rush" on the registries. The concern is that as applicants for IPv4 addresses do not expect to have another chance to go back to the registries for future requests, they will not provide realistic justifications for their last request.

If the situation is dire, why aren't people more concerned? This is likely the result of three factors. First, the value of an IP address is not market driven. If the value of an IP address were to grow with demand, people would take notice and would be able to calculate the cost versus the benefit of migrating to IPv6. Second,

---

11. For more information, see http://www.cisco.com/web/about/ac123/ac147/archived_issues/ipj_8-3/ipv4.html.

12. For more information, see http://www.potaroo.net/tools/ipv4/.

the Internet community "cried wolf" before and it turned out not to be an unsolvable problem. Third, because the Internet, like water and electricity, has become a utility service managed by others, users do not feel the need for strategic planning.

As discussed in the previous section, "Looking at the Numbers," the IPv4 address space cannot sustain the Internet's growth. For any long-term perspective, IPv6 becomes a natural choice. As with any limited resource, the IPv4 address space will be exhausted one day. IPv6 will pick up where IPv4 left off and it will plumb the Internet for a long period of time, accommodating a very large number of devices.

NOTE   Sixteen bytes or 128 bits can accommodate 340,282,366,920,938,463,463,374,607,431,768,211,456 IPv6 addresses, sufficient to keep engineers happy and to enchant trivia lovers with examples such as: There are enough IPv6 addresses for every proton in the Universe and 523 quadrillion addresses for each brain cell (number of cells per brain varies from person to person of course).

At the beginning of 2008, of the 255 possible /8 prefixes, more than 80 percent /8 IPv4 subnets were allocated to RIRs by IANA.[13] In turn, each RIR allocates address space to its members, service providers, government agencies, and enterprises. Each organization uses a certain percentage of the full address space assigned to it.

Answer: Yes, IPv4 represents a finite resource that will get exhausted. In the context of the current allocation policies, predictions are converging to an IPv4 address space exhaustion date between 2010 and 2015. Whether it is 2010 or 2015, the date is rather near. Would you postpone an IP upgrade to find out which prediction is correct?

---

13. http://www.iana.org/assignments/ipv4-address-space.

Are NAT Benefits Lost by Moving to IPv6?

Network Address Translation (NAT) use is a worldwide reality. It is the front end to enterprise and home networks. NAT was developed to conserve IPv4 addresses. Without its widespread use, the Internet would certainly have already exhausted its address space.

The private address space definition (RFC 1918, *Address Allocation for Private Internets*) and its usage (RFC 3022, *Traditional IP Network Address Translator [Traditional NAT]*) have been documented in several papers. The NAT operation is simple and effective—one globally known IPv4 address on the Internet with millions of "private" IPv4 addresses available for internal use. The process obscures or hides the actual IP addresses of host computers in the NAT environment. It also makes communication with them more complicated when it is initiated from outside the NAT domain. This is one of the reasons why IPv6 supporters regularly denounce the "dark side" of NAT, referencing IETF documents such as RFC 2993, *Architectural Implications of NAT*, and RFC 3027, *Protocol Complications with the IP Network Address Translator.*

The acceptance of NAT in the '90s as a solution to IPv4 address exhaustion, far before the availability of any IPv6 product, has pushed Internet users to ignore the increased level of complexity, its trade-offs (and potential costs), and the impact on applications and connectivity. Users became comfortable with NAT, to the point where they assigned it more functionality than it actually provides. A common NAT-related misconception is that it enhances security. This is an important factor to consider when developing an IPv6 transition strategy, as nobody wants to loose NAT's perceived benefits. To address all user concerns related to networks without NAT, the IETF developed RFC 4846, *Local Network Protection for IPv6*, which provides guidelines and explanations of IPv6 features and configurations that match the perceived benefits of NAT.

Answer: Although NAT breaks the fundamental end-to-end model of the original Internet, it is not the goal of this book to argue about the pros and cons of NAT. It is far more important for organizations that are using NAT in their environments to understand that none of the real and perceived benefits of NAT are lost in IPv6.

Is IPv6 Improving Routing?

The evolutionary and not revolutionary nature of the new protocol is probably best exemplified in the case of its routing protocols. No new, dramatic concepts were introduced. The IPv4 routing protocols were, however, rebuilt in a cleaner way. RIPv2 led to RIPng, OSPFv2 led to a similar but improved OSPFv3, and EIGRP, IS-IS, and BGP were extended to support IPv6.

The IPv6 routing protocols have no tricks to help alleviate the concerns about the size of the Internet routing tables. Considering the size of the Internet routing tables in Q1 2008 (+250,000 entries) and the lack of routing enhancements, some people argue that IPv6 is not good enough for a nest generation protocol.

Answer: Although the scalability of the Internet is indeed a pressing problem and the subject of many research efforts, we need to remember that during its inception and development, IPv6 was built to solve the addressing problems and not the routing problems. These goals were set in IETF with the agreement of the engineering community. Although the plentiful address resources could lead to a cleaner Internet, IPv6 is not better or worse than IPv4 in terms of dealing with the Internet's scalability.

A new generation of routers, including edge routers such as Cisco ASR 1000 series, is designed for both IPv4 and IPv6 and can support gigabytes of memory, amounting to millions of routes. This means these routers can comfortably cope with the growth of the Internet routing tables. The real challenges, however, relate to the speed of convergence and the stability of the Internet. All of these are areas for future innovation.

Does IPv6 Support Multihomed Sites?

It is often stated that multihoming of sites is an IPv6 problem. Multihoming is not a protocol problem. In the case of IPv6, the challenges are due to a set of prefix allocation policies enforced by the RIRs.

Multihoming is widely used by enterprises for the following reasons:

- **Connect sites of a network with global reach:** Organizations with multinational infrastructures will connect to multiple service providers in different countries.

- **Backup for the link to the SP:** An enterprise can have several links into the same provider that protect each other in the event of a failure.

- **Backup SP:** An enterprise can connect to several SPs in order to protect against SP failure.

Multihoming is a problem for IP in general and not for IPv6 alone. IPv4 faces the same issues with multihoming as IPv6. Current multihoming techniques impact the size of the Internet routing table. In February 2008, there were more than 250,000 entries in the IPv4 backbone BGP routing table.[14] The root cause of the problem is a lack of a good framework for prefix aggregation. IPv6 routing is based on the same protocols as IPv4, so all multihoming mechanisms available in IPv4 can be used in IPv6. The size of the IPv6 prefixes—which, within the Internet routing tables, is driven through prefix allocation policies—facilitates better address management and good aggregation.

Figure 2-4 is a summary of the IPv6 prefix allocation policies. The address space is managed by IANA, which allocates prefixes to the RIRs, which in turn allocate prefixes to ISPs on the provider dependent track or directly to organizations (enterprises, educational institutions, and so forth) on the Provider Independent track.

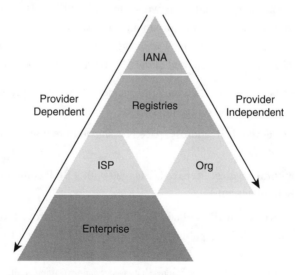

Figure 2-4   *IPv6 Address Allocation Policies*

14. http://bgp.potaroo.net/index-bgp.html.

A 2006 analysis of the IPv6 global routing tables, "Have We Reached 1000 Prefixes Yet? A Snapshot of the Global IPv6 Routing Table," presents the effectiveness of the policy approach at that stage in the deployment of IPv6.[15] Geoff Huston's well-respected BGP Update site tracks and analyzes historic IPv4 and IPv6 BGP routing information, a valuable resource for up-to-date information.

These policies enforced by Registries preempt the use of multihoming as done in IPv4. In the absence of a multihoming mechanism that would work in the context of IPv6, enterprises are faced with significant operational challenges when integrating IPv6. Whenever an enterprise is dissatisfied with its provider and wants to switch to another one, it would have to renumber its network; and this is an expensive proposition. The provider-dependent allocation policies are not acceptable to enterprises.

To avoid a slowdown in IPv6 adoption due to these concerns, new policies were adopted by the RIRs and they provision for Provider Independent (PI) address space,[16] which could be acquired directly from the RIR. These policies will help keep the IPv6 deployment momentum, but they do not solve the real problems of backbone routing table growth and organizations multihomed to several service providers. With a significantly larger address space, IPv6 can make the routing table problem considerably worse than it is in IPv4. The importance of this topic in the networking community mind is reflected in the support provided by IETF to research in this area. The list of suggestions and initiatives to solve the multihoming challenges was reported at the 53rd RIPE meeting and are

- **CIDR boundary:** The community decides on the longer prefix boundary that can be handled on the Internet.

- **Metro/regional:** IP address space is assigned to regions instead of organizations.

- **Community codes:** Prefixes are tagged with a BGP community attribute.

- **Published list of IPv6 blocks:** A list of prefixes approved for multihoming will be published, and filters will be opened for them.

15. http://www.ripe.net/ripe/meetings/ripe-55/presentations/doering-ipv6-routing.pdf.

16. http://www.arin.net/policy/archive/2005_1_orig.html.

- **Policy:** RIRs would implement policies that offer provider-independent address space. As of early 2008, all RIRs adopted a PI address space policy with the exception of RIPE (http://www.arin.net/policy/archive/2005_1_orig.html, http://www.afrinic.net/docs/policies/afpol-v6200701.htm, http://lacnic.net/documentos/lacnicx/LAC-2006-08-en.pdf, http://www.apnic.net/meetings/12/docs/proposal-ipv6-ixp.html).

- **IETF Multi6 WG:** This is the IETF working group that works on IPv6 multihoming solutions (http://ops.ietf.org/multi6/).

- **IETF Shim6 WG:** A shim layer that enables the decoupling between the IP address could be used by the application and used by transport (http://tools.ietf.org/wg/shim6/).

- **Global, Site, End-system (GSE):** Protocols that separate the user identifier from its locator.

- **Maximum prefix:** Each origin AS can advertise a limited number of prefixes.

Answer: The IPv6 protocol itself provides the same level of support for multihoming as IPv4 supports. Perceived challenges are just a reflection of address allocation policies implemented to enforce aggregation of prefixes in the Internet backbone routing table. IPv6 can leverage the same multihoming techniques as IPv4, and alternative mechanisms are being investigated in IETF.

Does IPv6 Deliver Plug-and-Play Autoconfiguration?

When mainframes and mini computers were the only devices running IP, autoconfiguration was not really an important feature, because devices were statically configured. With the proliferation of personal computers (PC), for scalable device management and reuse of resources, some dynamic autoconfiguration mechanisms became necessary. In IPv4, autoconfiguration relies on the Dynamic Host Configuration Protocol (DHCP) (see RFC 4776), which is today extensively used in both enterprises and service provider environments.

NOTE   The need and the benefit of a dynamic autoconfiguration mechanism was apparent to other networking protocols. For those who remember them, AppleTalk, IPX, or OSI ES-IS are now defunct networking protocols that had built-in autoprovisioning mechanisms. The users at the time, who were generally not networking proficient, were particularly fond of these features.

In RFC 1752, IPng specifically defined an acceptance technical criterion for the new protocol that focused on "configuration ease – The protocol must permit easy and largely distributed configuration and operation. Automatic configuration of hosts and routers is required." Not only is automatic configuration seen as mandatory, but the need for simple configuration mechanisms is also highlighted. The need for simplicity becomes more and more important when considering the simpler devices that are now using IP. These devices might operate in environments where dependencies on a server may not be acceptable.

IPv6 took on the challenge posed by IPng. It offers plug-and-play autoconfiguration beyond the capabilities offered by IPv4 in the sense that a stateless (or serverless) address autoconfiguration mechanism was defined as part of the Neighbor Discovery protocol (RFC 2461, updated by RFC 4681). This capability is available in addition to DHCPv6 (RFC 4776), the stateful address autoconfiguration that is similar to IPv4 DHCP.

Nevertheless, real plug-and-play is more than just acquiring an IP address to access the network. For full operation, an IP device might need information the server addresses for applications such as Domain Name System (DNS), Network Time Protocol (NTP), and so forth. This is currently delivered with the help of "stateless" DHCPv6, a process similar to IPv4. Nevertheless, although servers might not be fully eliminated, IPv6 devices can fully provision themselves in a stateless manner. Microsoft has capitalized on IPv6 autoconfiguration with Windows Vista. The operating system supports a Peer Name Resolution Protocol (PNRP) for identifying and securely communicating with other "peer" computers on the network. Windows Meeting Space is a built-in Vista application for information sharing and conferencing.

In addition to these specific provisioning mechanisms, DHCPv6 has also been expanded to deliver entire IPv6 prefixes to a device rather than deliver just a host address. This protocol extension, called DHCPv6 prefix delegation (RFC 3633), enables routers to autoconfigure their interfaces, a powerful tool that can be leveraged in broadband access networks to dynamically provision customer gateways.

Answer: It is true, IPv6 offers an enhanced plug-and-play autoconfiguration suite of protocols.

Does IPv6 Offer Better QoS?

Quality of service (QoS) in IP networks is delivered in the context of two architectures:

- **Differentiated Services (DiffServ):** Relies on each network element allocating resources to the forwarding of a packet based on a 6-bit classifier (differentiated code point) carried in the packet header

- **Integrated Services (IntServ):** Relies on the RSVP signaling protocol to set up resources along the path of packets with given transport requirements

- These architectural models are defined for both IPv4 and IPv6. IPv4 and IPv6 main headers include the same 8-bit field used for DiffServ, although they are named differently: Type of Service (ToS) in IPv4 versus Traffic Class in IPv6. IntServ for IPv6 requires an IPv6 implementation of RSVP.

Conceptually, QoS relates to applications. For example, to guarantee high quality for phone calls established over IP, VoIP packets get higher priority compared to other traffic types. This means that QoS policies should be independent of IP version and should depend exclusively on application types. Thus, in a dual-stack network, the same priority is assigned to the packets of a given application independent of the IP version it runs over. However, for those very specific conditions that require one IP version to be privileged over the other, it is possible to assign different priorities based on IP version.

Why do we read in some publication that IPv6 offers better QoS than IPv4? This is mainly driven by the presence of a 20-bit field named Flow Label in the main IPv6 header, a field that does not exist in IPv4. The Flow Label field, as specified in RFC 2460 and RFC 3697, is used by a source to label packets of the same flow. Its definition guarantees that the information carried has an end-to-end meaning; its value cannot be modified by intermediate systems. Although some interesting proposals do exist for the use of the Flow Label field, the field is currently unused and may not have practical value in the overall Internet where no definition of Flow Label value has been published or agreed upon by service providers. Nevertheless, these 20 bits in the main IP header are very precious real estate, so forms of Flow Label usage will surely be developed in the future.

Answer: IPv6 QoS is neither better nor worse than IPv4 QoS. It follows the same architectural models and faces the same inherent challenges. At this point in time, the presence of the 20-bit Flow Label field in the IPv6 header is not enough to justify the claim of better QoS.

Is IPv6 Required for Mobility?

Before addressing the topic, it is important to clarify what "mobility" really means for a given environment. Over the past few years, mobility became a "fashionable" term used in many marketing presentations. Nevertheless, it is not always related to IP. So, let's start with a few definitions:

- **Mobile client:** A mobile client is a device such as a laptop, PDA, smartphone, iPod, or sensor that regularly changes location but does not necessarily have its own network interface. For example, an Apple iPod will connect through a PC to download contents.

- **Mobile application:** An application that runs on a mobile device is a mobile application. Popular audio or video contents (for example, podcasts) consist of files that are downloaded to mobile devices and used later with no need for Internet connectivity. (By contrast, VoIP is an example of an application that requires the mobile client to be always connected.)

- **Wireless technologies:** They enable mobile devices and applications to be used in any covered location. There are licensed-band (3G/GPRS/Edge/EVDO/WiMAX/LTE) and unlicensed-band (Wi-Fi) technologies.

- **Layer 2 mobility:** A device moving within a single Layer 2 domain, such as the area covered by a single Wi-FI access point, has Layer 2 mobility.

- **Layer 3 mobility:** Also called IP Mobility, Layer 3 mobility addresses the case of a mobile device moving between multiple Layer 3 domains while keeping the same IP address. This capability supports persistency and transparency at the application level.

- **Layer 7 mobility:** A specific application with Layer 7 mobility may survive network reconfigurations and potentially address changes but with service interruption. An example of such an application is the Instant Messaging.

- **Mobile networks:** In a mobile network, mobility is provided simultaneously to a group of devices. The router providing network access to the devices moves across Layer 3 domains. The changes in the point of attachment for the router uplink have no effect on the interfaces that provide access to devices connected to the router.

- **Ad hoc networking:** This Layer 3 mobility feature set developed in the IETF under the MANET and Mobility EXTensions for IPv6 (MEXT) working groups enables mobile routers to self-organize their ad hoc connections with peers.

The mobility features relevant to an IP discussion are: Layer 3 mobility, mobile networks, and ad hoc networking. IP Mobility is generally synonymous with the IETF protocol suite called Mobile IP (MIP) that has been standardized for both IPv4 and IPv6. When considering the potential scope of deployment for MIP—for example, handheld devices compliant with standards from 3rd Generation Partnership Project (3GPP) and 3GPP2—it becomes evident that we are dealing with millions of mobile devices. This type of environment requires the large address space provided by IPv6. 3GPP has also addressed the delivery of converged voice, data, and video to mobile devices through the IP Multimedia Subsystem (IMS) standard. IMS requires IPv6 support, to ensure that each mobile phone is individually addressable with a persistent address for full bidirectional services.

There is more to MIPv6 than just the support of large-scale deployments. Mobile IPv6 leverages the IPv6 extension headers that are inherent to the protocol.

This makes IP mobility an integrated feature of the IPv6 protocol as required by RFC 1752 and enables it to easily add capabilities such as path optimization between mobile nodes and their communication peer.

Answer: No, IPv6 is not required for mobility. However, Layer 3 mobility, also named IP mobility, is integrated in the protocol rather than being an add-on, as in the case of IPv4. The market is developing new business models, new communities of interest, and new products based on standardized protocols like Mobile IPv6 (MIPv6) and Networks Mobility (NEMO). This will make mobility easier to deploy and capable of supporting a much larger number of more full-featured handsets and other new devices supporting multi-mode wireless radio, video, and VoIP. The use of IMS and other higher-level standards requiring IPv6 support will offer a platform for new marketable products and services not possible with IPv4.

Does IPv6 Provide Increased Security?

Today, security is certainly one of the biggest challenges faced by network managers. Any enhancement to security is always welcomed by operational teams. When reading that "IPv6 is more secure than IPv4," it is natural to become more interested in the new protocol. In fact, several past business cases have had as a supporting argument the increased security of IPv6. So, is IPv6 more secure than IPv4 or is it just a misunderstanding turned into an IPv6 marketing pitch?

The source of the enhanced IPv6 security claims can be traced back to the original version of the IPv6 specifications (RFC 1883), which states under "Security Considerations": "This document specifies that the IP Authentication Header [RFC-1826] and the IP Encapsulating Security Payload [RFC-1827] be used with IPv6, in conformance with the Security Architecture for the Internet Protocol [RFC-1825]."[17]

In an environment that eliminates the NAT gateway that manipulates a packet's payload, the use of AH and ESP headers might be perceived as a new security paradigm. End-to-end security is implemented based on IPsec with no intermediate devices manipulating the data. IPsec is becoming the de facto mechanism to protect IPv6 routing protocols such as OSPFv3.

17. http://www.ietf.org/rfc/rfc1883.txt.

In reality, IPv6 IPsec is not different from IPv4 IPsec. It offers the same level of protection and requires a key distribution infrastructure to be in place for full operation. With no universal key distribution mechanism available Internet wide, this architecture has no practical value for the overall Internet but it could meet the requirements for networks under a single management entity. It is also important to note that some devices might not be capable of doing encryption in a cost-effective way. Also, some features used in IPv4 (for example, WAN optimization) will not be possible if packet manipulation is not allowed. These devices and services would have to be excluded from an environment where end-to-end IPsec between nodes is the rule.

More importantly, communications security must be viewed holistically, at all layers of the OSI model. Different mechanisms and tools are deployed to secure each layer. For example, IEEE 802.1X is configured to protect an IEEE 802.11 infrastructure providing authentication mechanisms at Layer 2. At the same time, antivirus and antispam software protects the application layer.

NOTE   The most number of security threats, and the most damaging ones, target the layers above IP.

Based on the accumulated experience securing IPv4 networks, it would be extremely dangerous to narrow network security to IP and IPsec only. Such a strategy would lead to a world in which hosts exchange viruses in a very secure manner. When looking at Layer 3, however, it is true that IPv6 brings along new perspectives. IPv6 makes some things better but has the potential to make other things worse. We cannot state that the net sum makes IPv6 a more or a less secure protocol:

- **Better:** In IPv6, automated scanning and worm propagation is harder due to huge subnets. With a uniform and non-obvious distribution of host IDs, it is practically impossible for an attacker to perform successful reconnaissance.

- **Challenging:** New concepts in addressing and configuration and lack of familiarity with the technology can lead to incomplete or incorrectly applied security policies. When managing a dual-stack environment, potential vulnerabilities exist because both IPv4 and IPv6 need to be properly secured. Extension headers might open the door to new types of threats.

- **Different:** IPv4 Address Resolution Protocol (ARP) is replaced by IPv6 Neighbor Discovery (ND), both of which are unsecured by default. Unlike IPv4, IPv6 has a Secure Neighbor Discovery (SEND) protocol (RFC 3971), which improves security for ND.

NOTE The IPv4 security tools and features might not yet be available for IPv6, which exposes networks in the transitional phase.

Answer: No, IPv6 is not more secure than IPv4 as a protocol set. Most of the security challenges faced by IPv4 remain in IPv6 environments. Network managers must control the IPv6 traffic as they do for IPv4. IPsec can be leveraged to secure IPv6 environments when possible but a global network of IPsec peer-to-peer communication is far from becoming reality, if such a reality is ever possible or desired.

Is Renumbering Easier with IPv6?

Renumbering a network, assigning it a new addressing scheme, is a task dreaded by network managers. Renumbering, however, is a fact of life in the evolution of a business and is triggered by factors such as:

- Growth
- Acquisitions
- Large mergers
- Site transition

Although it is true that IPv6 autoconfiguration mechanisms help in the renumbering process, it is incorrect to state that IPv6 solved the renumbering problem. The actual change of IP addresses on the interfaces of hosts, routers, switches, and appliances represents only one step of the renumbering process. Other updates are generally required in order to restore full network operation:

- **IP address–dependent feature configuration:** Examples of such features are access control list (ACL) and addressing of resources such as AAA servers and network management servers.

- **Naming server:** All DNS entries must be updated to reflect the new address corresponding to a given name.

- **Network management applications:** All tools used to monitor the network must be updated.

To fully appreciate the implications of renumbering an IPv6 network, refer to RFC 4192, *Procedures for Renumbering an IPv6 Network Without a Flag Day*,[18] which documents a study done over the life of the European Commission–funded 6NET project in collaboration with Cisco Systems on this topic.

Answer: Renumbering is somewhat easier in IPv6; however, not all its aspects are simplified. The best recommendation is for organizations to use naming services, such as DNS, to the extent practical to minimize the impact of renumbering both in IPv4 and IPv6.

Summary

The key takeaway of this chapter is that IPv6 represents an evolution of IP, not a revolution. Its development reflects the lessons learned from IPv4 and the requirements of today's Internet. The primary benefit comes from increased resources, not from radical protocol changes, as sometimes claimed. The original design goals of the new protocol were also very specific about enabling a smooth transition over the years and facilitating a long-term coexistence of IPv4 and IPv6.

18. http://www.ietf.org/rfc/rfc4192.txt.

The commonly asked questions related to IPv6 that were answered in this chapter are summarized in Table 2-4. They provide a realistic perspective on the protocol.

Table 2-4 *Summary of Commonly Asked IPv6 Questions*

Question	Answer
Is IPv4 running out of addresses?	Yes. Current estimates indicate this will occur between 2010 and 2012.
Are NAT benefits lost when moving to IPv6?	No. Even though NAT is not available, its true or perceived benefits can be implemented in IPv6.
Is IPv6 improving routing?	No. Routing protocols for IPv6 are equivalent to their IPv4 counterparts.
Will the size of the Internet routing table be a problem for networking equipment?	No. New generations of routers can handle the growth of the Internet routing tables.
Does IPv6 support multihomed sites?	Yes. At protocol level, IPv6 can implement multihoming in the same way as IPv4. Challenges might be due to allocation policies.
Does IPv6 deliver plug-and-play autoconfiguration?	Yes. IPv6 offers unique autoconfiguration mechanisms.
Does IPv6 offer better QoS?	No. At this time, the IPv6 and IPv4 QoS implementations are similar.
Is IPv6 required for mobility?	No. However, IPv6 does implement improvements to the Mobile IP protocols.
Does IPv6 provide increased security?	No. Most security threats and mitigation policies are similar to IPv4.
Is renumbering easier with IPv6?	Yes. Some IPv6 features simplify renumbering; however, they do not address all aspects of renumbering.

As discussed, the IPv4 address space cannot sustain the growing number of Internet users and the many new ways in which the Internet is facilitating today's communications. This evolution was not envisioned by the initial developers of the TCP/IP protocol suite. The only real option to address the growth pressures faced by IP is IPv6, and the case for its adoption is made in this chapter. Although IPv6, similar to IPv4, is a live and evolving protocol, it has already reached the level of maturity needed for safe, large-scale deployments. In recognition of a need for IPv6, organizations worldwide are already deploying it or aggressively planning its deployment.

CHAPTER 3

The Economy of an IP Evolution

Over the past two decades, the Internet has become an integral part of our lives. Regardless of whether we see it as a source of knowledge or a source of entertainment, regardless of whether we experience it at work, via home broadband access in San Francisco, California, or in a tiny Internet café in New Delhi, India, we are aware of "the Internet." Most everyone can carry a conversation about one facet or another of this palpably vast resource.

The development of the Internet is one of the most successful examples of technology incubation and its rapid commercialization. It is an example of optimal collaboration between academia, government, and industry to create a new, open environment for the continued development and management of an information and communications resource. Its return on investment surpassed all expectations and is a testament to the value of government's sustained investment in fundamental and applied research. To put things in perspective, it took radio 38 years to attract 50 million listeners, it took television 13 years to attract 50 million viewers, and it took the Internet just 4 years to have 50 million users.[1]

The premise of the Internet started in 1962 with a series of memos by J. C. R. Licklinder on his vision of the "Galactic Network,"[2] a name that seems amazingly appropriate 46 years later. With the financial support of the Advanced Research Projects Agency (ARPA), the first network, ARPANET, was initiated on October 29, 1969. Used for the exchange of scientific data, this infrastructure led to the development of a new protocol, the Internet Protocol (IP). It replaced the original communications protocol used on ARPANET on January 1, 1983. Today's worldwide environment composed of infrastructure and information resources, the environment we call "the Internet," is operating with the help of IP. Although most people seem to be aware of the Internet, the fact that their favorite applications such as the World Wide Web, e-mail, telephony, and video on demand services are most likely using IP generally goes unnoticed by the vast majority of users.

The rapid growth and adoption of the Internet and IP can be attributed to some of its fundamental design and development principles, such as open architecture and open standards. In an open architecture, the individual networks are designed and operated independently based on the requirements of the users and services. The connectionless packet-switched nature of IP fits best in this environment.

1. Jonathan J. Gabay, *Successful Cybermarketing in a Week* (London: Hodder & Stoughton, 2000).

2. http://www.isoc.org/internet/history/brief.shtml#Introduction.

The openness of IP's standardization process is rather unique. It benefits from broad community participation and facilitates interoperability. This is a radical difference from other standardization bodies in which each country has a single vote in the decision-making process, an environment that lends itself more to political negotiations than to a focus on technology. The approach taken with standardizing IP makes the protocol nimble and easy to adapt to the requirements of new applications and services. The openness of the standardization process led IP to replace many traditional communications protocols and to continue its rapid growth. IP seems destined to be the underlying technology for most, if not all, communications services.

Over the years, the Internet has become a fundamental resource for our global economy; however, it is challenging to measure its direct impact in all economic areas.

The multitude of its uses and its large user base clearly imply that the Internet and what makes it work, IP, carry significant economic, social, legal, and even political value. At the same time, its governance, operation, and development principles set the Internet apart from other environments, making it difficult to model its evolution in economic terms. A 2006 workshop, "The Future of the Internet,"[3] organized by the Organization for Economic Cooperation and Development (OECD), reaffirmed the economic and strategic importance of the Internet while highlighting the many challenges it faces. Hugo Parr, the chair of OECD's Committee for Information, Computer, and Communications Policy (ICCP), concluded the meeting by summarizing the main points of the workshop, one of which was: "The basic features of interoperability and scalability of the Internet must be preserved. It needs to evolve to meet new demands (e.g., more users, torrents of data) but through evolution rather than drastic system changes."[4]

IPv6, the next version of the TCP/IP network layer, represents the pivotal element for an evolutionary step for the Internet that is being deployed increasingly through broadband and wireless media.

A technological evolution can, through the growth opportunities it offers, represent an inflexion point with significant business, economic, social, and

3. http://www.oecd.org/document/5/0,2340,en_2649_34223_36169989_1_1_1_1,00.html.

4. http://www.oecd.org/dataoecd/26/36/37422724.pdf, p. 23.

political implications. IPv6 facilitates the continued adoption of IP, enabling it to further benefit from economies of scale. In other words, IPv6 can support Tim O'Reilly's Web 2.0 framework:

> Web 2.0 is the business revolution in the computer industry caused by the move to the Internet as platform, and an attempt to understand the rules for success on that new platform. Chief among those rules is this: Build applications that harness network effects to get better the more people use them.

This chapter captures some of these aspects of IP evolution. The understanding and anticipation of an evolving Internet Protocol are shaping economic and political decisions worldwide at both a national and business organization level.

The Macroeconomic and National Perspective

The past few decades have seen tremendous developments in information and communications technology (ICT). These developments have lead to significantly increased capabilities available at lower prices. The computational capacity of devices grew by two orders of magnitude over the last three decades while the equipment prices decreased at a rate of 8 percent a year. This trend facilitates access to IT while increasing its contribution to users' productivity.

Early studies raised doubts about ICT's contribution to productivity in what was called a paradox of information technology.[5] ICT investment continued unabated and, by the end of the 1990s, its positive impact on the leading worldwide economies was evident.[6] The trend continues today. Based on the World Information Technology and Services Alliance (WITSA)[7] report *Digital Planet 2006: The Global Information Economy*, 2006 worldwide ICT spending

---

5. E. Brynjolfsson, "The Productivity Paradox of Information Technology: Review and Assessment," *Communications of ACM* (December 1993).

6. Paul Schreyer, "The Contribution of Information and Communication Technology to Output Growth: A Study of the G7 Countries," OECD, STI Working Papers 2 (March 2000).

7. http://www.witsa.org/.

topped $3 trillion and is estimated to reach $4 trillion by 2009. In this report, WITSA chairman George Newstrom concludes: "...ICT has become the indispensable technology for social and economic growth in developed and developing countries alike."

Figure 3-1 shows the history of ICT spending over the past decade in the United States and worldwide.

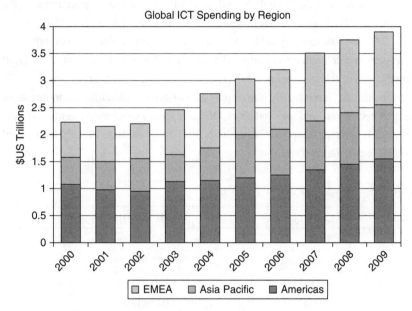

Figure 3-1   *Historic and Projected Global ICT Spending by Region*

ICT spending covers four areas:

- **Communications:** Includes audio, data networking, voice, and video equipment and products

- **Computer hardware:** Includes personal computers, workstations, servers, and so forth

- **Computer software:** Includes purchased or leased software for operating systems or specific applications

- **Computer services:** Includes managed services, consulting services, and so forth

The largest single category in ICT spending is communications products and services. Half of the U.S. ICT spending in 2006 was on communications. With IP becoming the primary communications protocol, it is fair to say that the significant investments in ICT reflect the increasing economic value and importance of IP.

WITSA data on individual national economies correlates the ICT investments and economic growth. The 2006 report indicates that in terms of ICT spending, China (10.4 percent 2006 GDP growth rate[8]) is targeted to surpass France (2.1 percent 2006 GDP growth rate) by 2007 and the United Kingdom (3.1 percent 2006 GDP growth rate) by 2008. A similar example is India (8.6 percent 2006 GDP growth rate), which is expected to replace Korea (4.6 percent 2006 GDP growth rate) in the top ten by 2007. This data highlights the importance of ICT investments and, intrinsically, the importance of communications technologies at the macroeconomic and national level. One measure of these investments and their outcome is Internet adoption and growth. The 2007 estimated GDPs for several countries are listed in Table 3-1.

Table 3-1   *Countries by GDP (2007 est)[a]*

Rank	Country	GDP (USD)
—	World	65.82 trillion
—	European Union	14.45 trillion
1	United States	13.86 trillion
2	China	7.04 trillion
3	Japan	4.35 trillion
4	India	2.97 trillion
5	Germany	2.83 trillion
6	United Kingdom	2.15 trillion
7	Russia	2.08 trillion
8	France	2.07 trillion
9	Brazil	1.84 trillion
10	Italy	1.80 trillion
11	Spain	1.36 trillion

8. http://www.witsa.org/digitalplanet/2006/DP2006_ExecSummary.pdf.

Table 3-1 *Countries by GDP (2007 est)^a (Continued)*

Rank	Country	GDP (USD)
12	Mexico	1.35 trillion
13	Canada	1.27 trillion
14	Korea, South	1.21 trillion

a. Source: *The World Factbook*, Central Intelligence Agency, https://www.cia.gov/library/
publications/the-world-factbook/rankorder/2001rank.html.

In the framework of the OSI layered model, Internet adoption and growth is shaped by several drivers:

- **Physical access:** This includes the availability of access and transport infrastructures such as DSL lines, cable, fiber, or wireless. For a long time, the high costs of deploying large-scale communications infrastructures were a major obstacle to adoption. However, rapid technological advancement has lead to less expensive, yet higher capacity media types that can support today's service needs.

- **IP transport:** Physical and media layers can support a variety of communications protocols. Over the past decade, IP replaced most competing protocols, becoming the dominant Layer 3 protocol. IP, however, risks becoming the victim of its own tremendous success if it cannot scale up to the worldwide needs.

- **Applications and services:** Applications and services are essential to generating feasible business cases that support the deployment and continued development of communications protocols.

Although drivers in each of the previous areas can be very important to the economic outlook, their interdependencies can significantly amplify their impact. For example, the wide availability of affordable broadband access provides the infrastructure for rapid adoption of bandwidth-demanding IP communications services such as high-definition video (HDV) content distribution. Although the government-sponsored telephone infrastructure provided the United States with a significant advantage in the early adoption of the Internet, other nations leapfrogged to newer and better technologies, positioning them to become leading adopters. In 2005, the United States was 16th in the world in terms of broadband access technologies penetration. The advantage of a modernized infrastructure would be further enhanced if the adoption of the next version of IP were aggressively pursued at the same time.

The importance of the Internet and, in particular, IP communications is undeniably significant in today's economy. As a consequence, social,[9] legal,[10] and governing issues related to IP communications and the Internet have become important as well. All these aspects gain a new dimension in the context of the IP evolution. From a technology perspective, IETF approached IPv6 as an opportunity for a new start to address the challenges and constraints experienced during IPv4's growth, and to lay the foundations of a new Internet. The IP evolution could, however, represent a significant inflexion point in all aspects related to Internet and IP communications. The question is: Will individuals, businesses, and the world seize the opportunity of a fresh start and if not, when will this opportunity present itself next?

The Global Information Society: WSIS

In a short period of time, the Internet adoption introduced IP in all aspects of our lives, whether we know it or not. The Internet's rapid adoption and its overall success can be credited to multiple factors but primarily to its operating and development principles. The Internet, as envisioned by its founders, is a network of networks and operates in a highly distributed, nonregulated manner. Its management and governance are developed and implemented locally by the user community. Technically, IP is developed bottom up, publicly in forums that are open and inclusive. The success of these principles is proven by the Internet's organic growth and its ability to adapt to the rapidly evolving world of communications services.

The principles that make the Internet so successful and the mentality they instill in its user community can become a challenge to existing institutions and

9. See Marleen Huysman and Volker Wulf, eds., *Social Capital and Information Technology* (The MIT Press, 2004).

10. Kaisor Basar and others, *IPv6: Legal Aspects of the New Internet Protocol* (Euro6IX, 2005), http://www.ipv6tf.org/pdf/ipv6legalaspects.pdf.

their governing policies. As its penetration increases, the Internet changes existent economic, legal, and political conditions in society. As discussed in Chapter 1, "The Business and Economic Importance of IP Communications," the Internet is a critical and strategic resource. It enables economies to grow internally while it facilitates globalization. It increases competitiveness within industries to the benefit of the users. The law, in the context of Internet communications and services, must revisit the concepts of privacy, intellectual property defense, and criminality. Freedom of speech and access to uncontrolled content takes a new dimension in the context of the Internet. The U.S. Department of Commerce controls the root resources, even though very loosely, but is also the subject of intense and highly politicized debates over Internet ownership.

If marketing benchmarks are used to measure Internet penetration, at the end of 2007, worldwide Internet penetration stood at 20 percent with signifying mass adoption only being achieved by less than 30 percent of the world population.[11] This is a measure of today's digital divide.

ICT and Internet adoption are essential to bridge this divide and to meet the United Nations (UN) Millennium Development Goals. It is a challenging task. At the same time, while understanding the Internet's enabling power and encouraging its rapid adoption, governments are fully aware of the challenges faced in terms of controlling it. This is a complex and difficult problem. How would a local, centralized entity manage and control a global, distributed environment? How would it justify the imposition of such control on an environment that proved to be admirably efficient, more so than regulated environments such as the telephone system?

The International Telecommunications Union (ITU), a UN organization, took the leadership role in organizing a two-part conference that would discuss the complexities and interdependencies of the Information Society in general and, among other topics, those of Internet adoption and governance. The World Summit on Information Society (WSIS) was endorsed by the UN General Assembly (Resolution 56/183) and organized in two stages (Geneva 2003 and Tunis 2005). The importance of this event was significant in potentially leading to fundamental changes to the operating and governing principles of the Internet. On this highly publicized topic, the adopted resolution was a compromise pleasing

---

11. http://www.internetworldstats.com/stats.htm.

both sides: those who favor the current governance model and those who want to change it.[12] Following are excerpts from the resolution:

- **Paragraph 55:** "We recognize that the existing arrangements for Internet governance have worked effectively to make the Internet the highly robust, dynamic and geographically diverse medium that it is today..."

- **Paragraph 68:** "We recognize that all governments should have an equal role and responsibility for international Internet governance and for ensuring the stability, security, and continuity of the Internet. We also recognize the need for development of public policy by governments in consultation with all stakeholders."

Although the need for another body to work on this topic continues to be debated,[13] WSIS also agreed to invite the UN secretary-general to convene a new forum for multi-stakeholder policy dialogue. Going forward, the Internet Governance Forum (IGF) will have to address concerns related to Internet ownership, impact of regulations, security, censorship, and maintaining a nimble development of IP technologies.

The advent of IPv6 and its deployment has the potential to be a unique inflexion point in the context of this discussion. In an IPv6 world, we can take advantage of the full potential of IP communications and applications; we can scale the IP infrastructure to support a truly global Information Society. IPv6 comes with significantly larger address resources that stimulate adoption. The IPv6 adoption dynamic is different from the IPv4 adoption dynamic. At the origin of the IPv4 adoption, Western countries were clearly leading the technology adoption through the sponsorship of their research and development community involved in IP standardization. Today, the Internet is a worldwide technology; the upgrade to IPv6 is market segment and region dependent, with leaders yet to be identified.

12. http://www.itu.int/wsis/documents/doc_multi.asp?lang=en&id=2266|2267.

13. "ITAA Comments to the U.S. Department of State on the Report of the Working Group on Internet Governance, June 2005," www.state.gov/documents/organization/50552.pdf.

To the extent to which address allocation is a measure of interest, the difference between IPv4 and IPv6 adoption is shown in Figure 3-2.[14]

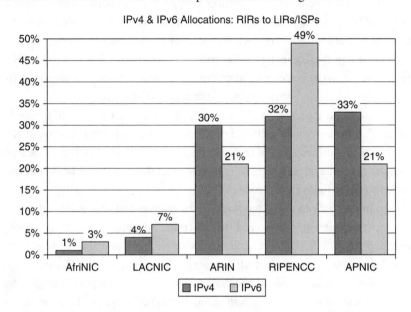

IPv4 & IPv6 Allocations: RIRs to LIRs/ISPs

Figure 3-2 *IPv6 Versus IPv4 Address Allocations per Regional Internet Registry*

Although the IPv4 Internet runs very well on entrenched, democratic, practice-proven policies and mechanisms, the next generation of the Internet could be a fresh start in all its aspects, including management. It is thus very likely that the IPv6 world will be the primary candidate for testing IGF proposals and policies.

The Internet community that built and continues to build this resource must be a significant and active stakeholder in both the process of IPv6 adoption and the process of shaping the governance principles of IPv6. This will ensure the rapid expansion of a practical Information Society and the continued success of the Internet to the benefit of people.

---

14. NRO, "Internet Numbers Status Report – December, 2007," available at http://www.nro.net/ statistics/index.html.

Stimulating Innovation

ICT is now a recognized, powerful enabler for all economic sectors. Investment in ICT is essential to maintaining competitiveness in a global economy. Extensive technology adoption increases exposure to business challenges that can be addressed in the context of advanced communications infrastructures. ICT enables each economic sector to adapt rapidly to new demands, to interface efficiently with partners, to open remote markets, and to innovate.

According to the 2006 WITSA report, the global market for ICT tops $3 trillion. This means that in itself, the development and commercialization of ICT is a significant business. While realizing the benefits of using ICT, governments recognize the value of producing ICT. To that end, businesses must be encouraged and supported to innovate and to lead.

The innovation process in the world of the Internet and IP is unique in nature. IP promotes open standards and architectures, meaning closed technology ownership is difficult if not counterproductive to maintain. Unlike other technologies, the dispersion of IP knowledge does not benefit from a single champion who could accelerate penetration. Standards are adopted through loose consensus and their value is proven through market adoption. In a sense, the Internet is a vast laboratory with all its users being allowed to propose and run experiments.

This observation, stemming from the Internet's mode of operation, leads to the conclusion that in the case of IP, creating a large IP infrastructure is essential to stimulating IP innovation. The environment educates and supports a savvy user base, which drives new requirements for applications and services. In turn, the requirements drive innovation in foundational, infrastructure technologies such as IP or access layer solutions. The same user base can be leveraged to trial and improve newly developed technologies. This environment, connected by the versatility of IP, becomes an incubator for innovation where economies of scale apply. Increased Internet adoption and a larger available infrastructure translate into an increased number of opportunities to innovate.

In this context, IPv6 is perfectly suited if not mandatory to support continued IP innovation:

- **Economies of scale:** IPv6 provides the resources to increase the scale of networks and to bring in more users with their demands and requirements. It also facilitates large-scale deployment of valuable services that were slow to the IPv4 market. Multicast-based content delivery is easier to deploy because there are virtually no limitations to the number of available global multicast groups.

- **Direct access to all devices:** IPv6 can eliminate devices that, in the name of IPv4 address conservation, broke the symmetry (ability to run bidirectional communications) of the Internet. With enough address space, all IPv6 devices can now be directly accessed, and that opens a new area of innovation: fully distributed applications and services.

- **New capabilities:** With new capabilities such as simple provisioning mechanisms and protocol extensibility, IPv6 enables communications infrastructures to offer new services that can drive innovation.

- **Easier market space to enter:** IPv6 expertise is not widespread. There is less competition in the IPv6 world than in the IPv4 world. This enables smaller companies to innovate and capture market share. This is the reason why some companies who want to enter the IP communications market focus on IPv6 rather than compete against established IPv4 vendors and providers.

Governments have a unique opportunity to stimulate innovation in their respective national economies. J. Farrell and G. Saloner have shown the importance of sponsorship in the process of stimulating and diffusing innovation.[15] This is an area where governments can take an active role through sponsorship and policies. Governments also can facilitate the establishment of centers of excellence where expertise is being developed and shared to facilitate the diffusion of technology and innovation. A very successful example is the

---

15. J. Farrell and G. Saloner, "Competition, Compatibility, and Standards: The Economics of Horses, Penguins and Lemmings," in *Product Standardization and Competitive Strategy*, ed. H. L. Gabel, 1–21 (Amsterdam: Elsevier Science, 1987).

6NET project sponsored by the European Union with Cisco as a leading partner.[16] The 6DISS project followed shortly thereafter.[17] These two projects were instrumental in increasing the IPv6 deployment and operational expertise worldwide. They also provided a setting for further development of the protocol. Government sponsorship can come in various forms and be applied according to specific national strategies, as discussed in Chapter 4, "IPv6 Adoption Strategies."

A government's decision to actively support and invest in IPv6 adoption today hinges on the perceived benefit and risks of being an early adopter. Early adopters need to invest significantly in the industry, and the rate of failure is generally high; however, laggards risk falling behind as they have to acquire infrastructure technologies and experience,[18] but the return on investment can be quite high for those who invest early. The deployment of IPv6 prepares a national infrastructure for a new wave of ICT based innovation.

Opportunities to Develop Local Industry

As discussed earlier, IPv6 adoption will stimulate innovation in a relatively greenfield environment. This makes it easier for new companies to penetrate the ICT markets with point products or entire solutions. With IPv6, the government's intention to develop a national ICT industry and promote ICT-based innovations can facilitate and support the growth of new companies.

National ICT companies focusing on IPv6 can leapfrog traditional, imported ICT technologies in either isolated and specialized areas or new ones. Governments can create national markets for these companies. Government-sponsored IPv6 research networks and new nationwide IPv6 infrastructures represent opportunities to shelter and sponsor new company growth. Equipment procurement for government projects also can favor an emerging national ICT industry, which can be competitive in IPv6. This trend has become evident in several countries around the world, as discussed in Chapter 4. The sooner such

16. http://www.6net.org.

17. http://www.6diss.org.

18. NTIA, "Technical and Economic Assessment of Internet Protocol Version 6 (IPv6)" (January 2006), available at http://www.ntia.doc.gov/ntiahome/ntiageneral/ipv6/.

national strategies are initiated, the higher the chance that incipient national industry will survive and lead in a next generation IP world.

The strategic economic importance of the IP evolution is significant by itself. This evolution, however, takes place in conjunction with revolutionary changes across multiple communications technologies with a tremendous compounded effect. Although national ICT industry emergence and growth is multifaceted, IPv6 can be a significant differentiator. IPv6 levels the playing field in the race for ICT leadership.

Enabling Education

Education is essential to shaping socially integrated citizens and competent contributors to the society. The education standards and practices become more important in a global society in which a highly educated workforce easily can be leveraged from all over the world. The success of an educated workforce is reflected in the competitiveness of the population.

Matching the digital revolution, educational concepts and practices have changed dramatically. Easy and rapid access to information, e-learning, and remotely accessed labs are just a few aspects of what is shaping up to be a radically new educational experience. The Internet is without a doubt the most important driver of change in the way we learn today. Efficient or not and whether we want it or not, students are taking advantage of the Internet. It is now up to the educators to systemize its use and to leverage the tools it offers to create innovative learning methodologies. These new approaches can improve the acquisition of fundamental knowledge, expand a student's cultural horizon through exposure to a larger world, and, more importantly, make the student Internet savvy. Reflecting the importance of ICT skills, the Educational Testing Service (ETS),[19] under the National Higher Education ICT Initiative, created the "ICT Literacy Assessment" test used to evaluate a student's ICT proficiency.

The Internet Age educational experience can become reality only when access to the Internet is available to most students. The development of new teaching techniques must be backed by robust and powerful IP infrastructures for

19. http://www.ets.org/.

schools that enable classrooms to benefit from them. Outdated IP infrastructures that are used for services such as e-mail, file transfers, and some Internet browsing should be replaced. The new IP infrastructures must have sufficient bandwidth to support audio and video content distribution, video conferencing, Voice over IP (VoIP) telephony, and collaborative applications. These networks must benefit from enough globally reachable addresses to provide access to all the resources they offer. Such upgrades become mandatory in order to enable new and efficient learning tools. Along with enhanced capabilities, the new school IP networks must have extended reach to provide access to all students, whether they are in a classroom or at a remote, sparsely populated location.

The deployment of such infrastructures requires government sponsorship, and IPv6 represents the perfect opportunity to transition schools into the Internet Age. A successful example of such an infrastructure upgrade is the deployment of IPv6 in all primary and secondary schools in Greece.[20] Covering approximately 13,000 nodes, this new network offers services such as broadband Internet access, e-mail, mailing lists, remote network access (dialup), personalized web portal and web hosting, content filtering, asynchronous distance learning, video on demand (VoD), teleconferencing, webcasting, electronic magazines, news, and discussion forums. The success of this effort encouraged other European countries to follow suite. Similarly, in the United States, ongoing state-level efforts to upgrade the school system IP infrastructure must include IPv6 deployment as well.

E-learning is now present in most U.S. higher-education institutions. Their campuses benefit from various IP-based services that help students with both administrative and academic activities. IPv6 is deployed in order to handle large numbers of devices and enable mobility between the classroom, libraries, and dormitories within campuses. Major national and regional research and education networks around the globe, such as Internet2 and RENATER, have been IPv6-enabled for years.[21] The next important step is to adjust engineering and computer science curriculum to include IPv6, to encourage and stimulate fundamental and applied research.

---

20. 6NET, *Cookbook on Deploying IPv6 in School Networks* (June 2005), http://www.6net.org/publications/deliverables/D5.14.pdf.

21. http://www.renater.fr/spip.php?rubrique156&lang=en.

NOTE	IPv6 is now part of all Cisco certification programs and is being included in the curriculum for all Cisco Networking Academies.

Recognizing the importance of technology in education, developing countries are enthusiastically embracing the idea of providing each child with a $100 laptop. But true worldwide education enablement comes with the networks that interconnect these laptops and provide them access to information. IPv6 has the resources to support such infrastructures in a scalable and cost-effective way. The value of the IP evolution resides in the fundamental business and social transformations that IPv6 is enabling.

The Business Perspective

Chapter 1 of this book highlights the strategic importance of IP infrastructures. More and more business-critical services and applications converge on IP. Businesses use IP for operational purposes (ordering, purchasing, inventory management, and so on) to support internal services (telephony, video conferencing, and so on) and to support services delivered to their customers. Hence, all business plans of an organization have, to one extent or another, an IT dimension; they observe IT implications and constraints. IT investments, while high at times, have proven justified.

The evolution of IP will continue to create both opportunities and challenges for all businesses. It is not so much about extraordinary new features or capabilities or about the killer application. It is more about addressing the resources necessary to efficiently support large infrastructures and the growing numbers of services and devices. Service providers need these resources to support the growth of their subscriber base. Enterprises, on the other hand, need these resources to support the convergence of services over their IP infrastructure.

Along with the quantitative benefits of a larger address space come qualitative benefits as well. A cleaner, well planned address scheme, for example, leads to reduced operational expenditure (OPEX). It could also reduce the costs and the downtime generated by mergers and acquisitions, which prove to be very challenging in the IPv4 world because address collisions complicate the process of integrating the IT infrastructures of independent organizations.

Last but not least, your customers and partners might pursue the IP evolution faster than expected. They will place requirements that might not be easy to meet overnight. Which U.S. service provider will be ready to offer IPv6 services to the federal agencies by 2008? Which enterprise will be able to interface smoothly with an ISP providing IPv6 access in an international market? The answers to such questions could dramatically change a market's competitive landscape.

The IT revolution is coming of age. Gone are the times of IT infrastructures built through disjointed projects on top of networks of networks. The sum of many of these tactical efforts does not match strategic needs anymore. So it is not surprising that everywhere you turn these days, everyone is talking about the Next Generation Networks (NGN) and, in a more complete picture, the next generation IT environments. Both enterprises and service providers are actively engaged in planning, designing, or implementing their future, holistic IT environments. And whether the benefits of the IP evolution are immediately apparent or not, businesses cannot ignore it. They must strategize with the future in mind. Regardless of the cost implications, which are discussed later in this chapter, or the timeline for its adoption, businesses can no longer ignore the IPv6 reality.

Addressing the Market Transformation and Needs

Over the past decade, IP communications have dramatically changed the market landscape for all businesses. The IP-enabled world is extending well beyond the current people-computer interactions to a broader context of object-to-object communications, where the connected "things" are devices, machines, information, services, and people. Always-on, always-connected resources, customers, suppliers, and partners create a new socioeconomic environment that demands new business models and business processes. These must be supported in turn by appropriately capable, integrated, and scalable information communications infrastructures.

Initially, businesses leveraged IP to optimize existent processes and functions. The focus was on very specific functions related to the primary scope of the business. This natural approach lead to the development of network "islands" customized to each market space, as shown in Figure 3-3.

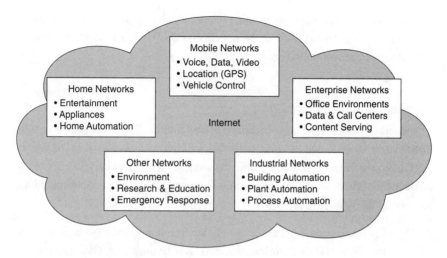

Figure 3-3   *The Internet Today*

Although IP is far from being fully leveraged within each of these islands, and the independent growth of each island remains a significant business opportunity, the larger opportunities are in integrating these islands. This is where the IP evolution delivers the most significant economic benefits and IPv6 becomes an essential component. Market segmentation has worked well for IP up to this point. However, it is now time to move away from market segmentation before it becomes counterproductive. This section explores some of today's market demands and the opportunities available to both service providers and enterprises.

The Convergence of IP-Based Communications

IP's ability to rapidly integrate new services and to deliver them in a cost-effective yet reliable way pushes both service providers and enterprises toward consolidating all their communications needs over a single protocol. A converged IT infrastructure would be easier and less expensive to manage. The service consolidation, however, increases the demand for IP addresses. An enterprise user now has multiple addresses for their devices and services. Fixed VoIP phone, fixed access for the PC, and Wi-Fi access for the laptop all require a different IP address. The combination of the market demand for converged services and the interest in options such as the deployment of thin clients (which requires double the number of IP addresses per host) leads to the conclusion that IPv6 is a necessary enabler for the service consolidation process.

The Demand for Information

Content has become the "currency of the Internet." Demand for access to information is growing in sync with the striking increase in the volume of information available. In meeting this demand, products and services related to content delivery are increasing at a dramatic rate and the delivery mechanisms are leveraging the IP infrastructures:

- **Entertainment:** Access providers are fine-tuning their business models to deliver HDTV premium channels over IP multicast. Over-the-top content providers such as YouTube built their audiences through free but lower-quality content and are now quickly morphing into a platform for business and political communications. A related move is the industry adoption of IP Multimedia Subsystem (IMS) standards. IMS is an enabler for application and content delivery of "triple play" services combining voice, video, and data over IP.

- **Educational:** Distance education is becoming a significant component in the curriculum of major universities. It is also the business object of greenfield educational institutions. The option to tailor the learning schedule around the personal schedule makes distance education very palatable to those interested in continuing their education or those seeking job- or business-related training.

- **Business:** Whether it is stock prices, news reports, plant operations, or inventory data, information reaches businesses entirely or partially over an IP infrastructure, and thus its availability is essential to the proper operation of the business.

- **Machine-to-machine (M2M):** Information is also a critical ingredient in M2M communications as industrial networks move from current-loop and bus systems to IP. The generation and use of static and real-time information opens the door to a wide spectrum of opportunities ranging from vehicle and building automation to innovations on more effective management and security of plant and process systems. The number of sensors, actuators, effectors, and annunciators in today's industrial environment is already huge and will explode as information from emerging sensor networks and nano-machines takes off. A scalable infrastructure is required to support these devices and enable them to acquire and provide relevant information.

An interesting dimension of this market is that many of the Internet consumers contribute content as well. A 2004 Pew Internet & American Life Project report[22] indicates that 44 percent of Internet users contribute their thoughts and information, while a related 2005 report[23] highlights that teens are even more involved in contributing to the Internet's information pool. Much of the content is exchanged through direct communication between users. Peer-to-peer communications, a growing contributor to the overall IP traffic, complicate the definition of business models that capitalize clearly on content distribution. Peer-to-peer communications also defy the traditional asymmetric traffic profile assumed for Internet users, requiring new considerations in designing the NGNs and in the development of the billing models. Although the customer base is very large, the challenge in this market space is to identify and develop the right business model and evolve the IP infrastructure to best support these services.

IPv6 is capable of bringing more content consumers into the market and providing them with more options to receive and transmit content. At the same time, an environment with all users having unique, globally reachable IPv6 addresses facilitates and stimulates peer-to-peer communications. This phenomenon can potentially drain revenue from today's services that count on IPv4's use of NAT and user communications that require a broker. Providers will have to generate value-added services that discourage a user's tendency to go for a similar service found free on the Internet. Higher quality would, for example, justify paying for the VoIP services offered by the access provider versus the free services available

22. Amanda Lenhart, John Horrigan, and Deborah Fallows, "Content Creation Online," http://www.pewinternet.org/pdfs/PIP_Content_Creation_Report.pdf.

23. Amanda Lenhart and Mary Madden, "Teen Content Creators and Consumers," http://www.pewinternet.org/pdfs/PIP_Teens_Content_Creation.pdf.

on the Internet. Initiative such as P4P Explicit Communications for Cooperative Control Between P2P and Network Providers is an other example of new service that could add value.

Social Networking

If its life is not measured in "Internet years," social networking can be considered a relatively new concept. At first sight it might be immediately filed in the entertainment/leisure category. However, it already proved itself to be much more than that.

Social networking experiments became unexpected tornado markets, bringing together incredible numbers of individuals. After being acquired by News Corp., MySpace was signing up 150,000 new users a day. Environments such as Second Life are exploring new sources of revenue from the captive audience they generate. This goes beyond simple entertainment. Cisco Systems, for example, purchased property and has a store in the Second Life virtual world. Going a step further on the path of trend validation, Cisco also purchased social networking technology from the privately owned Utah Street Networks, the operator of the social network site Tribe.net. Cisco plans to use the technology to build products for both consumers and enterprises.

Social networking will become a significant market driver in evolving the IP infrastructure. IPv6 can provide the resources necessary to efficiently support the social networking environments of the future and the markets they will develop.

Fixed-Mobile Convergence

The market demand for mobility has sharply increased since the early days of the first cell phones. Ericsson Research coined the phrase "Always Best Connected (ABC)" in 2001 for a model that allows seamless connectivity and handover across multiple access networks, including cellular, WLAN, and fixed networks.[24] The research explored emerging paradigms of integrated mobility including personal-area networks (PAN), Mobile Ad Hoc Networks (MANET),

---

24. http://adaptive.ucsd.edu/02_08_26_Eva_Topics_UCSD_2.pdf.

and Network Mobility (NEMO). The idea is to offer users the ability to connect anywhere, anytime, and with the device of their choice regardless of whether they are static or not. The transition between the access media types and between access points should be seamless for all services. Today's highly mobile, always connected individuals make these capabilities a market requirement.

Fixed-mobile convergence is a strategy aggressively pursued by both fixed-access providers and by mobile providers. This is the new telecom battleground.[25] Those who successfully implement fixed-mobile convergence will acquire a whole new market space to grow into. However, this convergence requires IP addressing resources beyond those provided by IPv4. IPv6 is the answer. It enables fixed-mobile convergence and is essential to the economic growth of access providers.

Servicing Networks for People

The increasing complexity and importance of today's networks generates great market demand for managed services. Enterprises of all sizes are interested in having someone—service providers or professional services organizations—manage their networks. Service providers are also tapping into the opportunities offered by home networks. New services such as security surveillance, health monitoring, and product tethering, together with existing services such as VoIP, video on demand, broadcast video, and Internet access, will lead to complex home networks that people depend on beyond entertainment. Subscribers are likely to rely more and more on someone else to manage this communications infrastructure.

The market size for these services is significant, yet it is not easy to make the service itself profitable. The large IPv6 address space offers globally unique addresses to all the devices managed, leading to simplified management models. To offer managed network services at home, the traditionally tight margins do not provide room for expensive provisioning tools and mechanisms. Some of the IPv6-specific provisioning mechanisms represent an opportunity to simplify the operational model and to keep a low post-sales cost for the service.

---

25. Wally Harris, "Convergence" (Ericsson AB, 2006), http://www.itu.int/ITU-D/imt-2000/documents/Algiers2006/Presentations/Day%203/Algiers_Presentation_37_WHariz.pdf.

Facilitating and Stimulating Growth

Over the past decade IP environments have been growing at unprecedented rates. This growth has been driven by multiple factors, which stretched the networks not only in size but also in the capabilities required to support new services.

Service Providers

The Internet's rapid adoption provides the service providers with a tremendous source of business growth. Internet access is no longer a luxury but a commodity in most household service portfolios. Figure 3-4 shows the growth from 2002 to 2007 in the number of high-speed access subscribers per 100 inhabitants of the member countries of the Organization for Economic Co-operation and Development (OECD).[26]

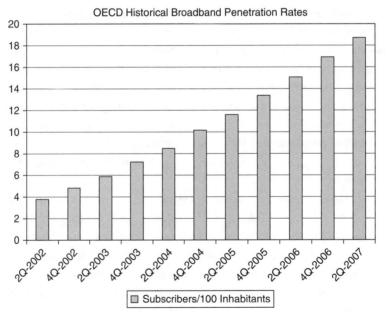

Figure 3-4 *Broadband Penetration in OECD Member Countries*

26. http://www.oecd.org/dataoecd/22/12/39574779.xls.

As much as the Internet is a driver for the IP adoption, this is just one aspect of IP's impact on the service provider's business growth. Cable operators use IP to manage their cable modems even if no Internet access service is provided. Without IP they would not be able to offer even basic cable TV service. Mobile providers rely more and more on IP to deliver services to the mobile handsets. VoIP services are a very high-growth business for both access providers such as Verizon and over-the-top service providers such as Vonage. With the availability of higher last-mile bandwidths, content providers have become very successful in delivering content over IP. These are just a few examples that show how embedded IP is in all aspects of the service provider business. With enough resources, IP can continue to both "push" business growth through new services and "pull" business growth by facilitating or stimulating the subscription to access services regardless of whether or not they involve IP services at first.

IPv4 opened up a whole new world of opportunities for service providers but it does not have the resources to support them in a clean, unfettered way at the present and anticipated growth rates. IPv6 becomes a necessity in enabling service providers to benefit from the economies of scales applied to the services we are familiar with today. But what about the IP services of tomorrow? Many revolve around managed services such as home and business security monitoring, home appliances monitoring and maintenance, health monitoring and telemedicine, and so forth, all of which open the door for an even larger business space. The IPv4 workaround options for IP address shortages, such as network address translation (NAT), significantly diminish a service provider's capability to leverage the economies of scale by making it difficult or impossible to communicate directly with network-connected customer devices and services. IPv6 must take center stage in any service provider NGN discussion.

Enterprises

Enterprise networks are less likely to reach the size of broadband or mobile service provider networks. Nevertheless, the number of devices enterprise networks need to integrate in their infrastructures is growing rapidly. On one hand, employees require more and more personal IP devices to perform their jobs. On the other hand, there are the IP devices that automate manufacturing processes or are used to monitor facilities.

Enterprise growing pains are often coming from mergers and acquisitions (M&A), short- or long-term joint venture (JV) arrangements, and inter-corporate connections to customers, suppliers, and business partners. If you have ever gone through such an event, you understand the magnitude of the problem. In today's fast-paced M&A and JV world, an organization's infrastructure can develop significant complexity and can quickly become unmanageable. The address collisions, address assignments, policies, and translation resources such as servers lead to the need for "creative" workaround solutions. The new business-to-business (B2B) connections cannot take downtime for a renumbering event. Even if things are made to work with several layers of NAT used internally, it will lead to a network that is almost impossible to scale up. The IT integration costs related to M&A and B2B relationships are significant and can be a burden to the swift success and ongoing operations of efficient electronic communications between organizations.

The next generation enterprise networks must be capable of handling mergers and acquisitions better. IPv6 offers the resources necessary to number enterprise networks and devices with globally unique addresses. It also offers the tools to facilitate a smoother renumbering process should one be necessary. The economic value for enterprises is significant, both in terms of reduced integration costs and in terms of reduced network operations and downtime costs. IPv6 facilitates enterprise growth.

Operations Simplifications

Managing and maintaining today's IT environments is a significant contributor to the OPEX of most medium-sized and large organizations. This applies to the infrastructure that supports internal processes and the infrastructure that offers services to customers. The expense proves to be justified by the returns generated through IT. However, the elimination of operation complexities and the subsequent reduction in IT operating costs remains a goal of every business.

On the one hand, improvements on the costs related to operations can be made through mechanisms or technologies emerging from our experience operating IPv4 networks for several decades. For the most part, such improvements can be integrated in any version of IP. On the other hand, there are significant cost-reduction opportunities in networks that can be centrally managed (no need for replication of resources within distinct administrative domains) and in all managed devices being accessible directly (devices are not hidden behind NAT).

IPv6 implements new provisioning mechanisms, some unmatched in IPv4, that can simplify operations. Most importantly, IPv6 offers the resources to build clean, scalable IT environments in which all devices are easily reachable and management policies can be implemented in the manner best suited for the situation. The cost-saving implications of these aspects of the IP evolution are significant and, together with the technical benefits, are very powerful incentives for IPv6 integration. Comcast was one of the first organizations to bank on the operational cost reductions generated by the use of IPv6 for infrastructure management. Comcast had several options to mitigate within IPv4 to address shortages it was experiencing. These solutions, however, entailed increased operational costs and would lead to constraints that could negatively impact growth in the future. IPv6 offered a much cleaner and less expensive solution.

Most enterprises are likely to be able to comfortably deploy a manageable environment with the resources provided by the private IPv4 address space (see RFC 1918, *Address Allocation for Private Internets*). This of course comes with the M&A-related challenges discussed earlier in this chapter. Very large enterprises, however, might start experiencing RFC 1918 shortages and would face decisions similar to the ones tackled by the large service providers.

Gaining Competitive Edge and Leadership

Competitive edge can be gained in two major ways:

- **Vision and strategic planning in implementing new services:** A business might have the foresight of a great opportunity and invest in it well ahead of its competitors. An example is the investment by Japanese access providers in building an infrastructure that supports the distribution of video content over IPv6 multicast. This gives them an edge over competing service providers that might not be able to scale the same service over their existent IPv4 infrastructures.

- **Readiness and nimble execution in meeting customer and market demands:** Opportunities and challenges might materialize within a market over a short period of time and they might be difficult to anticipate. Businesses that adapt quickly can gain a competitive edge. An example is the OMB and DoD IPv6 mandate that presented U.S. service providers with the challenge of meeting the IPv6 requirements by 2008 in order to keep their U.S. federal agencies as customers. The service provider with the best execution on meeting these requirements stands the chance of gaining significant market share.

Naturally, each of these approaches has benefits and drawbacks. The return on investing in a dramatically new idea can be very large while the risks may be significant. The important thing, however, is that both approaches can be optimally executed only in an IT environment that is flexible enough to rapidly integrate new services and that is sufficiently manageable and scalable to support their growth.

Competitiveness is not geographically bound anymore. In a global economy, the competitive edge is defined as much locally as it is in remote markets. If parts of the world will embrace the next generation of IP, global business will stay competitive only if their IT infrastructure will enable them to continue to interact with IPv6 customers or partners.

IPv6 in itself will rarely be the competitive differentiator. Instead, IPv6 enables the service provider or enterprise network to be more nimble and flexible in supporting the next big service opportunity or to adapt to rapid changes in their market. A well-planned IT infrastructure also will open the door for further innovation.

The Costs of an IP Evolution

The thought of transitioning such vast and operationally critical infrastructures as the IP networks from one version to another is daunting. At first sight the expected costs appear very large, and the question that immediately and naturally comes to everyone's mind is: What is the return on such a large investment?

The networking world and its IPv6 community lived for a very long time under the heavy weight of the return on investment (ROI) question; a question that became very common particularly during the Internet depression that started in early 2000. Although that is sometimes the right tactical, short-term question, there is always larger scope, strategic questions that should be considered, such as: How much can I scale up my current network and services and how easy is it to do? What operational cost reductions are generated in an environment with sufficient IP resources? Should we justify the enabling of our IP infrastructures to support IPv6, the adoption of a foundational technology, with just the traditional ROI calculation considerations? The answer to the IPv6 ROI is: None can be calculated easily. Instead we should ask ourselves: What are the costs of not integrating IPv6 in our networks? How can IPv6 better position us strategically?

You might have noticed a very important change in semantics from "transitioning" to "integrating." Transitioning from an IPv4 network today to an IPv6 network tomorrow is not a realistic goal and it is generally a goal that is difficult to justify both financially and technically. IPv6 is and will continue to be integrated in existing IPv4 infrastructures on a service by service basis. It will perform well-defined functions in a more cost-effective way, such as managing large numbers of devices, or it will support new, scalable services such as multicast-based content delivery. The corollary is that the network must be ready to support IPv6 to benefit from its use.

In the drawn-out process of marketing IPv6, the topic of its ROI was a constant trump card pulled out at the end of even the most exciting technical and visionary discussions. People balked under the pressure and entertained the idea that an ROI for IPv6 must be calculated before adoption will start.[27] This perspective is entrenched in the industry, as shown by a BT INS IT Industry Survey in early 2008.[28] Of the 310 respondents, two-thirds of which are located in the United States or Canada, 73 percent stated that there is not a strong enough ROI to deploy IPv6. This perspective, which went hand in hand with the obsessive search for the IPv6 killer app, is hiding the true value that IPv6 brings to our networks.

ROI calculations are generally applicable to service deployment and to network operation. IPv6 in itself is not a service; it only supports services. The

27. L-F. Pau, "IPv6 Return on Investment (R.O.I.) Analysis Framework at a Generic Level, and First Conclusions" (October 2002), available at https://ep.eur.nl/.

28. Rick Blum, "IPv6" (February 2008), available at http://www.ins.com/resources/surveys/.

deployment of services and the operation of networks benefit from the economies of scale. The economies of scale can be achieved only with sufficient infrastructure resources. IPv6 enables networks to increase the ROI on operations and services. This point has been clearly made by the cable operators who chose IPv6 to manage their infrastructure instead of choosing technically feasible but more expensive IPv4 options.

ROI for Services Supported by IPv6

In recent years U.S. cable TV multiple system operators (MSO) interconnected their various market-contained networks via powerful, nationwide backbones. Although private IPv4 address space was sufficient to manage the devices within a given market, in a consolidated environment, RFC 1918 (private address space) does not offer enough resources to manage the pooled devices.

From a technical perspective, the MSOs would always have the option of federating their nationwide network, reuse the private address space in each domain, and manage each domain independently. IPv6 would easily offer the cable providers the IP addresses they need to manage their devices in a single domain, but is it worth the trouble? A simple theoretical calculation on Comcast's environment, however, reveals the cost implications related to each scenario.

Based on a presentation delivered by Comcast's Brian Field at the University of Pennsylvania in November 2005, at the time there were 17.7 million subscribers, with the user distribution per converged regional-area network (CRAN) shown here:

- Four regions: 1.5 million subscribers

- Three regions: 1 to 1.5 million subscribers

- Nine regions: ~0.5 million subscribers

- Five regions: Less than 0.5 million subscribers

Assuming that in 2005 Comcast deployed the Cisco Network Registrar tool for provisioning services, the licensing costs (list price) would be $1,625,000 for supporting 5 million subscribers, $500,000 for 1 million subscribers, and $175,000 for 250,000 subscribers.

ROI for Services Supported by IPv6 (Continued)

In this simple, theoretical example, Comcast would spend $0.36 for provisioning each subscriber in a centralized model that could not be supported by IPv4. In a federated environment, the inefficiencies in the use of licenses raises the provisioning costs to $0.64 per subscriber. MSOs typically target a maximum cost of $0.50 per subscriber. These estimates do not include, for example, the cost savings for staff, which would also be reduced in a centralized model.

The major U.S. cable providers deploy IPv6 in order to manage their devices. They do not look at IPv6's ROI but rather at the increased ROI for all their services delivered over IPv4.

The same point has been made by Microsoft through its introduction of IPv6 in the Vista operating system. Although NAT traversal is a technically acceptable solution, maintaining it in networks where disparate implementations and more and more applications come to market becomes difficult. This often-silent aspect of NAT use erodes service and product revenues due to post-sales support costs, as exemplified in broadband access networks.

NOTE	When devices behind NAT need to be accessible from the Internet, a static address mapping must be performed in the home gateway. If the home user wants to be able to reach these devices by using their public address, an address returned by a DNS query, a further DNS/port mapping must be set up in the gateway performing the NAT functions. These configuration settings typically end up being addressed by either the access provider or the manufacturer of the home gateway. In both cases, these support costs reduce revenue per unit. With a clear move toward peer-to-peer applications and home users becoming content generators, these types of costs will become more apparent and difficult to sustain. This is without mentioning the challenges to deploy several NAT layers (NAT2) where NAT would be done on aggregation, quickly reaching the capacity limit of the model in terms of operations

Naturally there are costs involved with readying the network and its operation for IPv6, but these costs depend significantly on how well the process is planned and how far in advance the process is started. The planning aspects and the cost implications are discussed in Chapter 6, "Planning Your IPv6 Migration." It is as tempting to put a price tag on the IP evolution as it is dicey. For reference, a study by RTI International commissioned by the National Institute of Standards and Technology (NIST) estimates that in the United States alone, the incremental costs of integrating IPv6 will be $25.4 billion (in 2003 dollars) over 25 years. The "Executive Summary" of this report states:

> Although these cost estimates seem large, they are actually small relative to the overall expected expenditures on IT hardware and software, and even smaller relative to the expected value of potential market applications.[29]

This entire chapter highlights the value, the importance, and the need for more IP resources. This chapter offers a glimpse into the opportunities that would be lost were we not able to scale up our networks in a simple manner. This is the complex value that a foundational technology such as IPv6 builds into all aspects of a network's operation. Getting a network ready for IPv6 overnight, when a need is pressing or the alternatives are just not sustainable, is not cost effective and, at times, is technically impossible. The truly relevant question then becomes: What is the cost of not adopting IPv6?

Summary

IPv4 and its original killer application, the Internet, opened the door to a whole new world of communications, social interaction, and ways of conducting business. We have only begun to scratch the surface of possibilities. The value and importance of IP is recognized at both macro- and microeconomic levels; it is recognized by both individuals and governments. Today's IP infrastructures are critical, strategic assets.

29. Michael Gallaher and Brent Rowe, RTI International, "IPv6 Economic Impact Assessment" (October 2005), http://www.nist.gov/director/prog-ofc/report05-2.pdf.

Despite its overengineered opponents, IP won the race to become the convergence layer for most communications services over many media types. But its age and its own success put significant stress on the protocol. If nothing else, the protocol needs more resources to sustain its adoption and to continue to generate new ideas for its use. The evolution of IP brings renewed energy that generates tremendous opportunities for nations, businesses, and individuals. The economic result of this evolution can be dramatic, primarily because the economies of scale can now be truly leveraged from IP environments of today and tomorrow. The adoption of IPv6 has the potential to reshape markets and to redefine the leaders in IT innovation worldwide. The only question remaining is: What strategy does one embrace in adopting IPv6?

CHAPTER 4

IPv6 Adoption Strategies

Throughout this book we underline the engineering perspective on IPv6 as an evolutionary rather than a revolutionary step for the Internet Protocol. At the same time, we highlight the potentially revolutionary impact that the Internet growth associated with IPv6 can have on businesses and national economies. Chapter 3, "The Economy of an IP Evolution," detailed some of the opportunities offered by the adoption of the new protocol at both a national and an organizational level.

IPv6 integration sustains, and will very likely accelerate, the continued adoption of IP while expanding its scope and coverage. In the process, IPv6 reignites the competition for leadership in technological and business innovation, in progressive governance, and in information and communications technology (ICT)-driven enablement. In a world where governments and businesses are fully aware of the power of ICT, it is only natural to have strategies developed to deal with an inflexion point such as the IP upgrade.

This chapter reviews some of the IPv6 adoption strategies that emerged by the beginning of 2007 at both government and business levels. They match visions that capitalize on the opportunities and risks analyzed in Chapter 3 with market and technological realities.

The variety of environments and conditions in which IPv6 applies makes it impossible to identify a single, best approach to planning the IPv6 adoption. Instead, it is better to focus on identifying major trends and perspectives, and then learn from concrete examples. Some of the strategies discussed in this chapter can be recognized in the real-life case studies presented in Chapter 5, "Analysis of Business Cases for IPv6: Case Studies." In the end, IPv6 adoption can be a significant undertaking and naturally poses challenges. Some of these challenges are discussed at the end of this chapter.

National Strategies

The ICT revolution is a relatively young phenomenon. Businesses just started to see quantifiable returns toward the end of the 1990s and their investments in ICT have been growing exponentially ever since. The results of the adoption were soon reflected at the macroeconomic level. In most countries, ICT investments resulted in increased productivity and new access to remote markets. In a few countries, an entire ICT industry developed and became a significant contributor to the gross domestic product (GDP). As the Internet became part of every aspect of our lives, its economic value became almost incommensurable.

NOTE For more information about the impact of technologies on GDP, please visit http://www.itu.int/osg/spu/publications/digitalife/businessdigital.html.

Despite its short history, the ICT revolution and its catalyst IP delivered several important messages to governments around the world. The ICT infrastructure is

- **Locally strategic:** Business and government organizations rely on ICT.
- **Globally strategic:** ICT is essential in the economic integration of a global market.
- **An environment for innovation leadership:** Economies benefit significantly from national ICT industry and leadership. The United States stands as a conclusive example.

These lessons naturally led governments to develop strategies with respect to ICT adoption and enablement at the national level. As the foundation of today's ICT infrastructure, IP and the Internet are specifically addressed in these strategies. The Internet, unlike preceding communications infrastructures, came with new rules of management and development. Its technical development is pursued through personal contributions to a democratic forum, the Internet Engineering Task Force (IETF), a very different concept from organizations such as the International Telecommunication Union (ITU), European Telecommunications Standards Institute (ETSI), and International Organization for Standardization (ISO), in which each government has a representative and a vote. The new IETF model significantly reduced the influence of politics on standards and, along with it, governmental level control. Governments had to adapt their strategies to this new environment.

In the early years of the current decade, ICT-related national policies started to emphasize the importance of the IP upgrade. Without a doubt, the concerns over IPv4's limited resources rightfully justify the increasing focus on IPv6. In May 2007, the American Registry for Internet Numbers (ARIN) Board advised the Internet community about the impending need to migrate to IPv6 due to the depleting IPv4 address space.[1] Other Regional Internet Registries (RIR) have advertised similar policies on a unified, global basis. The general principles for addressing the "IPv4 countdown" are highlighted in Réseaux IP Européens (RIPE) policy proposal 2008-03, "Global Policy for the Allocation of the Remaining IPv4 Address Space,"[2] and in John Curran's draft RFC "An Internet Transition Plan," issued in January 2008.[3]

All RIRs and other Internet governing bodies have coordinated their efforts to ensure a unified approach to IPv4 address exhaustion and the phasing in of IPv6. These efforts include:

- **Global synchronization:** All five RIRs will proceed at the same time for measures on IPv4 address exhaustion.

- **An announcement of the date when the allocation is terminated:** A goal is to set the date when RIRs cease the allocation in accordance with a precise estimation and to announce the date far ahead of the termination date.

- **A promise to not make current address policy stricter for the remainder of IPv4 address lifetime:** Keeping the current allocation criteria as it is until the last date will ensure the steady provision of IPv4 address space.

- **A separation of discussions on "recycle" issues:** Recovery of unused address space should be discussed separately.

---

1. For more information on ARIN IPv6 recommendations, visit http://www.arin.net/announcements/20070521.html. For more information on AfriNIC IPv6 recommendations, consult http://www.afrinic.net/news/afltt-ipv6200707-0015.pdf.

2. http://www.ripe.net/ripe/policies/proposals/2008-03.html.

3. http://tools.ietf.org/html/draft-jcurran-v6transitionplan.

The economic implications of the migration are the subject of a recently initiated Organization for Economic Co-operation and Development (OECD) project that highlights the importance of a coordinated, strategic effort toward IPv6 integration as soon as possible.[4] In 2001, however, when the first national strategy on IPv6 emerged, the IPv4 address space exhaustion was not an acute concern and the market drivers were virtually nonexistent. In reality, the true driver for many of the national strategies that emerged in growing economies was this understanding of the opportunity offered by IPv6 to apply the lessons learned from IPv4 and take a more active role in ICT. This explains the apparent gap that existed for several years between national and business strategies on IPv6. This gap has been closing recently as IPv6 becomes a practical necessity and not just a long-term strategic vision.

The national perspectives on IPv6 vary both in scope and depth. They also reflect the specifics of various economies and sometimes align with larger economic and development plans.[5]

The national strategies that emerged between 2000 and 2007 can be grouped in three major categories:

- **Driving adoption through government mandates:** The government mandates IPv6 adoption within its governmental agencies, which in turn drives adoption in the organizations that interact with and support the government.

- **Sponsor adoption:** Implement fiscal and legislative policies that encourage and facilitate IPv6 adoption.

- **Support for national research:** Encourage and fund research activities that stimulate innovation and develop know-how.

Examples of such strategies are provided in the subsequent sections. Although the results of these strategies are hard to quantify and measure, they have

---

4. K. Perset and D. Ypsilanti, OECD, "Internet Address Space: Economic Considerations in the transition from IPv4 to IPv6," http://www.itaa.org/upload/es/docs/ OECD%20Economic%20Considerations%20in%20the%20IPv4%20to%20IPv6%20Transition.pdf.

5. See the Cisco Systems white paper "IPv6 and National Strategies on Information and Communication Technologies" (Sept. 2005), http://www.cisco.com/en/US/prod/collateral/iosswrel/ps6537/ ps6553/prod_white_paper0900aecd8032b2ad.html.

been successful both in raising IPv6 awareness despite market reluctance and in positioning countries as leaders in IPv6 knowledge, planning, and deployment.

Mandated Adoption

In 2003, the interest in IPv6 integration was almost nonexistent in the U.S. market. Even though ICT companies such as Cisco Systems, Apple Computer, and Microsoft were already developing IPv6-capable products, their requirements came primarily from non-U.S. customers. Despite tireless efforts by organizations such as the North American IPv6 Task Force[6] and the IPv6 Forum[7] to increase IPv6 awareness among businesses, and despite visibly increased attention paid to IPv6 in the Asian markets, there was virtually no interest in it in the U.S. beyond a distant monitoring of the protocol development. The market at the time remained fixated on being provided with ROI and applications that would justify the investments in IPv6.

All that changed dramatically on June 9, 2003, when John Stenbit, assistant secretary of defense, signed the memo mandating the integration of IPv6 in the IP infrastructure of the Department of Defense (DoD) agencies. The memo states:

> The DoD goal is to complete the transition to IPv6 for all inter and intra networking across DoD by FY 2008. To enable this transition, it is DoD policy for all Information Technology (IT) and National Security Systems (NSS) which make up the GIG that: As of October, 2003, all GIG assets being developed, procured or acquired shall be IPv6 capable (in addition to maintaining interoperability with IPv4 systems/capabilities). This explicitly includes all acquisitions that reach Milestone C after October 1, 2003. The next version of the Joint Technical Architecture (JTA) will reflect this requirement.[8]

DoD's push for IPv6 is clearly focused on the larger issue of defense strategies and technologies for the future. IPv6 is an explicitly required component

6. http://www.nav6tf.org/.

7. http://www.ipv6forum.com/.

8. Source: http://www.defenselink.mil/news/Jun2003/d20030609nii.pdf.

in the Net-Centric Operations and Warfare Reference Model (NCOW RM), the architecture for future Global Information Grid (GIG)-based operations going forward. IPv6 is the first of 12 transport design tenets in the National Information Infrastructure (NII) "Network-Centric Checklist" required to enable a network-centric military:[9]

> The Transport Infrastructure is a foundation for Net-Centric transformation in DoD and the Intelligence Community (IC). To realize the vision of a Global Information Grid, ASD/NII has called for a dependable, reliable, and ubiquitous network that eliminates stovepipes and responds to the dynamics of the operational scenario—bringing Power to the Edge. To construct the Transport Infrastructure DoD will:
>
> • Follow the Internet Model
> • Create the GIG from smaller component building blocks
> • Design with interoperability, evolvability, and simplicity in mind

Figure 4-1 highlights the major design tenets of DoD's Net-Centric Checklist.

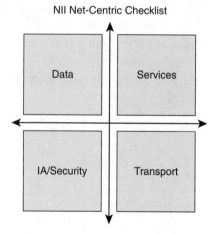

Figure 4-1 *NII Net-Centric Checklist—Major Design Tenets*

9. http://www.defenselink.mil/cio-nii/docs/NetCentric_Checklist_v2-1-3_.pdf.

The announcement was not the first sign of interest in IPv6. The DoD Defense Information Systems Agency (DISA) Center for Engineering acquired an IPv6 prefix in September 2000, and the Defense Research and Engineering Network (DREN) acquired an IPv6 prefix in June 2001. The mandate, however, defined a clear IPv6 path for DoD. At the same time, this policy was a veritable IPv6 earthquake across U.S. markets. It reverberated in the service providers' space, where shortly after the news became public, one service provider (SP) announced IPv6 service offerings.[10] It reverberated with the large government contractors who had to become IPv6 proficient and develop the ability to interface with their largest customers over IPv6. The procurement requirements identified by the mandate did not escape the ICT equipment and software companies. And the shock wave did not stop at U.S. borders. Within a relatively short time, the departments of defense of U.S. allies expressed support for similar, albeit smaller-scale initiatives. This mandate was a turning point for IPv6 adoption in the United States.

Many businesses soon took interest in IPv6, but it is important to note that they did it for one of two reasons: they were either afraid of losing one of their largest customers or they saw an opportunity to enter or even displace a competitor in this market space. There were not any great applications, but there was a key customer. And when the dust settled a little, it became apparent that the mandate was not backed financially. This tempered both the excitement and the concerns of the businesses that found themselves pushed toward IPv6. The spike in the 2003–2004 IPv6 prefix allocations in North America and its decline during the subsequent years probably reflect market reaction.

Figure 4-2 shows the IPv6 prefix allocation trend around DoD's mandate announcement.

10. Denise Pappalardo, "Verio Takes the Plunge on IPv6," *Network World*, July 7, 2003, http://www.networkworld.com/news/2003/0707verioipv6.html.

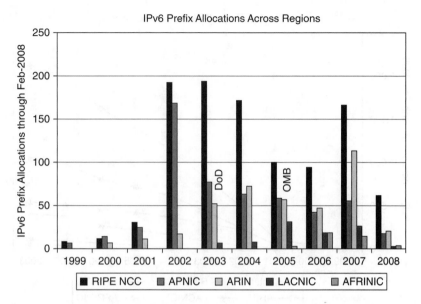

Figure 4-2   *Historical Data for IPv6 Prefix Allocation Across Regions*

NOTE   The data presented in Figure 4-2 is based on the Number Resource
Organization (NRO) "Internet Number Resource Report, December,
2007, available at http://www.nro.net/documents/presentations/
nro-jointstats-Dec07.

Although the intent of Figure 4-2 is to use the IPv6 prefix allocation statistics
to highlight U.S. market reactions to the DoD mandate, through other views, it
also provides interesting data about the IPv6 interest worldwide. Figure 4-3 shows
the cumulative IPv6 prefix allocation over time as of February 2008.

The analysis of the IPv6 prefix allocation by size provides another interesting
perspective. Figure 4-4 shows the allocation sizes in terms of /48 blocks (2^{80}
addresses) as of February 29, 2008.

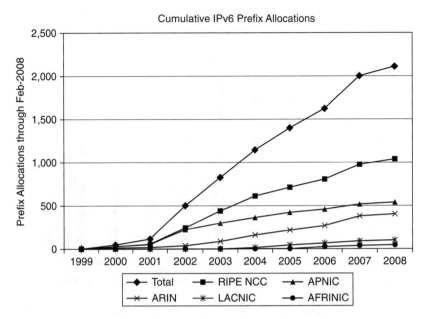

Figure 4-3 *Cumulative IPv6 Prefix Allocation Across Regions as of February 2008*

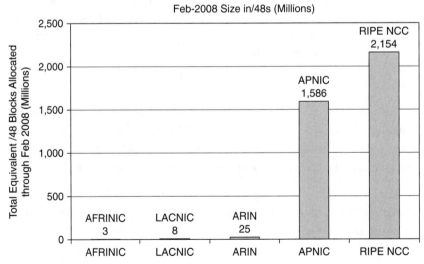

Figure 4-4 *Cumulative IPv6 Equivalent /48 prefix Allocation by RIR (February 2008)*

Detailed analysis of the 20 largest allocations (see Table 4-1) shows that APNIC (RIR for Asia Pacific) and RIPE NCC (RIR for Europe) have 20 out of the 20 allocations larger than /25. There are three strategic differences between the allocations of APNIC, RIPE NCC, and those of other RIRs:

- Large, country-specific and sub-RIR allocations, such as the European Regional Registry

- Larger carrier allocations to support fixed-mobile convergence and service to multiple countries (Deutsche Telekom AG, France Telecom, NTT, and others)

- Specific allocation of "portable" address blocks in Asia Pacific to support multihoming[11]

Despite developing a strong case for the need to move toward IPv6 and despite a logical strategy of IPv6 enablement through the regular refresh process by enforcing IPv6 requirements in the procurement process, DoD started to lose the audience it created through the announcement. Businesses were starting to retreat into a "wait and see" mode.

NOTE   It is important to note that making the case for IPv6 was not a small feat for DoD. After all, among the world's organizations, DoD owns the largest IPv4 address space and would probably be one of the most conservative organizations when it comes to inserting a new protocol in its environment. Nevertheless, after shaking off some of the IPv6 myths discussed in Chapter 2, DoD developed a strong, consistent set of arguments in support of IPv6 as a requirement for addressing all its assets (sensors, soldiers, tanks, ships, and planes) in its Global Information Grid (GIG), for supporting its vision of an integrated battlefield.

---

11. APNIC, "IPv6 Address Allocation and Assignment Policy," Sec. 5.8., "Portable Assignments," http://www.apnic.net/docs/policy/ipv6-address-policy.html#5.8.

Table 4-1   *Top 20 IPv6 Allocations by Size at the end of 2007[a]*

Prefix	Country	RIR	Netname
2003::/19	DE	RIPE NCC	DE-TELEKOM-20050113
2a01:c000::/19	FR	RIPE NCC	FR-TELECOM-20051230
2001:2000::/20	EU	RIPE NCC	EU-TELIANET-20040510
2001:8000::/20	AU	APNIC	TELSTRAINTERNET41-AU-20041202
2400::/20	KR	APNIC	KORNET-KRNIC-KR-20050601
2400:2000::/20	JP	APNIC	SBB-IPv6-20050712
2401:6000::/20	AU	APNIC	DEFENCE-DCC-MGMTCONFIG-20070810
2a01:2000::/20	IT	RIPE NCC	IT-INTERBUSINESS-20060516
2001:5000::/21	EU	RIPE NCC	EU-EN-20040910
2001:a000::/21	JP	APNIC	NTTWEST-IPv6-JPNIC-JP-20041201
2001:b000::/21	TW	APNIC	HINET-IPv6-TWNIC-TW-20060315
2a01:1000::/21	PL	RIPE NCC	PL-TPSA-20060201
2400:4000::/22	JP	APNIC	OCN-JPNIC-JP-20050815
2402::/22	KR	APNIC	KRENv6-20061020
2408::/22	JP	APNIC	APNIC-AP-ALLOCATED-PORTABLES8
2a00::/22	DE	RIPE NCC	DE-ARCOR-20050420
2a00:2000::/22	GB	RIPE NCC	UK-BTENT-20070829
2001:1c00::/23	NL	RIPE NCC	NL-BENELUX-20040510
2001:4600::/24	NO	RIPE NCC	NO-TELENOR-20041006
2a01:800::/24	DE	RIPE NCC	DE-ON-20060412

a. Source: Links to allocated IPv6 prefixes per RIR on RIPE NCC IPv6 statistics site - http://
   www.ripe.net/rs/ipv6/stats/index.html.

The important thing is that the U.S. government's strategy did not stop there, and in January 2004 the Department of Commerce (DoC) posted an RFC stating:

> The President's *National Strategy to Secure Cyberspace* directed the Secretary of Commerce to form a task force to examine the issues implicated by the deployment of Internet Protocol version 6 (IPv6) in the United States.[12]

12. http://www.ntia.doc.gov/ntiahome/frnotices/2004/ipv6rfcfinal.htm.

It requested comments on the benefits of IPv6 and the government's role in its adoption. The message of the recommendations received was "lead by example."

NOTE   The feedback received by DoC was interesting because it led to a different strategy from the one already being executed quite successfully in Japan. You can review the comments received at http://www.ntia.doc.gov/ntiahome/ntiageneral/ipv6/commentsindex.html.

The conclusions of DoC's RFC materialized on August 2, 2005, when Karen Evans of the Office of Management and Budget (OMB, an executive office of the president of the United States) issued a memorandum for the chief information officers with the subject: "Transition Planning for Internet Protocol Version 6 (IPv6)." It states, among other things, that OMB has "...set June 2008 as the date by which all agencies' infrastructure (network backbones) must be using IPv6 and agency networks must interface with this infrastructure" and that "[t]o avoid unnecessary costs in the future, you should, to the maximum extent practicable, ensure that all new IT procurements are IPv6 compliant."[13]

After much prep work and with the stroke of a pen, OMB memorandum M-05-22 created an opportunity for businesses to support the U.S. government's civilian agencies' implementation of IPv6. Incumbents and new businesses catering to these U.S. federal agencies found themselves again facing IPv6 requirements. ICT businesses had to meet mandate requirements, large telecom contracts up for renewal saw the addition of IPv6 service requirements, and integrators had to develop IPv6 expertise. Some relaxation occurred when it was found, once again, that the mandate was not backed financially and the terms of compliancy to the mandate were ambiguous. Hardware, software, and network SPs have not been able to ease up. The acquisition of IPv6-enabled products and services is being enforced through the Federal Acquisition Service (FAS) of the U.S. General Services Administration (GSA). Although full implementation of

---

13. OMB Memorandum M-05-22, http://www.whitehouse.gov/omb/memoranda/fy2005/m05-22.pdf.

IPv6 for U.S. federal agencies will not occur in 2008, IPv6 has become a requirement of network-enabled products and services purchased for U.S. government use.

NOTE Even in the case of civilian agencies, there was interest in IPv6 prior to the mandate. The U.S. Department of Energy (DOE), in support of its scientists, collaborators, and research facilities around the world, ran several IPv6 projects such as 6TAP (http://www-6bone.es.net/). DOE received an IPv6 prefix allocation (2001:400:/32) in August 1999 and its Energy Sciences Network (ESnet) currently runs IPv6 in its core backbone.

In June 2006, Market Connections, Inc. completed a federal market analysis commissioned by Cisco Systems.[14] The study revealed the way in which federal agencies viewed the mandates and their progress toward achieving the goals of the mandates. It is interesting to note that 39 percent of the respondents stated that they would have not implemented IPv6 prior to 2008 or later. Interestingly, a year later the Internet community converged in estimating IPv4 address space exhaustion in 2009, which, in hindsight, highlights the tremendous role played by the mandates in raising early awareness.

Figure 4-5 shows the progress made toward the 2008 mandate targets as measured through the poll conducted by Market Connections.

To their credit, both defense and civilian agencies continued to make progress despite some mandate ambiguities, some technical challenges inherent to a new protocol, and the lack of explicit funding to support its integration. The agencies developed both technical and planning expertise and, under the guidance of several forward-looking leaders, are developing services that leverage IPv6. With the 2008 target date getting closer, the "wait and see" approach is not an option anymore for the businesses that interact with the U.S. government. After all, the U.S. government is the largest enterprise in the world, with a 2007 estimated IT budget of $79 billion.

14. "IPv6 Survey: Taking the Federal Pulse on IPv6," http://www.cisco.com/web/strategy/docs/gov/
Cisco_IPv6_Report.ppt.

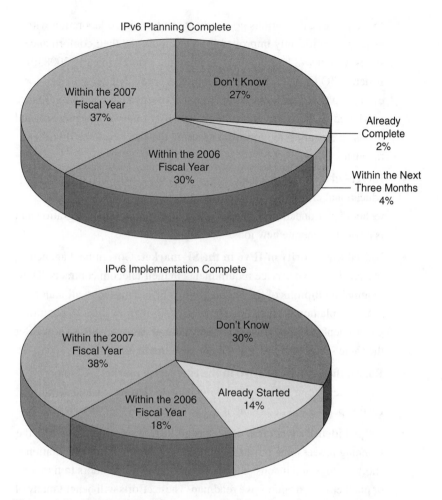

Figure 4-5 *Expected IPv6 Integration Timeline Based on the Market*
Connections Poll

The "adopt through mandate and lead the economy through example"
strategy has its challenges, but in the end it led to significant achievements:

- **Defined the IPv6 profile of networking equipment and devices:** After
  gaining experience with the protocol operation and its conformance testing, both defensive (DISA) and civilian (NIST) agencies identified the
  device IPv6 profile that will meet their respective mandate requirements.

In the process, the various government test labs, in collaboration with vendors, significantly improved IPv6 test tools and their conformance suites, which will have a great benefit to the market. In early 2008, the Federal CIO Council (http://www.cio.gov/) provided the guidance for evaluating IPv6 readiness in the context of the mandates.[15] This guidance was based on the experience accumulated over time with the protocol and it was an essential step toward measuring the success of the IPv6 mandates.

- **Increased technology education:** Both mandates kicked off huge educational efforts that quickly brought staffs up to speed on the technology. Education is a key element to any successful integration and is a way to generate new jobs.

- **Raised the priority of IPv6 in the SP market:** Government agencies placed clear IPv6 service requirements in their telecom contracts. They required multiprotocol (IPv4 plus IPv6) VPNs. This led to all major U.S. SPs planning and rolling out service for their existent or potential government customers. The exercise makes it easier for SPs to now offer the same services to the rest of their customer base.

- **Raised the priority of IPv6 in the enterprise market:** All major government contractors are working hard on developing and acquiring IPv6 expertise and deploying it at least in parts of their network.

- **Helped identify technical concerns and drive solutions:** Through the planning process, the government agencies identified implementation shortcomings and inconsistencies and worked with vendors to fix them or put them on an aggressive roadmap. These efforts will benefit many of the businesses that plan their own deployments.

- **Became a worldwide leader:** Many governments around the world are now closely monitoring the U.S. government's IPv6 strategy in order to understand the drivers, the possible options, and the applications to their own infrastructures.

15. William Jackson, "Guidance for Demonstrating IPv6 Capability," *Government Computer News*, February 28, 2008, http://www.gcn.com/online/vol1_no1/45891-1.html.

- **Increased protocol implementation consistency across networking products:** The U.S. government has been actively supporting the Moonv6 project (http://www.moonv6.org) that conducts extensive interoperability test work. These efforts also led to the accumulation of expertise on IPv6 deployments.

In a final analysis, the U.S. government mandates did more than just break the status quo; they actually forced the creative people in the government agencies and businesses alike to take a closer and more serious look at IPv6. In combination with enthusiastic early adopters, these idea incubators will lead to new services and new operational concepts and architectures. In fact, several other IPv6 adoption drivers have emerged in the U.S. market since 2003, as discussed later in this chapter.

Government-Sponsored Adoption

A government has many resources and instruments that can be leveraged to stimulate and accelerate the adoption of a technology or the deployment of an infrastructure deemed strategically important to the national economy. There are many examples where governments sponsored and drove technology adoption in the public sector. Looking at some of the modern technologies, examples include the public switched telephone network (PSTN) that provides universal access to phone service, the upgrade of broadcast TV to support high-definition TV (HDTV) programming, and the development of infrastructures that provide universal availability of IP broadband access. The adoption of IPv6, as an infrastructure technology, can be viewed in a similar context.

Government-driven mass-adoption projects have been and will always be complex. The premise of such efforts runs against the typical operation of the market they plan to change. These are strategic efforts that require significant investments with long-term returns, whereas the market is more concerned with tactical, short-term investments. The difference between the two perspectives is less relevant in the case of nationalized telecom industries or telecom industries in which the government still has a strong influence, but in these cases, the projects are generally not optimally managed and implemented. Driving completely privatized telecom industries is a more complex process; however, the implementation could be more efficient and innovative. In a fully privatized environment, government policies have to be more creative and must take into consideration the best use of public resources while making sure competitiveness is maintained in the new or upgraded market space.

NOTE   This is not a trivial effort, as shown by the recent efforts of the Australian government to ensure universal availability of broadband access while making sure access providers do not get a monopoly on these services.[16]

The complexities related to this type of government involvement in the market explain the variety of IPv6 adoption strategies that emerged around the world. Although most of them are framed in a general declaration of support, their practical aspects vary based on the specifics of each respective national economy. Moreover, it should be pointed out that these strategies apply primarily to the general population, the consumers, so they aim to influence SPs or manufacturers of appliances. Their effects on enterprise are not immediate and that is apparent in the case of IPv6.

Examples of various types and levels of government sponsorship for IPv6 adoption can be found in the national strategies of Japan, South Korea, the European Union, China, and India. This sponsorship is just one component of a larger-scope strategy for IPv6.

Japan and South Korea

The Japanese government was one of the first to highlight the national importance of ICT and, particularly, an IP access infrastructure. Japanese Prime Minister Yoshiro Mori's September 21, 2000, policy speech to the Japanese Parliament (Diet) was designed to strategically position the country for the 21st century, socially and economically. Prime Minister Mori identified "the IT revolution as a national movement" as the most important pillar in the rebirth of

16. http://www.dcita.gov.au/communications_for_consumers/internet/broadband_for_consumers/australian_government_broadband_initiatives.

Japan. Ubiquitous access to information was highlighted as a goal and responsibility of a public-private partnership:

> I shall boldly address the diverse range of issues we face, including the early realization of e-government, the computerization of school education and the development of systems compatible with the integration of communications and broadcasting, on the basis of discussion in the IT Strategy Council. We shall also aim to provide a telling international contribution to the development of the Internet through research and development of state-of-the-art Internet technologies and active participation in resolving global Internet issues in such areas as IP version 6 (IPv6).[17]

Japanese government action was swift. The Ministry of Internal Affairs and Communications (MIC) detailed its vision and plans in the "e-Japan Priority Policy Program" released on March 29, 2001.[18] While the primary focus was on the development of the broadband and IP access infrastructure, the policy highlighted the need for IPv6 and the steps taken to promote the migration to IPv6:

- **Financial incentives:** Following up on the e-Japan strategy adoption, for a period of two years, SPs benefited from reduced taxes on purchasing IPv6-enabled products. These incentives led Japanese ISPs to deploy IPv6 and deliver IPv6 services, either commercial or trials.[19]

- **Sponsor IPv6 integration and migration:** MIC is sponsoring the deployment of IPv6 for real-life use. The goal is to promote the technology and learn from the experiences. Some of the 2005 projects were: consultation services for residents (Taito, Tokyo), Taito City Assembly streaming live video relay services (Taito, Tokyo), health care at home support services (Asahikawa, Hokkaido), push-type information provision services for residents (Osaka), IPv6 multiservices in Security-Town (Kawasaki, Kanagawa), IPv6 multiservice in school security

17. http://www.kantei.go.jp/foreign/souri/mori/2000/0921policy.html.

18. http://www.kantei.go.jp/foreign/it/network/priority/index.html.

19. http://www.ipv6style.jp/en/statistics/services/index.shtml.

solutions (Tokyo), and office building automation services (Tokyo). The results and the lessons learned from the projects are highlighted in the October 20, 2005, *MIC Communications News* newsletter.[20]

- **Establish international recognition for IPv6 expertise and develop international partnerships:** The Japanese government sponsors the dissemination of IPv6 information and expertise while the research organizations it sponsors are involved in IPv6 projects worldwide. It aggressively pursues international collaboration such as the IPv6-related memorandum signed with China and India.

- **Fund research on the protocol, its deployment and its use:** Japan invested on average $10-13 million a year on research efforts such as the WIDE project (http://www.wide.ad.jp/).

With the e-Japan project leading to Japan being one of the countries with the widest-coverage, highest-speed, and cheapest Internet environments, the focus moved to leveraging this infrastructure. The u-Japan Policy builds on e-Japan to realize a ubiquitous network society by 2010 in which "anyone can easily access and use a network any time from anywhere and from any appliance."[21] IPv6 represents the cornerstone of this strategy.

The results of Japan's IPv6 strategy have been significant:

- **Country with the largest IPv6 deployments:** The leading broadband access providers in Japan deployed IPv6 in production. NTT-Communications has been offering IPv6 service internationally (including U.S. service). IPv6 was deployed primarily in the SP market space.[22]

- **The local ICT industry:** Several new or existing Japanese manufacturers developed new products focused on IPv6 that cater to the requirements of local IPv6 deployments. These manufacturers are competing aggressively with traditional leaders in the local ICT market space.

20. "Broad Outlines of FY 2006 ICT Policy Principles," http://www.soumu.go.jp/joho_tsusin/eng/Releases/NewsLetter/Vol16/Vol16_01/Vol16_01.pdf.

21. http://www.soumu.go.jp/menu_02/ict/u-japan_en/index.html.

22. http://www.ipv6style.jp/en/statistics/services/index.shtml.

- **Leading innovator in IPv6 services and applications:** In the IPv6 Japan deployment, a favorable environment was created in which businesses developed new services, applications, and devices that leverage IPv6. The IPv6 Promotion Council (http://www.v6pc.jp/en/index.phtml) runs a showroom in Tokyo called Galleria v6, where companies present their IPv6-enabled devices.

- **Established leader in IPv6 knowledge and expertise:** Japan can claim the longest and the most diverse experience in developing open source IPv6 stacks, testing IPv6 implementations for conformance and interoperability (the TAHI suites), and deploying and operating IPv6 networks. Japan successfully used IPv6 as an opportunity to raise the profile of its engineers within the IETF. This goal was achieved through increased and active participation and through significant contributions that leveraged the IPv6 expertise developed in Japan.

Although the government's policies alone are likely not the only reason Japan became the leading nation in IPv6 adoption and expertise, the policies created an environment that raised awareness early on and actively supported the process along the way. The strategy had a significant impact in the SP and consumer market, but at the time of this writing it does not seem to have had measurable effects on enterprises.

South Korea

South Korea's strategy on IPv6 shares many similarities with Japan's. Korea had specific per capita GDP goals and was aware of the increasingly positive effect of ICT on the Korean economy, including its exports and trade surplus. The government emphasized the importance of ICT and actively supported the development of the IP infrastructure. The Korean Ministry of Information and Communication (MIC) drew up the IT839 Strategy in 2003 to specifically focus on services, infrastructure, and technology products. These are the elements that comprise the vertical and horizontal value chain of the ICT industry.

South Korea's IT839 program identified eight services, three infrastructures (including IPv6), and nine growth engines for areas of national development. As with Japan, South Korea sought direct involvement in international standards organizations that are shaping the future. By 2004, ICT was contributing over 30 percent of the country's total production and trade exports.[23] By June 2006, Korea was the number four OECD country in the world in terms of both Internet access and broadband access penetration, a position it still holds.[24]

Similar to Japan, the importance and opportunity of IPv6 was recognized early, with the MIC establishing the "Next Internet Infrastructure Constructing Plan by Diffusing IPv6" in 2001. In 2004, a nationwide trial service was created called KOREAv6. At the Korean IPv6 Summit in July 2004, deputy director of the Korean MIC, Kwan Bok Jo, detailed Korea's strategic direction with IPv6 in a presentation titled "Government IPv6 Policy and Strategy in KOREA6."[25] The Korean government, however, did not plan to support the IPv6 adoption through financial incentives.

A 2006 study revealed the effects of the Korean government's IPv6 strategy.[26] Of the 34 companies surveyed, 17 percent implemented IPv6, 11 percent had no plans to implement IPv6 in the near future, while the rest were in planning stages, with implementation expected to start within two years. Respondents stated that the government policies influenced positively their adoption decisions and established IPv6 as a technology norm. These companies recognized IPv6 as the prevailing technology in the region but felt that the business value of IPv6 had not been clearly demonstrated. These conclusions indicate that government policy support might not be sufficient to get the market buy in. Without concrete examples and leadership, despite understanding the message, businesses might take longer to go into actual implementation phase. Addressing this market perception, in September 2007, MIC initiated the IPv6 Model Project, which

23. Hong Koo Kim, "ICT Standardization Strategy in Korea," http://www.ttc.or.jp/j/info/sympo/doc/TTC_20thSympo_06.pdf.

24. Source: OECD Broadband subscribers per 100 inhabitants, by technology, June 2007. http://www.oecd.org/dataoecd/21/35/39574709.xls.

25. http://ipv6.or.kr/summit2004/proceeding/5.%20Technical%20I/TSI-3.pdf.

26. Anat Hovav, Yoo Jung Kim "Determinants of IP Version 6 Adoption" in Proceedings of the International Multi-Conference on Computing in the Global Information Technology (ICCGI'06), http://ieeexplore.ieee.org/iel5/4124012/4124013/04124028.pdf?tp=&isnumber=4124013 &arnumber=4124028

provides examples of IPv6-based services.[27] Government agencies, enterprises, local self-governing bodies, communications enterprises, and equipment manufacturers together would invest over \$4 billion (42 percent provided by the government and 58 percent by the private sector) in the project by the end of 2007.

European Union

The European Union publicly stated as early as 2001 that IPv4 is stifling its economic growth. The challenge does not come just from the effects of future address resource depletion. The European Union holds a leadership position in mobile GSM technologies and deployment but it lags behind the United States in the ICT sector, particularly in the area of IP communications. This is despite the fact that member states had significant contributions to the development of the IPv4 Internet that is mass adopted in the EU market. IPv6 by itself or in combination with the mobile technologies expertise and infrastructure is recognized as an opportunity to take a leadership role. The e-Europe policy highlights, within a larger context, the EU's IPv6 adoption strategy.[28]

As will become apparent in the subsequent sections, most efforts and financial resources were directed toward research projects. Nevertheless, investments are being made in projects that leverage or promote IPv6. The U-2010 project (http://www.u-2010.eu/) will provide the integration of emergency response resources for better and faster resolution of incidents, and the infrastructure for this integration will be IPv6-based. The 6DISS project (http://www.6diss.org/) established the European Union as a center of IPv6 expertise by disseminating across the world the expertise accumulated through various European-sponsored projects, primarily 6NET (www.6net.org). The Go4IT project (http://www.go4-it.org/) develops the infrastructure for a standardized approach to IP conformance testing. The European Union is a leader for many other communications technologies, but it still has to achieve the same stature for the Internet Protocol. IPv6 offers a unique opportunity to provide IP leadership.

---

27. Hyo-Jeoung Kim, "Korean IT Enterprises on a Mission to Popularize IPv6," *ZDNet Korea*, August 31, 2007, http://www.zdnet.co.kr/etc/eyeon/network/0,39036963,39160893,00.htm.

28. Erkki Liikanen, "Towards the Next Generation Internet" (speech, Brussels, January 15, 2004), http://europa.eu/rapid/pressReleasesAction.do?reference=SPEECH/04/18&format=HTML&aged=0 &language=EN&guiLanguage=en.

It is difficult to measure the immediate effects of the e-Europe strategy on IPv6 adoption in the European Union. Several successful research efforts and several highly publicized projects such as U-2010 did establish the European Union as a leader in the IPv6 community. On the other hand, there are few known large-scale commercial deployments even though RIPE NCC has the largest IPv6 address allocation. There is no definitive explanation for the large address space allocated in Europe. Large SPs such as France Telecom and Deutsche Telecom acquired significant address space (/19) that can be used for pan-European, converged IP infrastructures.

China

The rapid adoption of the Internet and the accelerated growth and modernization of the economy make IP addresses a strategic resource for China. IPv6 is a natural solution, although the inadequacy of the remaining IPv4 address space is not the primary driver. Chinese companies are receiving the IPv4 addresses requested from APNIC. The Chinese government views the adoption of IPv6 as an opportunity to take a leadership role, both in terms of technology and governance, in the new Internet. This is also viewed as an opportunity to develop the national ICT industry.

Although the government sponsored research on IPv6 for a long time, the first major step taken in implementing the national strategy on IPv6 was the launch of the China Next Generation Internet (CNGI) in November 2003. The government invested over $170 million in this project, which involved eight ministries, five major national carriers (China Telecom, China Unicom, China Netcom/CSTNET, China Mobile, China RailCom), and several national research networks, including CERNET. The core network was completed in 2005 and a panel of experts certified it in September 2006, hailing it as a major strategic achievement.[29] The public announcement of this important milestone placed little emphasis on the availability of IP addresses. Instead, it highlighted the fact that the infrastructure was a first in the world, that it was built with domestic routers, and that it used Chinese-developed technologies.

29. "China Leads Next Generation Internet Development," *Xinhuanet*, September 24, 2006, http://news.xinhuanet.com/english/2006-09/24/content_5130188.htm.

CNGI is materializing as a first step in the government's strategy to build an information-based country supported by an IPv6 infrastructure. It also provides the environment for the implementation of IPv6-related policies. IPv6 is a high-priority topic on the national economic and social development plan for the 2006–2010 period. The CNGI network will be showcased as the communications platform for the 2008 Olympics in Beijing.[30]

India

Similar to the infrastructure of other large Asian economies, India's infrastructure requires significant resources. There are several drivers for strategic interest in IPv6. A significant portion of the GDP comes from Internet-enabled businesses offering service to remote markets. IP interconnection must be maintained regardless of the IP version preferred by the customers. Although the percentage of population with Internet access at home is smaller and its substitute is communal access points such as Internet cafes and mobile phones, adoption is widespread. To support the existing and rapidly growing infrastructure offering IP-based services, India will require the address resources of IPv6.

The importance of IPv6 was recognized at the governmental level by the release in August 2005 of a consultation paper compiled by the Telecom Regulatory Authority of India (TRAI).[31] It provides recommendations on the integration of and migration to IPv6. In November 2006, this paper was followed by a proposal to establish a government-sponsored conformance test environment in the Telecommunication Engineering Center (TEC).[32] This environment is tasked with certifying the IPv6 readiness, in accordance with the TRAI recommendations, of IP communications equipment vendors. TEC (http://www.tec.gov.in/) is part of the Department of Telecom and its role is to specify common standards for telecom network equipment, identify generic and interface

30. Kaushik Das, "IPv6 and the 2008 Beijing Olympics," IPv6.com, http://www.ipv6.com/articles/general/IPv6-Olympics-2008.htm.

31. "Issues Relating to Transition from IPv4 to IPv6 in India," http://www.trai.gov.in/trai/upload/ConsultationPapers/6/conspaper26aug05.pdf.

32. "Invitation for Expression of Interest (EoI) for Participation in Programme for Establishing IPV6 Test & Certification Lab in Telecommunication Engineering Centre (TEC) India," http://www.tec.gov.in/List/IPV6_EOI_%20draft%20final.pdf.

requirements, issue interface and service approvals, formulate standards, and interact with multilateral international agencies such as APT, ETSI, and ITU. The IPv6 conformance work is a first step by TEC in exerting its role in India's strategy for IPv6 adoption. It will lead to more detailed criteria for product selection and establish a baseline at the national level.

National Research Environments and Projects

The Internet and the World Wide Web emerged from successful research projects sponsored by the U.S. government. The tremendous return on that investment is impossible to measure. Sponsoring research projects and environments remains one of the most important and least expensive tools available to governments to stimulate innovation and maintain scientific and technological competitiveness. IPv6 will be the foundation of the next generation Internet. Why not repeat the research sponsored experiments proven to work, experiments similar to the ones that led to the IPv4 Internet? This perspective is adopted by many governments around the world who sponsor many research projects on the next generation Internet. Even the U.S. DoD, after a long hiatus, declared in the context of its IPv6 strategy the intent to be active in Internet-related projects and IPv6 development. All national strategies focused on IPv6 adoption have a research sponsorship dimension.

Because IPv6 is a foundational technology with a large scope, there are many areas that require investigation, evaluation, and deployment expertise. To highlight the diversity of topics covered by national research projects, we list here just a few examples:

- **United States:** It is difficult to measure the U.S. government investment in IPv6-related research. Its support for such projects is for the most part indirect. For example, Moonv6 is one of the prominent projects supported by the government through active participation in its activities focused on IPv6 interoperability testing. The project is run by the University of New Hampshire, which has a long tradition in interoperability testing, in collaboration with many other organizations. Internet2 established a wide range of IPv6 goals, such as to support and encourage development of advanced applications using IPv6, create a national infrastructure to support IPv6, educate the Internet2 IPv6 user base, support interconnectivity, and transport during the initial stages of IPv6 deployment. Another example is National LambdaRail, Inc. (NLR), which "is advancing the research, clinical, and educational goals of members and other institutions by establishing and maintaining a unique nationwide network infrastructure that is owned and controlled by the U.S. research community."[33] NLR supports many services across its network, including IPv4 unicast, IPv4 multicast, IPv6 unicast, and IPv6 multicast.[34]

- **European Union:** In the context of the European Union's ICT Framework Program (http://cordis.europa.eu/ist/), funding of over $216 million was provided to several research projects: 6NET, GEANT, Euro6IX, 6INIT, 6DISS, and Go4IT. These projects focused on developing deployment experience, protocol knowledge, and new applications and services. The 6NET project was a tremendous success, providing the IPv6 community with a wealth of knowledge in IPv6 deployment and providing new protocol improvements. The 6DISS project disseminates the expertise accumulated in the 6NET project throughout the world. The EU-sponsored projects actively brought together universities and industry partners from around the world into successful collaborative efforts.

- **Japan:** The government invested on average $10–13 million a year on research efforts such as the WIDE project (http://www.wide.ad.jp/).

- **Korea:** The Korean government invested $81 million to support several national research projects: KOREN, KREONET2, 6NGIX, and TEIN (Trans Eurasia Information Network).

33. http://www.nlr.net/about/.

34. Tom West, NLR CEO, "2007 Summary Report for NLR," www.nlr.net/docs/ NLR%20Summary%20Report%202007%20080208.pdf.

- **China:** According to "A Case Study on IPv6 Implementation in the North Asian Triangle" by Say Joe:

  > China's IPv6 projects started in 1998 with the China Education and Research Net (CERNET) initiative. Beijing Internet Institute (BII) established an IPv6 R&D Center in 1999. In 2000, BII interconnected their IPv6 testbed with the 6 BONE. It also built BII-BUPT NGN Lab with Beijing University of Post and Telecommunications (BUPT) in 2001. In 2002, BII and Research Institute of Telecommunication Transmission (RITT) inaugurated IPv6 Telecom Trial Network (6TNET), the first and biggest IPv6 multivendor, multi-operator project in China. BII also built up the first commercial IPv6 network for China Telecom in the same year. Thereafter, China Telecom's Beijing, Shanghai, and Guangzhou IPv6 trial projects have been launched.[35]

  CERNET-2 was launched in late December 2004, connecting 20 cities and university campuses with a pure IPv6 network.[36]

The intent is not to provide an exhaustive list of national research environments and projects but rather to highlight some of the prominent ones and the investments made by governments in support of IPv6-related research. This is another mechanism that, in conjunction with mandated adoption and government-sponsored adoption (discussed earlier in this section), can be used to implement national strategies on IPv6 adoption.

IPv6 is a fundamental, infrastructure technology and its adoption is often challenged by short-term business constraints. For this reason, a national, strategic vision is essential. Most often, government develops and drives such a perspective. However, professional associations can also single out constraints for national development and promote strategic, long-term solutions. For example, the

35. http://icsa.cs.up.ac.za/issa/2004/Proceedings/Full/027.pdf.

36. Chinese Academy of Sciences, "Scientists Select 2004 Top 10 S&T Achievements in China," January 18, 2005, http://english.cas.cn/english/news/detailnewsb.asp?InfoNo=25329.

National ICT Industry Alliance (NICTIA, http://www.nictia.org.au/), a consortium of 20 Australian industry associations, launched on May 21, 2007, with a 12-point, 10-year strategic vision for increasing Australia's ICT competitiveness. IPv6 adoption is a component of this strategy. In this instance, the industry recognized the need for a national ICT strategy, took a leadership role in defining it, and is partnering with the government to implement it. This type of national-level effort, whether driven by the government or professional associations, raises the awareness level about the importance of ICT and particularly IPv6; such efforts help businesses plan for it and adopt it early enough to maintain international competitiveness.

Business Strategies

Forward-thinking organizations are constantly evaluating industry trends in an effort to best position themselves economically for the future. Their strategic investments often involve establishing the foundation required for future product and service development. However, strategic investments are in constant tension with the economic and tactical competitive demands to reduce costs and minimize disruptive changes. Visions and strategies for the IPv6 transition should consider the intersections of cost, revenue, risk, timing, and dependencies.

There are three prerequisites, represented graphically in Figure 4-6, for broad deployment of communications-based products and services: standards, platforms, and networks. Businesses should consider the maturity level of these areas when developing their strategies. In the end, it is all about the timing.

NOTE   Broad commercialization and deployment of network-centric applications and services requires a minimum level of relevant maturity in international standards, platform adoption of standards, and local/global network transport.

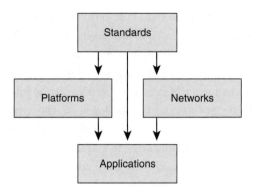

Figure 4-6 *Prerequisites for Communications Technologies Deployment*

There are some general timing-related questions that every organization should seriously consider when planning for IPv6. The answers will vary for different industries and market strategies:

- **When will IPv6 be needed?** This assessment should consider mandated adoption, competitive position goals, application- and vendor-driven requirements, and industry trends. This may be a combination of objective and subjective perspectives.

- **How long will it take?** Basic understanding of IPv6 and the transition process is required for this assessment. Sometimes there are dependencies that are beyond the control of the enterprise. For example, economic global deployment of IPv6 applications and services will require a combination of mature standards, IPv6-enabled platforms, and availability of network transport. If one of the required components is not available, workaround solutions should be part of the strategic planning.

- **When do I start?** To determine the starting time reference, do the simple math of subtracting the time to get to IPv6 from the date when it will be needed. For many organizations, doing an honest assessment indicates the ideal start time may have already passed. For example, companies that are deploying current versions of Windows, MAC, and Linux operating systems may already have IPv6 packets and services running on their LANs.

- **What are the dependencies?** In some cases, the IPv6 strategy will be modulated by actions of others, such as standards processes or availability of specific features in common computing and network platforms. In other cases, the dependencies are internal, such as the deployment of DNS services that support IPv6 and the verification of end-to-end, host-to-host communications over a network with IPv6 turned on.

- **Can I do something today to make the future easier?** An organization may not need IPv6 within a few years. However, often times an organization can take steps in the short term to make the eventual transition less expensive and less painful. This includes purchasing standards and developing applications that are IP-version agnostic.

Defining the Standards

Many organizations find that involvement in defining new standards or extending existing standards might be a required step to the development of new products and services. Traditional standards bodies as well as industry-specific consortia are places where this is common. A "standards ecosystem" has evolved where parallel standards development efforts are interdependent. The core IPv6 standards are the basis for changes in several other standards. Although there is no immediate ROI for involvement in standards organizations, enterprises make the strategic commitment to standards participation as an integral part of developing existing markets and growing new ones. As mentioned earlier in this chapter, end-user adoption will not occur until standards have reached an acceptable level of stability and are included in products:

- **IETF IPv6 standards:** The IETF is responsible for the specification and standardization of several Internet standards, including IPv6. Within the IETF, the IPv6 Working Group's focus is to complete the standardization of the IPv6 protocols, to review and update the IPv6 specifications based on implementation and deployment experience, and to advance them on the standardization track as appropriate. There are several standards that make up the IPv6 protocol. Although IETF participation is on an individual basis, interested organizations often sponsor the time and expenses of their employees as standards are envisioned, debated, refined, and finalized. Subsequent revisions of the specifications go through a similar cycle as the standards are revised based on real-life deployment experience. Organizations that sell products and services based on Internet technologies participate in IETF standards activities based on the standards' relevance to their products and strategic objectives. Over time, the collaborative process involving people and companies with different perspectives ensures some level of functionality required for broad interoperability. Contributors to the IETF standards process also have the opportunity to ensure that the new standards integrate well with their product evolution.

- **ITU:** ITU is the leading UN agency for ICT. The Next Generation Network Global Standards Initiative (NGN-GSI) focuses on developing the detailed standards necessary for NGN deployment to give SPs the means to offer the wide range of services expected in NGN. NGN-GSI harmonizes, in collaboration with other bodies, different approaches to NGN architectures worldwide.

- **Cellular industry:** The 3rd Generation Partnership Project (3GPP) is a collaboration agreement between a number of telecommunications standards bodies, including ARIB, CCSA, ETSI, ATIS, TTA, and TTC, that supports radio access technologies used throughout the world. Its roots are with ETSI. These roots include cellular standards such as Global System for Mobile communications (GSM), General Packet Radio Service (GPRS), and Enhanced Data rates for GSM Evolution (EDGE). 3GPP2 is a sister organization born out of the ITU's International Mobile Telecommunications IMT-2000 initiative. 3GPP2 focuses on Asian and North American global specifications for ANSI/TIA/EIA-41 Cellular Radio Telecommunication Intersystem Operations network evolution to 3G. 3GPP2 is a consortium formed between five standards development organizations: ARIB, CCSA, TIA, TTA, and TTC. Market advice is provided by the CDMA Development Group (CDG), IPv6 Forum, and International 450 Association (IA 450).

Both 3GPP and 3GPP2 are collaborating in the development of IP-based converged core networks. The commercial goal is to have a technical base for providing sets of services that can be delivered to mobile users seamlessly across multiple access technologies. The foundational standard is the IP Multimedia Subsystem (IMS). The target converged services include VoIP, web, video, and nonsession-based services. With the rapidly growing number of devices, IPv6 support is a mandatory part of the IMS specification. From ETSI (http://www.etsi.org/tispan/), "Building upon the work already done by 3GPP in creating the SIP-based IMS (IP Multimedia Subsystem), TISPAN [Telecoms & Internet converged Services & Protocols for Advanced Network] and 3GPP are now working together to define a harmonized IMS-centric core for both wireless and wireline networks." The vision is clearly ubiquitous, access-independent converged services across multiple networks, fixed and mobile.

- **Cable television industry:** Cable Television Laboratories, Inc. (CableLabs, http://www.cablelabs.com//) is a nonprofit research and development consortium established by cable operators and dedicated to pursuing new cable telecommunications technologies that will help its members integrate technical advancements into their business objectives in a very competitive market. Delivery of new products and services is critical to market share positioning against alternative delivery operators, such as satellite, DSL, and wireless broadband. CableLabs' R&D efforts are solidified in widely adopted cable industry standards such as Data Over Cable Service Interface Specification (DOCSIS). The evolution of DOCSIS and other CableLabs standards goes beyond the original delivery of residential television services to include HDTV, broadband Internet services, and VoIP. CableLabs also incorporates standards from other organizations. As movement to an Internet-based world continues, CableLabs standards have changed to include IPv6. The protocol must be supported in DOCSIS 3.0. These standards are implemented by the providers of equipment and services to the cable industry, such as cable modems, customer premises terminals, and central office equipment.

- **Sensors industry:** IEEE standard 802.15.4 was developed for low data rate wireless personal-area network (WPAN) use such as long-life battery-powered sensors. The ZigBee Alliance (http://www.zigbee.org) has developed higher-layer proprietary protocols based on the 802.15.4 standard for wireless monitoring and control products. There is a license fee associated with the ZigBee specifications. Standardization efforts for

IPv6 have been initiated in this area as well. Several companies, including Intel, Microsoft, and Arch Rock, that are interested in seamless communications between wired and wireless sensors have initiated RFC 4944, *Transmission of IPv6 Packets over IEEE 802.15.4 Networks.*[37]

There are dozens of other standards organizations that are including IPv6 in their new and revised standards, just as they have with the introduction and evolution of IPv4. Organizations that are dependent on IPv6 as part of their products' future have a strong incentive to be an integral part of the standards ecosystem.

Standards change over time or are replaced over time based on innovation and the experience of people using and developing standards-based products and services. The evolution of standards is a natural part of the process and not unique to IPv6. While basic IPv6 standards are mature and stable enough for enterprise deployment, other IPv6 standards are still being debated in the standards organizations and have not yet reached the level of maturity needed for production use. Standards organizations are actively working on completing standards work in areas where there is the greatest interest and demand. Some examples of maturing or incomplete IPv6 standards are in the areas of multihoming, mobility, and multiple access hand-offs.

Organizations developing products and services related to or depending on emerging standards should consider active participation in the standards processes. Organizations deploying or planning to deploy IPv6 should start with the basic mature standards as they develop their internal competence.

Creating Infrastructure Platforms

The basic deployment of new networking protocols depends, at a minimum, on network elements and host computers supporting the technology. Enabling computing and network platforms to support IPv6 is not an end in itself, but it is an important step in creating environments that lead to further innovations in services, applications, and product development. Market demand, however, is essential in driving the industry to continue adding IPv6 capabilities to products.

37. http://www.ietf.org/rfc/rfc4944.txt.

The "build it and they will come" approach, which requires an initial, strategic investment with no immediate returns, rarely creates a relevant market for significant investment in IPv6-related product development. Technical-, business-, and mandate-driven adoption created an increasing market demand for IPv6 support, which translated into the availability of devices that support or have well-defined road maps for integrating IPv6 features. Software and hardware is now being designed for IPv6 or with IPv6 in mind. Moreover, development and test environments have been updated to support and facilitate IPv6 integration in products.

As the standards mature and developers gain experience, the number of IPv6 features in platforms has continued to grow since the turn of the century in the following ways:

- **Computing software platforms:** In 2001, most operating system developers had included basic IPv6 features in their products and/or OS road maps. The introduction of initial IPv6 features has often been in the form of OS-related software development kits (SDK). After initial experience and feedback is obtained, more mature and advanced features have become native to the operating systems. Today IPv6 is relatively full-featured in the most current version of all major client and server OSs: Microsoft Windows Vista, Windows Server 2008, Windows Server 2003, Windows XP, Windows CE (4.1 and later), Red Hat Linux (7 and later) and FreeBSD (4 and later), HP-UX, Apple MAC OS, Ubuntu, Sun Solaris (8 and later), Tru64 UNIX, and Symbian (7 and later). Some OSs, such as MAC OS X and Windows Vista, are now harvesting IPv6-enabled capabilities to perform new system-level functions such as device and service discovery on LANs. This is the foundation for higher-level applications discussed in the following sections.

- **Computing hardware platforms:** Computer hardware platforms and computer processor chip set manufacturers are often not directly responsible for higher-level network protocols in their system design. However, they actively work with the OS suppliers to ensure that their products will work in harmony when IPv6 is enabled in the OS. The strategy for hardware and chip manufacturers is to collaborate in ways that ensure that the hardware is IPv6 capable when required by the OS.

Often this translates into simply performing routine testing (such as whether an Ethernet adapter with advanced features such as TCP off-load will support IPv6). In other cases, revisions to code may need to be made (for example, network binding across interfaces).

- **Network platforms:** Network processor chip set manufacturers have the additional target of enabling IPv6 packet processing in hardware. Most major network platform manufacturers, such as Cisco, Foundry, Juniper, Alaxala, Huawei, and Nortel, have supported IPv6 in their products over the past few years. This strategy is based, in part, on the firm belief that IPv6 is a basic product-survival requirement for the future. Many network platform companies are responsible for hardware and software design and packaging. IPv6 in networking products has frequently started with a software-based implementation. For optimum performance, IPv6 code for functions such as routing is best done in application-specific integrated circuits (ASIC). Support of IPv6 in network platforms is not a trivial endeavor. In fact, hardware must be designed with IPv6 in mind; otherwise, the performance of the platform can be significantly impacted under common forwarding conditions. For example, on a network platform not fully designed for IPv6, any router interface with an access control list (ACL) applied to it, ACL filtering based on upper-layer protocol information, might result or packet with extension headers being dropped or punted into the software path instead of being switched in hardware. The prudent strategic approach is for hardware to be designed with IPv6 in mind. Although the pace has been tempered by customer demand and standards maturity, the future ubiquity of IPv6 is clear.

- **DNS services:** Name resolution is a cornerstone to today's Internet economy. On July 20, 2004, the Internet Corporation for Assigned Names and Numbers (ICANN) announced that IPv6 AAAA records for the Japan (.jp) and Korea (.kr) country code Top Level Domain (ccTLD) name servers became visible in the root zone file. The strategy in ICANN's announcement was clear:

  > By taking this significant step forward in the transition to IPv6, ICANN is supporting the innovations through which the Internet evolves to meet the growing needs of a global

economy... Recognizing the importance of IPv6 to the Internet community, ICANN has coordinated with its Root Server System Advisory Committee, Top Level Domain managers, Security and Stability Advisory Committee, and other interested parties in careful analysis of this issue. After a period of thorough examination, the decision was made to move forward with deployment of the IPv6 address records in the manner prescribed by the community.[38]

- **Industrial networking platforms:** Several of the control systems standards associated with building, plant, and process automation are moving from proprietary and industry group–specific protocols to IP as a basis for communications. There are enormous numbers of sensors, effectors, actuators, and other controls that will benefit from IPv6 features.

  However, industrial networking has been slower than enterprise network platforms in embedding native IPv6 support. Part of the delay is the task of converging a large variety of industrial network protocols, several of which are proprietary. There is also the large installed base of legacy systems that may be in service for 15+ years. It was discovered in the NATO SilkRoad IPv6 over satellite project experiment that integration of IPv6 often is only possible with next generation products. Legacy satellite technology was not capable of handling IPv6 for non-Internet-related devices such as satellite encoders or security encryptors.[39] RUNES (Reconfigurable Ubiquitous Networked Embedded Systems) is an EU 6th Framework Program. To date, "RUNES is the largest ever European-led project enabling the creation of large-scale, widely distributed, heterogeneous networked embedded systems that interoperate and adapt to their environments."[40] The RUNES program developed and demonstrated an adaptive middleware platform and application development tool set to support abstracted interaction

---

38. http://www.icann.org/announcements/announcement-20jul04.htm.

39. Wolfgang Fritsche, "Deploying IPv6 over Satellite," September 23, 2004, http://www.ist-ipv6.org/presentations/m12/IABG-Manchester.pdf.

40. "The RUNES Project" brochure, http://www.ist-runes.org/docs/brochures/RUNES_brochure.pdf.

between developers and the controls environment. RUNES work activities carefully examined trends in industrial networking. Figure 4-7 highlights the high-level trends in industrial control networks.[41]

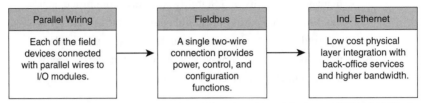

Source: Wireless communication technologies in industrial monitoring and control, koumpis@vodera.com, TCCL March 2006 Meeting
http://www.ist-runes.org/docs/presentations/2006-03-30_tccl_koumpis.pdf.

Figure 4-7   *Evolution of Control Networks*

NOTE   A wireless communications technology in industrial monitoring and control is a compelling industrial network trend. Vision, technical, organizational, and social issues were concisely covered at the March 2006 TCCL meeting.[42]

The RUNES research and middleware platform also emphasized flexibility, installation, and operational advantages of wireless control networks. The RUNES final demonstration included a presentation that focused on IPv6 and network mobility within a control systems environment.[43] The demonstration scenario describes control platforms that include Mobile IPv6 (MIPv6), Network Mobility (NEMO), IPv6 over Low power WPANs (6LoWPAN), and fixed and mobile IPv6-enabled gateways.

41. "The RUNES Project" brochure, http://www.ist-runes.org/docs/brochures/RUNES_brochure.pdf.

42. Costis Koumpis, "Wireless Communication Technologies in Industrial Monitoring and Control," March 2006, http://www.ist-runes.org/docs/presentations/2006-03-30_tccl_koumpis.pdf.

43. Socrates Varakliotis, Manish Lad, and Peter Kirstein, "RUNES Final Demo, IPv6 and RUNES," June 19, 2007, http://www.u-2010.eu/fileadmin/user_upload/documents/U2010_RUNESIPv6DemoStory_v7.pdf.

- **Interoperability validation:** Development of a new IP protocol version that impacts any equipment speaking IP requires a strong validation to guarantee compliancy and interoperability. This is being achieved for IPv6 through different worldwide efforts that go from validating a specific set of standard's implementation on a given product and software release (for example, IPv6 Ready Logo, www.ipv6ready.org), to operations done on large scale and over a long period of time, such as the experimental 6bone infrastructure (1996–2006) and 6NET (2001–2005), resulting in collaterals published for the rest of the industry.

Product development should ideally be strategically guided by the balance between clear industry direction, anticipated project life, and projected value to customers. Many organizations in the business of creating infrastructure platforms that attach to an IP-based network have already completed required changes to make IPv6 a native feature of their products. Others are behind the strategic effort of including IPv6 as a base component of the products they sell. Lagging platform companies are in the potential position of losing market share to others that fully support IPv6. Organizations purchasing infrastructure platforms should insist that the products they buy fully support IPv6 features they will need during the life of the product in their organization.

Addressing Specific Customer Requirements

A sometimes reactive but powerful reason for technology adoption is demand-based, where customers will pay for a service or product only when it contains specific features. Some organizations have a business need for IPv6. Others take an early planner or even early adopter role and initiate the IPv6 integration process that translates into concrete product requirements. In certain cases, policies, fiscal incentives, or mandates lead organizations to demand IPv6-enabled products, IPv6-capable applications, and IPv6 services. These adopters and planners are interacting with other businesses, which now must consider IPv6 to meet customer needs. There are several examples of businesses placing concrete IPv6 requirements before their providers of hardware and software.

NOTE   Sometimes IPv6 requirements simply come "along for the ride" with the implementation of other products and services. There are many such examples, from new cable services to the deployment of Windows Vista. For example, in December 2007, Free, one of the most innovative European Broadband SPs, added IPv6 services free to the installed base, enabling nearly three million homes.[44]

Requiring Operating System Integration of Applications

Although some organizations are already reacting to IPv6, as in the case of those driven by mandates, other companies are already responding to the current and anticipated demand for IPv6-enabled products. The timing is important. The requirements for OS "certified" applications are a natural customer expectation as new OSs become more widely used. Compliance with the integration requirements of these popular OSs is necessary for many products in the market. Apple MAC OS X 10.3, Microsoft Windows Mobile, Windows Vista, and Windows Server 2008 have IPv6 enabled by default as a directional networking change to enable device and service discovery as well as other functions that are not easy to implement in IPv4 due to various constraints such as having to deal with NAT.

Apple and Microsoft have developed conformance tests as part of their current Logo programs, and in some cases in relation to their redistribution licensing programs. The current versions of their Logo programs require demonstrated compliance with specific IPv6 features. Organizations and consumers that are going through the natural transition to the current versions of OSs will demand products that support all the features of the OS, including IPv6. This is an indirect driver for the manufacturers to develop, deliver, and support IPv6-enabled products. Logo program compliance, such as Apple Bonjour Conformance test 1.2.3 and Microsoft's Premium "Certified for Windows Vista" programs, are starting to yield a new batch of more mature IPv6-enabled products. Customers naturally gravitate to products they know will work with their new OS.

---

44. "Free Deploys IPv6," December 12, 2007, press release, http://www.iliad.fr/en/presse/2007/CP_IPv6_121207_eng.pdf.

Requiring Zero Impact of IPv6

At a minimum, organizations deploying IPv6 expect products to operate (not break) when IPv6 is enabled. Many legacy applications will continue to operate over IPv4 when IPv6 is enabled on the hosts and the network operates in a dual-stack environment. However, organizations that are testing or implementing an IPv6-enabled environment will find that a few commercial applications will fail if IPv6 is enabled on hosts and networks. This usually is caused by poor and/or inadequate coding practices that are dependent on IPv4. For example, configuration files or applications will require human updates before they will run over IPv6 when IPv4 addresses are used in configuration files instead of using DNS, or applications doing IPv4-specific network calls rather than using the OS for communications functions. Customer shifts to competing IPv6-aware products will cause product supplies to react with required fixes.

Requirements Driven by Mandate Responses

In the United States, government-mandated and government-sponsored IPv6 adoptions have provided clear direction that some form of change will be required. The U.S. federal mandates were even more prescriptive, with specific target dates. Earlier in 2007, the U.S. GSA awarded two very large ten-year "Networx" contracts to "The Nextworx program offers comprehensive, best value telecommunications providing for new technologies, industry partners and ways to achieve a more efficient, and effective government."[45] Networx Universal was awarded to AT&T, Verizon Business Services, and Qwest Government Services. Networx Enterprise was awarded to the same carriers plus Level 3 Communications and Sprint Nextel.

Networx contains IPv6-specific requirements in 39 of 52 services. GSA issued the Networx RFP to the industry in May 2005. Each company bidding for the Networx contract had to address the five questions at the beginning of this "Business Strategy" section.

In the case of Networx, the carriers had a clear interest in upgrading their networks to provide the required levels of IPv6 capabilities, a job that was

---

45. http://www.gsa.gov/Portal/gsa/ep/channelView.do?pageTypeId=8199&channelPage=%2Fep%2Fchannel%2FgsaOverview.jsp&channelId=-16201.

probably easier for the companies that started the IPv6 deployment process earlier. The "follow the money" approach will result in IPv6 availability for U.S. federal customers before broad commercial and residential deployments. However, the experience gained by the large-scale federal deployment will generally be directly applicable to future nongovernment IPv6 services.

The adoption efforts at the federal level naturally led to increased pressure on network equipment and software vendors to provide support for IPv6 that is comprehensive, has high performance, has high scalability, and is uniform across platforms. Whether demonstrated in product or promised on road maps, IPv6 became, under the demands of federal customers, more important to the industry.

U.S. government departments and agencies are also aware that they will need assistance in their IPv6 evolution, and they are counting on vendors and system integrators to help fill any gaps to ensure they meet mandated milestones. This creates demand for other types of IPv6 services and expertise, a driver for investment in IPv6 within the professional services market.

Establishing Leadership Through New Services

Growth in market share and revenue is often derived by the introduction of new products and services. Market introduction timing needs to match anticipated customer demand. Introduction too late may cause a company to lose position relative to its competition. Long-term loss of revenue may be one result. Development of a product or service too early may divert funds from other critical areas, or result in a product that is based on an immature foundation, requiring additional update funds. Organizations are starting to improve their leadership position by capitalizing on the foundation of IPv6 in their new product and service development. These are a few concrete examples:

- **IPv6 multicast at New York University:** In 2005, NYU became the first end site in North America with global, native IPv6 multicast connectivity. With over 50 research centers, NYU is a Category I Research University with a long tradition of innovation dating back to the early 1800s. The NYU deployment of IPv6 was done in close collaboration with NYSERNet, Internet2, and equipment suppliers such as Cisco. While native IPv6 multicast across the Internet was just a first step supporting research at the university, it laid the foundation for additional research in IPv6-enabled applications and services. Specific areas of interest for NYU researchers include Source-Specific Multicast (SSM), Embedded RP (multicast routing rendezvous point), Digital Video over IP (DVoIP), conferencing, and Multicast Listener Discovery (MLD). IPv6 activities and successes have continued to affirm NYU's leadership as a research university.

- **Scaling up the network infrastructure at Comcast:** Comcast's interest in IPv6 is based on a couple of solutions to current operational challenges and lays the foundation for new innovative services. At the June 2006 NANOG conference, Comcast's Alain Durand presented a change in the giant cable company's network management strategy based on IPv6. The challenge is managing 100+ million IP addresses.[46] With a start in 2005, Comcast's initial focus has been to deploy IPv6 on the control plane for the management and operation of its edge devices. The architecture includes dual-stack at the core, transitioning over time to dual-stack at the edges with a logical incremental deployment approach. Transitions of this scale are complex, but are seen by Comcast as a necessary, core component for their future. The 100 million IP addresses (20 million video customers, 2.5 set-top boxes per customer, and 2 IP addresses per set-top box) are just its current portfolio. Future growth areas will come through additional subscribers (including mergers and acquisitions), introduction of new converged services such as data and voice, and by offering higher-bandwidth services. The cable industry standards foundation for the new services is found in DOCSIS 3.0 developed by CableLabs. DOCSIS 3.0 provides channel bonding, dramatically increases both upstream (120+ Mbps) and downstream (160–480 Mbps) transmission speeds, complies with IMS specifications, and requires IPv6 support. Comcast's IPv6 strategy recognizes industry trends, current operational challenges, and future revenue opportunities.

46. http://www.nanog.org/mtg-0606/pdf/alain-durand.pdf.

Establishing Leadership Through Innovation

Not all IPv6 adoption efforts are mandated or driven by fears of address exhaustion. There is a lot of innovation happening on IPv6. In some cases IPv6 simply provides the resources for a cleaner implementation of an idea, while in others it offers protocol capabilities that lead to better solutions. A better understanding of IPv6, familiarity and experience with it, and sometimes an IPv6-enabled test or development environment naturally lead to new ideas. These new ideas translate into new products, applications, or services that enable new companies to leapfrog incumbents and gain leadership in certain markets.

Three very interesting examples of innovative but strategic use of IPv6 in new applications and products are described here:

- **Facilities management:** Matsushita's Shiodome Building and NTT's Saitama Building have been operational for a few years with advanced IPv6-based facilities control systems. Matsushita has been targeting home automation and building automation innovations for years, with over 100 commercial products on the market today, including the IPv6-ready FreeFit for Lighting Controller and Icont for Gate Management System. The technologies are the foundation for its industry-leading innovations: web, IPv6, and sensor networking.

NOTE   In a 2005 briefing at the Asia Pacific Regional Internet Conference on Operational Technologies, Matsushita highlighted some specific strategies about IPv6 technology and its leadership position:[47]

1 IPv6 is not [a] "Magic wand." The user is demanding a clear advantage.

2 Energy conservation request is one of the big demand[s] for BA [Building Automation] systems.

3 Internet and ISP are ready to provide IPv6 services. But IPv6 products do not meet solutions for HA [Home Automation] system[s] and BA system[s].

47. Noriaki Fujiwara, "IPv6 and Facility Management," February, 24, 2005, http://www.apricot.net/apricot2005/slides/C3-6_1.pdf.

4 Create the solution that meets users' demands.

- 4-1 Clear advantage
- 4-2 Labor saving of engineering
- 4-3 Security and safety
- 4-4 Self-actualization

5 IP centric system will be a major solution.

6 PLC [Programmable Logic Controller] and Wireless will be key technologies.

- **Sensor networks:** Several companies are actively pursuing IPv6 in conjunction with sensors. The IEEE standard 802.15.4 has been around for several years as the base network protocol for low-power WPANs. The use of 802.15.4 has grown significantly through proprietary/licensed developments of the ZigBee Alliance. However, Arch Rock, Intel, Microsoft, and others have started a parallel standards-based effort in the IETF called 6LoWPAN for the transmission of IPv6 packets over IEEE 802.15.4 physical and MAC layers.[48] This innovative approach has two distinct advantages. First, 6LoWPAN is standards based, eliminating what can be significant license fees associated with large-scale ZigBee certified deployments in facilities with thousands of sensors. Second, the use of 6LoWPAN eliminates the mapping and translation to get data from a sensor, through the sensor network, to the service or application that will consume or act on the sensor data. While this is an enabling building block for Intel and Microsoft, Arch Rock Primer Pack/IP is already delivering commercial implementation of 6LoWPAN. Arch Rock (U.S.) and Sensinode (Finland) conducted the first successful interoperability demonstration of the IETF 6LoWPAN standard for IPv6 communications over the IEEE 802.15.4 low-power radio in late July 2007.[49] The

---

48. http://www.ietf.org/html.charters/6lowpan-charter.html.

49. "Arch Rock, Sensinode Conduct First Interoperability Test of IETF 6LoWPAN Standard," July 31, 2007, press release, http://www.archrock.com/news_events/press_releases/2007.07.31.php.

strategy of these companies is to be first to market through involvement in the standards process and early standards integration in commercial products.

Sometimes IPv6 represents nothing more than a larger resource of addresses. Other times IPv6 offers clear advantages over IPv4. In either case, innovative companies must keep IPv6 in mind when developing products and solutions for the future. This strategic approach makes them more competitive and can provide them a leadership role in their market space.

Be a Follower

If you are a follower, the problems you face are that you might loose leadership and that early adopters might not solve the problems specific to your environment. A rapid IPv6 ramp-up is not simple, and can be expensive. And, there may be little time left to wait. Being a follower creates a downstream impact of having to react to certain change. Having an unidentified protocol running on an enterprise network can be a potential security threat, if undetected. Current versions of several shipping OSs have IPv6 enabled by default. A few applications might not work properly if IPv6 is enabled end to end.

Organizations will need to make changes to accommodate IPv6 at some point—it is a matter of time. Some straightforward planning and a little effort today can make the future transition much easier. There are a few simple positioning strategies that followers should be adopting now. The level of effort and investment is relatively low, and will make the eventual transition to IPv6 smoother and less costly.

Making minor adjustments to existing processes is often the most effective strategy to address IPv6 as a follower. The changes align (if unexpected adoption drivers do not require quick adoption) with the normal hardware and software life cycle of moving from a development of engineering and testing environments through quality assurance, and then into production. Figure 4-8 highlights the typical packaging that takes place as a product or service moves from its beginning into operation. The organization accepting the turnover package can be viewed as a gatekeeper.

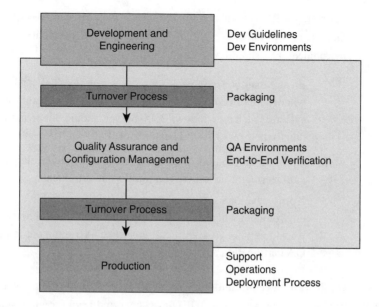

Figure 4-8   *Turnover Points for the Process of Technology Integration*

Followers can act on some of the process points shown in Figure 4-8 to ease the integration of IPv6 and prepare for its adoption:

- **Quality assurance/configuration management:** Followers should use their quality assurance/configuration management gatekeeper as a starting point, and move upstream from there. The initial focus should be to simply ensure that hardware and software moving through QA will not fail or introduce security risks when IPv6 is enabled on the hosts and network in a dual-stack configuration. Applications usually go through testing/QA processes prior to deployment in an organization's production environment. The testing/QA environments should be IPv6-enabled end to end. This includes clients, servers, and the network. IPv6 should be part of relevant test plans and QA sign-offs. Verify that all applications will function correctly with IPv6 enabled end to end. Testing to ensure all applications are IP protocol-agnostic is a low-cost, low-risk strategy to prepare for IPv6 deployment in the future. This will avoid "surprises" when the new protocol is eventually turned up in the production environment. QA should perform the following steps:

1   Ensure that the testing environment is running dual-stack, where supported on hosts and networks. Legacy operating systems, such as Windows 2000 Server, should not be included due to their lack of solid support for IPv6.

2   Update requirements of turnover packages from developers/ engineering to include minimum IPv6 requirements.

3   Notify developers that their products will be tested in an environment where IPv6 is enabled on the hosts and network. End-to-end network verification will be a requirement to pass QA certification.

- **Application development environment:** Java SDKs and integrated development environments (IDE) have supported IPv6 for a few years now. Developers should have IPv6 enabled on their computers and networks. Microsoft is starting to support IPv6 with .NET Framework 1.1 and Visual Studio 2003. There are a few very minor configuration changes that are required to configure the developer workstation and development environment to create IP-version-agnostic code. Newer versions of the IDE have enhanced IPv6 features and support available.

- **Application code:** The popular open source community collaboration site SourceForge.net lists over 100 IPv6 projects, with over 25 showing an activity rating greater than 80 percent. Structures, API parameters, and other development components will change slightly in a protocol-agnostic application. For example, the function call gethostbyname() must be replaced by the Internet protocol-neutral getaddrinfo() function call. Microsoft has a compile-time flag IPV6STRICT to ensure source code will meet IPv4 and IPv6 requirements. Hard-coded IP addresses should be avoided. Use DNS for name resolution instead. Databases used for IP source/destination address logging should also be modified if there is inadequate room to store the larger IPv6 addresses.

- **Protocol-agnostic applications:** In-house developed applications often go unchanged for several years. Financially prudent and strategic thinking organizations realize the value of reducing the number of times an application is modified. With this in mind, consider making IPv6 an additional (usually very small) part of new application development requirements and any application modifications. The minor investment now will usually eliminate an IPv6-only application revision in the future. Most applications rely on the OS for network services and will be immune to the introduction of IPv6 in the network. However, some applications and application development environments have specific APIs, definitions, structures, services, or functions that work only in an IPv4 environment.

Today, most products and their development and test environments are IPv6 capable. Many of the implementations and products have been hardened in production. As more stacks and applications come to market at an accelerated rate, some of these products might be less reliable. Going forward, conformance evaluations could become a necessary tool in ensuring quality of IPv6 implementations.

The actions taken to insert IPv6-specific requirements in the process, depicted in Figure 4-8, are a valuable and sometimes inexpensive precursor of the IPv6 integration. Together with other actions, they can pave the road for the IPv6 adoption. Following are some of the actions:

- **Basic education and awareness:** Organizations make sound business decisions based on knowledge. The decisions around IPv6 are no exception. IPv6 will impact many parts of the organization over time; it is not just a network change. An understanding of the amount of time and effort to make the transition should be factored into future network, application, infrastructure, and training budgets.

- **Knowledge of the starting points:** An honest gap analysis is helpful in any technology transition. Organizations should have current IT inventory to help assess what systems will need to change when IPv6 implementation is started.

- **Leverage of the gatekeepers:** IT product and service life cycles include natural turnover points (gatekeepers) as systems move from development through QA into production.

Organizations in a follower position should at least put some short-term effort into the "upstream" areas of hardware, software, and service acquisition, development, and deployment. The short-term goal should be to simply stop doing anything that perpetuates a mandatory dependence on IPv4.

IPv6 Adoption Challenges

At the beginning of 2008, a decade since the IPv6 core specifications became IETF draft standard documents (August 10, 1998), IPv6 commercial adoption remains limited and confined to walled gardens, albeit some quite large ones. This chapter shows that many people give a lot of thought to IPv6 adoption and that both national and business strategies are being developed and implemented in its support. Nevertheless, we naturally wonder: Why has it taken so long? What are the IPv6 adoption challenges? Analyzing and understanding these challenges is essential for two reasons. On one hand, the IPv6 enthusiasts can better support and prepare their adoption plans; on the other, skeptics might postpone a serious investigation of IPv6 for their organization based on an apparent lack of interest from the market.

There are two ways to analyze the IPv6 adoption challenges: a short, informal way that simply lists some of the issues raised by the market, and a formal, more systematic way based on business and economic models. The former approach is practical. The latter is a theme of research in itself. This section briefly provides both perspectives.

Industry Perspective

The primary challenges to IPv6 adoption come from wrong perspectives and major misunderstandings with respect to its role and its value. Throughout this book, we have highlighted these problems and addressed them; following are some of the primary problems:

- **IPv6 is *not* a feature:** One common perspective is that IPv6 is a feature that can be turned on to provide new capabilities. The problem with this perspective is that it greatly underestimates the task of integrating IPv6 and it minimizes the potential of an IPv6 environment. IPv6 is not a feature; it is the infrastructure of future IP services and communications.

- **Search for a well-defined ROI:** The apparent lack of ROI and killer applications was, and in many cases still is, a major barrier to adoption. In the search for ROI and killer apps that would justify adoption, we ended up with fabricated myths about IPv6 capabilities and we missed the larger picture: the fact that IPv6's primary role is to help us scale our IP environments to meet the needs of the NGNs. In this fundamental, infrastructure role, IPv6 implies a far more complex ROI calculation, if any can be practically calculated. After all, what is the value of the overall Internet business today in its current size? What would it be when scaled up with the resources provided by IPv6? The exhaustion of the RFC 1918 address space provides a great example: You do not need a killer app to deploy IPv6. You simply have to deploy IPv6.

These two misconceptions along with a set of obstacles distracted the industry from addressing more concrete and valuable challenges. The commonly quoted obstacles are independent of market space and their perception will inevitably change in time:

- **Lack of pressure to adopt IPv6:** NAT and CIDR postponed the immediate need for IPv6, but this reprieve was greatly misunderstood. How many times have we heard in the response to a warning about IPv4 address space exhaustion: "I have been hearing this for several years now and it did not happen. If nothing else, they will come up with another workaround."? The exhaustion of the IPv4 private addresses was already painfully experienced by large networks. As of May 2007, the prediction for the global pool exhaustion is around 2010. There is no time left to come up with workarounds, test them, put them in a product, and deploy them. The pressure to adopt will only increase.

- **Lack of apparent use:** This perspective relates to the lack of a killer app, as discussed in the previous list. In reality, SPs and enterprises have found use for IPv6 such as content delivery or facilities maintenance. These are not killer apps but they are examples of cost-effective ways to use IPv6.

- **Costs involved in adoption:** In the context of the two arguments identified at the start of this list, virtually any investment in IPv6 would be perceived as an unjustifiable cost. Of course, this argument relates, to a certain extent, to the search for ROI. With more and more organizations developing adoption plans, the true costs of integration have been more clearly defined and quantified. Early planning was proven to significantly reduce costs.

- **Perceived technology challenges:** Another common question that we hear is: Is IPv6 reliable? Chapter 2 debunked several of the myths that point to technology shortcomings. Many times, sensational news in ICT-related publications presents the problems out of context, generating misgivings toward IPv6. As an example, in May 2007, an apparent IPv6 security problem—the potential use of source routing for denial-of-service attacks—was discovered and made big news. In reality, the same security problem exists on IPv4, but, being well known, most if not all IPv4 implementations disable IPv4 source routing by default. Although IPv6 implementations continue to mature, in this particular case, most networking equipment manufacturers already implemented IPv6 countermeasures similar to the ones on IPv4. Most true challenges with IPv6 come in the context of its use in ways IPv4 could not be used, for the next generation services and architectures.

- **Availability of IPv6-ready products:** The definition of "IPv6 ready" depends on the product. As mentioned previously, IPv6 is not a feature, but it is similar to IPv4, a package of features. The definition of readiness revolves around the contents of that list. Organizations planning to deploy IPv6 can indeed run into product or feature gaps. Although manufacturers with global coverage have been developing IPv6-ready products for a long time, manufacturers with a localized market or covering very specific market segments might have started to introduce IPv6 in their products only recently. Moreover, the investment in feature development is market driven, so the later a given market or IP environment type started to plan for IPv6, the more likely it is that features specific to that market might not yet be available.

- **Lack of trained staff:** The number of IPv6 subject matter experts (SME) is limited today, and most network operations teams lack familiarity with the protocol. Training is often listed among the top costs for adoption. Public training, such as seminars offered by the 6DISS project, is not sufficient to raise the appropriate level of protocol knowledge in a timely manner. Consultant firms, however, have been stepping up their course offerings and expanding the coursework coverage.

The June 2006 market study performed by Market Connections provides a concrete and quantitative example of top IPv6 adoption challenges for a given market segment discussed on page 102 of this chapter.[50]

Figure 4-9 shows the impact that various challenges have on IPv6 adoption as perceived by the U.S. federal agencies.

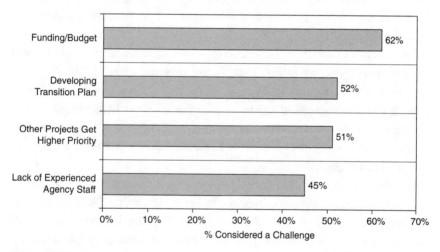

Figure 4-9 *Top IPv6 Adoption Challenges Based on the Market Connections Poll*

Some obstacles are just a matter of perception and some are challenges that must be actively addressed. The minor ones relate to deploying IPv6 in the context of the principles and frameworks of today's IPv4 network. The more interesting ones relate to deploying IPv6 based on new principles and in the context of new architectures.

50. "IPv6 Survey: Taking the Federal Pulse on IPv6," http://wwwcisco.com/web/strategy/docs/gov/ cisco_IPv6_Report.ppt.

Academic Perspective

As the Internet became an unprecedented business phenomenon it generated more and more interest. One attraction was to model from an economic perspective its unique mode of operation and the opportunities it generates. Another attraction was to investigate the diffusion of new ideas in this environment with unique characteristics for innovation and standardization. Over the past decade, economics and innovation diffusion theories have been jointly leveraged to model various aspects of the Internet evolution. Independent of the various models that were proposed, our analysis of the IPv6 adoption challenges benefits from the systematic approach developed in this field of research.

The 2004 paper "A Model of Internet Standards Adoption: The Case of IPv6" provides a list of factors influencing adoption.[51] The most relevant factors to our analysis are part of the "Environmental proliferation" category, which, as defined by the authors of the paper, reflects the spread of IPv6 in the population of potential adopters. These factors are also complemented by a set of technology-focused factors of which we include: compatibility, triability, observability, and relative technological advantage. These factors are summarized in Table 4-1 along with explanations that take into consideration the infrastructure, not the feature role, of IPv6. The perceived impact of each factor on the IPv6 adoption varies from region to region and from market to market. Table 4-2 lists the concrete results of a 2006 study that surveyed 34 Korean companies discussed in the South Korea section in this chapter.[52]

In the end, the academic analysis of today's state of the industry highlights similar challenges as the ones discussed earlier in the chapter. Nevertheless, this formalized framework is essential in comparing IPv6 adoption to the adoption of other technologies, or in comparing adoption trends and conditions across markets and across the world.

51. Anat Hovav, Ravi Patnayakuni, and David Schuff, "A Model of Internet Standards Adoption: The Case of IPv6," *Information Systems Journal* 14, no. 3 (July 2004): 265–294.

52. Anat Hovav, Yoo Jung Kim "Determinants of IP Version 6 Adoption" in Proceedings of the International Multi-Conference on Computing in the Global Information Technology (ICCG1'06), http://ieeexplore.ieee.org/ie15/4124012/04124028.pdf?tp=&isnumber=4124013&arnumber=4124028.

Table 4-2 *Technology Adoption Factors and Their Impact in IPv6 Adoption*

Adoption Factor	Explanation	Korean Perception of Impact on IPv6 Adoption
Prior technology drag	The more established the existing infrastructure is the higher the apparent costs of deploying a new one. High drag adversely impacts adoption even if the new standard is superior. This is true even though the industry is not yet talking about a full migration to IPv6 but rather about an integration of IPv6.	High
Inertia	If the prior standard is well established, most feature and application development focuses on this standard generating high inertia, which adversely impacts adoption.	High
Perception of sunk costs	High capital and equipment loses due to upgrades required by the new protocol will negatively impact adoption.	Medium
Crisis	An impending need for the capabilities or resources of the new standard stimulates adoption.	Low
Network externalities	Refers to the level of adoption by other organizations. The more organizations that adopt the standard the fewer the challenges that will be experienced and the easier to justify and design adoption plans. Lack of network externalities adversely impacts adoption.	High
Sponsorship	Government sponsorship of adoption reduces the barriers to adoption. Financial support is generally valuable because it offsets adoption costs. Governments can also mandate adoption and force its proliferation.	Medium
Compatibility	Little compatibility between the new and the old protocol adversely impacts adoption.	High
Observability and triability	The ability to quantify and observe the benefits of the new protocol helps make the value more apparent to a wider audience.	Low
Relative technological advantage	The new protocol can sometimes directly or indirectly provide a competitive advantage for an organization.	Medium

Summary

IP infrastructures have become strategic resources, so their growth and evolution is of critical importance at all levels: global, national, organizational, and personal. IPv6 represents a major evolutionary step for IP, one that is becoming either a necessity for some organizations and nations or an opportunity for others. But, this does not mean IPv6 is *the* final achievement. In the larger context of IT strategies, nations and businesses must develop IPv6 adoption plans. They must decide based on industry trends and future growth goals how soon IPv6 should be integrated in the IP infrastructures.

This chapter reviews IPv6 adoption strategies that emerged primarily between 2000 and 2008. They reflect the multitude of drivers for the IPv6 adoption and the perspective taken on IPv6 by various countries and businesses. Although these strategies fit in the theoretical frameworks of technology adoption, they bare the unique aspects of the adoption of infrastructure technologies, technologies for which business cases have to be developed by taking into consideration many aspects of the IT environment.

Several conclusions can be drawn from analyzing the IPv6 strategies developed as of 2008:

- **National strategies have a positive effect:** Government support of IPv6 adoption is a good driver for raising industries' interest in an infrastructure technology. The implementations of national strategies are different from one country to another. However, the ones showing results involve concrete actions (mandates, policies, requirements, and so on) and partnerships with the industry.

- **Globalization helps IPv6 strategies:** The global economy exposes IT product vendors to regional or vertical markets that may have specific IPv6 requirements. A business case and a strategy can be developed at first around these requirements and later can be expanded and applied to the entire market.

- **There might be consequences to late adoption:** In the case of an infrastructure technology such as IPv6, a "late adopter" has to accept the decisions made by others with respect to the structure and use of the protocol. Late adoption also will imply a slower start on IP innovation.

- **Plenty of room for innovation:** IPv6 opens the door to many innovations and new business development.

The IPv6 strategies covered in this chapter are representative of a certain stage in the IPv6 adoption process. They continue, however, to evolve as more and more organizations discover their integration needs and take the time to make IPv6 part of their larger IT strategy.

The IPv6 adoption strategies discussed in this chapter are reflected in the concrete case studies presented in Chapter 5. Although not an easy task, the development of these strategies represents the first step in the complex process of integrating IPv6 in existing IT environments.

Analysis of Business Cases for IPv6: Case Studies

This chapter would not have been as informative and practically useful as it is without the expert and enthusiastic help provided by the representatives of the featured organizations. It was an honor to work with everyone and we are grateful for their guidance and support.

—Patrick Grossetete, Ciprian Popoviciu, and Fred Wettling

Up to this point, this book has provided an objective review of the benefits and challenges of IPv6, a review of business and economic aspects of an IP-enabled world, and a mix of theoretical and practical analyses of IPv6 adoption strategies. Although the information provided comes from our experience with large-scale deployments, deployments that do exist but usually as services in a closed environment or "walled-in garden," nothing can replace the value of case studies based on actual organizations that must demonstrate the real-life business value of IPv6. A natural corollary of the previous chapters offers a collection of case studies that materialize in the context of specific market conditions. These case studies may also help you to discover similarities between the described experiences and business values and requirements in your own organization.

The case studies show all IPv6 planning steps in the context of the business, operational, and technical realities of actual organizations. The time dimension is equally important because it shows the determining factors and the progression of an organization from the "interested in IPv6" stage to the "IPv6 planner" stage and finally to the "IPv6-enabled" stage. With the approach of the U.S. OMB mandate deadline, the approaching exhaustion date for the IPv4 global address space, and the emergence of IPv6 applications and of OSs with IPv6 turned on and preferred by default, more and more organizations are publicizing their IPv6 efforts and documenting their experiences.[1] This rapidly increasing database of experiences and expertise can be used to illustrate and validate the points made in this book.

---

1. See, for example, John Eldridge, Tan C. Hu, and Lawrence F. Tolendino, "A Report on FY06 IPv6 Deployment Activities and Issues at Sandia National Laboratories," June 2006, http://www.prod.sandia.gov/cgi-bin/techlib/access-control.pl/2006/063635.pdf, and William Jackson, "Lockheed to Begin IPv6 Transition as 'Pathfinder' for Government Clients," *Government Computer News*, August 29, 2007, http://www.gcn.com/online/vol1_no1/44960-1.html.

The case studies presented in this chapter, however, capture multiple aspects related to planning and implementing the IPv6 integration. In selecting and developing these case studies, we had the following specific goals:

- **Select a broad spectrum:** Select as many organizations as possible that represent major markets and various governmental institutions. Until recently, this was not possible because of the inhomogeneous level of IPv6 readiness and interest across markets.

- **Present a global perspective:** Select organizations with national coverage from all regions (the United States and others), as well as global organizations.

- **Present an objective perspective:** The organizations featured in the case studies were not selected based on their favorable perspective on IPv6. They were selected to focus on the business impact. The goal is not to sell IPv6. Hence, the reader will find enthusiastic early adopters and aggressive early planners and organizations that have only long-term plans for IPv6. The goal is to provide a realistic assessment of the need for IPv6.

- **Combine business and engineering perspectives:** The individuals who assisted the authors in developing the case studies represent business, marketing, and engineering communities. The goal is to highlight what makes business and engineering sense when developing an IPv6 strategy.

Table 5-1 summarizes the case studies covered in this chapter and the individuals who generously guided and assisted us in preparing them.

NOTE	Several other organizations have valuable experiences to share related to planning and deploying IPv6. We believe the selected case studies offer the variety and relevancy necessary to cover most aspects of IPv6 adoption from a technology, market, and historical perspective.

The case studies were developed in collaboration with representatives of the featured organizations. They were initially drafted around the answers provided to

Table 5-1 *List of Case Studies Presented*

Market	Organization	Contributors
Service Providers		
Broadband access provider	Comcast	Alain Durand
Carriers	Sprint	Wesley George
	Tata Communications	Yves Poppe, Anne-Marie Legoff, Raju Raghavan
IT utilities provider	SAVVIS	Robert LeBlanc, Wen Wang
Mobile providers	Bouygues Telecom	Lionel Hoffmann
Enterprises		
Education and research	Greek School Network	Athanassios Liakopoulos, Dimitrios Kalogeras
Financial	Consolidated market perspective	Patrick Grossetete
Government	Consolidated market perspective	Ciprian Popoviciu and Patrick Grossetete
Information technologies	Cisco Systems	Craig Huegen
Global Engineering & Construction	Bechtel	Fred Wettling
Startup—sensor networks	Arch Rock	Roland Acra
Professional Services	Command Information	Yurie Rich

a questionnaire developed specifically for the two major categories: service provider and enterprise. Along with the answers to these questions, the respondents provided additional historical, background, and future planning information to help build the timeline of the IPv6 efforts. Publicly available material was leveraged and referenced whenever it was found useful in the development of the case study.

The case studies share a similar structure that is designed to describe the starting (IPv4 infrastructure and services) and ending (IPv6 strategy, implementation plans, and deployment) points of an organization's IPv6 experience. This approach is intended to help readers identify similarities between their environments and their IT goals and those of the organizations covered in the case studies. The technical details of the IPv6 deployments have been left out intentionally.

Such information is already extensively covered in existing literature such as *Deploying IPv6 Networks*, by Ciprian Popoviciu, Eric Levy-Abegnoli, and Patrick Grossetete (Cisco Press, 2006). Most of the case studies in this chapter have the following structure:

- **Company profile:** Provides an overview of the company profile, the scope of its business, and its size and market coverage. The goal is to help the reader relate to the business goals of the featured organization.

- **Network and IT profile:** Provides an overview of the IT environment and the way it supports the business goals of the organization. It reviews the type of devices and the OSs deployed and the applications used. The goal is to help the reader recognize aspects of their own IT environment in that of the case study, including hardware and software.

- **IP infrastructure characteristics:** Provides an overview of the IP aspects of the IT environment, listing any challenges experienced or envisioned. This section touches on the addressing scheme, renumbering, and management considerations. It should bring forth some challenges faced by the readers in their own environments.

- **Perspective on IPv6:** Presents this organization's perspective on IPv6 as a technology and on the IPv6 adoption trends within its market space. It reflects its appreciation of the level of urgency in adopting IPv6 in order to stay competitive.

- **The case for IPv6:** Combines the perspective on IPv6 covered in the previous section with the early or late adopter position considered by the organization and any specific drivers or opportunities it identified in relation to IPv6. The result of this information leads to the creation of a case for IPv6 adoption, which comprises motivation, goals, and timelines.

- **IPv6 planning and implementation:** The case made for IPv6 adoption shapes the adoption strategy and its implementation. There are, however, many other determining factors that must be considered, such as alignment of timelines, alignment with other IT initiatives to reduce impact and costs, availability of resources, and so forth. In reflecting the strategy implementation stages of the featured organizations, for some case studies this section is heavy on the planning side while for others it focuses on both planning and deployment.

- **Lessons learned:** Concludes the case study with the main lessons learned by the organization. Whether the organization was already operating IPv6 services or just planning for them at the time of this writing, there are lessons that have been learned from the process.

Departures from this structure were warranted in certain situations by the specifics of the market or the specifics of the organization featured in the case study.

NOTE   In certain case studies, the internal deployment of IPv6 is not as relevant as the company's investment in developing IPv6-based technologies and services. Startup or consulting companies, for example, might develop a significant part of their business model around IPv6, which can provide valuable insight, whereas their internal adoption of IPv6 might be of less interest.

You can choose to go over the case study of an organization whose IT environment and market drivers are most similar to those of your own organization, as this will provide immediate value to your own IPv6 efforts. At the same time, it is recommended that you read the other case studies as well, because they will likely offer a perspective on the challenges faced by some of the upstream or downstream business partners and providers with whom your organization interacts and on whom it might depend.

Without further ado, here are the case studies organized based on major market segments. Their title identifies the market they represent and the name of the featured organization.

Service Providers

The Internet would never reach a "production ready" status for IPv6 without the service providers' infrastructures becoming able to forward IPv6 traffic natively. This section contains case studies from forward-thinking ISPs willing to discuss their IPv6 planning.

Broadband Access Provider: Comcast

In the context of this book's focus on IP, one might be tempted to think of broadband access providers just in terms of the Internet access services they offer. In reality, access providers deliver significant amounts of bandwidth to home users and businesses. Regardless of whether it is delivered over the existing telephone line, over coaxial cable, or over optical fiber, the major asset is the pipe they have all the way to our home or our business. Originally, the access infrastructure was typically built for a specific purpose (for example, to offer telephony service or cable television), and for the most part, it is still used to deliver those services. The adoption of IP, however, offered the specialized providers the capability to deliver a variety of new services on top of the existent infrastructure. Today, broadband access providers are leveraging the bandwidth real estate they built into the subscriber premises to offer a wide range of services such as Internet access, Voice over IP (VoIP), and video on demand over a single protocol: IP. In a natural evolution of this environment, the new broadband access infrastructures, such as fiber to the home (FTTH), are designed to fully leverage IP as the consolidating layer for service delivery.

The combined demand for primary services such as television (and more recently HDTV) programs in the case of cable companies and the rapid adoption of IP services led to tremendous growth rates for broadband providers. To sustain this growth, to increase capacity, and to reduce operational costs, broadband access providers have been working aggressively to deploy their Next Generation Networks (NGN). These new infrastructures must support millions of devices and a wide range of IP services. For both of these reasons, they would benefit from IPv6:

- **Device management:** The large number of devices that are more efficiently managed in a single administrative domain require more addresses than what is available via RFC 1918, the 24.0.0.0 address space, or what would be available from the IPv4 global address space.

- **New services:** New services can be enabled on IPv6 for dedicated services purposes or to take advantage of the resources offered by IPv6.

One way or the other, broadband access providers stand to gain significantly through IPv6 integration. With the rapid growth of their customer base, these providers might need to adopt IPv6 sooner than they think. Lack of IP addresses can stifle growth in the number of managed subscribers or new services that can be offered. But the integration of IPv6 might not be straightforward, either, because media-specific capabilities or necessary IPv6 features might not be available. The sooner the planning for IPv6 starts, the higher the probability that its integration will be completed in the scope of deployment.

This case study covers the leading U.S. cable access provider, Comcast, which took a leadership position in planning and deploying IPv6. The case study was developed with the assistance of Alain Durand, Director of Advanced Engineering and IPv6 Architect at Comcast.

Company Profile

According to its corporate information page:

> Comcast was founded in 1963 as a single-system cable operation. Today, we're the country's largest provider of cable services—and one of the world's leading communications companies. We're focused on broadband cable, commerce, and content. We deliver digital services, provide faster Internet and clearer broadband phone service, and develop and deliver innovative programming[2]

Comcast is a diversified, privately owned corporation. The primary source of revenue is the cable services it provides. Comcast is the largest cable provider in the United States, with over 24 million cable customers, 15 million digital cable customers, 13 million high-speed Internet customers, and 4 million voice customers as of January 31, 2008. Its corporate profile is summarized in Table 5-2.

Table 5-2   *Comcast Corporate Profile Overview*

Profile Category	Status/Value
Organization	Comcast
Industry	Cable network operator and content provider
Number of employees	90,000 (December 2007)

2. http://www.comcast.com/Corporate/About/CorporateInfo/CorporateInfo.html.

Table 5-2 *Comcast Corporate Profile Overview (Continued)*

Profile Category	Status/Value
Geography	National, covers 39 U.S. states and District of Columbia
Revenue	$30.9 billion (December 2007)
Total market share	44 percent

NOTE All data in Table 5-2 is current as of January 31, 2008. The market share data is provided for the third quarter of 2007 as reported in the "High-Speed Access Report" produced by Information Gatekeepers, Inc. (http://www.igigroup.com/).

Comcast is not only the largest U.S. multiple system operator (MSO), but also a leader in setting the direction for the market from both a business and technology perspective. Comcast must stay at the forefront of networking technologies to support the wide spectrum of services it offers to its large customer base (cable TV, high-speed Internet access, and VoIP). Comcast is one of the leading partners in the CableLabs consortium (http://www.cablelabs.com/), in which it actively drives and contributes to the definition of the cable industry standards such as the Data Over Cable Service Interface Specification (DOCSIS).[3] As a major user of IP, Comcast is actively contributing to the evolution of DOCSIS and Internet Engineering Task Force (IETF) standards. Today, Comcast is recognized worldwide as a leader in IPv6 adoption, and it needs IPv6, as will be shown in this case study, to support the rapid growth of its customer base and the devices deployed.

Network and IT Profile

In terms of the number of IP devices, Comcast operates one of the largest infrastructures in the world. Comcast's infrastructure is made out of at least 21 converged regional-area networks (CRAN) that provide cable TV and IP services to the subscribers in a market or a region. The CRANs are connected by a

---

3. http://www.cablelabs.com/specifications/doc30.html.

common, high-speed backbone that enables them to share high-bandwidth content and information. The access network is a DOCSIS-based, bridged cable environment.

The OSs currently deployed in Comcast's infrastructure and those it plans to use going forward are listed in Table 5-3.

Table 5-3   *Comcast IP Infrastructure Profile—Operating Systems*

Device Type	Today	Future
PC, workstations and servers	Windows 2003, Windows XP	TBD
	Linux	TBD
	Solaris	TBD
Set-top boxes	DOCSIS 1.0, 2.0	DOCSIS 3.0
Routers and switches	Cisco IOS and IOS-XR	Cisco IOS and IOS-XR

Comcast's IT infrastructure deploys a variety of network and user management applications. Most of these applications are customized versions of commercially available applications. The back-office systems are important to Comcast's operation and require particular design considerations because of the very large infrastructure operated by Comcast.

IP Infrastructure Characteristics

In the past, Comcast's CRANs were relatively independent and were independently managed. In that context, the RFC 1918–defined IP address space was sufficient to manage the devices in each market. With its rapid growth, Comcast naturally moved toward a consolidated environment by building a high-speed, nationwide backbone network that integrates all CRANs into a single administrative domain. In this new environment, RFC 1918 addresses (or a similar space, such as 24.0.0.0) are insufficient for the pooled devices.

Comcast's current IPv4 address management has the following characteristics:

- **Address lifetime:** Most endpoints (cable modems, set-top boxes, VoIP devices) are dynamically assigned temporary addresses. Network elements use fixed IP addresses.

- **Address types:** Both global IPv4 addresses and private (RFC 1918) IPv4 addresses are used.

- **Global IPv4 addresses management:** Comcast exhausted the RFC 1918 address space and is currently using global IPv4 addresses to manage its devices. Comcast is often applying to American Registry for Internet Numbers (ARIN) for additional global IPv4 address space.

NOTE   Comcast ran out of the RFC 1918 address space in July 2005. Ever since, it has been using global IPv4 addresses just for managing devices and not for IP services.

The most significant challenge Comcast sees to the existent IP infrastructure is the lack of IPv4 addresses, primarily to manage the devices that provide services. Note that even though a customer might subscribe only to cable TV service and not to IP services, Comcast will burn IPv4 addresses in order to manage its cable modems and set-top boxes. In this sense, lack of IP addresses would limit company growth and not just its diversification of service offerings.

Perspective on IPv6

In Comcast's vision, IPv6 and its early adoption would provide Comcast the following benefits:

- **Resolve address shortage challenges:** IPv6 is the only long-term solution to the IP address needs of large infrastructures. The adoption of IPv6 for device management will eliminate obstacles to growth and will reduce operational costs.

- **Gain competitive advantage:** The integration of IPv6 and DOCSIS 3.0 into an access provider's network is inevitable and will take time. The impact will be from the core network to the set-top boxes and other customer premises devices. All access providers will have to make the investment at some point to remain viable. Early planning and deployment of IPv6 provides a competitive advantage over organizations that have to integrate it under pressure and over a short period of time. Cable providers compete against DSL and FTTH providers.

- **Prepare for future services:** A tested and proven IPv6-enabled infra-structure enables access providers to easily turn on services better suited or only supported for IPv6. With the natural refresh of the Windows OS in the subscriber base, Vista will become prevalent in homes, leading to an increase in use, with or without the user being aware of it, of IPv6.

The three benefits are listed in the order of their relevancy and priority for Comcast. In the short term, the use of IPv6 in device management solves a pressing problem, which also provides a competitive edge. In the long term, the use of IPv6 for service delivery will be considered on a service-by-service basis. Comcast's perspective on IPv6 is clearly highlighted by its CTO, David Fellows:

> IPv6 implementation is a critical tool for our industry as we seek both to expand our triple play offerings and to extend into new areas. It also will allow cable operators to effectively manage the proliferation of devices that are capturing consumer interest, including portable media players, cellular phones, gaming consoles, PDAs and others.[4]

The Case for IPv6

Comcast was the first company worldwide to point out that IPv4 address space, private or global, was insufficient to manage today's large networks. Its rapidly growing customer base and the consolidation of its markets presented Comcast with a real challenge. By July 2005, Comcast exhausted the resource it was using for device management, the private IPv4 address space.

---

4. "CableLabs Issues DOCSIS 3.0 Specifications Enabling 160 Mbps," CableLabs press release, August 7, 2006, http://www.cablelabs.com/news/pr/2006/06_pr_docsis30_080706.html.

A diligent and thorough analysis of the solution space led to several options, which are summarized in Table 5-4.[5]

Table 5-4 *Comcast's Solutions for the Depletion of IP Addresses Used in Device Management*

Solution	Description	Impact
Use of public IPv4 addresses	Apply for global address space from ARIN.	Minimal impact deployment wise. However, it is facing the depletion of the global address space.
Use of dark space	The address space that has not been allocated by the registries or that has been allocated but is not in use is called "dark space." The U.S. government and several large North American universities are examples of organizations that own large dark or unused address spaces.	Minimal impact deployment wise. However, it places additional operational requirements to avoid leaks and conflicts.
Federalized network	This solution divides the entire network into independent domains or segments. Each domain can reuse the same private IP addresses as long as they are isolated from each other.	High deployment impact, because the network needs to be redesigned. High operational costs, because management cannot be done within a single administrative domain.
IPv6	Use IPv6 addresses to manage devices.	Medium-to-high, short-term transition impact. However, IPv6 deployment is expected to occur sooner or later anyway. Lower operational costs, because all management functions can be centralized.

Comcast chose the natural, long-term solution, which is to deploy IPv6. The case made for IPv6 is as follows: leverage the larger address space in order to manage large-scale networks in a cost-effective way and provide the foundation for new services.

5. Alain Durand, "Managing 100+ Million IP Addresses," presented at NANOG 37, June 2006, http://www.nanog.org/mtg-0606/pdf/alain-durand.pdf.

NOTE Focusing on using IPv6 for management purposes first is a practical approach to the integration of a new protocol. The management traffic uses little resources, so it will have little impact on the services delivered over IPv4. As confidence grows in the new protocol, its use can be extended to service delivery.

The business case for IPv6 in Comcast's network is pragmatic and realistic. It provides a new perspective on IPv6 adoption where in the context of today's large networks even the private IPv4 address space represents a constraint.

IPv6 Planning and Implementation

Comcast developed its strategy for the IPv6 integration within the framework of several guiding principles that reflect general good practices and the specifics of its goals:

- **IPv6 must be part of the roadmap:** A policy decision has been made to consistently pursue the IPv6 integration in all elements of the IT infrastructure. IPv6 is an integral part of roadmaps and product purchasing requirements.

- **Incremental deployment:** The infrastructure is not transitioned to IPv6 but, instead, IPv6 is incrementally integrated in it. In the context of device management, IPv6 will be used to manage new customers while existing customers continue to be managed over IPv4.

- **Minimal disruption:** The integration of IPv6 and its use should have minimal impact on IPv4 and the services it supports.

- **Maintain the security of the network:** Even though in its initial use, IPv6 will operate only within Comcast's network, a closed and controlled environment, security remains a concern.

From a technology perspective, Comcast chose a dual-stack approach to the deployment of IPv6. The network elements, from core all the way to cable modems, must support both IPv6 and IPv4. The integration of IPv6 will start with the core and spread toward the edge of the network.

NOTE   This approach runs counter to the predictions made by the IPv6 community that the protocol will be deployed at the edge first, in small islands that are interconnected over the core via tunnels. Comcast targets a large-scale deployment however it is highly dependent on the timely availability of commercial products availability to meet their deployment goals. The networking devices used in the core of the network have been supporting IPv6 for a very long time in a stable manner. The edge products such as cable modem termination systems (CMTS) and cable modems, however, had no IPv6 support at the time these plans were laid out, so it made sense to start deploying IPv6 in the core and move outward toward the edge.

The back-end systems used to manage the network and the customers must also support both IPv6 and IPv4. The IPv6-based device management environment follows the same model and architecture as the one currently used with IPv4.

The implementation of the IPv6 integration strategy is not straightforward, especially for an early adopter. Some of the standards, products, and services that Comcast planned on using were not available at the optimal time. As a result, Comcast had to adjust its schedules and manage a higher level of complexity. Comcast had to manage several timelines in order to achieve optimal and rapid deployment of IPv6, including:

- **IPv6 support in DOCSIS:** DOCSIS is the technology standard for delivering data services over cable networks. At the time Comcast initiated its IPv6 plans, DOCSIS did not support the new protocol. Comcast, as a member of CableLabs, the standardization body for DOCSIS, together with other MSOs and networking equipment manufacturers, had to actively pursue the integration of IPv6 in the latest version of the specification: DOCSIS 3.0. The new DOCSIS 3.0 standard directly supports concurrent IPv4-only, dual-stack, and IPv6-only environments. The contributions made to the DOCSIS standard by Comcast and other members of the CableLabs consortium have paved a practical path for the complimentary transition to IPv6 and DOCSIS 3.0.

- **Availability of networking products supporting IPv6:** Although major networking equipment manufacturers have been supporting IPv6 in their products for several years, the cable-specific equipment (CMTS, cable modems) did not integrate IPv6 because it was not even supported by the media-relevant standards. In parallel with pursuing the development of DOCSIS 3.0, Comcast had to work closely with gear manufacturers to produce compliant networking equipment as soon as possible. It could not afford to wait for a serialized process that would take too much time. The market analysis predicts that 60 percent of the cable products will support DOCSIS 3.0 by 2011, but Comcast wanted to move faster.[6] It worked closely with vendors to see prototypes of DOCSIS 3.0–compliant equipment, even before the DOCSIS 3.0 specification was released. The Comcast positioning effort benefited Comcast's early adoption approach and also helped CMTS and cable modem equipment manufacturers get practical guidance on product requirements. This is just one example of how the ripple effect of an early adopter significantly influences the industry.

- **Back-end systems support for IPv6:** For back-end systems, Comcast uses customized, off-the-shelf products that must be able to manage both IPv4 and IPv6 endpoints. The products available in the market do not always meet the needs of Comcast's environment and at the large scale of its production deployment.

- **IPv6 deployment in the network core:** Comcast had to inventory the existent infrastructure, to investigate the architecture it wanted to use and to put in place a deployment plan.

- **Training:** IPv6 knowledge is very limited and experience with the protocol is virtually nonexistent, so Comcast had to put in place a program that would timely bring its staff up to speed on IPv6.

While managing these timelines toward an early IPv6 solution to its device management problem, Comcast had to put in place a temporary alternative because

---

6. ABI Research, "DOCSIS 3.0 Network Equipment Penetration to Reach 60% by 2011," August 23, 2006, http://www.abiresearch.com/abiprdisplay.jsp?pressid=710.

it exhausted the RFC 1918 address space. Until the IPv6 solution becomes fully operational, Comcast is using global IPv4 addresses for device management. This means that it has to apply to ARIN for new address space on a regular basis.

With all these considerations, Comcast put in place the IPv6 integration strategy summarized in Table 5-5.

Table 5-5 *Comcast's Strategy for Deploying IPv6*

Phase 1 (2003–2006)	Phase 2 (2007–2008)	Phase 3 (2009 Onward)
Actively contribute to the development of DOCSIS 3.0 and its inclusion of IPv6.	Work with back-end system vendors to integrate the necessary IPv6 support.	Plan and deploy service offering over IPv6.
Work closely with vendors to integrate IPv6 support in all products of interest.	Work with networking vendors to integrate IPv6 support in cable products and set-top boxes.	
Perform network inventory to asses IPv6 readiness.	Run tests and interop events to evaluate design options for the edge of the network.	
Acquire IPv6 address space.		
Perform tests on most suitable approaches to the deployment of IPv6 in the network core.	Deploy IPv6 in the network access layer and start using IPv6 for device management.	
Review security policies.		
Complete the deployment of IPv6 in the network core.		

NOTE   Comcast understood the value of IPv6 early. It acquired its global IPv6 address space from ARIN in January 2003: IPv6 prefix 2001:558::/32.

Comcast took a strategic and holistic approach to the process of IPv6 integration and did not focus on just a quick solution for the problem faced. The IPv6 integration was planned for the long run. Comcast understood that it requires tighter acceptance rules in order to deal with its varying levels of implementation maturity. Comcast viewed the integration of IPv6 as an opportunity to improve the infrastructure and its operating policies, and it took this opportunity to strengthen its policies going forward. Various IP design options were considered and tested. Comcast took a closer look at its product acceptance policies and formalized them, raising the bar in terms of both requirements and evaluation.

An area that Comcast had to pay particular attention to during its strategy planning was training. IPv6 is a new technology and most engineers are not familiar with its specifics. The success of the IPv6 deployment depended on the ability of the operations staff to manage the new protocol. The training efforts employed included academic-style courses, web-based classes, and hands-on experience. The appropriate level of training was provided to each member of the technical staff based on the functions they perform and their responsibilities.

NOTE   The Society of Cable Telecommunications Engineers (SCTE; http://www.scte.org/) in partnership with Cisco developed a web-based course dedicated specifically to IPv6 in cable environments and called "IPv6: Impact on Cable Networks."

The IPv6 integration process continues at Comcast in line with its strategy and shaped by the progress made in each of the timelines mentioned earlier. As an early adopter, Comcast naturally faced many challenges along the way. At the beginning of 2007, the main challenges listed by Alain Durand were

- IPv6 support in back-end systems
- Training

Nevertheless, Comcast overcame many challenges in its deployment of IPv6, and the experience it gained along the way provided Comcast with competitive advantage over other cable providers that rushed to deploy IPv6. Comcast's active role in the IPv6 community earned it worldwide recognition as a leader in deployment and innovation.

With the IPv6 infrastructure operational end to end and stable in the 2007 to 2008 timeframe, Comcast will be well positioned. It will have the knowledge and expertise to easily integrate new and old services during its transition and steadily introduce new and improved services over IPv6.

Lessons Learned

As an early IPv6 adopter in the MSO market space, Comcast has to deal with many technology, product, and policy challenges that are natural for a new technology. Comcast developed a strategy that took all these elements into consideration and its approach was validated by the lessons learned:

- **IPv6 can solve problems today:** As the large cable providers have shown, one does not have to assiduously search for a reason to deploy IPv6, but rather keep it in mind as a possible solution to technical problems. IPv6 is the natural solution to scaling up today's networks in terms of the number of nodes and variety of services.

- **The value of early planning:** Comcast's experience shows how important it is to plan the IPv6 integration early, particularly in the case of early adoption within a market segment. Many elements and details that are relevant to the IPv6 deployment might not be readily available or properly addressed. Products must be updated through the refresh cycle and training must be started early.

- **The value of a phased approach:** A phased approach is essential in mitigating the various timelines that confine the integration plans.

Comcast's efforts on planning and deploying IPv6, efforts justified by a clear need and vision for its future large-scale network, are now studied by many organizations. Comcast not only resolved a pressing technical problem with IPv6, it also helped push its market segment toward a natural upgrade of IP. The experience gained is unmatched and the infrastructure deployed prepares Comcast for the upcoming innovations in IP-based services.

Service Provider: Sprint Nextel

Sprint has been testing IPv6 applications with customers for over a decade. With the expansion of IP infrastructures worldwide, IP addresses have become strained, particularly with the emergence of "always on" applications. The general availability of IPv6 will not only expand that address space but will add an additional level of security, will foster network efficiencies and will accommodate application growth. Our Federal customers are leading that transition.

—Tony D'Agata, Vice President, Federal Government and Public Sector

Service providers must always monitor the technology developments in data, voice, and video communications in order to design new services for their customers or respond timely to customer demands. Service providers cannot afford to be adoption laggards, but they can choose how early of an adopter they want to be. In the case of IPv6, carriers have studied the protocol suite for years to prepare for customers who request various types and levels of IPv6-based services. These customers might run tests on the new protocol, run trial services, observe adoption mandates, or deploy IPv6 in production. To remain viable for those customers, and knowing that the deployment of a new service takes time, service providers have to conclude their IPv6 evaluation at least in sync with, if not ahead of, the early adopters across all markets they support. The level of IPv6 awareness by service providers reflects to a certain extent the interest in the technology among consumers, enterprises, and even other service providers. For this reason, a case study on a major U.S. service provider, one with a large and varied customer base, is instructive in understanding both its IPv6 adoption strategy and the IPv6 adoption drivers across the U.S. market.

Although production-level deployment of IPv6 in service provider networks can be precipitated by major industry drivers, the approach to IPv6 integration and adoption can be a significant differentiator. Early involvement with the protocol evaluation, participation in industry-wide trials and test environments, and offering trial IPv6 services can provide invaluable experience and expertise that can be leveraged not only in the design of production services but also in guiding customers in their adoption efforts. For this reason, a service provider's past involvement with the IPv6 efforts is as valuable as its future plans to offer IPv6 services.

Service providers also have an influential role in the market's perception of a technology and its adoption. Through their participation in standardization bodies (IETF), governing bodies (Regional Internet Registries [RIR]), and service provider–specific bodies (North American Network Operators' Group [NANOG]), service providers can champion the adoption of IPv6 and accelerate its adoption. Service providers can also distance themselves from participation and, by doing so, increase adoption drag. The perspective taken by service providers on IPv6 and their adoption roadmaps are thus important not only to the market segment they belong to, but to the overall industry.

For this market segment, we selected Sprint Nextel, one of the largest U.S. and international service and mobile providers. Sprint Nextel has a diverse set of customers with a wide spectrum of IPv6 service requirements. It has a long history of involvement in IPv6 protocol development, standardization, testing, and deployment. Building on its IPv6 experience and early services, Sprint Nextel continues to implement its strategy, leading to a diverse portfolio of production-level IPv6 services. Sprint will begin testing IPv6 on its Peerless IP (PIP) network in the fourth quarter of 2007 with limited rollout in early 2008. General availability on all Sprint wireline networks is planned by the end of 2008 or early 2009.

This case study was developed with the assistance of Wesley George, Sprint IP Engineering.

Company Profile

According to its corporate information page:

> Sprint Nextel offers a comprehensive range of wireless and wireline communications services bringing the freedom of mobility to consumers, businesses and government users. Sprint Nextel is widely recognized for developing, engineering and deploying innovative technologies, including two robust wireless networks serving 54 million customers at the end of 2007; industry-leading mobile data services; instant national and international push-to-talk capabilities; and a global Tier 1 Internet backbone.[7]

---

7. http://www2.sprint.com/mr/aboutsprint.do.

Sprint offers a wide spectrum of data, mobile, and voice services. Its corporate profile is summarized in Table 5-6.

Table 5-6   *Sprint Nextel Corporate Profile Overview*

Profile Category	Status/Value
Organization	Sprint Nextel
Industry	Telecommunications
Number of employees	~60,000
Geography	Global, covers over 25 countries, bilateral service to 137 counties
Revenue	$41 billion net operating

NOTE   The information provided in Table 5-6 is current as of September 2007 (see http://www.sprint.com).

Sprint Nextel offers a full suite of telecommunications services:

- **Voice:** Sprint Nextel offers both wireline and wireless voice services, including cable resale. It also provides instant national and international push-to-talk capabilities.

- **Data:** Sprint Nextel offers IP Layer 3 Multiprotocol Label Switching (MPLS) Virtual Private Networks (VPN) with a transport differentiator (unicast and multicast), L2TPv3-based VPNs (Layer 2 services), and dedicated IP access (unicast and multicast).

- **Mobile:** Sprint Nextel offers wireless content (streaming media, downloads, portal) and wireless Internet access.

- **Managed services:** Sprint Nextel offers managed network services, managed security, and managed IP telephony. It offers simplification and convergence of legacy internal data networks (which includes OSS, OAM&P, call center, and corporate networks).

The typical customers for the voice services are consumers and businesses requiring long-distance and wireless service, as well as enterprises adopting IP telephony. Sprint Nextel also offers switching and back-office services to cable providers. The typical customers for the data services are multinational and U.S. enterprises, Internet content providers, and Tier 2 and Tier 3 ISPs.

Network and IT Profile

Sprint Nextel owns and manages an end-to-end IP infrastructure. The network covers the Americas, Europe, Middle East, Africa, and Asia Pacific. MPLS and IP coverage is provided through the Sprint network and other partners in 137 countries. Ethernet access for IP services is provided in 25 U.S. markets as of the fourth quarter of 2007 and is expanding in 2008. Internationally, as of 2007, Ethernet access is offered in 13 countries and is expanding in 2008. The Sprint Nextel infrastructure has over 300 remote sites and 15,000 cell sites.

Sprint's infrastructure consists of several distinct networks supporting various services. These networks are referenced throughout this case study:

- **SprintLink:** The common IP backbone of Sprint's networks and the Tier 1 dedicated IP access network.

- **iDEN:** Motorola-based network that supports Nextel's premerger voice services.

NOTE   The iDEN network was the first ever large-scale deployment of Mobile IPv4 (MIPv4). It was built with Cisco IOS MIPv4 Cisco Home Agents.

- **Sprint PCS:** The CDMA-based wireless voice and data network that supports Sprint's premerger wireless voice/data services.

- **GMPLS:** Sprint's global MPLS VPN.

- **PIP:** A completely independent network that provides VPN services. It was built primarily to support customers who have requirements for their data that precludes it from being transmitted across a public network (government, medical/financial institutions, and so on). It is a domestic-only network and is the first place where IPv6 VPNs will be enabled, primarily to support federal customers under the Office of Management and Budget (OMB) mandate.

Sprint recently committed to spending $1 billion in 2007 and between $1.5 and $2 billion in 2008 to deploy a nationwide 4G next generation broadband wireless network based on WiMAX (Worldwide Interoperability for Microwave Access) IEEE 802.16e-2005 technology that is expected to exceed 100 million subscribers by 2014.[8] This network is called XOHM (http://www.xohm.com/) and will provide Sprint Nextel customers a nationwide mobile data network that is designed to offer faster speeds, lower costs, greater convenience, and enhanced multimedia quality. At 100 million subscribers (projected), this environment will require addressing resources that can be provided only by IPv6.

The infrastructure integrates over 10,000 devices and is built on a variety of networking equipment and devices running a wide spectrum of OSs. The OSs currently deployed in Sprint's infrastructure and those planned to be used going forward are listed in Table 5-7.

Table 5-7   Sprint Nextel Infrastructure Overview

Device Type	Today	Future
PC, workstations	Windows 2003, Windows XP	Windows Vista, Windows Server 2008
Servers	Linux, AIX, HP-UX, Solaris	Linux, AIX, HP-UX, Solaris
Routers and switches	Cisco 12.0(32SY), 12.2, IOS-XR	Cisco 12.0S, 12.2S family, IOS-XR

Sprint Nextel manages approximately 1500 network devices supporting wireline services and an additional 2000 network devices for wireless services (which does not include wireless radio access network [RAN] elements at each cell site). In addition, Sprint manages approximately 40,000 enterprise devices on

8. http://www.maravedis-bwa.com/PressRelease-and-LTE-Converge.html.

behalf of its customer base. The infrastructure is managed using in-house-developed applications (60 percent of the total number of management applications) and off-the-shelf applications (40 percent of the total number of management applications). Sprint is shifting focus toward off-the-shelf options and is in the process of transitioning 20 to 30 percent of the applications from in-house-developed to off-the-shelf applications. This process will minimize the IPv6 integration challenges due to internally developed applications that are not IP version agnostic and will shift attention from internal development processes to application procurement requirements.

The primary challenges faced by Sprint Nextel with its current infrastructure are software stability, feature velocity, end of life for hardware, and an increasing need for IP address space.

IP Infrastructure Characteristics

The addressing scheme of Sprint's network reflects its diversity. Most of the infrastructure and the corporate network primarily use private addresses. The iDEN network uses private IP addresses, while the SprintLink network and its management elements use public IP addresses. Sprint PCS is assigning global IPv4 addresses to its mobile nodes. The IP infrastructure has been stable and the addressing scheme appropriate. The network was renumbered less than five times over its lifetime, primarily due to growth, mergers, and acquisitions.

With such a large and growing infrastructure and a diverse service portfolio, Sprint Nextel naturally experiences the strain on the IPv4 address resources. IPv4 address shortages are witnessed in various aspects of Sprint's business (providing Tier 1 services, managing wireless devices, providing VoIP services, and providing managed services), manifesting themselves differently in various parts of Sprint's environment. Although the SprintLink and Sprint PCS networks have not run out of IPv4 address space, the shortage of global addresses is made apparent by increased RIR scrutiny on Sprint's requests for new address space. On the other hand, the iDEN network is experiencing actual address shortages driven by the increasing number of supported handsets, each one of them being assigned a static IP address.

Sprint is able to address each type of IP shortage based on service and environment characteristics by applying the following techniques:

- **Segmentation:** Networks are segmented either through VPNs or Network Address Translation (NAT) to enable reuse of the RFC 1918 address space.

- **Pool resizing:** IPv4 address resources are redistributed among regions in order to adapt to the geographical distribution of wireless IP users.

- **Address lifetime adjustments:** The dynamically allocated addresses are more aggressively managed by temporary reductions of idle timeouts.

These workarounds are not sustainable in the long term due to the added operational costs. The prevalence of "always on" mobile devices driven by VoIP, collaborative applications, and "push" services makes the address reuse workaround unsustainable even for the immediate future. These changes in address space utilization pose not only an operational issue that keeps reuse from being sustainable, but also a technology and service offering issue. The workarounds would also not scale to meet the customer base growth. As mentioned earlier, this is particularly the case in Sprint's new XOHM environment, which is targeting 100 million subscribers. Sprint investigated long-term, scalable, and cost-effective solutions to these problems even before the address shortages became apparent. In this context, Sprint investigated IPv6 and became closely involved with the development and testing of the protocol early on. This early investment in IPv6 provided Sprint with the experience needed to develop solutions not only for the emerging addressing constraints but also for the IPv6 services required by the market.

Perspective on IPv6

Sprint's perspective on IPv6 reflects its long-term investigation of the protocol suite and its exposure to a wide spectrum of customers with varied service requirements. From a protocol analysis perspective, Sprint identifies several benefits of IPv6 adoption:

- **Address space scalability:** IPv6 offers sufficient resources to address the needs of users and to provide new IP-based services to a growing range of device types. The address space enables more scalable and simplified address schemes that reduce operational costs.

- **Improved security:** IPv6 can help in some areas of a security architecture. One example is the reduced vulnerability to external reconnaissance due to the large number of hosts typical for IPv6 subnets. It is important to note that mobile networks will heavily leverage SIP for VoIP and IP Multimedia Subsystem (IMS)-based services. Technologies such as STUN/TURN, which are required to facilitate NAT traversal, are fairly complex to implement. The elimination of NAT thus reduces operational and troubleshooting costs and facilitates the deployment of new applications and appliances.

- **Mobility:** Mobile IPv6 (MIPv6) is of particular interest to mobile providers. On one hand, the global address resources simplify deployments; on the other, the protocol improvements over MIPv4 (eliminating the need for foreign agents, simple local provisioning mechanisms such as SLAAC, and the availability of route optimization options) lead to more scalable deployments. Most importantly, a deployed IPv6 network is automatically ready to support MIPv6-based services.

- **Packet processing optimizations:** IPv6's main header is simplified, which leads to packet processing efficiencies. Options and extensions are handled in a more structured way. Fragmentation is streamlined and removed from intermediary network elements. Flow label might lead to new quality of service (QoS) architectures, but until its use is better defined, QoS will be applied in the same way in IPv6 as in IPv4, thus requiring no IPv6-specific changes to be made in the network.

As a Tier 1 mobile and voice provider, Sprint is exposed to the requirements and interests of many types of customers. This shapes its market perspective, which includes three major drivers for IPv6 adoption in the service provider environment:

- **IPv4 address space exhaustion:** As mentioned in the previous section, the signs of a depleting global IPv4 address space are becoming evident while the number of devices requiring long-lived IP addresses is rapidly increasing.

- **Mandated adoption in United States**: The OMB mandate led to a new set of requests for IPv6 services from the federal government. IPv6 support becomes essential to maintaining and acquiring federal customers and subsequently their partners.

- **Managed services:** Businesses will require not only IPv6 connectivity but IPv6-enabled managed services as well.

Sprint estimates that by 2008, at least 70 percent of its market segment will have started to investigate IPv6. Sprint expects that at least 70 percent of its market segment will have started adopting IPv6 by 2009–2010. Sprint started supporting the 6bone IPv6 test environment in 1996 and has worked on production-level services ever since. It will provide global IPv6 Internet access and will start offering VPNv6 services on the PIP network in the beginning of 2008. Sprint's goal is for its network to be fully dual-stack by 2009.

NOTE   The 2009 target date applies to Sprint's entire infrastructure. This includes the wireless network, for which it is challenging to get acceptable IPv6 support for devices (particularly non-smartphone handsets) in the near future.

The Case for IPv6

The adoption of a technology or a protocol with such significant implications but to which it is not straightforward to tie immediate revenue is a complex process. This is particularly true early in the adoption process when the technology lacks a clear champion, be it service provider, enterprise, consumer, or even equipment vendor. Although technologists might be interested and even supportive, the marketing team, usually tasked with making the "case" for adoption and deployment, is faced with a "chicken and egg" situation. For this reason, it is important to make a clear distinction between "interest in IPv6" and "having a business case for IPv6."

Sprint showed technical interest in IPv6 early. It has been actively involved in the standardization and testing of IPv6 since 1997, both to gain experience with deploying and supporting IPv6 and to identify areas where the protocol still has problems that need to be solved. In support of 6bone, Sprint acquired 6bone IPv6 address space (3ffe:2900::/24) and overlaid an IPv6 test environment on top of its IPv4 SprintLink infrastructure with the help of generic routing encapsulation (GRE) tunnels. SprintLink IPv4 customers were offered the possibility to connect to the 6bone network at no additional cost.

Figure 5-1 depicts the topology of the IPv6 overlay deployed in the SprintLink network.

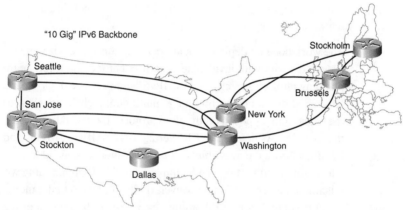

Figure 5-1   *Sprint's Testbed Network*

In 1998, Sprint's IPv6 evaluation network had 15 customers; in 1999 it had 40, and by the end of 2000 it had 110. Between 2000 and 2002 the environment had four more IPv6-capable points of presence (PoP) added: Brussels, Washington DC, San Jose, and New York City. During this period Sprint was turning up two to three customers per week. In 2000 and again in 2002 Sprint acquired global IPv6 address space (2001:440::/32) from ARIN. In May 2004, the number of IPv6 tunneled connections was 300 and the number of native connections was 2; however, the frequency of requests for IPv6 services slowed down considerably to roughly one per week. The customer base continued to expand to eventually reach 400 customers across the entire network shown in Figure 5-1. Sprint continues to offer IPv6 services over the original environment under the 2001:440::/32 prefix even after 6bone was retired on June 6, 2006 (http://www.6bone.net/). Sprint has seen interest in IPv6 service, especially native IPv6, increasing dramatically over the last 6 to 12 months, first driven by the OMB mandate, and then by ARIN's announcement on May 21, 2007.[9]

NOTE   Sprint has been active in the IETF Next Generation Transition (NGTrans) and IP Next Generation (IPng) working groups and co-authored RFC 2772, *6Bone Backbone Routing Guidelines.*[10] Sprint engaged in other IPv6 evaluation efforts outside of 6bone, as well. It provided engineering support to the Moonv6 project (http://www.moonv6.org/).

The work done on deploying and operating this test environment provided Sprint with invaluable expertise that it could leverage in planning an IPv6 strategy and the IPv6-based service deployment. RFC 2772 did in fact highlight the multihoming challenges due to the constraints imposed on the IPv6 protocol by the address allocation policies. As detailed in Chapter 2, "IPv4 or IPv6—Myths and Realities," with the availability of provider independent address allocation, multihoming can be implemented in IPv6 the same way it is implemented in IPv4. However, IETF still has to find a more scalable solution for multihoming, regardless of the version of IP.

Sprint has actively participated in standards work and test environments in the context of the general principles of customer demand and broad commercial scalability required for the introduction of a new infrastructure protocol such as IPv6. It believes in customer preparation and scalability:

- **Be prepared for customers:** Sprint's customers will be deploying IPv6 for many different reasons. Sprint must complete its own deployment in order to effectively serve customer needs. The sooner the production deployment of IPv6 is in place, the better Sprint is prepared to assist customers with their deployments, both from a service availability

---

9. "ARIN Board Advises Internet Community on Migration to IPv6," http://www.arin.net/announcements/20070521.html.

10. "SprintLink IPv6 Services; Overview," http://www.sprintv6.net/Sprintv6.html.

perspective and the consulting/managed services perspective. The same concepts apply to the internal planning of the IPv6 deployment. Sprint's IP core must be IPv6-enabled first in order to support IPv6 services enabled on Sprint's various infrastructures that offer specific services (mobile, VPN, and so on).

- **Determine and improve behavior at scale:** The sum total of IPv6 deployments today is nowhere near the scale of the global IPv4 networks, in either traffic level or number of networks/routes. Existent large-scale deployments of IPv6 are not open to the Internet. Until more large network providers begin ubiquitous deployments of IPv6 and open them to the global Internet, there will not be a wide enough environment to understand all aspects of IPv6's behavior at Internet scale, nor to wring out possible remaining issues that must be solved for the protocol to fully replace IPv4.

NOTE	At the beginning of 2008, there were roughly 250,000 IPv4 Internet routes compared to around 1000 IPv6 routes. Comparison of Iv4 and IPv6 topology can be evaluated from the CAIDA website.[11]

- **Prepare for innovation:** IPv6 will provide new capabilities to networks and networked applications. Ultimately, these new capabilities will improve existing services while opening the door for new, innovative ones. While driven by other factors (customer demand, address exhaustion), early adoption provides Sprint with an environment in which it can pursue innovative ideas and enable customers to try out and improve them.

- **Establish leadership:** Early engagement in standardization and testing efforts helps identify Sprint as a leader in the industry.

- **Guide vendors:** Sprint started to work closely with vendors to ensure IPv6 readiness of products. It provided requirements for IPv6 features in products and performed trials of wireline and wireless equipment.

11. CAIDA, "Visualizing IPv4 Internet Topology at a Macroscopic Scale, Visualizing IPv6 AS-level Internet Topology 2008" http://www.caida.org/research/topology/as_core_network/ and http://www.caida.org/research/topology/as_core_network/ipv6.xml.

In the end, however, the investigation of the protocol, the result of a relatively small investment, has to evolve to full commitment to the protocol adoption in order to have IPv6 deployed in production. This transition requires a business case. Because a service provider of Sprint's size covers several different markets, there might be multiple business cases for the adoption of IPv6, each specific to part of Sprint's business.

By mid-2007, two major drivers for IPv6 adoption in the U.S. service provider market emerged:

- **Request for service from federal agencies:** The OMB mandate requiring the infrastructures of civilian federal agencies to become IPv6 capable by June 2008 led to concrete demand for production-level IPv6 services. The requirements are coming not only from civilian federal agencies and through the Networx contract, but also from organizations working with or for the federal government. To maintain market share with these customers, service providers had to provide IPv6 services in time for the OMB-mandated deadline.

- **IPv4 address shortage:** In the case of wireless services, Sprint is seeing a change in the IP usage profile from short hold times of pooled addresses (casual data access) to longer hold times. These changes are driven by new applications requiring always-on connectivity and by new user habits. These changes dramatically decrease the ability to oversubscribe IP address resources for wireless devices. IPv6 represents the clean solution for addressing the growth in terms of number of subscribers, the demands of new applications, and the future Fixed Mobile Convergence (FMC).

These two drivers created two clear and distinct business cases for the adoption of IPv6 in two of Sprint's infrastructures: the wireline services infrastructure must be enhanced to support dedicated IPv6 Internet access and IPv6 VPNs, and the mobile services infrastructure must be upgraded to deliver information and services to mobile users over IPv6. The former business case had a clear timeline associated with its implementation, to become operational before June 2008 to help federal customers meet the OMB mandate requirements. In the absence of a killer IPv6-based application for the mobile services, the timeline for the latter business case is defined by Sprint.

The experience gained with the IPv6 evaluation network helps Sprint expand the business case for IPv6 in the context of the knowledge needs of federal agencies migrating to IPv6. Sprint can provide IPv6 planning, deployment, and operation consultancy services.

IPv6 Planning and Implementation

Based on internal requirements, on market demand, and on its vision for the future service offerings, Sprint has a multifaceted business case for IPv6 that targets the following overall services:

- **Enable existing services for IPv6:** Enable SprintLink for dual-stack to support the Internet access services initially offered over the IPv6 evaluation network. Provide VPNv6 services to enterprises. Offer managed services for IPv6-capable customer premises equipment.

- **Value-added services:** With rapidly approaching depletion of the IPv4 address space, it is unlikely that all the IP devices will manage to become dual-stack. In this case, solutions will need to be offered to customers who need to access IPv4-only resources from IPv6-only hosts and vice versa. These solutions could either focus on a more efficient use of existing IPv4 address space and temporarily employ additional IPv4 NATs or focus on IPv6-to-IPv4 protocol translation and employ application-level gateways. In either case, scale and complexity considerations would make many users unable or unwilling to manage these solutions. This represents a service opportunity for service providers.

- **Content distribution:** Offload device-to-device and device-to-content/ service IP connectivity in the wireless space to use IPv6.

- **IPv6 consulting:** Provide IPv6 planning and deployment guidance based on Sprint's extensive and long experience with the protocol. As mentioned in the company profile, Sprint is managing over 40,000 enterprise devices. These organizations and potential new customers will benefit from Sprint's advice on deploying IPv6.

The two main business cases mentioned in the previous section require relatively independent strategies. They are driven by different timelines; and they are implemented in distinct infrastructures. Although the two deployments leverage knowledge and some back-office work from each other, it makes sense to discuss their planning and implementation independently. Nevertheless, both implementations are rooted in Sprint's early efforts of investigating, developing, and deploying IPv6. The evolution of these efforts and the migration of the resulting infrastructure to a full production, dual-stack network represent the third major planning/implementation timeline of Sprint's IPv6 efforts worth documenting independently.

NOTE   As an incumbent IPv4 Tier 1 provider, it is important for Sprint to maintain and grow the number of its IPv6 peering points. Competing service providers see IPv6 as an opportunity to take a leadership position in the IPv6 Tier 1 market.

The IPv6 Evaluation Network (AS6175), which was initiated by Sprint's engagement in the 6bone project, is shown in Figure 5-1. (Additional details can be found at Sprint's IPv6 web page, http://www.sprintv6.net/, and particularly in its IPv6 position paper.[12]) The routers in the diagram are IPv6 standalone routers connected through GRE tunnels over the IPv4 infrastructure (SprintLink, AS1239), with which they do not interact in terms of control plane. Subscribers access the evaluation network via GRE or IPv6 in IPv4 tunnels. They can receive /48 prefix allocations from Sprint's 2001:440::/32 pool or they can attach with their own prefix (allocated by an RIR). Routing is provided via fully meshed iBGP.[13] Sprint's IPv6 evaluation network provides global reachability by peering with many other IPv6 networks.[14] Peering sessions are established with over 600 autonomous systems, primarily via IPv6-over-IPv4 tunnels, but in some instances

12. http://www.sprintv6.net/Sprintv6.html.

13. "IPv6 BGP Operational Report from SprintV6," http://www.sprintv6.net/aspath/bgp.html.

14. CAIDA, "Visualizing IPv6 AS-level Internet Topology 2008," http://www.caida.org/research/topology/as_core_network/ipv6.xml.

they are established natively at peering points such as The Stokab in Stockholm, Sweden, and AMS-IX in Amsterdam, Netherlands. As the number of IPv6 Internet users grows, the evaluation network will be integrated into the SprintLink infrastructure by enabling it for dual-stack, and most peering sessions will be established natively over IPv6.

NOTE   Why did Sprint take this approach to building the IPv6 evaluation network? Following are some reasons:

- **Dedicated routers:** The dedicated routers could be operated with software that supports the necessary IPv6 features yet not be constrained by having to run the software certified for the production network. They also ensure the maximum possible independence of the overlay from the production network.

- **Equipment reuse:** Can reuse lower-end, depreciated equipment requiring minimal capital investment.

- **Little traffic:** The tunnel approach was appropriate and sufficient because customers were primarily interested in feature experimentation and not in bandwidth-demanding applications. A bandwidth utilization snapshot taken at the end of 2003 indicated that the IPv6 customer traffic on the evaluation network was 0.006 percent of the IPv4 traffic on SprintLink.

Table 5-8 summarizes Sprint's phased approach to deploying IPv6 access services.

NOTE   Sprint acquired the first block of IPv6 addresses from ARIN in 2002. The original allocation met the policies at that time and was 2001:440::/35; it then changed to /32 in accordance with the RIR allocation policy updates. Sprint uses this to number its testbed IPv6 network and to allocate /48s to customers on this network. In December 2006, Sprint acquired the prefix 2600::/29, which will be used for Sprint's deployment of IPv6 into its production networks.

Table 5-8   *Sprint's Strategy for Deploying IPv6 Access Services*

Phase 1 (1997–2002)	Phase 2 (2002–2007)	Phase 3 (2008–2009)
1997: Deploy IPv6 network in support of 6bone. Acquire 6bone address space.	2004: Include IPv6 requirements into purchasing policies.	2008: Enable IPv6 everywhere that it is supported, use transition technologies (tunneling/gateways) to cover gaps, drive both internal and external development to support IPv6 in all new projects, and justify exceptions that must remain IPv4-only.
1998: Offer IPv6 access at no extra cost to SprintLink IPv4 customers.	December 2006: Acquire global IPv6 address space for the production services.	
2002: Acquire global IPv6 address space from ARIN.	2006: Initiate infrastructure inventory, a process expected to last until the end of 2007.	2009: Infrastructure completely operating in dual-stack mode.
	2006: Start internal back-office development and testing for IPv6 on network elements.	

The enterprise-focused services, which are particularly relevant in relation to the OMB mandate, will be offered in the form of MPLS IPv6 VPNs (RFC 4659) over Sprint's PIP network. Corresponding VPNv6 services follow on the global MPLS network, which is supported by the SprintLink rather than PIP platform. For these services, Sprint deployed dedicated Cisco 12000 series Gigabit Switch Routers (GSR) running Cisco IOS-XR as dual-stack provider edge (PE) routers. At first, the current IPv4-only PE routers will remain on IOS. Sprint's plan is to upgrade its existing PE devices to IOS-XR once feature parity, code quality, and customer demand are appropriate for deployment to the overall network. Existing customer Virtual Routing and Forwarding (VRF) tables will be upgraded to multiprotocol VRF operation whenever IPv6 support is requested. The service is offered on PIP as of Q4, 2007, to trial customers and will be fully operational prior to June 2008.

NOTE   Sprint's VPNv6 services have the following characteristics:

- **VPNv6 access:** Access to the VPNv6 services is offered over similar media types and encapsulations as for IPv4.

- **Topologies:** Familiar IPv4 VPN service topologies are available for VPNv6.

- **Customer-facing routing:** The VPNv6 service supports eBGP, IPv6 EIGRP, and static routing on the PE-CE interface. Open Shortest Path First version 3 (OSPFv3) support will be added at a later time.

The solution was extensively tested over a period of two months in an environment that included five sites.

Prior to enabling SprintLink for dual-stack and deploying VPNv6 services over its PIP network, Sprint updated its purchasing policies in 2005 to include IPv6 requirements. The requirements were specific and were based on Sprint's experience evaluating the protocol and the envisioned needs. Using the OMB mandate date as the target for VPNv6 service readiness, the requirements had to be communicated as early as possible in order to account for the time required by vendors to implement missing requirements and harden the features, for the time required by Sprint to thoroughly test the equipment and the end-to-end solution, and for the time required for deployment and trials. Sprint also initiated an IPv6-oriented inventory of its infrastructure, primarily SprintLink, because for the VPNv6 services Sprint decided to deploy new, dedicated, dual-stack PE routers.

Table 5-9 summarizes Sprint's phased approach to deploying IPv6 services to enterprises and the federal agencies.

Finally, the third business case and strategy/implementation review is for deploying IPv6 in the mobile environment. This project is on a less aggressive timeline than the enterprise services, which observe externally imposed deadlines. Nevertheless, this deployment is essential in supporting the growth of Sprint's mobile customer base and the diversification of the services offered.

Table 5-9   *Sprint's Strategy for Deploying IPv6 Services for Enterprises*

Phase 1 (2004–2007)	Phase 2 (2008)	Phase 3 (2009 Onward)
2004: Include IPv6 requirements into purchasing policies. 2006: Acquire global IPv6 address space for the production services. 2006: Start internal back-office development and testing for IPv6 on network elements. 2006: Initiate infrastructure inventory, a process expected to last until the end of 2007. 2007: Perform VPNv6 code testing and network tests. 2007: Initial deployment of the VPNv6 functionality on PE routers. 2007: Offer trial IPv6 VPN services on the PIP network.	Expand the deployment of VPNv6 services. Offer dual-stack dedicated Internet access. Offer Networx services: Managed Network Services (MNS) and Customer Specific Design and Engineering Services (CSDES). VPNv6 services ready to support the requirements of the OMB mandate before June 2008.	2009: Infrastructure fully enabled to provide IPv6 services to enterprises. Continue to offer consultancy services and to develop managed services.

Table 5-10 summarizes Sprint's phased approach to deploying IPv6 to support mobile services.

Table 5-10   *Sprint's Strategy for Deploying IPv6 Services for Mobile Users*

Phase 1 (2004–2006)	Phase 2 (2002–2007)	Phase 3 (2008–2009)
Early discussions about IPv6 support for future applications.	Initiate infrastructure inventory, a process expected to last until the end of 2007. Start internal back-office development and testing for IPv6 on wireless elements. Push new projects and services to be IPv6-ready on day 1 and justify any exceptions that must remain IPv4-only.	Enable IPv6 on as much infrastructure as possible, and begin testing end-to-end IPv6 on the wireless network. 2009: Infrastructure fully enabled to provide IPv6 services seamlessly across both the wireline and wireless network.

NOTE   It is important to note that currently the IETF is actively working on the options and requirements of deploying IPv6 over WiMAX. This work is conducted in the 16ng IETF working group.

Building on its experience with using MIP in the iDEN environment, Sprint plans to deploy MIPv6 in its new XOHM network to deliver pervasive and seamless mobility to its customers. Trial tests of MIPv6 were started in 2007.

The primary challenges experienced by Sprint in implementing its IPv6 strategy across all three projects discussed are as follows:

- **Lack of pervasive support for IPv6 features:** Many vendors support IPv6 on paper, but do not support it in a scalable, high-performance manner or do not support all of the features needed. For example, it is challenging to get acceptable IPv6 support in wireless devices, especially non-smartphone handsets within the deployment timeframe envisioned by Sprint. Although IPv6 should not be viewed as a feature but as a fundamental transport capability, many vendors expect early adopters to support financially the development necessary for IPv6.

- **Network management challenges:** Support for features and tools necessary to manage IPv6 does not keep up the pace with deployments of the dual-stack routers.

Nevertheless, building on the IPv6 Internet access services offered over the IPv6 evaluation network and the extensive testing done to demonstrate the capabilities, scalability, and performance of the VPNv6 solution, Sprint expects all of its infrastructure to be IPv6-enabled by 2009.

Lessons Learned

Sprint's long involvement in the development, evaluation, and deployment of IPv6 led it to acquire a wealth of information and expertise. The most important lessons learned throughout this evolution from 6bone participant to provider of production-level IPv6 services are described here:

- **Gain early familiarity with the protocol:** Early deployment through testbed networks and involvement in the standards bodies are critical in ensuring that you gain experience prior to production implementation, and that the protocol has real applications for your particular business needs.

- **Take a realistic perspective on the protocol:** IPv6 brings improvements in some aspects of the protocol, such as addressing and "plug-and-play" capabilities for appliances, but its capabilities should be well understood and evaluated in a realistic manner.

NOTE   Refer to Chapter 2 for an analysis of the IPv4-IPv6 myths and realities.

- **The need for expertise with large-scale deployments:** IPv6 has long suffered from a lack of legitimate deployment drivers. This has slowed the large-scale Internet deployment necessary to truly shake down the protocol and drive final solutions to the still-outstanding issues and challenges associated with IPv6.

- **Demand for IPv6 is not uniform across market segments:** Some markets have articulated clear demand for IPv6 while others do not yet see a need for its deployment. Service providers thus need to address the specific IPv6 requirements of their customers as they emerge. It is time for providers to start taking a serious look at their implementation strategy or else risk being behind the curve. Addressing the early service requirements helps Sprint prepare for a future in which the demand for IPv6 support is pervasive.

Combining its IPv6 expertise and experience with a realistic perspective on the capabilities of the protocol, Sprint developed an IPv6 strategy that enables it to address its short- and long-term needs. The deployment follows the principle of the "when and where needed" approach while new infrastructures are built with IPv6 in mind.

Tier 1 Service Provider: Tata Communications

As a Tier 1 provider of IP wholesale transit services, early adoption of IPv6 has provided us a powerful differentiator in the market place. Now it is the turn of national and regional networks to also reap the benefits of early adoption with their enterprise and retail customer base. Private enterprise networks themselves now start to identify competitive advantages that early use of IPv6 will bring them within their respective industry sectors.

—Yves Poppe, Director Business Development, Tata Communications

To a certain extent, Tier 1 providers can be viewed as a barometer of the Internet's current state as well as its evolution. They provide transit between the sites of the same service provider or large enterprise or they interconnect various service providers. In that sense, they represent the Internet backbone. Their infrastructures have to support the types and levels of traffic that characterize users' interest at the time. They must also anticipate trends and demand in order to adapt their infrastructure accordingly. For example, recent projects aimed at expanding the capacity of Tier 1 networks reflect the rapid growth in bandwidth demand driven by new usages of the Internet. Applications such as YouTube not only increased users' appetites for content, they also enabled users to generate and provide content. Social networks supported by applications such as MySpace create large-scale user groups exchanging large amounts of information in a peer-to-peer model. These realities of today's Internet are reflected in the type and quantity of traffic that traverses Tier 1 provider networks.

Tier 1 providers aggregate the IP transport requirements of service providers and large enterprises and, implicitly, the requirements of their customers. Moreover, the traditionally large geographical footprint of their networks enables them to capture the IP requirements not only within individual countries, but also across various regions around the world. In this sense, Tier 1 service providers are well positioned to reflect the IPv6 interest in the overall service provider market space. This of course should not be considered the only factor in judging overall interest in IPv6. Adoption trends have shown that Tier 1 providers are not exposed to all IPv6 deployments. At the time of this writing, the content available on the IPv6 Internet is limited and the availability of IPv6 Internet access service is limited. Many of the known large-scale regional service provider IPv6 deployments are taking a "walled-in garden" approach in which IPv6 is used to support just an internally managed service such as multicast-based content distribution. These deployments would not be visible on the backbone of the Internet. Nevertheless, Tier 1 providers, while handling other types of IPv6 transport requests, will be the first to observe the mapping of the Internet content into both versions of IP and to observe the inevitable opening of the garden walls.

By staying a step ahead of their customers in terms of infrastructure support for various traffic types and traffic profiles, Tier 1 providers are natural early adopters of certain technologies and products. This is definitely the case with a network layer protocol such as IPv6. Their planning and deployment experience provide the interesting perspective of the IPv6 early adopters. Tier 1 providers typically offer a large portfolio of services and operate national, domestic networks as well. This provides an added value to their perspective on user requirements and, in particular, interest in IPv6.

This case study covers one of the largest, global communications companies, Tata Communications, formerly known as VSNL (Videsh Sanchar Nigam Limited) International and referred as such in the rest of this case study. It is a leading international IPv6 connectivity provider over its Tier 1 global network. The service was and continues to be built based on the IPv6 early adopter experience gained by one of VSNL's acquisitions, Teleglobe. Along with its global, Tier 1 network, Tata Communications operates an extensive domestic network in India covering more than 120 cities. Tata Communications was also selected as the second network operator in South Africa under the name Neotel. The case study was developed with the assistance of Yves Poppe, Director of Business Development, Tata Communications; Anne-Marie Legoff, Senior Product Manager of IPv4 and IPv6 services; and Raju Raghavan, from the Tata Communications Global IP MPLS Engineering Center. The successful deployment of IPv6 in the global Tata Communications network was and continues to be the result of the relentless dedication of the engineering and operations staff, with a particular mention to Nenad Pudar of the AS6453 engineering team.

Company Profile

According to its corporate information page:

> Tata Communications promotes communications solutions to the global carrier and enterprise markets by leveraging our extensive undersea and satellite network capabilities in India and around the globe.
>
> Tata Communications Global Network spans across 4 continents and comprises major ownership in 206,356km of terrestrial network fiber and subsea cable. Through our principal ownership status in SMW-3, SMW-4, SAFE, TIC (100% owned) and capacity ownership in FLAG and I2I, Tata Communications offers the greatest diversity for connectivity services to India. This is coupled with a powerful domestic network that covers over 300 cities in India and a comprehensive portfolio of managed services that makes Tata Communications the most reliable provider of solutions to, from and within India.
>
> Tata Communications owns and operates TGN, which offers unparalleled connectivity solutions on the Trans-Atlantic, Trans-Pacific and intra-European routes. This multi-terabit system allows Tata Communications to offer carriers and enterprises connectivity from speeds of 64K to 10Gbpps and provides commercial flexibility using features like global capacity portability.[15]

VSNL International was integrated in Tata Communications in 2008. It offers a wide spectrum of data, mobile, and voice services. Its corporate profile is summarized in Table 5-11.

---

15. http://www.tatacommunications.com.

Table 5-11   *Tata Communications Corporate Profile Overview*

Profile Category	Status/Value
Organization	Tata Communications (formerly VSNL International)
Industry	Telecommunications
Number of employees	5000
Geography	Global, covers over 200 countries across 300 POPs
Revenue	$1.04 billion
Total market share	The world's largest wholesale voice carrier, 11 percent of the global voice market share; largest transpacific capacity owner, with 7.68-terabit subsea cable system; leading transcontinental IP wholesale transit provider

NOTE   The revenue figure covers both VSNL International and VSNL India and it was reported in 2006 under the former VSNL website. Today, information on Tata Communications is available at http://www.tatacommunications.com.

NOTE   Tata Communications is part of the Tata Group, which also includes Tata Consultancy Services (TCS), Asia's largest software and systems integration services company, covering 33 countries across 5 continents and a key player in high-growth international markets.

Tata Communications offers a large spectrum of services, including the following:[16]

- **Voice:** The world's largest international wholesale carrier with more than 415 combined direct and bilateral relationships with leading international voice telecommunications providers and more than 17 billion

---

16. http://www.tatacommunications.com/providers/, http://www.tatacommunications.com/enterprise/.

minutes annually of international wholesale voice traffic. Principal provider of public international telecommunications services in India, linking the domestic network to over 240 territories worldwide.

- **Data:** Tier 1 IP service provider and international IPv6 connectivity leader. Principal provider of international data services in India leveraging both Metro-Ethernet and cable infrastructures.

- **Mobile:** Connection to over 400 mobile operators worldwide. Principal provider of signaling conversion services to enable GSM roaming to and from North America. Offering content delivery services.

These services are provided over a large, legacy-free infrastructure built around a global MPLS network. Tata Communications owns 206,356 km of terrestrial network fiber and subsea cable. It operates 300 POPs in 200 countries and has access to five geostationary satellites through 30 dedicated Earth stations. Tata Communications owns over 100 subsea and terrestrial cable systems and has full ownership of Tata Indicom Cable. The buildout and growth of this infrastructure was marked by two major acquisitions: Tyco Global Network (acquisition completed on July 1, 2005) and Teleglobe (acquisition completed on February 13, 2006).

As of June 2007, 85 percent of Tata Communications IP infrastructure is IPv6-enabled.

Network and IT Profile

Tata Communications operates a Tier 1 global network under AS6453 and operates an extensive domestic network in India covering more than 120 cities under AS4755. Tata Communications was also chosen as the second network operator in South Africa under the name Neotel. Neotel is in the process of building a domestic countrywide IP network under AS36937 and will connect to the local AS6453 PoP. AS6453 comprises 80 POPs in 25 countries. The POPs are connected via a globe-spanning MPLS backbone of multiple 10-Gigabit transcontinental and continental connections. The backbone capacity is 700+ Gbps and carries more then 380 petabits globally per month. Tata Communications global IP backbone is shown in Figure 5-2.

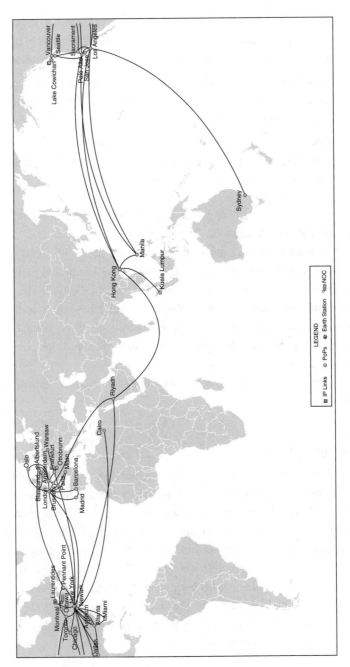

Figure 5-2 *Tata Communications Backbone Network*

Tata Communications India domestic network operates under AS4755, covering over 120 cities. The AS4755 network consists of eight regions converging into eight Tier 1 POPs. This portion of Tata Communications network is shown in Figure 5-3.

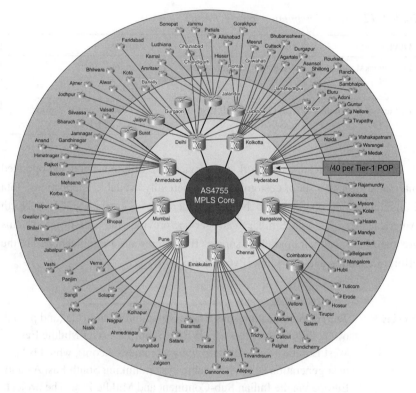

Figure 5-3   *Tata Communications India Domestic Network*

This IP infrastructure guarantees Tata Communications global and national IP networks' readiness for Internet's next growth phase and its associated revenue opportunities. The terabit-level transoceanic cable capacity owned by the company (100+ subsea cables and a total of 206,356 km of combined terrestrial fiber and subsea cable) guarantees Layer 1 capacity that is capable of easily accommodating periods of the most explosive traffic growth.

The infrastructure is built on a variety of networking equipment and devices running a wide spectrum of OSs. The OSs currently deployed in Tata Communications infrastructure and those planned to be used going forward are listed in Table 5-12.

Table 5-12   *Tata Communications IT Profile*

Device Type	Today	Future
PCs, workstations	Windows 2003, Windows XP	Windows Vista
	Solaris	TBD
Routers and switches	JUNOS, Cisco IOS and IOS-XR, iSOS, FTOS	JUNOS, Cisco IOS and IOS-XR, FTOS

Tata Communications network and services are fully managed and operated internally through a set of customized, commercially available applications. Tata Communications operates two Network Operations Centers (NOC) in North America and one in Asia. Similar to any service provider, the back-office systems are important, and their upgrade to support IPv6 represents a significant part of the effort of enabling and providing IPv6 services.

NOTE   Tata Communications has a network administrator role (and partial ownership) in the SEA-ME-WE-4 (South East Asia-Middle East-West Europe 4) project (http://www.seamewe4.com), which is "a next generation submarine cable system linking South East Asia to Europe via the Indian Sub-Continent and Middle East. The project aims to take these regions to the forefront of global communication by significantly increasing the bandwidth and global connectivity of users along its route between Singapore and France."

IP Infrastructure Characteristics

As a global, Tier 1 carriers' carrier, Tata Communications does not experience significant pressure due to the IPv4 address space constraints. All peers and all major customers connect autonomous system to autonomous system using BGP and manage their own address space. Evidently, networks connecting multitudes of end users and end devices are significantly more exposed to the looming address shortage.

A more important consideration in the design and operation of a global network such as Tata Communications is to minimize round-trip times for traffic originating and terminating in a given region. In this context, Tata Communications has to optimally use the address blocks issued by the various RIRs within the various parts of the world where it has a presence. VSNL AS6453 covers IPv4 address allocations from various RIRs, and the same approach is being taken for IPv6. Indeed, the Tata Communications/Teleglobe network has IPv6 address blocks (/32s) from the ARIN, RIPE NCC, AfriNIC, and APNIC registries. Optimal integration of these allocations is done through a routing design that leverages a set of route reflectors.

In the case of the regional Indian and South African access IP networks, the situation is different because they are more exposed to potential address shortages. IPv4 address shortages are of particular concern in rapidly developing regions such as China and India. Both the Indian and South African domestic networks have acquired their IPv4 and IPv6 address allocations from APNIC and AfriNIC, respectively.

Perspective on IPv6

The type of services offered and the global footprint of its network naturally expose Tata Communications to varied customer demands. This is also true in the case of IPv6 requirements. Tata Communications sees requests for IPv6 support generated by:

- **IPv4 address space depletion:** It is now a quasi-certainty that the world will be running out of IPv4 addresses, with the address shortage being particularly acute in major developing economies such as China and India. The plethora of addresses available in IPv6 will sustain the continued growth of these economies and will allow restoration of the end-to-end principle and the allocation of permanent IP addresses. This will make possible IP address–based billing, unique identification of goods, operation of sensor and monitoring networks, and so on. By covering

India and other Asian markets, Tata Communications expects to see rapid increase in demand for IPv6 support as its customers run out of IPv4 address space.

- **International IPv6 adoption:** IPv6 adoption around the world is driven by various factors other than the impending depletion of IPv4 address space. Drivers can be service- or deployment-specific benefits, early adoption, or mandated adoption. Some of these environments will require Tier 1 support for IPv6 in order to interconnect sites or to connect to customers and partners.

- **The needs of next generation mobile networks:** IPv6 is a prerequisite for the inclusion of major new mobile application families, Mobile Ad Hoc Networks (MANET), and Network Mobility (NEMO). IPv6 is a mandatory component in the upcoming IMS for the mobile 3G world and also for the ITU-T defined NGNs. As a major mobile provider, VSNL must be prepared for the IPv6 requirements of this environment.

- **Pursuit of competitive advantage:** Tata Communications customers are starting to look at IPv6 as a differentiator. They might initially deploy IPv6 exclusively within their network or part of their network but those deployments will quickly be followed by requests for IPv6 transit services or support for tunneled service in order to reach the IPv6 Internet.

In its Tier 1 provider and mobile provider roles, Tata Communications sees the value and the importance of having an IPv6-ready infrastructure. Even before large-scale adoption becomes apparent at the Tier 2 service provider level, Tier 1 providers will pick up the service requests of small-scale deployments. Tata Communications has to be prepared to address the IPv6 connectivity needs of early adopters and the service requirements of early planners who, even though they expect to deploy IPv6 in one to two years, make IPv6 support a requirement when signing long-term service contracts.

The Case for IPv6

Tata Communications global presence exposed it early on to various levels of request for and interest in IPv6. Based on this market feedback, the business case for offering IPv6 connectivity at Tier 1 level was evident as long as the new service was incremental and had no impact on existent services. From a global Tier 1 network perspective, IPv6 was viewed as a powerful differentiator in the marketplace and an enabler to increase its customer base by attracting customers planning for a future IPv6 deployment.

The February 2006 acquisition of Teleglobe was essential in strengthening and simplifying the business case for IPv6. The acquisition provided significant and worldwide-recognized IPv6 expertise in deploying IPv6 in an incremental, nondisruptive way. Moreover, Teleglobe provided Tata Communications with an operational Tier 1 IPv6 service. This service could be expanded across the rest of Tata Communications infrastructure based on customer demand.

The second facilitator in building the case for IPv6 was an ongoing network upgrade project. Even though it was driven by bandwidth demand generated through IPv4 traffic, the network upgrade was performed with IPv6 in mind, thus providing the opportunity to achieve IPv6 readiness at no additional costs.

In 2006, Tata Communications IPv6 business case was validated by the market. Of about 60 major Requests For Quotations (RFQ) answered by Tata Communications in 2006, 50 had questions about IPv6 support, about half gave points for IPv6 support in the evaluation, and 10 had IPv6 as a mandatory factor, or even as an exclusion factor in the case of noncompliancy.

Tata Communications is expanding its business case for IPv6 to include its entire infrastructure, including the national networks in India and South Africa.

IPv6 Planning and Implementation

Tata Communications IPv6 planning and implementation had a strong head start through the knowledge and the operational service acquired through Teleglobe.

Teleglobe was an early promoter of IPv6. As a member of the Canadian Research and Education (CA*net4) network Technical Advisory Board, collaborating with CANARIE, Inc. (http://www.canarie.ca/) who manages CA*net4, Teleglobe supported the development of 6TAP (http://www.6tap.net/) in Chicago, a native IPv6 peering point cofunded by CANARIE, Inc. and ESnet (http://www.es.net/). The 6TAP peering router was a Cisco 7206 router running an initial prototype of Cisco IOS IPv6 code. Teleglobe hosted the first IPv6 node for Surfnet (http://www.surfnet.nl/en), the Netherlands National Research and Education (NREN) network, connected to the Chicago 6TAP located at The Science, Technology, And Research Transit Access Point, or STAR TAP (http://www.startap.net/startap/). The infrastructure is depicted in Figure 5-4.

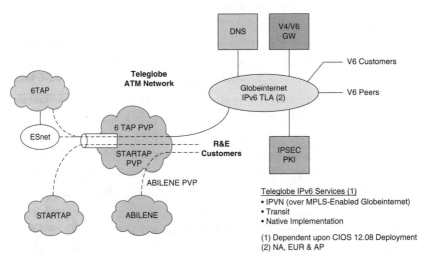

Figure 5-4   *Tata Communications IPv6 Test Network in 2000*

Teleglobe facilitated the world's first intercontinental native IPv6 connection in 1998 between the Communications Research Centre (CRC) in Ottawa and Berkom in Berlin. It also took an active role in promoting and championing IPv6. Teleglobe became a founding member of the IPv6 Forum in 1999.

At the March 2000 Telluride IPv6 Forum meeting, Teleglobe presented its initial IPv6 service plans, and in 2003 it provided an initial IPv6 service based on the Hexago tunnel broker transition mechanism. This initial offering was followed by a gradual deployment of IPv6 over MPLS using the Cisco 6PE feature, which became RFC 4798 in January 2007. The production-level, high-performance service was introduced in January 2004. It is important to note that while other IPv6 service announcements at that time, triggered by DoD's mandate, were typically tunnel based, Teleglobe's service was based on a scalable high-performance integration mechanism.

Starting with the original Teleglobe infrastructure, Tata Communications continues to expand the IPv6 coverage across its network in a dual-stack approach.

The deployment of a full dual-stack network, core and access, has accelerated in 2006, facilitated by the current phase of high growth in Internet traffic, due essentially to the user-generated-content phenomenon driven by applications such as YouTube and MySpace. This traffic growth, although essentially IPv4 in nature, provided a sufficient business case for upgrading the network with new, top of the line interface cards. The line cards were selected so that they also support IPv6 hardware acceleration, which enables Tata Communications network to deliver high-performance, scalable IPv6 services.

NOTE	From a technical perspective, the integration of IPv6 has the following characteristics:

- **For AS6453:** The global network evolved from a 6PE environment to a dual-stack network, including core. Native IPv6 peering has been established with major Tier 1 and Tier 2 providers. Peering is through public peering (dedicated for IPv6 or dual-stack) or private dual-stack peering.

- **For AS4755:** For the domestic IP network in India covering more than 120 cities, Tata Communications decided to leverage existent MPLS cores to deliver IPv6 connectivity with the help of 6PE, similar to Teleglobe's early approach in AS6453. It is also deploying a dual-stack network where the Interior Gateway Protocol (IGP) selected is multitopology Intermediate System-to-Intermediate System (IS-IS). The addressing scheme allocates a /44 per POP with a /48 reserved for infrastructure purposes and a /56 allocated per router. Customer allocations are /48 or longer. A detailed analysis of the scalability requirements of this design was performed for all platforms in its network. The edge routers (Metro Ethernet POPs and PE routers) are dual-stack routers and the IGP used is OSPF. The IPv6 addressing scheme in this part of the network takes a hierarchical approach with a /40 allocated per region. The AS4755 network consists of eight regions within India converging into eight Tier 1 POPs. The /40 per region is further subdivided into /44s and allocated to the Tier 2 and Tier 3 POPs that in turn converge into the regional Tier 1 POPs.

Table 5-13 summarizes Tata Communications phased approach to IPv6 deployment.

Table 5-13 *Tata Communications' Strategy for Deploying IPv6*

Phase 1 (1998–2004)	Phase 2 (2005–2008)	Phase 3 (2008 Onward)
1998: Teleglobe is involved with the IPv6 research networks supporting 6TAP. Teleglobe provides dedicated links for IPv6 connectivity. 1999: Teleglobe is a founder of the IPv6 Forum. 2003: Teleglobe provides initial service based on Hexgao tunnel broker. 2004: Teleglobe announces full IPv6 service based on Cisco 6PE.	Performed a detailed inventory of the hardware and software deployed in the network. Memory requirements, hardware forwarding of IPv6, and scalability capabilities of devices and line cards were evaluated for the two major vendors deployed in the network: Cisco and Juniper. 2006: Network upgrade driven by IPv4 bandwidth requirements leads to an IPv6-capable infrastructure. Both core and access layers are enabled for dual-stack, IPv4/IPv6. In areas operating around an MPLS core, IPv6 services are deployed using 6PE.	Dual-stack, core and access. IPv6 support mandatory for NGN deployment in the context of IP convergence. Generalized IPv6 support for enterprise markets.

NOTE   Teleglobe acquired its first IPv6 prefix from ARIN on March 5, 2003: 2001:5A0::/32. In the meantime, given the global nature of its network (AS6453), Teleglobe obtained an IPv6 prefix from APNIC, 2405:2000::/32, one from AfriNIC, 2001:42c8::/32, and one from RIPE NCC, 2a01:3e0::/32.

For the domestic network in India (AS4755), Tata Communications IP was allocated prefix 2403::/32 by APNIC while for the domestic network in South Africa (AS36937), Neotel was allocated prefix 2001:42a8::/32 by AfriNIC.

Figure 5-5 shows the current options available to Tata Communications customers to connect via IPv6.

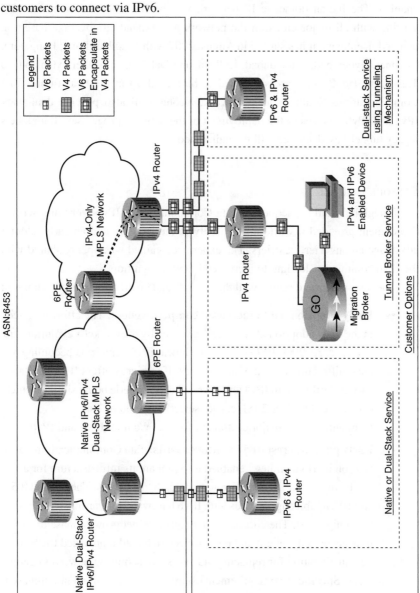

Figure 5-5 *IPv6 Access Options for Tata Communications Customers*

As of June 2007, approximately 85 percent of the network is fully dual-stack enabled. The Indian domestic IP network will be IPv6-enabled based on 6PE starting with all major cities on the network and expanding coverage based on demand. Deployment has started in August 2007 with Mumbai, Pune, Bangalore, Chennai, Hyderabad, Ahmedabad, Kolkata, and Delhi and a further extensions to Tier-1 and Tier-2 cities are scheduled to be turned up in the near future. Tata Communications South African network, Neotel, will also provide dual-stack IPv4 and IPv6 services as the deployment of the network progresses. Teleglobe's legacy tunnel-based service will be maintained.

Lessons Learned

Teleglobe's and subsequently Tata Communications IPv6 work and service deployment provided it with high visibility in the industry and an early adopter advantage among Tier 1 carriers. The experience gained was openly shared with the IPv6 community, leading to increased brand recognition.

The lessons learned reflect well the benefits and challenges of early adoption:

- **Early adoption led to increased competitiveness:** The effort invested in the early adoption of IPv6 was rewarded by the market's evolution and response. As 2006 RFQ stats have shown, IPv6 support is becoming a clear differentiator in the marketplace. If carrier A offers IPv4 only and carrier B offers both IPv4 and IPv6, all other criteria being similar, which carrier would a Tier 2 ISP carrier select? Over 30 of Tata Communications major customers connect via both IPv4 and IPv6.

- **Early planning resulted in reduced costs:** Tata Communications early start on its IPv6 strategy enabled it to prepare its infrastructure for a production-level IPv6 service with no dedicated costs. The needed 2.5- and 10-Gigabit engine cards with IPv6 hardware-forwarding capabilities had a high cost. The current tremendous Internet growth phase due to user-generated content and peer-to-peer-rich media provided the business justification for replacing old cards and acquiring new 10-Gigabit cards. Specific IPv6 requirements were placed on equipment purchased to upgrade the network's bandwidth capacity, which led in turn to an infrastructure with better IPv6 performance.

- **Product availability challenges:** The major challenge in the early phase was the sometimes ambiguous position of leading equipment suppliers with regard to the time frames for IPv6 support of their equipment. Statements like "it is not necessary to be a leader, but to be a good follower" sometimes reflected the degree of readiness or of planning. The success of early adoption depends significantly on working closely with leading suppliers to convey the value of features needed. Strategic relationships with vendors facilitate the prioritization of product capabilities early enough and in spite of the market's perceptions at the time.

NOTE   The strategic relationships remain important even after the first phases of deployment. Early adopters will continue to need features and capabilities ahead of the rest of the industry. As an example, in Tata Communications case, after the IPv6 infrastructure was deployed, occasional challenges related to network management, such as the availability of statistical and network monitoring tools supporting IPv6, remain a problem.

Tata Communications took an IPv6 early adopter role as differentiator in the global IP transit wholesale market segment, anticipating an uptake of dual-stack IPv4 and IPv6 demand. This allowed the company to build early IPv6 expertise and experience and to reduce adoption risks. Mandating IPv6 support in the procurement process reduced deployment costs by integrating its IPv6 strategy into the purchasing policies of ongoing network upgrade projects. The implementation of its IPv6 strategy led Tata Communications to become a leading provider of international IPv6 connectivity.

IT Utility Service: SAVVIS

Due to the ever-changing industry standards, vendor product enhancements, and compliance requirements, IT departments are strained to keep pace while staying within their budgets. IPv6 adds yet another level of complexity to this environment, virtually touching most aspects of IT. SAVVIS provides a complete portfolio of products and services that deliver a secure, managed IT infrastructure, built to respond to these strategic IT challenges, including IPv6. Anticipating increasing demand for IPv6, the infrastructure was designed with the new protocol in mind, enabling SAVVIS to easily include support for the new protocol in its portfolio.

—Bob LeBlanc, Vice President, Strategic Alliances

The importance of IT, particularly IP, communications and IP services in today's economy is the premise of the case made for the IPv6 upgrade. For most organizations, the IT environment plays a mission-critical role in their business yet it is not revenue generating. Operating the IP infrastructures and managing the IP services demand significant resources and expertise. In some cases it makes business sense to manage these resources internally. More and more organizations, however, choose to outsource this element of their operation, or aspects of it, to companies who specialize in providing and running IT services. Such IT utility services companies provide storage resources, web and application hosting services, IP connectivity between sites and IP VPN services, as well as security and consulting services. Overall, their services can move IT from being a "cost of doing business" to becoming a "revenue enhancing" organization.

IT utility services companies cater primarily to large and medium-sized enterprises. Because IP is ubiquitous, these IT utility companies are well positioned to provide various types of services to any organization regardless of size or focus. By the very nature of their business, global IT utility services providers serve over a wide spectrum of target markets. As this case study shows, SAVVIS, the IT utility services company featured in this case study, competes with traditional IP service providers such as AT&T and Verizon in IP VPN service offering while competing with IBM and EDS in hosting services. The broad portfolio of services exposes companies such as SAVVIS to both the opportunities and challenges faced by their customers. This makes their perspective and strategy on IPv6 particularly interesting and meaningful. IT utility services companies must stay a step ahead of their customers in both IPv6 knowledge and service offering readiness.

As mentioned, this case study covers one of the leading global IT utility service providers: SAVVIS. This case study was developed with the assistance of Bob LeBlanc, Vice President of Strategic Alliance at SAVVIS, and Wen Wang, Network Architect at SAVVIS.

Company Profile

According to its corporate information page:

> SAVVIS, Inc. (NASDAQ: SVVS) is a global IT utility services provider that leads the industry in delivering secure, reliable, and scalable hosting, network, and application services. SAVVIS' strategic approach combines the use of virtualization technology, a utility services model, and automated software management and provisioning systems. SAVVIS solutions enable customers to focus on their core business while SAVVIS ensures the quality of their IT infrastructure. With an IT services platform that extends to 45 countries, SAVVIS is one of the world's largest providers of IP computing services.[17]

SAVVIS is a public company focused on providing IT-related services through IP products and services spanning network offerings such as Internet and IP VPNs; a full hosting portfolio that ranges from co-location, through managed hosting, to utility compute and storage services; and a broad Managed Security Services products set that includes cloud- and premises-based security offerings. Additionally, SAVVIS has an advanced level of professional consulting services. SAVVIS has over 5000 customers in 45 countries. Its 2006 revenue was $764 million. As reported on the Company Information section of its website, in 2005 SAVVIS was identified by IDC as a market share leader in hosting along with IBM, EDS, and AT&T and was identified by In-Stat/MDR as a market share leader in IP VPN services along with AT&T and MCI. SAVVIS was positioned in the "Leader" quadrant in Gartner's Pan European Web Hosting Magic Quadrant 2006 and as the "Leader" in Gartner's North American Web Hosting Magic Quadrant for 2006. Its corporate profile is summarized in Table 5-14.

17. http://www.savvis.net/corp/Company+Information/.

Table 5-14 *SAVVIS Corporate Profile Overview*

Profile Category	Status/Value
Organization	SAVVIS, Inc.
Industry	IT infrastructure services provider (integrated hosting, IP connectivity, security, and consulting services)
Number of employees	2200+
Geography	Global: North America, EMEA, and PACRIM
Revenue	$794 million (2007)

NOTE Financial data is as of December 31, 2007, and was taken from SAVVIS' Form 10-K SEC filing, available at http://www.sec.gov/Archives/edgar/data/1058444/000119312508038596/d10k.htm.

SAVVIS has consistently increased its market share in the services offered, and to support this expansion, it started building its NGN, designated Application Transport Network (ATN), which will augment its existing infrastructure. SAVVIS also places significant focus on providing services to the U.S. government through SAVVIS Federal Systems, a company headquartered in Herndon, Virginia. The nature of its business, IT utility services, its global coverage, and the close attention it pays to the requirements of the federal market have exposed SAVVIS to IPv6 early on. Its equipment purchasing policies included IPv6 requirements as early as 2002 and its ATN is built to support both IPv4 and IPv6 services.

Network and IT Profile

SAVVIS operates one of the largest, global, wholly owned infrastructures, operating in 110 cities from 45 countries. It has over 1.4 million square feet of data center space under management from 24 managed data centers distributed around the world, and plans to add several new data centers by the end of 2007 and into

2008. The infrastructure interconnects over 32,000 network elements/circuits, hosts/servers, and storage devices. Connectivity is provided over a Tier 1 OC-192 MPLS backbone operated by SAVVIS with industry-leading 99.99 percent availability Service Level Agreements (SLA), which reduces the need for expensive backup circuits and ensures optimal performance. The features offered by this infrastructure are leveraged to deliver and optimize a wide variety of services offered by SAVVIS:

- Public Internet
- Private IP VPN
- Financial platform services
- Co-location
- Managed hosting
- Utility compute and storage services
- Security services
- Professional services

SAVVIS' ATN integrates the networking and hosting infrastructures into a single, high-bandwidth, high-availability, QoS-enabled platform. Both unicast- and multicast-based services are supported. This service-oriented network enables SAVVIS to deliver the enterprise applications needed by businesses and government agencies.

The conceptual structure of the ATN is shown in Figure 5-6.

The OSs currently deployed in SAVVIS' infrastructure and those it plans to use going forward are listed in Table 5-15.

SAVVIS uses a sophisticated combination of network management, billing, and provisioning tools, most of which are commercial off-the-shelf (COTS) products that are adapted to its needs while augmented with others that are built in house, to ensure seamless delivery of its IT services to its customers.

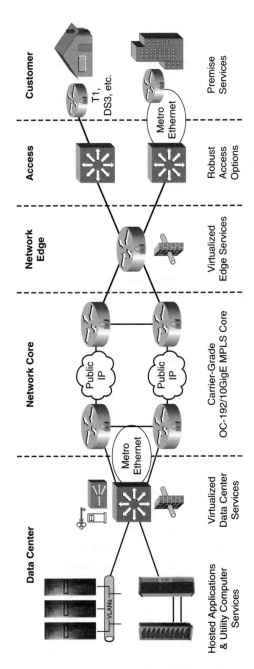

Figure 5-6 *Conceptual Representation of SAVVIS' Application Transport Network*

Table 5-15   *SAVVIS IP Infrastructure Profile—Operating Systems*

Device Type	Today	Future
PC, workstations	Windows 2003, Windows XP	Windows Vista
	Solaris	
Servers	HP DLx w/ Windows 2000 and RedHat Linux SUN w/ Solaris Egenera w/ Windows 2000 and RedHat Linux	HP DLx w/ Windows and RedHat Linux SUN w/ Solaris Egenera w/ Windows and RedHat Linux HP C-class w/ Windows and Linux
Storage Area Networking	3Par nServ Series Hitachi AMS and USP	3Par nServ Series Hitachi AMS and USP EMC Symetric
Routers and switches	Juniper M-Series w/ JUNOS Cisco IOS Nortel SER w/ iSOS	Juniper M-Series w/ JUNOS Cisco IOS and XR-IOS

IP Infrastructure Characteristics

SAVVIS' IP infrastructure is the foundation of its service offering. It is used to provide connectivity; to deliver mission-critical, time-sensitive services such as financial market data, video, and VoIP applications; to deliver high-bandwidth content; and to host and deliver software as a service (SaaS) applications. All these services, with specific and complex requirements, are delivered over a single quality-enabled secure network infrastructure that enables SAVVIS to offer its customers greater value and improved performance by converging its own infrastructures.

SAVVIS' current IPv4 address management has the following characteristics:

- **Address types used:** SAVVIS currently provides its customers both globally routable IP addresses and private (RFC 1918) IPv4 addresses.

- **Addressing constraints:** Historically, SAVVIS has not experienced constraints with respect to its IPv4 global address allocation. SAVVIS was a pioneer in the use of virtualization technology. One of the features that it has offered with the Intelligent IP Network services since early

2001 is the use of network-based security and VPN services. These services include NAT functionality, which has enabled SAVVIS to avoid having to perform IP address renumbering in its network. SAVVIS' ATN services will continue the use of virtualized services and include the ability to fully support IPv6.

The most significant challenge regarding SAVVIS' infrastructure does not come from the number of devices and IP address constraints; it comes from its need for higher access capacity and alternate QoS options. For this reason, SAVVIS started building its new network, which provides the capacity and functionality necessary to support and scale up its service offering.

Perspective on IPv6

A large variety of customers and the global span of its network exposes SAVVIS to the IT requirements of multiple industries and world regions. SAVVIS' perspective on IPv6 reflects its presence across various markets and the demands of its customers:

- **Connectivity requirements:** Current trends predict that IANA, the Internet Assigned Numbers Authority, the organization responsible for the allocation of IP addresses down to the RIRs (ARIN, APNIC, AfriNIC, RIPE NCC, and LACNIC), will have exhausted the remaining available IPv4 addresses sometime in 2009. Additionally, prospects and customers have requested support for both IPv4 and IPv6 access and connectivity. IPv6 is often listed in RFQs as a mandatory requirement when looking for Layer 3 VPN services and Internet access. Customer interest is expected to increase throughout 2008.

- **Mandate government adoption:** IPv6 adoption mandates led to clear requirements for IPv6 support. In the United States, SAVVIS Federal Systems sees clear business opportunities driven by the IPv6 mandates at all levels, from networking and applications services to professional services.

The emerging need to provide IPv6 connectivity is a driver to enable the infrastructure to support the new protocol. SAVVIS is also exploring other opportunities of leveraging an IPv6-capable infrastructure. It is investigating the feasibility of using IPv6 as the base technology for VoIP and other emerging access methods. In its drive to support managed services within corporate networks, SAVVIS must be prepared to handle IPv6 in enterprise environments. Overall, IPv6 can prove to be a catalyst for SAVVIS' drive toward additional virtualized services.[18] It eliminates resource constraints and makes the replacement of certain appliances with virtualized services more natural. The design and capabilities of SAVVIS' NGN reflect its perspective on IPv6 as an important transport protocol that will support existent and new IP services.

SAVVIS perceives the adoption of IPv6 as a very important step in gaining a strategic advantage over its competition. Adopting IPv6 enables SAVVIS to attract customers from the competition by offering, along with competitive IPv4 services, the support of IPv6 connectivity and services. The steps taken by SAVVIS in planning for IPv6 reflect its early adopter position with respect to IPv6.

The Case for IPv6

SAVVIS sees IPv6 both as a necessity in addressing growing customer demand and as an opportunity to increase its market share. In this context and in a first phase of its IPv6 strategy, SAVVIS identified the support of IPv6 as a clear market differentiator and, as such, a business case for providing dual-stack, IPv4 and IPv6 connectivity for its public Internet access and private IP VPN services. Defining this business case was made easy by the fact that SAVVIS was embarking at the time on building its NGN.[19] As an added benefit, with some nominal additional planning, the overall costs of having a dual-stack next generation infrastructure were minimal. By proactively placing IPv6-related requirements in networking equipment gear purchase requests, SAVVIS was able to ready its new infrastructure for IPv6 without significant additional cost. In 2006 Brian Doerr made public SAVVIS' IPv6 goals: "We will be ready to release a product based on IPv6 in 2008."[20]

---

18. http://www.networkworld.com/newsletters/isp/2007/0108isp1.html.

19. Carolyn Duffy Marsan, "SAVVIS Chooses Cisco for Network Upgrade," *Computerworld*, December 20, 2006, http://www.computerworld.com.au/index.php/ id;1289971788;fp;4194304;fpid;1.

20. See note 19 above.

SAVVIS' dual-stack ATN enables it to address near-term customer needs and provides an environment in which to pilot and evaluate the delivery of existent and new services over IPv6. The experience gained by managing this infrastructure and by providing IPv6 connectivity enables SAVVIS to further expand and develop its IPv6 strategy.

IPv6 Planning and Implementation

An early interest in IPv6 and active evaluation of the protocol provided SAVVIS with invaluable expertise and insight in the technology. SAVVIS connected to the 6bone experimental infrastructure as early as 2001. The experience gained through this work was leveraged by SAVVIS in shaping its IPv6 adoption and deployment strategy.

NOTE	6bone assigned the 3FFE:1300:4::/48 prefix to SAVVIS in mid-2001. Savvis received its 2001:460::/32 prefix from ARIN in 2004.

Moving IPv6 from protocol trials to its introduction into production and to service offering required detailed planning. The IPv6 deployment strategy and plan developed by SAVVIS followed common best practices observed throughout the industry:

- **Consistent approach:** Deploy IPv6 consistently across the infrastructure in order to provide access to service throughout the network footprint. All network planning activities should include the IPv6 strategy targets.

- **Incremental deployment:** The infrastructure should be readied to support IPv6 even though IPv6 will be turned on incrementally, based on service demand.

- **Minimal disruption:** IPv6 services should have no impact on the existing, revenue-generating IPv4 services.

- **Maintain the security of the network:** Enabling the infrastructure to support IPv6 and the deployment of new services and OSs that use IPv6 should not reduce the security of the network or of the services provided.

NOTE	SAVVIS intends to provide both IPv4 and IPv6 services to endpoints.

Many of these guiding principles were intrinsically observed and followed by SAVVIS because it tied the deployment of IPv6 to the deployment of its ATN. This enabled SAVVIS to design the future infrastructure with the dual-stack services support in mind and to mitigate any challenges during the planning phase. For the first phase of its IPv6 strategy, providing IPv6 connectivity for its public Internet access and private IP VPN services, SAVVIS is leveraging the capabilities of the MPLS core to seamlessly integrate IPv6 services on its new network infrastructure. This approach, typical for providers with MPLS cores, in conjunction with the selected Cisco CRS-1 platform enables SAVVIS to offer high-performance, scalable IPv6 services deployed incrementally to meet customer demand, with minimal impact on the existing infrastructure. This strategy requires no changes in the core of the network and only configuration changes on the PE routers.

NOTE	SAVVIS evaluated the 6PE (RFC 4798) and 6VPE (RFC 4659) features during extensive tests executed on the target platform.

This approach enables SAVVIS to extend to IPv6 all the capabilities sought for IPv4 through its new core network deployment. SAVVIS anticipates providing the same quality of service and functionality over IPv6 as it does over IPv4. Initially the deployment and services will be contained within SAVVIS' network, while peering with other providers over IPv6 will be initiated later. This approach reflects the U.S. market trend that sees higher customer demand for multiprotocol (IPv4 and IPv6) private IP VPN services than demand for Internet access services. Moreover, an initially contained service limits exposure to any unforeseen, IPv6-related threats.

As a result of its initial 6bone engagement started in 2001, SAVVIS gained valuable expertise early on. This expertise enabled SAVVIS to start implementing elements of its IPv6 plan by updating purchasing policies to include IPv6 requirements, and by updating security policies to address potential IPv6-based threats. SAVVIS developed the design of its dual-stack edge network and went beyond testing individual IPv6 features to testing its planned design from a system perspective.

NOTE   SAVVIS typically requires a stringent 12-month testing and validation process to certify features, software, and hardware for its production environment. This was taken into consideration when planning the date for public offering of IPv6 services.

With all these considerations, SAVVIS put in place the IPv6 integration strategy summarized in Table 5-16.

Table 5-16   *SAVVIS' Strategy for Deploying IPv6*

Phase 1 (2001–2006)	Phase 2 (2007–2008)	Phase 3 (2009 Onward)
6bone subscription and initial IPv6 evaluation.	Test the operation, performance, and scalability of the IPv6 features planned for the deployment (6PE and 6VPE).	Deploy new services over IPv6 as they are introduced by vendors and accepted or driven by market demands.
Define the IPv6 requirements for the new network.		
Update networking equipment purchasing policies to reflect IPv6 requirements.	Initiate the process of certifying the IPv6 solution and the hardware and software supporting it.	
Acquire an IPv6 prefix from ARIN.	Enable the ATN to be dual-stack.	
Design the IPv6 support within the ATN.	Offer IPv6 connectivity for Internet access and Layer 3 VPN services.	
Develop the IPv6 integration plan in the context of the ATN deployment.		
Update security policies to address IPv6-specific threats.		

NOTE	SAVVIS applied for an IPv6 prefix to ARIN in 2004, and was allocated 2001:460::/32.

SAVVIS intends to make the IPv6 services operational by mid-2008 over the ATN infrastructure. The primary challenge it sees to the deployment of IPv6 relates to the tools necessary to manage the dual-stack infrastructure and to provision and operate the IPv6 services. Many vendors are finalizing enhancements of their off-the-shelf tools to account for IPv6. SAVVIS is testing these enhancements, as well as internally developing specialized tools so that its IPv6 support will be at the same level as the current IPv4 support.

Lessons Learned

SAVVIS' IPv6 strategy, planning, and implementation provided several valuable lessons:

- **IPv6 demand is real:** In its interaction with various customers, primarily as a Tier 1 network provider, SAVVIS realized that having an IPv6-capable infrastructure is critical in maintaining existing customers and increasing the customer base. IPv6 is requested today even though customers may not be planning its deployment for another one to two years.

- **The opportunity to deploy IPv6 in a cost-effective way**: IPv6 support in the NGNs is an essential requirement for future infrastructures. With early and focused planning, ongoing network infrastructure enhancement projects represent a unique opportunity to deploy IPv6 at minimal additional costs.

- **Early planning:** Early planning of the IPv6 strategy enabled SAVVIS to take full advantage of the new network deployment project in deploying IPv6. It led to higher-value solutions and a natural integration through the new infrastructure.

SAVVIS' new application delivery network is built to respond to the needs of modern IT environments. One such need that is currently emerging in various markets is the support of IPv6 transport, services, and applications. SAVVIS designed its new infrastructure with IPv6 in mind and is preparing the tools needed to support IP version–agnostic services.

Mobile Provider: Bouygues Telecom

IP is certainly one of the key successes of the future world of convergence between telcos and IT departments that has already been on the move for several years through the evolution of traditional TDM networks to New Generation Networks. More specifically, the adoption of the new version of IP, IPv6, is of crucial importance because its new features, especially its unlimited capabilities of addressing, are required for future growth. As a consequence, IPv6 will play a major role by enabling the new multimedia applications and services of the future of social networking and mobility (P2P applications, connected objects, and so forth).

It is time to be conscious that without the availability of a large set of IPv6 terminals, IPv6 equipment from the different suppliers, and IPv6 web applications and servers from the different editors or application developers, it is difficult for a operator to consider a large commercial deployment of IPv6 services.

—Lionel Hoffmann, Technical Director of Bouygues Telecom

Demand for mobile voice services has seen dramatic growth during the first decade of the new millennium. In July 2007 the counter of GSM and 3GSM users posted by GSM World (http://www.gsmworld.com) had passed 3.0 billion. The rapid adoption is due to several factors. The service is a perfect fit for today's "on the move" world; it provides telephony services along with other communications applications and services. On the other hand, technological advancements have made the service easily and inexpensively available to a large part of the population. Costs of deploying and operating mobile wireless infrastructures have decreased because they can support higher densities of users. Frequency reclamation processes at the national level have offered providers new resources to expand their coverage and the ability to multiplex more and more subscribers. Roaming service agreements between mobile providers have also been a significant adoption catalyst that has increased subscriber accessibility. While the benefits of the service are the primary driver for its adoption, price has been a significant catalyst lately in the service reaching lower-income populations. A typical example is in India, where the most expensive component is the handset itself and the mobile services can be afforded by virtually everyone.

The landscape of mobile services has changed significantly. Without a doubt the handset represents a powerful device to reach users and deliver a wide range of services beyond basic voice communications, and service providers have been capitalizing on the opportunity. Today's mobile phones provide text messaging, audio and video on demand, Internet access, and content (such as pictures or video) uploading services, just to mention a few. The important aspect of this expansion of the service offering is that these additional services are delivered over IP. IP has become the service delivery infrastructure for most services in the mobile environment. It is only a matter of time before this consolidation is taken to its natural conclusion: voice is just another application delivered over IP on top of this media type. This vision enables a far richer service offering with a better integration of the services offered, and is defined in the 3GPP specifications (http://www.3gpp.org/specs/specs.htm).

This is an example of another major communications industry converging toward IP. More importantly, considering the large number of devices that have to be assigned an IP address and the fact that these devices are holding these addresses for longer periods of time, mobile providers became major consumers of IP address space. Would this demand for IP addresses make mobile providers strong candidates for IPv6 adoption?

Today's mobile provider networks are most often a set of domains that can use overlapping addresses for subscribers. The mobile phones do not have to hold an IP address for a very long time due to their "client" role in the applications supported, so address reuse through dynamic allocation has been a practical solution. These environment characteristics explain the current architecture of most mobile service provider networks, where private addresses are reused in multiple domains bordered with a NAT gateway. This approach eliminates IP addressing worries and subsequently a pressing need for IPv6. The evolution of the technology and services, however, is changing the design requirements for the mobile environments. There are several major drivers for IPv6 adoption in this market segment:

- **Voice over IP:** With voice becoming another IP-based service, the mobile devices require unique addresses that they will hold for a long period of time as they move from one domain to another.

- **New applications:** New applications that have the mobile phone play a "server" role or are involved in "peer-to-peer" communications also demand fixed and global IP addresses.

- **High density of users:** Continued adoption leads to high densities of subscribers in each IP domain, with subscribers holding on to their addresses for longer periods of time. In the case of large mobile providers, this implies limited address-reuse opportunities within a given IP administrative domain. Further segmentation of the IP domain is not a practical or cost-effective solution.

NOTE   To provide a sense of the scale of a mobile provider's user base, it is interesting to note that in France, where mobile services have almost a 100 percent penetration rate with approximately 60 million subscribers, a provider that has 20 percent of the market will not have sufficient RFC 1918 IPv4 addresses to uniquely address all the mobile phones it is managing.

- **3GPP Standards:** The 3rd Generation Partnership Projects, 3GPP (http://www.3gpp.org/) and 3GPP2 (http://www.3gpp2.org/), develop the standards for the next generation mobile networks. These standards recommend IPv6 support in the IMS and the UMTS Terrestrial Remote Access Network (UTRAN). The primary reason for selecting IPv6 is its larger address space that enables providers to assign a unique address to each handset. Other IPv6 features and capabilities are also leveraged.

The mobile industry is becoming a prime candidate for IPv6 adoption. Although not all elements of the end-to-end environment will support IPv6 yet, a recent market survey indicates that most recent high-end mobile handsets get IPv6 support from their OS release, enabling a potential focus to serve enterprise fleet and high-end consumer markets with new services.

NOTE	The three OSs typically used in mobile phones are Linux (http://www.linux.org/), Symbian (http://www.symbian.com), and Windows Mobile (http://www.microsoft.com/windowsmobile/default.mspx). They all support IPv6. Most of today's medium- and high-end mobile phones have an IP stack and thus support IPv6, but this is not yet true for low-end mass-market handsets.

Another important phenomenon in this market space is the drive toward converged fixed mobile services. There is a clear distinction between services offered through wireline providers (broadband access, for example) and services offered through mobile providers, a distinction that is apparent to subscribers who have to switch between the two services. With mobile phones supporting multiple radio technologies such as Wi-Fi and 3G, Fixed Mobile Convergence (FMC) will enable users to seamlessly switch from the mobile access networks to their less expensive home access networks. This becomes possible as home gateways integrate more wireless technologies such as WI-FI, 2G, 3G, and so on. Consequently, one of the key challenges, in addition to the need for multiple addresses at home, is the seamless mobility between these access technologies. IPv6 is certainly an enabler in achieving seamless handover between the various access environments.

This market strategy is starting to become reality with large mobile providers offering the feature over their own or over partner broadband access networks. FMC will further the addressing constraints on the mobile network architectures. In fact, it is believed that the key to its implementation might be the use of IPv6 mobility.

So where do mobile providers stand with respect to enabling their infrastructure for IPv6 and offering IPv6-based services? What level of urgency does IPv6 deployment have in their planning and strategy? Perspectives differ, reflecting market and technology realities. Here we offer the opinion of a fast-growing and proactive provider that does not pursue early adopter strategies.

This case study covers the third-largest mobile provider in France: Bouygues Telecom. The case study was developed with the assistance of Lionel Hoffmann, Technical Director of Bouygues Telecom.

Company Profile

According to its corporate information page, Bouygues Telecom was created in 1994 by the Bouygues Group, an organization with focus on traditional (construction, transport) infrastructure development. Bouygues Telecom was the first mobile operator to introduce the talk-plan concept to the French market, in 1996. Through several innovative service plans and services, such as Short Message Service (SMS) messaging and music downloads through a partnership with Universal Music, Bouygues Telecom developed an installed base of 8.7 million French customers by 2007. Its goal is to become the "preferred brand of mobile communication services."

Bouygues Telecom also offers high-bandwidth access services over its national network, which covers over 98 percent of the population of France and offers bandwidth capacity for data transfer that is five times faster than the standard General Packet Radio Service (GPRS) network. In 2005 Bouygues Telecom launched broadband service based on i-mode (technology licensed from NTT DoCoMo), and by the end of 2006, it had over 1.7 million subscribers. Both consumers and enterprises are offered high-bandwidth access anywhere in France.

Bouygues Telecom's corporate profile is summarized in Table 5-17.

NOTE   All data in the table is up to date as of the end of 2007.

Table 5-17 *Bouygues Telecom Corporate Profile Overview*

Profile Category	Status/Value
Organization	Bouygues Telecom
Industry	Mobile provider
Number of employees	7400
Geography	National, France
Revenue	Euro 4.8 billion
Total market share	17 percent

Bouygues Telecom was a newcomer to the French mobile market, which until 1996 was split between Société Française du Radiotéléphone and France Telecom Mobiles (currently known as Orange France). From its inception, Bouygues Telecom was one of the fastest-growing mobile providers in Europe.

Network and IT Profile

Bouygues Telecom's network covers over 98 percent of France's population and has more than 40 sites (core network POPs) with over 10,000 network elements. The OSs currently deployed in its infrastructure and those it plans to use going forward are listed in Table 5-18.

Table 5-18 *Bouygues Telecom IP Infrastructure Profile—Operating Systems*

Device Type	Today	Future
CS and PS core network	Ericsson devices & products (Mobile Switching Service Center Server [MSC-S], Transit Switching Centre [TSC], Media Gateway for Mobile Networks [M-MGw], Serving GPRS Support Node [SGSN], Gateway GPRS Support Node [GGSN], etc.)	No public plans
PC and workstations	Windows XP	Windows Vista
Servers	Unix	Window Server 2008
Routers and switches	Cisco IOS and IOS-XR	Cisco IOS and IOS-XR

Bouygues Telecom uses HP OpenView solutions to supervise the IP equipment and infrastructure operation. The HP OpenView TeMIP Fault Management and Real-Time Operations solution is used for alarm handling and event logging. InfoVista products, together with in-house-developed tools, is used for managing the performance of the IP environment. If tomorrow gigabytes of user traffic is transiting over IPv6, the in-house-developed billing applications that are IP based must be modified to understand the IPv6 traffic.

IP Infrastructure Characteristics

For its IP infrastructure, Bouygues Telecom uses primarily private address space. Similar to other mobile provider deployments, it is using private address space for subscriber services, access usually being provided through a proxy device.

Bouygues Telecom's current IPv4 address management has the following characteristics:

- **Address lifetime:** User devices are dynamically addressed using Dynamic Host Configuration Protocol (DHCP). Network elements use fixed IP addresses.

- **Address types:** Both global IPv4 addresses and private (RFC 1918) IPv4 addresses are used. For the internal infrastructure, 20 percent of the addresses are global and the rest are private. For subscribers, only 10 to 15 percent are assigned public addresses for direct access to the Internet, the rest are using private addresses.

Most of the applications deployed use a proxy or relay device to access the public domain so the use of private addresses is perfectly appropriate and sufficient for the time being. Bouygues Telecom did not have to go through any major renumbering since its inception so it did not experience challenges in that sense. Bouygues Telecom's move toward an all-IP, NGN does not in itself imply that globally unique IP addresses are needed for the mobile phones. To Bouygues Telecom it is clear that there are no needs to move to IPv6 for the infrastructure sake. The potential driver is IP addressing of the subscriber's terminals. For the time being however, the driver is still expected to be new end to end applications.

The network operator and ISP landscape is going to be changed dramatically in the coming years with VoIP traffic growing more and more and with the global explosion of triple- and quad-play offerings and packages. These changes are perceived to be a major driver for the adoption of IPv6 with its significant addressing resources.

Perspective on IPv6

Bouygues Telecom took interest in IPv6 for what it believes are some of the new protocol's benefits:

- **Address space:** The large address space can help reestablish the end-to-end paradigm of services. Moreover, with the recent announcement of ADSL service[21] offering, Bouygues Telecom is better positioned to offer fixed-mobile converged services. FMC will add significant pressure to the IPv6 private address space.

- **MIPv6:** As an important technology in FMC, particular attention was given to the added features available with MIPv6 compared to those available with MIPv4.

NOTE   MIP has been chosen and specified by 3GPP as one of the potential solutions for seamless mobility between 3GPP access networks (Edge, 3G, HSPA, E-HSPA) and non-3GPP access networks (WI-FI, WiMAX).

- **End-to-end security:** The evolution to an "all-IP" framework raises critical security issues from the perspective of mobile operators. An end-to-end IP model with expected hardware evolution of MIP terminals and IP phones should secure the subscriber's traffic automatically. Equipment and network design rules must provide mandatory security mechanisms to protect against attacks without complex software being added on handsets.

21. "Bouygues to Launch National ADSL Service; Launches Wholesale Tender," CommsUpdate, July 11, 2007, http://www.telegeography.com/cu/article.php?article_id=18658.

Although Bouygues Telecom sees the potential benefits of IPv6, it does not see them imminently driving adoption within its market space. Nevertheless, as a leading mobile provider, Bouygues Telecom is already investigating IPv6 and the value it can bring to its service offering and operations. In the same context, Bouygues Telecom continuously monitors its markets to validate the need to integrate IPv6.

NOTE   Bouygues Telecom's evaluation of market readiness represents a conservative perspective on IPv6 adoption compared to an often-stated opinion that IPv6 will be rapidly integrated in mobile provider networks. Although in principle IPv6 appears to be a clear fit in mobile provider networks, because it should improve the services at the user level, its deployment must take into consideration many practical aspects. Particularly important is the readiness of all elements that are required in providing the service, including GPRS Support Node (GGSN), authentication, provisioning, billing systems, and applications.

Several mobile providers around the world are known to be currently testing IPv6 in lab environments. Some European providers are also planning IPv6-based NGNs that would provide contiguous coverage for users, eliminating the need for roaming. However, at the time of this writing, there is no known IPv6 service being offered by mobile providers even though IPv6 traffic tunneled over IPv4 has been detected on current networks.

The Case for IPv6

Bouygues Telecom's conservative perspective on the IPv6 adoption in the mobile market is reflected in its internal IPv6 strategy. Bouygues Telecom sees no benefit in pursuing IPv6 as an early adopter; it believes there are no immediate customer benefits. In fact, at the time of this writing Bouygues Telecom does not expect to turn IPv6 on for a commercial launch within its network prior to 2010.

Nevertheless, Bouygues Telecom continues to investigate the opportunities offered by IPv6 and to prepare for its integration. IPv6 is considered in planning future network elements, products, and services. Some of the services for which IPv6 is considered as beneficial follow:

- **Push technologies and applications:** Work on machine-to-machine and mobile-to-mobile applications indicates that IPv6 could be an enabler in this area.

- **Multicast-based applications:** Multicast-based content delivery services could be deployed over IPv6 as a new network overlay.

- **Voice over IP:** VoIP is believed to be the service most likely to leverage IPv6 at the user level.

Bouygues Telecom remains concerned with the potential impact that an unpredictable shortage of IPv4 addresses or a new and popular peer-to-peer, IPv6-only application would have on its business. Traditionally, it needs one year to deploy a new service into production, so to minimize the impact of the eventualities mentioned, Bouygues Telecom has been focusing on preparing its infrastructure from end to end for a smooth and inexpensive integration of IPv6.

IPv6 Planning

Although Bouygues Telecom is taking IPv6 into consideration in all its future service and new technology product planning, it is focused primarily on achieving IPv6 readiness in an efficient and cost-effective way. Because it does not pursue an early adopter strategy, Bouygues Telecom must be prepared to quickly adapt to IPv6-related market trends. In this context, its IPv6 planning involved the following measures:

- **IPv6-related infrastructure inventory:** A detailed evaluation of the IPv6 capabilities of the infrastructure and different equipments was performed. The impact of deploying IPv6 in the current environment is in the process of being evaluated.

NOTE   Bouygues Telecom's network is MPLS based, which means that IPv6 can be deployed with minimal impact using 6PE or 6VPE mechanisms.

- **Purchasing policies update:** To ready its infrastructure for an IPv6 deployment, Bouygues Telecom took advantage of its long-term IPv6 plans. It updated its purchasing policies to have strict IPv6 requirements applied to its various suppliers. Having these policy updates in place early on leads to an inexpensive upgrade of the network toward becoming IPv6 capable.

- **Gap analysis and feature monitoring:** Bouygues Telecom performed a protocol evaluation to identify the feature and product support gaps that would prove to be challenging to deploying IPv6.

NOTE   Based on its protocol analysis and the available implementations and products on the market, Bouygues Telecom identified two major challenges to the deployment of IPv6:

- **Lack of IPv6 support in various elements of the mobile network:** An operational IPv6 deployment implies protocol support in multiple elements of the network. Bouygues Telecom's concern relates particularly to the IPv6 support in the back-end systems and mobile terminals that are essential to service offering.

- **Lack of IPv6 management:** Lack of management tools or an overall incomplete IPv6 management framework presents challenges to deploying a production IPv6-based service. Some of the missing IPv6 features in HP OpenView have been listed as an example.

These considerations led Bouygues Telecom to put in place the IPv6 integration strategy summarized in Table 5-19.

NOTE   At the time of this writing, Bouygues Telecom is in the process of registering for an IPv6 prefix with the European RIR: RIPE NCC.

Table 5-19   *Bouygues Telecom's Strategy for Deploying IPv6*

Phase 1 (2002–2007)	Phase 2 (2008–2010)	Phase 3 (2010 Onward)
Active member of the French National IPv6 Task Force.	Evaluate the impacts of IPv6 on the existing infrastructure.	Possible service launch.
Internal trials for evaluating the technology and support for an end-to-end service.	Design the architecture of IPv6-based services.	
	Test the targeted IPv6 deployment design.	
Perform network inventory to asses IPv6 readiness.	Acquire IPv6 prefix.	
Review security and product purchasing requirement policies.		

NOTE   During the testing phases of an IPv6 strategy, it is important to evaluate a service deployment in an end-to-end environment that involves all elements of a mobile network. Bouygues Telecom's focus on this approach enabled it to identify the essential elements lacking IPv6 support today and plan its deployment accordingly.

Cisco Systems conducted successful end-to-end tests in collaboration with major mobile phone manufacturers to demonstrate IPv6 readiness of mobile network equipment.

Lessons Learned

Bouygues Telecom's long-term experience and work with IPv6 helped it to evaluate the market direction and the business opportunities and challenges presented by the adoption of the new version of IP. Several lessons crystallized along the way:

- **Technology education:** Early investment in understanding the technology proved valuable in realistically estimating its potential and challenges within the mobile provider environment. This investment translated into savings related to other aspects of planning and deployment.

- **Understanding and following vendor roadmaps:** Bouygues Telecom identified early on the IPv6 needs of its environment. This information became a scorecard for tracking production-level, IPv6 readiness of equipment and applications. It also helped Bouygues Telecom work with vendors to integrate needed features.

- **Conducting trials:** While Bouygues Telecom studied the impact of IPv6 service, it performed extensive trials on the technology to understand it in absolute terms as well as in the context of its own environment. The experience gained proved invaluable to many other aspects of IPv6 planning efforts.

- **Measuring and evaluating the impact of IPv6 integration in existing infrastructure:** Technology analyses and benchmarking efforts were found to be very important in evaluating the potential impact of IPv6 to existent services. This work is an important step connecting trial efforts and production-level deployment.

- **Fixed/mobile convergence strategy:** Tying IPv6 to other major initiatives helps provide context for some of the IPv6 drivers and its adoption strategy. It also helps coordinate resources, requirements, and schedules between these projects.

The IPv6 strategy development and the deployment plans are ongoing efforts modulated by the market and internal service development activities. Bouygues Telecom took the necessary steps to ready its environment for a smooth and cost-effective integration of IPv6. Under these conditions, Bouygues Telecom positioned itself to react timely to IPv6 service requests and to deploy quickly should new IPv6-specific services or applications emerge.

Enterprises

An enterprise's decision of whether or not to adopt IPv6 is tied to its IT strategies supporting the requirements of its business and market segment. This section presents case studies from several market segments with the collaboration of enterprises who have agreed to discuss their IPv6 planning.

Education: Greek School Network

> By exposing young students to advanced networking technologies such as IPv6, we influence the communication and collaboration paradigms of future Citizens.
>
> —Dr. Athanassios Liakopoulos, Network Operation & Support Manager, and Dr. Dimitrios Kalogeras, Senior Researcher

Formal education represents an essential component of individual and societal development. At all levels of the education system, schools provide the information and training that helps individuals acquire fundamental and highly specialized expertise and skills. Schools also prepare individuals to become members of society and citizens of the world. These general principles are observed by a vast majority of schools and learning environments, which otherwise are quite diverse due to specificities related to societal characteristics, culture, geography, resources, and pedagogical approach. In a gross simplification, the education process can be characterized as transfer of information.

The educational systems and the didactical methodologies they employ evolved over time. Their evolution was driven primarily by changes in human knowledge, scientific and cultural advancements, and developments in pedagogical sciences. Education has seen very few significant changes in the means of conveying information. The discovery of printing and the availability of printed material led of course to the most significant changes in the means of delivering information. As new modes of communications emerged, such as telephony, radio, and TV, they peripherally made their way into the tool set of educators. For the most part, however, the transfer of formal information followed the ancient "educator to pupils" or "server to user" model.

The beginning of this millennium brought along new means to produce and exchange information that are being rapidly adopted by society. The Internet provides access to a wealth of information, both good and bad, while simplified means to generate content provides the opportunity to openly contribute to this wealth of information. In a relatively short time, the digital revolution changed the way people access information, the way information is delivered to them, and the way content is being generated. This environment enables users to combine several types of content (data, voice, video) and to leverage various resources to create a more complex and more powerful user experience. As members of the information society, students of all levels, ages, and backgrounds are individually leveraging these resources to complement the education process. These resources, however, can become significantly more powerful and efficient if they are systematically integrated in the formal education process. They would help to enhance the effectiveness of information transfer and to prepare the next generation of citizens for the information society.

Information technologies are leveraged in a limited way in today's schools. The services typically available and used are e-mail and web browsing. The schools of tomorrow will have to take full advantage of the resources provided by the IT revolution to achieve modern educational goals and to meet the requirements of a diverse student population:

- **Enhance the transfer of information:** Combine types and sources of content to generate a more intense and memorable learning experience.

- **Enable new ways of collaboration:** Provide an environment that allows students in primary or secondary schools, within the same country or between different countries, to collaborate on educational or youth-related activities. In addition, enable educators to collaborate with students independent of their relative location.

- **Facilitate the transfer of information:** Make valuable knowledge resources such as unique presentations and emeritus educators available to students in remote and sometimes isolated schools. Facilitate the exchange of educational material between school communities. Support remote education.

- **Support education beyond school hours:** Enable educators to assist students after the regular school hours to complete projects, to improve, or to pursue topics of interest beyond the requirements of the regular classes.

- **Stimulate cross-boundary social interaction:** Build links between school communities in different countries. Expose young students and individuals who progressively form their character to different cultures, nationalities, and races without any prejudice.

- **Security:** Leverage surveillance and other mechanisms and tools to secure schools and enhance youth protection. Provide parents with ways to nonintrusively monitor their children's behavior and assess the school level of security.

Educational institutions and state and local education systems around the world are upgrading their IT infrastructures to enable students and faculty to make better use of these opportunities. Even if IT is not always tightly integrated in the education process (for now it might be simply used by students using their laptops or PDAs to access class resources), the availability of an advanced IT infrastructure will provide an environment for the development of new applications and services for students and educators. Because this environment is in its incipient phases of leveraging the true potential of IP-based services and is in the process of being upgraded, it makes sense to ask: Why not enable it in the process to support IPv6 as well?

IPv6 represents an excellent opportunity for the school environment. It provides plenty of resources to deploy services and to experiment with new ones, and it can provide a parallel infrastructure dedicated exclusively to services developed and provided for educational purposes. This environment will also help students familiarize themselves, should they be interested in digital communications, with the next generation of the IP protocol. As shown through the experience captured in this case study, enabling the infrastructure of a nationwide school system to support IPv6 is not as expensive as might be expected, especially when combined with ongoing upgrade projects. Many National Research and Education Networks (NREN) have deployed IPv6. These infrastructures are interconnected via international networks that currently support IPv6 as well. The challenge is to extend these infrastructures to primary and secondary schools.

This case study covers an organization that initiated a pioneering project to build the infrastructure for the applications and services needed in the educational environment of the future: Greek School Network. It is developed with the assistance of Dr. Athanassios Liakopoulos, Network Operation Manager, Greek Research and Technology Network (GRNET), and Dr. Dimitrios Kalogeras, Senior Researcher, GRNET. Both are members of the technical and scientific committee of the Greek School Network.

Organization Profile

The Greek School Network (GSN) is the educational intranet of the Ministry for National Education and Religious Affairs of Greece (http://www.sch.gr/). It provides IP connectivity and IT services to the majority of primary and secondary schools in Greece. The GSN environment facilitates the development of new learning communities and the integration of IT technologies and services in the educational process.

The profile of the GSN is summarized in Table 5-20.

Table 5-20   *Greek School Network Profile Overview*

Profile Category	Status/Value
Organization	Greek School Network
Industry	Education
Users	54,000 teachers
Geography	National
Coverage	6000 primary schools
	4000 secondary schools
	2500 administration units

NOTE	Data listed in Table 5-20 is up to date as of June 2006.[22]

One of the interesting aspects of the GSN environment is the fact that it has a challenging geographical footprint. Providing nationwide IP connectivity and IT services to thousands of schools—some of them located in tiny villages over the mountains or the islands of the Greek archipelago—is not a trivial task. On the other hand, this represents a perfect example of an environment where IP can be leveraged to provide the same level of instruction to all students, regardless of location. The government of Greece invested significantly in upgrading the IT infrastructure and promoting services that support remote education. One of the main objectives was to provide the same level of support for IP services to all schools around Greece regardless of their location, either in large cities or in isolated villages.

Network and IT Profile

The GSN provides connectivity to the vast majority of schools and administrative units throughout Greece. The services provided by GSN are as follows:

- **Basic services:** Dial-up access, proxy/cache, web filtering, web page generator, web hosting, portal, e-mail (POP3, IMAP, web mail), forums, news, and instant messenger.

- **Advanced services:** E-learning tools, video on demand, secure content delivery, real-time services, teleconferencing, and VoIP.

- **Infrastructure services:** Domain Name System (DNS), directory services (Lightweight Directory Access Protocol [LDAP]), user registration services, statistics, help desk, Geographical Information System (GIS), and remote control (http://www.sch.gr/en/index.php).

The GSN has a traditional, hierarchical design. It does not operate its own backbone but rather leverages the backbone network of the Greek NREN

22. Athanasios Liakopoulos, Kostas Kalevras, and Dimitrios Kalogeras, "Deploying IPv6 Services over Broadband Connections: The Greek School Network Case," http://www.terena.nl/events/tnc2006/core/getfile.php?file_id=862.

(GRNET; http://www.grnet.gr/en). GSN connects to GRNET via eight POPs over Fast or Gigabit Ethernet links. The distribution layer has 8 primary and 43 secondary nodes, with the equipment being hosted by the national telecommunications operator. The links in the distribution layer have speed ranging from 256 kbps to 5 Mbps and are implemented over ATM, E1, and fractional E1. The distribution layer also hosts nine data centers spread around the country.

Figure 5-7 shows a simplified topology of the GSN, which highlights the backbone and the distribution links. Even if the network continually evolves, as more interconnection links are established or upgraded, the hierarchical topology of the GSN will remain the same.

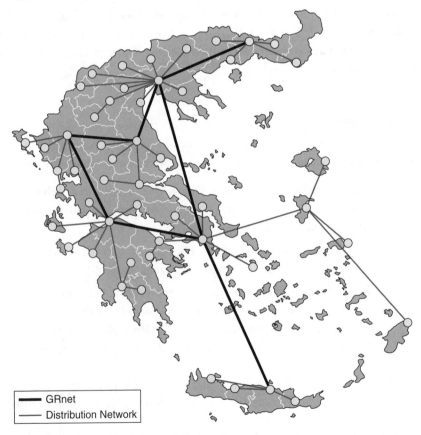

Figure 5-7 *Greek School Network*

GSN manages over 13,000 access routers and provides network access over the following media types: dial-up (PSTN or ISDN), ADSL, leased line (SDSL or VDSL), and wireless.

The overall GSN asset distribution is summarized in Table 5-21.

Table 5-21   *Greek School Network IT Profile—Assets*

Device Type	Number of Devices
Managed workstations and PCs	~80,000
Servers	88
GRNET core routers and switches	90 routers and 32 switches
Access routers	Over 13,000
Unmanaged devices	One per school

The OSs currently deployed in GSN's infrastructure and those it plans to use going forward are listed in Table 5-22.

Table 5-22   *Greek School Network IT Profile—Operating Systems*

Device Type	Today	Future
PC and workstations	Windows 2003, Windows XP	Windows Vista (from 2007)
	Linux	Linux
	Solaris	
Servers	Windows Server 2003	Windows Server 2008
Routers and switches	Cisco IOS	Cisco IOS

The GSN is actively upgrading its infrastructure to provide higher access bandwidth for schools that can support advanced, media-rich communication. It is also adding or expanding the coverage of new services such as VoIP and content distribution.

IP Infrastructure Characteristics

GSN's IP infrastructure has to contend with limited address resources. This means that each school uses NAT and PAT to translate the private addresses used locally. The overall IPv4 address management has the following characteristics:

- **Address lifetime:** The vast majority of PCs (endpoints) in the school labs are dynamically assigned temporary addresses. Usually, one server and a videoconferencing system are the only nodes using a fixed IPv4 address.

- **Address types:** GSN is using both global IPv4 addresses and private (RFC 1918) IPv4 addresses within schools and administrative offices.

- **Global IPv4 addresses management:** The number of endpoints assigned global IPv4 addresses is not changing rapidly, so GSN does not have to request IPv4 address space often.

From the infrastructure management point of view, addressing a dispersed set of routers for remote access is not a simple task, especially considering that the managed access should not be a member of the LAN address space. From the user point of view, PAT-like addressing may potentially limit P2P applications. The reason is that P2P applications use dynamic ports, which cannot easily pass through NAT devices. In addition, NAT adds complexity to the management and operation of the network. Such an environment is not well suited for delivering content over multicast, a service that would be beneficial to the education process.

GSN found the limited IPv4 address space constraining in terms of service deployment, ease of managing connectivity and services, and maintaining a contiguous, well-aggregated address scheme. For example, in many school networks, only one IPv4 address could be allocated for local servers while the access router (aka customer premises equipment, or CPE) supported only one internal LAN. Under these conditions, deployment of new services required changes in the router's configuration on a per-case basis, leading to extensive service deployment delays and increased network management overhead.

Perspective on IPv6

Leading technologists from GSN and GRNET, such as Dr. Kalogeras and Dr. Liakopoulos, have been actively involved in various national and pan-European projects related to the IPv6 protocol suite since 2000. Apart from the national projects, they participated in the major efforts such 6NET (http://www.6net.org) and 6DISS (http://www.6diss.org). They also took a leadership role in promoting and supporting IPv6 activities in South-Eastern Europe (http://www.seeren.org).

This involvement reflects a clear, positive perspective toward IPv6 among leading GSN experts. The open, bidirectional exchange of information and expertise between GSN and various IPv6 projects facilitated GSN's development of its IPv6 strategy and established GSN as a leading European case study on IPv6 adoption. The initial work done in deploying IPv6 in GSN was documented in a 6NET deliverable.[23]

The Case for IPv6

In its effort to modernize its IT infrastructure and to provide new, media-rich, interactive services, GSN took IPv6 into consideration early on. GSN sees IPv6 providing the following benefits to its environment:[24]

- **Removing addressing constraints:** IPv6 provides sufficient global addresses for all of GSN's needs. It leads to the elimination of NAT/PAT and to the simplification of managing devices and services. Network resources such as national and local servers can now be assigned fixed global addresses. It also facilitates the deployment of a simple, unfragmented addressing scheme.

- **Enabling peer-to-peer applications:** Peer-to-peer, virtualization applications are perceived to be a major enabler in the future educational environment. IPv6 would provide a suitable environment for the development and the deployment of such applications.

- **Mitigating management and security issues:** IPv6 can simplify the deployment and management of networking equipment at remote schools and locations. Security policies implementation can be simplified by using an addressing scheme that can clearly identify various types of user groups and services.

23. Karaliotas Tasos and others, "Cookbook on Deploying IPv6 in School Networks," June 15, 2005, http://www.6net.org/publications/deliverables/D5.14.pdf.

24. See note 22 above.

- **Stimulating innovation:** An IPv6-enabled infrastructure within the Greek schools provides students with an environment in which they can use the new protocol, get familiar with it, and develop new applications for it. An IPv6 GSN would also enhance the impact and value of other IPv6-enabled networks within Greece, such as GRNET. A typical example is the One Laptop per Child (OLPC) project, the aim of which is widespread utilization of computers by students at the moderate price of approximately $100. OLPC uses IPv6 technology for minimization of bootstrapping.

The GSN committed to IPv6 early and, thus, had the opportunity to tie the deployment of the new protocol to ongoing infrastructure upgrades. The ensuing cost savings provided an additional argument in support of its IPv6 vision and strategy. GSN collaborates closely with the other IPv6 efforts in Greece to leverage the economies of scale provided by the joint infrastructures. GSN is using the GRNET IPv6 network for its backbone connectivity. It also provides valuable feedback to other commercial and national initiatives. On the commercial side, the GSN experience and expertise was shared with the Technical Chamber of Greece (http://www.tee.gr), which was one of the first commercial ISPs in Greece to started investigating the deployment of IPv6 production services to its ADSL customers. Upstream IPv6 connectivity was established in 2007 while tunnel-based solutions are under trial. The GSN experience provided feedback to other national projects, such as the DIODOS ("diodos" translates into "passage") project (http://www.diodos.net.gr/). DIODOS was established under the authority of the Ministry of Development, the Ministry of National Education and Religious Affairs, and the Ministry of Transport and Communications, and it is implemented by the General Secretariat for Research and Technology with the support of GRNET. The goals of the project are as follows:[25]

- **Enhance the education process at the university level:** The project would provide students with broadband access and the resources supporting applications such as tele-teaching, collaboration, videoconferencing, virtual labs, and rich-content multimedia.

25. Athanassios Liakopoulos, "IPv6 Broadband Access to University Students in Greece: The DIODOS Project," 2006, http://www.6diss.org/workshops/ipv6td/liakopoulos-diodos.pdf.

- **Stimulate broadband adoption in Greece:** Provide subsidized broadband access service to students to encourage adoption and to stimulate access providers to develop the necessary infrastructure.

Based on GSN's IPv6 experience, DIODOS initiated a proposal for offering IPv6 services over the broadband access made available to students.

IPv6 Planning and Implementation

GSN's goal is to deploy a wide range of services over IPv6, including mapping some of the existing IPv4 services:

- **E-mail:** Services are accessible through the POP3 and IMAP protocols, as well as the World Wide Web.
- **Web hosting:** Web hosting is available for static and dynamic pages.
- **GSN web portal:** The web portal offers news services and personalized access to telecommunications and informatics services.
- **Web proxy and web filtering:** Web proxy and filtering services ensure optimal performance with centralized content-filtering administration.
- **AAA services:** Shared authentication, authorization, and accounting services are used to manage and secure network access.
- **Instant message services:** Services are provided that enable real-time asynchronous peer-to-peer communications over the Internet, generally using text-based conversation.
- **Directory services:** LDAP services are used for user authentication and authorization.

As mentioned earlier, GSN benefits from having a core of IPv6 experts who are able to define the architecture of the envisioned IPv6 deployment, establish the optimal strategy for the IPv6 integration, and detail its implementation steps. The following are the phases of the IPv6 deployment in GSN:

- **Define IPv6 addressing plan:** Acquire the IPv6 address space from the Local Internet Registry (LIR) and define the addressing scheme.
- **Upgrade the core and distribution network:** In both of these layers, the approach was to implement a dual-stack environment and to avoid the use of tunnels.

NOTE	No major problems were encountered with IPv6 support in the commercial platforms used in GSN's environment.

- **Select address allocation mechanisms:** At the access layer, access routers from multiple vendors are used and they exhibited different capabilities. GSN had to evaluate various provisioning tools, preferring those that minimize the management process. DHCP-PD is used whenever possible.

- **Enable IPv6 services:** Identify and evaluate the commercial software and applications that support the services targeted for IPv6.

- **Update management tools:** Identify the tools that can be used to manage the IPv6 infrastructure and services.

- **Provide IPv6 services to a small group of schools:** IPv6 support requirements narrowed down the initial phase of the deployment to schools with broadband access and new CPE. For the trial sites, at first establish connectivity to the access routers and then extend the IPv6 services to the hosts on the school LANs.

- **Extend IPv6 services to the other schools:** Extending IPv6 access to other educational networks is planned.

In line with the defined strategy, by June 2006 the GSN IPv6 deployment made great progress while handling the challenges specific to its environment and providing valuable operational lessons.[26] These lessons include:

- **IPv6 addressing plan:** Acquired 2001:648::/35 from the LIR. Multiple /48s are assigned for each POP, a /62 is assigned for each school, and /64s are used for LANs.

- **Core and distribution network upgrade:** The routers in all GSN's major POPs were dual-stack and enabled in two phases with minimal hardware upgrades, such as memory upgrades. Peering was established with GRNET. OSPFv3 is the IPv6 IGP used. Secondary distribution

26. Manos Varvarigos, "Greek Schools's IPv6 Network," http://www.ipv6.eu/admin/bildbank/
uploads/Documents/Vienna_June_2006/Session_3_Manos_Varvarigos_-_CTI.pdf.

nodes were not enabled for IPv6 due to hardware/software limitations. This lead to the decision to trial the deployment at schools with broadband access and newer equipment.

- **Select address allocation mechanisms:** At the access layer, access routers from multiple vendors are used and they exhibited different capabilities. GSN had to evaluate various provisioning tools, preferring those minimizing the management process. DHCP-PD is used whenever possible.

- **Enable IPv6 services:** Servers for the targeted services were upgraded and configured in dual-stack mode. DNS records were updated and DNS services enabled in the network.

- **Provide IPv6 services to a small group of schools:** Pilot service was initiated in 50 schools and it was later extended to 300 schools.

To address some of the hardware and software challenges experienced, the GSN made a long-term plan to enhance the hardware infrastructure across the distribution and access layers of the network. In parallel to IPv6-trials performed, access circuits were upgraded from PSTN/ISDN to ADSL for all schools by the end of 2006. This reduced the congestion in the access links and allowed the provision of interactive and bandwidth-consuming multimedia applications. Following the hardware upgrade schedule, by the end of 2007, approximately one-third of the schools were using IPv6-enabled routers able to support multiple internal VLANs. This will require reconsidering the management and security policies, such as access lists, applied in internal networks. Midterm plans include the development of tools to automatically manage the configuration and software upgrade of thousands of access routers, school servers, and (possibly) PC labs, including the operating system. Some of the management challenges can be addressed using static global IPv6 addresses instead of using NAT/PAT translation techniques.

The phases of GSN's strategy and the implementation timeline are described in Table 5-23.

Table 5-23   *Greek School Network's Strategy for Deploying IPv6*

Phase 1 (2004–2005)	Phase 2 (2006–2007)	Phase 3 (2008 Onward)
Acquire IPv6 address space. Start IPv6 trials in xDSL environment. Upgrade core and distribution networks. Enable IPv6 routing protocols in the core and distribution layers. Upgrade basic networking services to support IPv6, such as DNS, HTTP, SMTP, and so on. Set the specifications for future upgrade phases.	Trial deployment of IPv6 interconnection services in 500+ schools. Provide broadband interconnection circuits in all schools. Investigate and improve management schemas and service provisioning using IPv6. Set a long-term plan for hardware and software upgrades.	Large deployment of IPv6-enabled access routers. Operate IPv6-enabled PC labs. Develop new multimedia applications and virtual cooperative environments for educational purposes.

NOTE   GRNET, as an LIR of RIPE NCC, has permanently assigned to GSN the IPv6 address prefix 2001:648::/32 in 2005.

This phased approach enabled GSN to minimize deployment costs by correlating it with ongoing equipment upgrades. It also enabled GSN to minimize the impact on the IPv4 services provided while new IPv6 services were gradually added to its service portfolio. In addition, network engineers and system administrators were gradually involved in the deployment process of IPv6 services without requiring any increase of the available resources for the operation of the production network.

Lessons Learned

The deployment of IPv6 in the GSN proved to be a positive and valuable experience. This deployment is often referenced as a standard case study for deploying IPv6 in educational environments. Within Greece, the project stimulated other IPv6 efforts that involved public and private sectors. The success of the project sparked similar initiatives in other European countries. The government's support for GSN's IPv6 project amounts to a successful national strategy of leading by example, both internally and internationally.

The most important lessons learned from GSN's IPv6 experience are as follows:

- **The value of pilot projects:** IPv6 deployments should start with pilot projects, which provide valuable technical experience and an environment in which to evaluate early on the deployment strategy. Pilot projects are easy to manage and control. They allow an enterprise to evaluate tangible benefits, analyze missing functionality in the deployed infrastructure, and identify potential risks. Avoid enabling IPv6 services in the production network prior to investigating their management and security implications. The active participation in the 6NET project and the collaboration with other IPv6 efforts such as SEEREN (http://www.seeren. org/) provided valuable protocol and deployment experience.

- **The value of correlating the deployment with the equipment upgrade process:** This leads to reduced costs for the deployment and to avoiding the use of unplanned solutions to work around limitations of old equipment. Early correlation of the two efforts helps to avoid the slowdown of the IPv6 deployment due to unsuitable equipment that has not yet been upgraded.

- **IPv6 technology is mature:** GSN was able to enable IPv6 services in the core and distribution networks without degrading the already deployed production IPv4 services. In most cases, the increase in the infrastructure management efforts was marginal. However, avoid upgrading the networking infrastructure for IPv6-technology per se.

- **IPv6 applications or services were built using open source software:** The open source software has good support of IPv6. For technical and financial reasons, GSN has chosen to enhance its infrastructure using open source software. In some cases, upgrading services to support IPv6 did not require any software upgrades but only changes in the configuration. When necessary, GSN extended management tools or end-user applications to fully support IPv6 features.

- **Raise awareness of IPv6 technology:** Identify any strategic advantages from the introduction of IPv6 technology in the operation of an educational organization. Clearly explain these advantages to the administrative and technical personnel to achieve their commitment to long-term IPv6 deployment plans.

The GSN case is a successful example that proves that smooth transition to IPv6 is feasible for a large-scale network if a ground plan is identified and dedication to well-understood targets is achieved by key administration and technical personnel.

Factice World Bank—Exploratory Case Study

It was impossible to find a financial institution fully dedicated to the IPv6 integration; however, several were investigating the potential technology benefits and challenges. This exploratory case study tries to be as close as possible from all comments received by the people interviewed at the financial institutions.

—Patrick Grossetete, Chip Popoviciu, Fred Wettling

Social networking is one of today's buzz words, but the concept is rather old. There is one "social network" that has been in place for hundreds of years: the financial system. Although bartering represents the oldest trading system, a system that exists today as well, the true revolution came when value started to be quantified through commonly accepted objects such as beads, shells, or bones. These objects were the foundation of primitive financial systems established for small communities. Money, a further and more generic abstraction, offered the means to scale up the financial system, which evolved to have global coverage. Today, the financial system represents a pillar of the worldwide economy. In recent decades, the evolution of the information and networking technologies has enabled financial institutions to optimize, control, and secure the financial operations across the planet. Without a properly operating financial system, the modern, global economy would collapse. The financial system relies on IT to interconnect resources and to provide services at all levels of its operation:

- **Individuals:** Individuals interact with the financial system through bank accounts that store money, and through financial vehicles and other means that enable them to manage their assets.

- **Businesses:** Businesses interact with the financial system through their regular operation and by providing the information that helps the financial markets valuate them.

- **Governments:** Governments control the financial system at the national level through policies that support its operation, growth, and stability.

- **Global:** Globally the financial system relies on a set of international agreements enforced by dedicated institutions with the support of the participating governments.

Today's global economy organized itself around global financial centers located in large cities. The centers host the representatives of the world and regional financial institutions. This structure bares close similarity to the Internet exchange points, where providers can quickly and efficiently exchange information. Because the financial centers require extensive communications resources, it is not a coincidence that their growth correlates with the availability of state-of-the-art telecommunication services.

With tens of thousands of financial institutions spread around the world, communication among them is essential to the daily flow of transactions that shape modern economy.

NOTE	In their company profiles, the leading electronic payment companies, MasterCard Worldwide[27] and Visa Inc.[28], indicate they have more than 20,000 financial partners across 200 countries whose networks and clearing centers are used to process electronic payment transactions.

---

27. http://www.mastercard.com/us/company/en/docs/MasterCard%20FAQ.pdf.

28. http://www.corporate.visa.com/av/pdf/Visa_Inc_Overview.pdf.

When focusing solely on the private banking sector, it becomes immediately clear how important a versatile networking infrastructure is to the financial organizations. This is generally true regardless of their size (in terms of capitalization, structure, asset management, and so on), but it is particularly evident in the case of the most popular institutions in private banking. Table 5-24 summarizes the profiles of some of the leading financial organizations in 2006-2007 to illustrate the importance of networking in supporting their infrastructure.

Table 5-24   *Private Banking Sector Profile Examples*

Company	Revenue (US$ Millions)	Presence	Employees
UBS	107,834.8	50+ countries	80,000
Citigroup	146,777.0	8140 branches, approximately 19,100 automated teller machines, 708 automated lending machines, and the Internet	332,000
HSBC	115,361.0	80 countries 10,000 offices	296,000
Credit Agricole	128,481.3	55 countries 39 regional banks 9000 branches	152,000
Societe Generale	84,485.7	42 countries Over 2900 branches	120,000
ABN Amro	71,217.8	Over 4000 branches in 52 countries	100,000
Savings Bank of Russia	8,284.0	Central head office Regional head offices (17) Branches (819) Subbranches (19,341)	250,000
Industrial and Commercial Bank of China	36,832.9	18,764 domestic branches 106 overseas branches 1165 agencies around the globe	351,000

Table 5-24   *Private Banking Sector Profile Examples (Continued)*

Company	Revenue (US$ Millions)	Presence	Employees
Bank of China	30,750.8	27 countries and regions	232,000
		11,241 domestic and overseas branches and outlets	
		37 tier one branches	
		283 tier two branches	
		10,277 outlets in domestic operation	
		643 branches, subsidiaries, and representative offices in overseas operation	

These financial institutions have a large geographical footprint, with all their branches and employees requiring adequate telecommunications resources to support their operations. Network size, however, is not the only challenge. Consider the type of communications specific to the financial environment such as financial transactions, stock quotes, and market updates. The IT infrastructure must support errorless communications and multicast-based applications, it must support time-sensitive services, and in certain areas it must be highly redundant to avoid downtime at all costs. This is why the IT infrastructure is a strategic, mission-critical asset for financial institutions.

Company Profile

We were unable to find an appropriate contact in this market space who was willing or able to publicly present an IPv6 adoption plan. This is not surprising, because financial institutions traditionally shy away from the early adopter spotlight. Therefore, this case study differs from all the others in that it is not tied to a real organization. Financial institutions operate IT environments with specific requirements and characteristics. They must balance the drivers described in the previous section with the implications of deploying a new protocol. This balance relates not only to the technological aspects, but also to the perception of their customers and partners regarding the security and stability of the IT environment.

Because the interest in IPv6 has been steadily increasing in the financial market, we chose to discuss the integration drivers and considerations within this market space through a fictional case study. Nevertheless, the case was developed based on information acquired by interviewing several Cisco customers who are actively studying and monitoring IPv6 but are not ready to publicly share their IPv6 strategy.

The fictional financial institution analyzed in this case study is called Factice World Bank (FWB). Its corporate profile is summarized in Table 5-25.

Table 5-25   *Factice World Bank Corporate Profile Overview*

Profile Category	Status/Value
Organization	Factice World Bank
Industry	Commercial and personal banking
Number of employees	43,000
Geography	Global
Revenue	$6.5 billion
Presence	35 countries
	9000 branch offices
	12,000 ATMs
	Internet banking

IT Profile

The OSs currently deployed in FWB's infrastructure and those it plans to use going forward are listed in Table 5-26.

Table 5-26   *Factice World Bank IT Profile—Operating Systems*

Device Type	Today	Future
PC and workstations	Windows Server 2003, Windows XP	Windows Vista and Windows Server 2008
	IBM zSeries	IBM zSeries
	Sun Solaris 8	Sun Solaris 10
	HP-UX 10	HP-UX 11

Table 5-26 *Factice World Bank IT Profile—Operating Systems (Continued)*

Device Type	Today	Future
Servers	Windows Server 2003	Windows Server 2008
IP phones	Cisco	Cisco
Smartphones	Nokia, RIM	Nokia, RIM, Samsung
Routers and switches	Cisco IOS, CatOS	Cisco IOS, IOS-XE, and NX-OS

The IT department is running around 3000 applications over the Internet, 80 percent of which were developed in house. More recently, IP telephony was deployed in all branches using the Cisco Unified Communications solution.

The applications currently deployed are summarized in Table 5-27.

Table 5-27 *Factice World Bank IT Profile—Applications*

Application Type	Facility
E-mail	Microsoft Messaging Application Programming Interface (MAPI), remote-procedure call (RPC), HTTP with SSL encryption (HTTPS), POP3, and Lightweight Directory Access Protocol (LDAP)
File/print sharing	Common Internet File System (CIFS)
Web-based tools	HTTP
Stock quotes and market info	Multicast based

IP Infrastructure Characteristics

FWB's IT infrastructure is still largely heterogeneous because it has made a few acquisitions over the past four years. Nevertheless, the IT department decided to standardize the deployment of Cisco equipment for campus and WAN routers. The merger of regional banks, opening and closing of branch offices, and starting new overseas operations are part of the IT department's regular activities. To support its branch operations, FWB has negotiated the outsourcing of its WAN to a global ISP that is able to cover all of FWB's operational theaters. The campus infrastructures are still managed by FWB IT teams. Security is the responsibility of a dedicated team that is in charge of defining policies and regulations, managing incidents and Product Security Incident Response Team (PSIRT) alerts, and propagating certified fixes. This team works closely with its ISP to manage security in the WAN portion of its infrastructure.

Address management is not optimized as a result of several mergers. It has the following characteristics:

- **Private address space:** Most PCs and workstations dynamically receive their IPv4 address from the RFC 1918 private address space via DHCP. The process was put in place to help with the mandatory renumbering that occurred as part of mergers. Several private subnets are set aside and used for the IP telephony deployment. Access to the Internet is authorized through proxy servers.

- **Global IPv4 addresses:** FWB uses a Class B and several Class C networks that are assigned to public servers and networking devices. Those addresses are manually configured and published in DNS records.

Aside from the fragmented address space, FWB's IT department envisions challenges to the IPv4 infrastructure due to an increasing number and continuing diversification of deployed devices:

- **Wireless access:** With wireless access, PCs require twice as many addresses even when docked. This has led to several address shortages that required manual interventions and further fragmentation of the addressing scheme.

- **IP telephony:** Using Cisco Unified Communications applications led to a rapidly increasing number of devices requiring IP addresses for long periods of time.

- **Smartphones:** Around 30 percent of the workforce and 100 percent of managers are equipped with smartphones, enabling them to always stay connected for e-mail and trading applications. These devices require long-lived addresses as well.

FWB expects the rhythm of acquiring businesses will continue to be strong for several years. The integration of these businesses will be challenging for the IT department. Although a restructured IPv4 addressing scheme would be very beneficial, it would be very difficult if not impossible to implement because it would lead to a major restructuring of the intranet with all the negative implications of the inevitable downtime. The integration of a new IP version is seen as an opportunity to define new design rules and addressing architectures that are more flexible and scalable.

Perspective on IPv6

Although financial institutions have always taken a conservative position regarding the adoption of new technologies—a perspective that is expected due to the potential impact on security and the stability of the environment—similar to other businesses, they are moving toward IP-based convergence of communications services and applications, so sooner or later an analysis of IPv6's benefits and challenges is inevitable. This analysis provides several reasons to consider the integration of IPv6 in the IT environment of financial institutions, including:

- **Simpler and better internal addressing scheme:** The large population of employees requires a well-defined addressing plan to connect all personal computers, servers, and workstations over the intranet. Introduction of technologies such as IEEE 802.11 (Wi-Fi) often doubles the IP address space needs.

- **Convergence of the intranet:** The convergence of data, voice, and video over IP adds some stress on the internal addressing resources, which now have to cover large numbers of devices used in IP telephony, video conferencing, video surveillance, and sensors to increase operational efficiency and security.

- **Financial market consolidation and expansion:** A significant number of mergers and acquisitions is leading to a consolidation of the financial market. This process presents the IT departments with the challenge of merging IP infrastructures. This process not only is challenging in the case of IPv4 but also leads to increasing demand placed on the address provisioning and management resources. The consolidation of the financial market is complemented by continued expansion into new regions or countries. A good example is the expansion of the European financial institutions in the new member states. This expansion leads as well to increased demand for address space.

- **Evolution of ATM services:** Very often, private banks manage a network of automated teller machines (ATM), a network that may be far larger than the network connecting their branch offices. Previously deployed over X.25 networks, the ATM machines migrated to using IP. Once again, although not connected to the Internet, the ATMs represent another consumer of IP addresses. Another area of development is the deployment of "mobile ATM" using technology such as Mobile IP and Network Mobility (NEMO). Leveraging IPv6, these technologies would allow the deployment of temporary ATM services in locations such as beaches and cultural events.

- **Internet banking:** With consumers adopting Internet and broadband technologies, the financial institutions have to offer Internet-based services. Over the years, making 24-hour banking available to customers became a competitive differentiator for the financial institutions. Some financial institutions conduct most of their personal banking business over the Internet. This means that financial institutions must adjust their customer-facing infrastructure and services to the communications protocols available to their customers. For example, if IPv6 is widely adopted in Asia, a financial institution doing business in the region would certainly need to support access to its online banking services over IPv6 or else risk losing customers to competitors.

- **Mobile banking:** The evolution of mobile phone services and smartcard technologies opened the door for new financial services. To put in perspective the importance of such services, some regions in the world have a better penetration rate for mobile phones than for bank accounts. Financial services over mobile phones represent a new opportunity to develop business. These services can be implemented by using a lite client model, which requires the front-end server infrastructures to be fully capable of accessing always-on devices in a secure fashion. Many always-on devices, as in the case of mobile phones, require IP address resources at a scale unavailable through IPv4. The environment will become reality due to many other services targeted for the mobile phones, and it most likely will use IPv6.

These arguments, along with external events such as ARIN's recommendation to consider IPv6 and even denial of requests for IPv4 address space, drove financial institutions around the world to pay close attention to IPv6. Although financial institutions shy away from being at the bleeding edge of technology adoption, they cannot afford to be far behind on the adoption curve either. The integration of IPv6 was not seen as an immediate necessity in 2007, but market monitoring and contingency planning have become important to almost all large financial institutions around the world.

"No Case" for IPv6

Identifying a business case for IPv6 was not at all an objective for FWB's IT team. In fact, it has considered the technology to be not mature enough and reserved for researchers and universities. Recently, however, the IT team started to consider IPv6 as a "must do" topic following various external events, such as press articles, presentations from vendors such as Cisco and Microsoft, reports from analysts, an adoption mandate from U.S. federal agencies, and the opening of Internet banking operations in Japan, where consumers have access to IPv6 services.

FWB's main drivers to learn more about the IPv6 technology are as follows:

* **Security:** The default integration of IPv6 in new OSs such as Microsoft Windows Vista, Windows Server 2008, Windows Mobile 6, and Symbian forces the security team to evaluate new potential attack vectors. Even without an identified application for IPv6, the availability of this new protocol on devices operating on its network could not be ignored.

NOTE　　Although IPv6 traffic might represent only a low percentage of the Internet traffic and although IPv6 is not largely deployed in production environments by organizations, several PSIRT alerts have already been generated by vendors. Several of the potential denial-of-service attacks used IPv6 over IPv4 tunnels as a way to bypass existing security policies.

- **New operating systems:** The migration to Microsoft Windows Vista and Windows Server 2008 clusters is driven by FWB's partnership with Microsoft, the vendor for most of its applications and the infrastructure for most of its internally developed applications. New frameworks such as Windows Peer-to-Peer Networking and Layer 3 clustering offer opportunities to enhance applications but require an IPv6 environment.
- **International Internet banking:** Triggered by the recently launched commercial operations in Japan, the IT department was tasked to evaluate the implications on Internet banking of the IPv6 broadband services offered by Japanese ISPs to their home users.

These points drove FWB to take a closer look at IPv6, to analyze the market, the potential challenges, and the potential opportunities. None of these topics are drivers for immediate integration of IPv6 but they must be analyzed and a strategy to address them must be identified.

IPv6 Planning and Implementation

To manage the various challenges described in the previous section, FWB's IT team concluded that the time had come to evaluate the IPv6 technology, understand its current level of development and adoption, and build the necessary contingency plans. This exercise created the opportunity for the IT team to review the current architecture, deployed several years back, and update its requirements and policies to deal with the challenges faced in today's rapidly evolving IT world. IPv6 offered the opportunity to roll out an overlay design based on updated requirements while having minimal impact on the existing environment. The IT team can deploy FWB's NGN in parallel with the existent one. The phased approach taken to integrate IPv6 is described in Table 5-28.

Table 5-28   *Factice World Bank's Strategy for Internal Deployment of IPv6*

Phase 1 (2006–2008)	Phase 2 (2008–2010)	Phase 3 (2010 Onward)
Learn about the IPv6 technology to evaluate its integration options.	Acquire IPv6 addressing space and define address allocation policies.	Deploy Microsoft Windows Vista and Server 2008 as the main OSs.
Add IPv6 requirements to purchasing policies.	Identify applications or appliances that could be trialed over IPv6.	Managed WAN services support IPv6.
Block and monitor IPv6 traffic to and from the Intranet.	Evaluate the impact of deploying Microsoft Windows Vista and Server 2008 in terms of IPv6.	Online Internet banking services are made available over IPv6.
Require equipment vendors, managed services organizations, and service providers to present their IPv6 roadmap.	Foster collaboration and policies to get application developers to integrate IPv6.	Deployment of new services and appliances is done over IPv6.
Define an architecture that enables a cleaner addressing scheme to deal with acquisitions.	Upgrade security appliances to support IPv6.	
	Initiate Internet banking services trials in Japan.	

FWB's schedule summarized in Table 5-28 provides ample time for getting the organization ready for the IPv6 integration. The early planning leads to reduced deployment costs and smooth coexistence with IPv4.

Lessons Learned

Although migration to IPv6 has never been considered imminent or a high-priority project by the IT team, the impact IPv6 can have on the industry and the market forced the team to investigate the technology and the implications of its deployment internally and globally. After the IT team mastered the technology and gained confidence in its capabilities, there is no reason not to leverage it for the applications that could benefit from it.

The most important lessons learned from FWB's IPv6 investigation are as follows:

- **The value of closed collaboration with vendors and ISPs:** Engaging early with networking and software vendors was essential in closely evaluating the direction of the market, the upcoming features and capabilities, and the aspects of IPv6 that would be of particular interest to this market segment. The interaction with ISPs was valuable in evaluating the level of support that can be expected should the IPv6 integration become urgent.

- **The value of an early, phased approach:** The phased approach is found very helpful in assigning the appropriate amount and type of resources at the right time to the IPv6 integration process. The investments made in this effort have been spread out and organized so that readiness is achieved timely in case unexpected market drivers require deployment. By starting early, the IT department at FWB was able to set aside ample time to evaluate the protocol internally and in interaction with primary vendors and to investigate fully the opportunities offered by the IP upgrade.

- **Some challenges remain:** The evaluation of the new protocol highlighted a few areas that could be viewed as challenging. The developments in the area of multihoming routing deaggregation policy from RIRs will be monitored by the IT department. Although FWB has no problems acquiring its own /32 address space from ARIN, multihoming techniques better than the existing IPv4 ones would be very valuable. The operations and security aspects of the IPv6 integration are also perceived as work in progress.

FWB is not in a hurry to deploy IPv6, but it keeps up with the technology trends and addresses external drivers for IPv6 adoption. FWB will not be an early adopter but at least it will have a strategy in place to address the need for the IPv6 integration. It will get its environment ready for IPv6 to respond to any sudden shift in the protocol adoption within the financial market driven by unique applications or requirements. The IT department at FWB takes the event of an IP upgrade very seriously and has taken plenty of time to prepare for it and make the most out of it.

Government Agencies—Early Adopters

An August 2, 2005, memorandum from the Executive Office of the President, Office of Management and Budget, triggered an intense wave of activity to address the strategic deployment of IPv6 within all U.S. federal agencies:

> As I stated in my testimony of June 29, 2005, before the House Committee on Government Reform, we have set June 2008 as the date by which all agencies' infrastructure (network backbones) must be using IPv6 and agency networks must interface with this infrastructure. This memorandum and its attachments provide guidance to the agencies to ensure an orderly and secure transition from Internet Protocol Version 4 (IPv4) to Version 6 (IPv6). Since the Internet Protocol is core to an agency's IT infrastructure, beginning in February, 2006 OMB will use the Enterprise Architecture Assessment Framework to evaluate agency IPv6 transition planning and progress, IP device inventory completeness, and impact analysis thoroughness....[29]

> —Karen S. Evans, Administrator

This case study aggregates IPv6 deployment observations in several U.S. federal agencies.

Economic development is spurred by and relies on infrastructures that support various economic activities. Infrastructures that have a national-level impact typically must cover a large geographical footprint and provide accessibility to a significant part of the population before their economic value becomes apparent. For these reasons, they require tremendous initial investment before a return on investment (ROI) is definable and feasibility is proven. The development of strategic infrastructures requires long-term vision, in the range of 15 to 20 years, and significant commitment, which is why it is generally initiated and supported by governments. In the end, however, the investments lead to better use of existing technologies and the creation of a fertile innovation environment.

---

29. "Transition Planning for Internet Protocol Version 6 (IPv6)," OMB Memorandum M-05-22, http://www.whitehouse.gov/omb/memoranda/fy2005/m05-22.pdf.

The history of U.S. economic development offers multiple examples of such strategic infrastructures that led to technological revolutions and explosive economic growth. An often cited example is the development of the U.S. highway system. Its history highlights some aspects that are interesting in the context of this book:[30]

- **Federal-Aid Highway Act of 1938:** Supported the first study of a system of highways. The study, conducted under the auspices of the Bureau of Public Roads, concluded that this system could not be self-supporting. It advocated a 26,700-mile network of roads instead.

- **Federal-Aid Highway Act of 1944:** Chartered a "National System of Interstate Highways" leading to a 40,000-mile network of roads. Highway agencies and the DoD planned the nationwide routes.

- **Federal-Aid Highway Act of 1954:** Set aside $175 million for the construction of an interstate highway system, but significantly more was needed to build the infrastructure envisioned by President Eisenhower.

- **Federal-Aid Highway Act of 1956:** Authorized a $25 billion budget for the project, with the federal government's share being 90 percent.

The highway system was an essential element in U.S. economic growth, highlighting the importance of government's involvement in these types of long-term strategic projects. Other important infrastructures have since been built that share many of the traits already mentioned. For these reasons, they are often used as examples in planning and supporting the development of new infrastructures. A parallel is sometimes drawn between the U.S. highway system and the adoption and deployment of IPv6. Despite certain similarities, the comparison is not truly applicable. The deployment of a national broadband access infrastructure relates much more closely to the highway system. IPv6 is just an enabler of such a broadband access infrastructure.

---

30. See the Highway History web page of the U.S. Department of Transportation Federal Highway Administration, http://www.fhwa.DOT.gov/infrastructure/history.htm.

NOTE	No specific funds were authorized for the construction of the U.S. highway system before 1954 but progress was still made, albeit slowly. Similarly, IPv6's adoption in the United States was triggered by the DoD's (and later the federal government's) vision and commitment, yet no funds were allocated for it. Federal progress has been made, and its adoption was indirectly financed through the IPv6 requirements placed in the U.S. General Services Administration's Networx program.[31]

This short overview of a major infrastructure was not intended to provide just a historical perspective and some lessons learned. Traditional infrastructures are also entering the information age. As an example, the auto, shipping, and air transportation industries continue to grow along with the economy while evolving to integrate IT technologies that enable them to optimize operations and deliver additional services. As ICT, and in particular IP, continues to be integrated and leveraged in these large infrastructures, more and more resources are required for the many elements involved in the system: cars, ships, trains, airplanes, sensors for vehicles and infrastructures, and so forth. In this context, IPv6 becomes a catalyst for the continued growth of these infrastructures and opens the door for supporting the new services described in the "Transportation" section of Chapter 2. These IP-enabled infrastructures will not only operate more efficiently by intelligently and dynamically avoiding congestion and improving safety, they will also make the most of the capabilities of IP-enabled vehicles.

Transportation is just one example from which IPv6 adoption can learn valuable lessons and for which IPv6 will become indispensable. In the United States, this bidirectional relationship between existing, traditional, national infrastructures and IPv6 is particularly interesting because the OMB mandates practically set a timetable for IPv6 planning for all the government agencies managing or overseeing these infrastructures. Independent of their own vision about the role of IP and, more specifically, IPv6 in their environments, agencies such as the Department of Transportation (DOT), Department of Energy (DOE),

31. "Networx Overview," http://www.gsa.gov/Portal/gsa/ep/contentView.do?
lcontentType=GSA_OVERVIEW&contentId=16100.

Department of Education, and Social Security Administration (SSA) had to start preparing for the June 2008 deadline. The work done by the federal agencies toward IPv6 adoption will be invaluable to the national economy in general and IPv6 adoption in particular.

This case study takes a general look at the strategies and plans of the U.S. federal agencies toward the adoption of IPv6. It draws from the varied experiences and perspectives of several agencies that took a leadership role in new technology integration and summarizes publicly available data related to their adoption plans. This case study is also based on data provided by the Market Connections, Inc. federal market analysis completed in June 2006, commissioned by Cisco Systems.[32]

Company Profile

The U.S. government is the largest enterprise in the world and comprises large individual departments incorporating many employees supported by extensive ICT infrastructures. The 2007 federal budget outlays were $2.6 trillion for 1175 agencies employing 5 million people. The whole U.S. government spent over $60 billion on IT, more than the IT expenditure of the entire Fortune 1000. Individual departments are of the size of large businesses. DOT has approximately 60,000 employees and a 2008 budget of approximately $67 billion.[33] DOE has approximately 15,000 permanent employees (complemented by a very large number of contractors) and a 2008 budget of approximately $24.3 billion.[34] The SSA has approximately 62,000 employees and a 2008 budget of $657 billion.[35]

Along with managing and operating the infrastructures they are responsible for, government agencies invest in research and development that enables them to evolve and adapt. DOT has an R&D strategy and a set of emerging research

---

32. "IPv6 Survey: Taking the Federal Pulse on IPv6," http://www.cisco.com/web/strategy/docs/gov/Cisco_IPv6_Report.ppt.

33. http://www.dot.gov/about_dot.html.

34. http://www.energy.gov/about/budget.htm.

35. http://www.ssa.gov/.

priorities identified in its 2006–2010 strategic plan.[36] DOE covers, by its mission, a wide range of scientific and technological research areas.[37]

Federal agencies are pursuing these R&D efforts in partnership with other civilian and defense federal agencies, with universities, and in coordination with other projects. Some of these projects address the realities of today's world, such as the ways in which various infrastructures would deal with dramatic events like flu pandemics, natural disasters, or terrorist attacks, or the ways in which they can support sources of energy and the devices utilizing them, and so on.

IT Profile

ICT in general and more and more IP networks represent an essential infrastructure for today's optimal operation of the government. Some of the technologies currently used are in the process of being updated and upgraded to support the requirements and scale of today's communications applications. One example is the effort of modernizing the Federal Aviation Administration (FAA) infrastructure to support the demands and the scale of today's air traffic environment, an effort similar to that of the European EUROCONTROL Network Sub-Domain project.[38]

The IT environments of the U.S. federal agencies run over extensive IP infrastructures supporting thousands of workstations, PCs, and VoIP phones at many locations. The SSA, for example, operates 1500 locations nationwide.[39]

U.S. civilian federal agencies usually use a variety of common, enterprise-specific applications. Some of them are procured off the shelf while others are developed in house. Their IT environments are usually managed internally while security is ensured through the network engineering groups in partnership with dedicated cybersecurity groups.

36. U.S. Department of Transportation Research and Innovative Technology Administration, "Transportation Research, Development and Technology Strategic Plan: 2006–2010," 2006, http://www.rita.DOT.gov/publications/transportation_rd_t_strategic_plan/pdf/entire.pdf.

37. DOE Science and Technology web page, http://www.energy.gov/sciencetech/index.htm.

38. http://www.eurocontrol.int/communications/public/standard_page/com_network.html.

39. Carolyn Duffy Marsan, "Five IPv6 Tips from an Early Adopter," *Network World*, July 26, 2006, http://www.networkworld.com/newsletters/isp/2006/0724isp1.html.

NOTE   Although the release of Microsoft's new OS, Windows Vista, is considered one of the catalysts for IPv6 adoption, some federal agencies have decided to postpone its integration in their environments, citing security concerns and lack of business needs.[40] This may sound like negative news for Microsoft, but this approach is not different from that taken by enterprises toward any new OS release adoption, generally waiting for the first service pack before moving it into production. It is likely that the Vista evaluation efforts started in 2007 will be followed by deployment in the 2008–2009 timeframe following the publication of Vista SP1 in March 2008.

Based on the Market Connections survey, the IT problems of most interest to the decision makers in this sector are as follows (in the order of their identified importance):

- Privacy and security of communications

- Quality of service

- Network performance

- Network management

- Cost of operations

- Interoperability

Each agency, however, might have a slightly different set of priorities, especially when it comes to R&D. As an example, the IT priorities considered by DOT for the fiscal year 2007 reflect its active efforts to enhance the infrastructure and expand the services offered to its departments. Here is a list of initiatives selected from the DOT CIO's "Potential FY07 IT Initiatives" presentation:[41]

- Encryption of Data at Rest on Mobile Devices

- Proliferation of Voice/Video over IP

---

40. Jason Miller, "Agencies Uncertain About Move to Vista," *Federal Computer Week* (online edition), March 12, 2007, http://www.fcw.com/print/13_7/news/97891-1.html.

41. Tim Schmidt, Chief Technology Officer, U.S. Dept. of Transportation

- Secure Remote Access

- Logical Access Control Integration

- Implementation of IPv6 by 2008

- Role-Base Access Control

- Wide Area Network Consolidation

- Virtualization

- Basic Customer "Self-Service" Tools and Capabilities

- Analysis of thick/thin/Internet based desktop clients—possible transition to stateless clients

- Transportation "Congestion" technology and advisory support

- Service Oriented Architectures

While DOE defined its own 2008–2010 IT strategy,[42] it is also involved in various IT R&D efforts together with other federal agencies within a larger scope of the federal Networking and Information Technology Research and Development (NITRD) initiatives.[43]

IP Infrastructure Characteristics

For the most part, federal agencies have a similar perspective on the address characteristics in the design of IP infrastructures, which are

- **Address lifetime:** Most endpoints are dynamically assigned temporary addresses via DHCP, while network elements use fixed IP addresses.

- **Address types:** Both global IPv4 addresses and private IPv4 addresses are used. RFC 1918 addresses are used for all internal applications.

With large initial allocations of global IPv4 address space (SSA owns a Class A allocation), this IP address management strategy proved sufficient for the agencies' needs. The addressing scheme and management rarely if ever require

42. "Information Resource Management Strategic Plan: FY2008–2010," http://cio.energy.gov/documents/DOE_IRM_Strategic_Plan_FY2008-2010_FINAL.pdf.

43. http://www.nitrd.gov/pubs/2008supplement/08Supp_FINAL-August.pdf.

any renumbering events. While most of the time they did not experience addressing constraint pressures, some of the agencies are expecting to see shortages in the future due primarily to multiple overlays in their networks such as the wireless services infrastructure, the fixed-line services infrastructure, and management of network devices, each with its own dedicated IPv4 address space. Further challenges are expected from enabling new services and the expansion of some of the existing ones (Ultra-Mobile PC, VoIP, monitoring devices, and sensors). The address shortages represent a practical (although not pressing) reason for taking interest in IPv6.

Perspective on IPv6

The perspective on IPv6 in this U.S. market segment was significantly crystallized by the OMB mandate. Here are a few common major U.S. federal agency responses to the OMB message:

- **Interest:** A large majority of the federal agencies are investigating IPv6 and planning to meet the mandate deadline.

- **Drivers:** The primary immediate driver remains the OMB mandate.

- **Deployment:** In the context of the OMB mandate requirements, the federal environment infrastructure should have IPv6 capabilities by June 2008. From an operational perspective, however, IPv6-based products and business solutions will emerge within and across the organizational boundaries two to three years past June 2008.

Although the OMB mandate is an important short-term driver for IPv6 adoption within the federal agencies, the Market Connections study indicates that at least 53 percent of the persons surveyed were somewhat or very likely to consider IPv6 independently of the mandate. IT strategists and technologists investigated the potential benefits and opportunities offered by IPv6. They came up with the following list of strategic benefits:

- **Provide a solution to the IP address shortage:** Addressing challenges are expected in the context of increasing infrastructure and increasing the number and types of devices connected to it.

- **Support for future service infrastructures:** IPv6 is seen to be very well suited to support the mass numbers of new services and new devices. In the case of DOT, IPv6 can provide the infrastructure for the services developed within the Intelligent Transportation Systems (ITS), the Vehicle Infrastructure Integration (VII) project, and the Next Generation Air Transportation System (NextGen). The Energy Sciences Network (ESnet), which is part of DOE, is one of the early adopters of IPv6. In February 2007 it established an IPv6 peering agreement with Global Crossing to extend the IPv6 services offered to its users.[44]

NOTE	More details on ITS and the related IEEE standards can be found in the "Intelligent Transportation Systems Standards Fact Sheet."[45]
	NextGen represents FAA's plan to modernize the National Airspace System through 2025. FAA plans to implement its next generation infrastructure goals through Performance-Based Navigation (PBN).[46] FAA pursues harmonization of NextGen with other similar projects such as EUROCONTROL. It is important to note that EUROCONTROL is actively pursuing the use of IPv6.[47]
	ESnet started using IPv6 as early as 1999.

- **Support large-scale networks:** IPv6 is investigated within the NITRD efforts related to scaling up the Internet DOE, for example, is a participant in these efforts.

44. "U.S. Department of Energy's ESnet Peers with Global Crossing to Support IPv6 Traffic Exchange," Global Crossing press release, February 19, 2007, http://www.globalcrossing.com/news/2007/february/19.aspx.

45. http://www.standards.its.dot.gov/fact_sheetp.asp?f=80.

46. "RNAV and RNP Evolution Through 2025," February 8, 2008, http://www.faa.gov/news/fact_sheets/news_story.cfm?newsId=8768.

47. Eivan Cerasi, "EUROCONTROL IPv6 Addressing and Autonomous System Numbers," ICAO ACP Sub-Working Group N-1 Working Paper 1108, November 9, 2006, http://roland.grc.nasa.gov/~ivancic/papers_presentations/2007/WP1108%20EUROCONTROL%20IPv6%20ASN%20Addressing_final.doc.

NOTE   For more information on the Large Scale Networking (LSN) efforts, refer to http://www.nitrd.gov/pubs/2008supplement/08-Supp-Web/ TOC%20Pages/08supp-LSN.pdf.

In spite of the common perception that the federal agencies are looking at the technology only because of the mandate, the innovation efforts actually started before the mandate and their focus goes beyond the requirements and the deadline imposed by it. Federal agencies understand that IPv6 adoption is necessary and include the technology in their planning. The adoption schedule, however, has to balance needs, costs, and availability of products. In 2007, the most pressing networking and application challenges were IP telephony and videoconferencing. Although IPv6 is taken into consideration in the search for a solution, these challenges must be addressed quickly and might not have hardened IPv6 solutions.

The Case for IPv6

At first sight it could be argued that the case for IPv6 was made for all civilian federal agencies by the OMB mandate. To a certain extent this is true; however, various agencies had an IPv6 vision or even worked on it for some time prior to the mandate. DOE is a good example. It acquired an IPv6 prefix in August 3, 1999, and performed experiments and tests within its ESnet. DOT acquired IPv6 address space as early as October 25, 2004, before the OMB mandate was announced. The mandate did provide a justification for early planning, but many agencies built a longer-term case for IPv6 adoption.

NOTE   In 1999, ESnet managed the main IPv6 peering point for 6bone (http://www.6tap.net).

The case made for IPv6 by federal agencies generally reflects both short- and long-term drivers:

- **Meet the OMB mandate requirements:** Every department must meet the requirements of the OMB mandate independent of its own considerations and plans for IPv6. The mandate helped accelerate and justify some of the IPv6 activities.

- **IPv6 is necessary for the future infrastructures:** IPv6's address resources are necessary for the multiple devices that are part of DOT's future ITS, VII project, and NextGen. Sensors, cameras, and other surveillance devices will have to be integrated in the IP infrastructure to monitor the assets and resources managed by DOE. IPv6 has the necessary addressing resources to integrate all these devices and reestablish a secure peer-to-peer model that opens the door to a new set of applications.

NOTE   IPv6 is taken into consideration in the R&D efforts of the agencies. DOT organizations, for example, include IPv6 requirements and support in technology analysis and research activities they lead. As an example, the Dedicated Short-Range Communications (DSRC) project (targeted for use in various aspects of transportation), originally sponsored by DOT and later migrated to the IEEE Standards Development Organization, has explicit IPv6 support requirements.

DOE's Oak Ridge National Laboratory is running the SensorNet project (http://www.sensornet.gov/), which could leverage 6LoWPAN sensor technologies.

The OMB mandate is a driver for an early update of the infrastructure and achieving IPv6 readiness. The business case for IPv6 adoption at production level reflects individual department goals and the specificities of the sector they cover. In this respect, individual business cases will show a certain level of variance and a longer-term perspective with a target of 2010 and beyond.

IPv6 Planning and Implementation

Federal agencies consist of multiple departments and organizations with specific needs and requirements. For this reason, these departments might develop their own IPv6 adoption strategies, though these plans will have to fit within the overall plan defined for the entire agency.

As an example, DOT's IPv6 plans can be correlated with information available through links in the R&D Information table of DOT's FY 2006 E-Government Act Report. Below is a summary of key IPv6 points aggregated from the DOT R&D sites.[48]

- **Forward and backward compatibility of systems:** IPv6 is backward compatible with IPv4 systems by design. IPv4 hosts must be able to communicate over IPv6 networks, which should represent minimum problems, given IPv6's design. The reverse presents a bit more involved examination. IPv6 must be able to communicate over an IPv4 connection and retain enough information to transition back to an IPv6 network, or through gateways communicate directly to an IPv4 network.

- **Transition existing applications:** The magnitude of accomplishing a change from IPv4 to IPv6 will entail a significant project management effort and coordination with internal and external resources.

- **Providing IP mobility:** IPv6 states it will allow for more secure network interaction and connectivity. This will permit DOT employees access to secure resources within the DOT network. Enabling IPv6 mobility will also provide the additional capability to support more robust remote access and telecommuting.

- **Procuring equipment to support IPv6 natively:** Devices/equipment will have to have dual capability in order to enable the smooth transition to IPv6—future procurements will need to ensure this dual capability and support backward compatibility.

- **Training the technical staff to implement:** Training in the basic understanding of the standard and its capabilities is important now, as well as in the transition strategies. DOT will develop a transition plan that has some flexibility to change as technology and best practices emerge.

48. http://www.dot.gov/webpoliciesnotices/dotegovactreport2006.pdf.

- **Having COTS applications that support IPv6 features:** Microsoft COTS products are predominant on DOT desktops and, to a lesser degree as server and database software. Microsoft has ensured that existing applications that support IPv4 will be able to run under IPv6 but without all the functionality/benefits of the new standards.

- **Application vendors:** Other application vendors will also be required to provide IPv6 support for any network centric application that will connect using the IP protocols.

DOT's global IPv6 strategy was detailed by each of its organizations and adapted to their specific needs. A good example in this context is the plan put in place by the FAA, which mapped DOT's IPv6 strategy to its own organization. On June 14, 2006, the FAA released its internal IPv6 Guidance memorandum stating:

> The purpose of this memorandum is to establish the Internet Protocol Version 6 (IPv6) guidance for the Federal Aviation Administration (FAA). This guidance will promote compliance with the attached documents: Department of Transportation's (DOT) IPv6 guidance memorandum, dated October 4, 2005, entitled DOT's Transition Planning for Internet Protocol Version 6 (IPv6); DOT's guidance memorandum, dated October 1, 2004, Guidelines for Information Technology (IT) Purchases; and the Office of Management and Budget's (OMB) guidance memorandum dated August 2, 2005, Transition Planning for Internet Protocol Version 6 (IPv6).

The memorandum also establishes one of the important steps in the IPv6 planning, providing the purchasing guidance that enables the organization to update equipment and applications to support IPv6:

> To facilitate this transition, it is the responsibility of the staff offices and lines of business to ensure that all future information technology procurements can use both IPv4 and IPv6 or uses native IPv6 protocol for communication with FAA networks. The procurement of IPv6 compatible IT will allow FAA to accomplish the transition to IPv6 through technology refresh cycles and spread the overall cost of this transition over a number of years.

The "2006 FAA R&D Annual Review" details its perspective and strategy on IPv6:[49]

> FAA planners also integrated IPv6 objectives into the Agency's Information Resources Management strategic plan and modified its Acquisition Management System policy to include language requiring IPv6 compatibility in future networking procurements. In addition, the FAA IPv6 Steering Committee developed an IPv6 Transition Plan that includes an IPv6 transition strategy, impact analysis, and asset inventory. The Steering Committee is currently working to:
>
> Define the IPv6 address allocation/management process,
>
> Define security strategy for IPv6 Internet Access Points,
>
> Establish IPv6 test beds at major centers,
>
> Test IPv6 hardware/software products,
>
> Develop configuration guidelines,
>
> Demonstrate 4 to 6 tunneling between IPv6 "clouds," and
>
> Develop detail transition plans and schedules thru June 2008.

The strategy outlined in the R&D review is concretely reflected in the FAA's Information Services Business Plans. In the 2006 business plan, the IPv6 inventory activities are listed as one of three activities in a proposed IT Asset Management Program. For 2006, two IPv6 transition activities were explicitly identified:

- Develop a final IPv6 inventory by June 30, 2006
- Develop an IPv6 transition plan by September 30, 2006

49. http://research.faa.gov/downloads/publications/annual/rdreview_annual_2006.pdf.

The IPv6 planning activities continued to be detailed in the 2007 business plan. The "IPv6 Transition Activities" section proposes the following:

- **Policies update:** Include the IPv6 objectives in FAA's Information Resources Management (IRM) strategic plan and in the Acquisition Management System (AMS) policies.

- **Progress update:** Quarterly IPv6 transition status reports will be sent to OMB.

FAA's IPv6 strategy and plans were developed within the framework established by the parent organization, DOT. Nevertheless, FAA's IPv6 efforts have aspects specific to its area of operation. Its interest in IPv6 matches similar interest by its European counterpart, EUROCONTROL, which pursues IPv6 for its future IT infrastructure.[50] For these organizations, IPv6 represents an opportunity to address the communications needs of today and of future air traffic control infrastructures.

NOTE	In November 25, 2004, DOT acquired its global IPv6 address space: 2001:19E8::/32.

DOE is the earliest adopter of IPv6 among U.S. civilian federal agencies. Its ESnet was a natural host for the new technology. IPv6 transport services are offered to DOE's researchers and the DOE-administered research laboratories. It was the OMB mandate, however, that kick-started the integration of IPv6-specific activities in the IT plans of various DOE organizations and projects. One such example is the FY2007–2008 plan of the Stockpile Stewardship Program (SSP) to integrate IPv6 in the Advanced Simulation and Computing (ASC) program, which is an essential environment for SSP's operation.[51] Another example is the extensive work done by Sandia National Laboratories (SNL) in collaboration with

---

50. Eivan Cerasi, "Focus on Air Traffic Control," June 2006, http://www.ipv6.eu/admin/bildbank/uploads/Documents/Vienna_June_2006/Session_4_Eivan_Cerasi_-_Eurocontrol.pdf.

51. "Advanced Simulation and Computing FY07–08 Implementation Plan," Volume 2, Rev. 0.5, October 18, 2006, http://www.llnl.gov/tid/lof/documents/pdf/338124.pdf.

ASC to investigate the benefits and challenges of deploying IPv6 and to make recommendations on adoption strategy.[52] SNL's report on IPv6 activities identifies the adoption steps followed or planned as of June 2006:

- **Understand and observe the NIST specifications:** Special consideration was given to the NIST guidelines in identifying the official interpretation of IPv6 readiness. It was recommended to identify the IPv6 readiness characteristics specific to SNL.

- **Develop an IPv6 addressing scheme:** The IPv6 addressing architecture was analyzed along with the various address provisioning tools available in IPv6 to decide which will best suit this environment. The decision process was thoroughly documented.

- **Test the environment:** A small-scale test environment was set up to test router, host, DNS, and NTP configurations and operation. Applications were also evaluated. WAN testing was performed in collaboration with ASC. The results of the tests executed were thoroughly documented.

- **Evaluate IPv6 integration costs:** The network hardware costs for the SNL environment were estimated at approximately $1 million. Other costs related to the integration of IPv6 were identified.

- **Define the deployment schedule:** A detailed plan and schedule was put in place for the rollout of IPv6 throughout the entire infrastructure.

Such efforts with various organizations and programs provide a wealth of expertise and experience that can help the entire department define an envelope strategy and plan for the integration of IPv6 according to the perceived need and demand. This plan will of course have to meet the OMB mandate requirements by June 2008.

NOTE	DOE was one of the first U.S. civilian federal agencies to acquire IPv6 address space. In August 1999, it received 2001:400::/32 from ARIN.

52. John M. Eldridge and others, "A Report on IPv6 Deployment Activities and Issues at Sandia National Laboratories: FY2007," June 2006, http://www.prod.sandia.gov/cgi-bin/techlib/access-control.pl/2007/074476.pdf.

SSA emerged as one of the early adopters of IPv6 within the U.S. government. Without benefiting from additional, dedicated funding, SSA defined and implemented a well-planned IPv6 integration strategy. Its work and experiences were well publicized in various magazines catering to IT specialists in the government agencies. One of these articles identifies SSA's IPv6 integration strategy and long term plans for:[53]

- **Inventory:** SSA performed an extensive inventory of its infrastructure to identify the devices requiring hardware and software upgrades to support the required IPv6 features.

- **Hardware and software upgrade:** Upgrades were actively pursued through the regular refresh cycles, thus ensuring the IPv6 readiness of the infrastructure backbone without additional costs.

- **Testing:** An environment consisting of 20 to 30 routers running dual-stack was set up to gain familiarity with the protocol and identify deployment and operational challenges.

- **Request dual-stack services from SP:** SSA placed clear requirements with its service providers for upgrading its WAN connectivity to dual-stack.

- **Training:** SSA started training its IT staff early and by July 2007 it had 150 of its engineers go through basic IPv6 training.

In the long term, SSA plans are to meet the OMB mandate June 2008 deadline by enabling IPv6 in its backbone. By 2010 SSA plans to offer dual-stack services to other agencies over its extranet. SSA expects to have all its field offices dual-stacked by 2012.

NOTE   In February 2004, SSA received the IPv6 address allocation 2001:1930::/32.

---

53. Carolyn Duffy Marsan, "Government Agency Details Its Experience of IPv6 Deployment," *Network World*, July 19, 2006, http://www.networkworld.com/newsletters/isp/2006/0717isp1.html.

Most planning and implementation efforts revolve around deploying IPv6 in campus networks. From a WAN connectivity perspective, IPv6 transport service availability does not appear to generally be a concern. Commitment to support IPv6 was one of the selection criteria for service providers bidding for governments Networx contracts. It is expected that major U.S. providers will offer IPv6 services in time to meet the OMB mandate deadline.

Overall, the IPv6 activities of various U.S. government agencies highlighted several challenges:

- **Security:** Security remains one of the items at the top of the list of concerns for IPv6 adopters. Concerns relate to new, IPv6-specific threats and to what is perceived to be inadequate support for needed security features.

- **Applications dependency on IPv4:** Applications inventory reveals that many applications are not IP version agnostic and that adapting them would be difficult and costly.

- **Equipment support for IPv6:** Not all features and capabilities required or of interest are available in networking and IT equipment. Vendors are waiting for market demand before developing some of these features.

- **IPv6 support in standards:** Government agencies implement and observe many technical standards not related to IETF where IPv6 was developed. It was found that some of these non-IETF standards might lack support for IPv6, which in turn implies that related products will not support the new version of IP either.

- **Compatibility with corporate information systems:** Compatibility of IPv6 with the existing IT frameworks needs to be analyzed in detail to fully understand the technical and policy implications of its deployment.

While these challenges might be experienced by most agencies, early evaluations of the new protocol are essential in identifying challenging aspects that are specific to each environment.

It is important to highlight the value of the work done by both NIST and JITC in defining what "IPv6 capable" means for the U.S. federal agencies, civilian and defense respectively. Prior to the release of recommendations by NIST[54] and JITC[55], the IPv6 strategies of the federal agencies had a hard time crystallizing around a more concrete target than the general requirements of the OMB and DoD mandates. The documents from NIST and JITC went beyond being a mere list of all IPv6-related RFCs to identify realistic targets and expectations for feature support in the context of the mandates. These documents and all their subsequent revisions that integrate the industry feedback are valuable references for any organization planning to deploy IPv6.

Lessons Learned

Many of the federal agencies who took on the role of IPv6 early adopter have often done the same thing in the past with other technologies or applications. These organizations are familiar with both the challenges and opportunities of early adoption and have generally demonstrated strong commitment to modernizing their IT infrastructures and to pursuing new IP-enabled services.

While some of these agencies started evaluating IPv6 before 2005, the OMB mandate provides additional momentum and validation for their efforts. They not only took on the task of figuring out the challenges of deploying IPv6 within their environments, they also actively shared their experience with other agencies, thus acting as catalysts for IPv6 efforts across the entire U.S. government agencies. The lessons they learned at various stages along the road of implementing their IPv6 strategy are for the most part applicable to all the other agencies.

SSA identified the following tips related to IPv6 adoption:[56]

- **Update the IPv4 environment:** Start the IPv6 adoption by cleaning the existing IPv4 environment and by bringing it up to some of the latest, proven IPv4 technologies. This first step will simplify the integration of IPv6 in a modern and competitive architecture.

54. Stephen Nightingale and others, "A Profile for IPv6 in the U.S. Government (Draft) – Version 1.0," February 22, 2007 (NIST Special Publication 500-267), http://www.antd.nist.gov/usgv6-v1-draft.pdf.

55. David B. Green, ed., "DoD IPv6 Standard Profiles for IPv6 Capable Products Version 1.0 (Release Candidate)," May 1, 2006, http://jitc.fhu.disa.mil/adv_ip/register/docs/disr_ipv6_product_profile_draft.pdf.

56. See note 39 earlier.

- **Dual-stack strategy:** Based on its vision of the IP infrastructure and the results of its lab tests, SSA prefers a dual-stack approach to deploying IPv6.

- **Leverage the tech refresh cycle:** Use the standard refresh cycle in conjunction with purchasing policy updates to make the infrastructure hardware and software IPv6 ready.

- **Go slow:** It is important to start the IPv6 adoption process early in order to learn about its capabilities, to investigate the various integration options, to test its readiness for the targeted environment, and to have sufficient time to take advantage of refresh cycles for upgrades. IPv6 deployment is a multiyear, complex process.

Nevertheless, identifying concrete applications and services that would immediately benefit from IPv6 within an agency such as SSA is not always easy.[57] The deployment of IPv6, however, does provide an environment for continued innovation while meeting the mandate deadlines.

Other lessons learned that were mentioned by several agencies include the following:

- **Availability of equipment with required IPv6 features and capabilities:** Several of the devices currently in the infrastructure and targeted to support the dual-stack deployment do not meet the expectations of certain federal agencies. By starting early to work closely with product vendors, federal agencies can help prioritize development to address their needs timely.

- **Applications availability:** This point, highlighted explicitly by SSA's experience but identified by other agencies as well, refers to the difficulty to identify the services and applications that should be enabled right away over IPv6. In many cases, applications of interest are not implemented over IPv6.

---

57. Carolyn Duffy Marsan, "An Inconvenient Truth About IPv6," *Network World*, August 2, 2006, http://www.networkworld.com/newsletters/isp/2006/0731isp1.html?page=1.

- **IPv6 and other standards:** IPv6 is only a foundation technology. To get IPv6 included in all standards observed and implemented by the federal agencies, the protocol has to be mastered by the IT staff participating in the non-IETF standards bodies.

- **Security and management remain a concern:** Many agencies identified security and network management as the most significant challenges in relation to IPv6 network transport. This is primarily due to inconsistent support of features and lack of well-defined architectures for these aspects of IPv6, other than the ones currently in place for IPv4.

In spite of all the challenges, early adopters are forging the way toward wide adoption of IPv6 within the U.S. government IT environment. Its future infrastructure stands to benefit greatly from the new protocol and the IP convergence of communications technologies. A phased approach to the IPv6 integration will ensure the success of the deployment. At first the focus should be on meeting the OMB mandate deadline of June 2008 and readying the infrastructure for IPv6. After that will come more complex steps with the deployment of applications and services over the IPv6-enabled network.

Information Technology—Networking: Cisco Systems

> To keep the human network running as the global growth engine it has become, we must integrate and transition to IPv6. IPv4 simply cannot keep up with the potential change that the network will create.

—Craig Huegen, Cisco, Director IT Network Architecture

The Internet Protocol has become an intrinsic component of most if not all information communications technology companies today. For evident business reasons, they are naturally aware, through the requirements placed on their products, of changes and developments of IP. Although applications developers can be to a certain extent independent of the lower-layer protocols, IP is at the center of business for networking equipment manufacturers. IPv6 awareness is without a doubt very high in this market segment.

Awareness, however, does not equate to the business priority of IPv6 superseding that of other technologies. The need for IPv6 support might be closely monitored but it has to fit in product roadmaps together with ongoing market requests for new IPv4 features. The integration of IPv6 in networking products requires significant and sustained investment. It requires engineering resources that would be used otherwise to implement or improve IPv4 features. It requires hardware design with IPv6 in mind in order to deal with the new protocol's specific characteristics. The decision to make these investments must be backed up by business demand.

Before 2003, companies with a geographically limited market space—focused on U.S. enterprises, for example—most likely experienced little pressure to support and implement IPv6 in their products. On the other hand, as early as 2000, businesses with global market coverage were exposed to strong IPv6 support requirements from theaters such as Asia-Pacific and Europe despite little interest from other regions. This drove some networking companies to start early on to integrate IPv6 in their product lines according to demand.

Customers expect the networking equipment to perform in IPv6 at least as well as it does in IPv4. Such level of feature and performance parity requires multiple product development cycles. To stay competitive, networking equipment manufacturers do not have the luxury to wait for market adoption acceleration or, even worse, for mass adoption due to IPv4 address exhaustion. They must start early to develop the IPv6 expertise and to systematically integrate it in products. Along with product planning, networking companies must plan the deployment of IPv6 over their internal IT infrastructures. Their adoption of IPv6 is essential for several reasons:

- **Infrastructure for IPv6 developers and testers:** Development and test groups working on IPv6 require a certain level of internal and external IPv6 connectivity and accessibility.

- **Improve IPv6 support in products:** The internal IT infrastructure most likely leverages networking equipment manufactured by the company. Internal use helps test and improve the product in parallel with the market.

- **IPv6 expertise of customer support organization:** The support organization must receive IPv6 training and develop the expertise to reproduce customers' issues and provide configuration assistance. To perform their job function, support engineers might also have to connect to a given customer site via IPv6.

- **Marketing:** Demonstrate successful deployment and operation by, to put it in simple terms, "drinking your own wine."

- **Online experience:** Similar to many other companies today, networking companies rely on the Internet to conduct their business and interact with customers (provide information or sell products). Lack of IPv6 support by the company Internet portal will lead to lost customers and business.

The focus of this case study is not a networking company's planning of IPv6 support on products but rather its business case for integrating IPv6 in its own IT infrastructure.

There are many networking equipment manufacturers worldwide and their level of IPv6 readiness varies. Whereas some have not yet started to integrate IPv6 in products, others are focusing primarily on IPv6, seeing it as an opportunity to gain technology leadership and break into a highly competitive market space. The same variety characterizes the internal adoption of IPv6.

This case study covers the leading networking equipment manufacturer: Cisco Systems, Inc. It is developed with the assistance of Craig Huegen, Director IT Network Architecture.

Company Profile

According to its corporate information page:

> Cisco Systems, Inc. is the worldwide leader in networking for the Internet. Today, networks are an essential part of business, education, government and home communications, and Cisco Internet Protocol-based (IP) networking solutions are the foundation of these networks. Cisco hardware, software, and service offerings are used to create Internet solutions that allow individuals, companies, and countries to increase productivity, improve customer satisfac-

tion and strengthen competitive advantage. The Cisco name has become synonymous with the Internet, as well as with the productivity improvements that Internet business solutions provide. At Cisco, our vision is to change the way people work, live, play and learn.[58]

Cisco grew with the Internet from its beginnings to become the leading provider of networking equipment. It naturally evolved alongside IP from a data-forwarding-centric product line to providing end-to-end solutions for delivering voice, audio, and video services. This growth brought Cisco closer and closer to the consumer and to multimedia services, a trend reflected in its most notable recent acquisitions: Linksys and Scientific Atlanta.

Cisco Systems corporate profile is summarized in Table 5-29.

Table 5-29 *Cisco Systems Corporate Profile Overview*

Profile Category	Status/Value
Organization	Cisco Systems, Inc.
Industry	Networking and communications
Number of employees	63,050
Geography	Global
Revenue	$34.9 billion
Total market share per segment	73% routers; 73% Ethernet switches; 65% WLAN; 51% home networking; 23% VoIP

NOTE All data in Table 5-29 is up to date as of the end of Cisco Systems' fiscal year in 2007. The sources for the market share data are Dell'Oro Group (http://www.delloro.com/), Synergy Research Group (http://www.srgresearch.com/), and NPD Group (http://www.npd.com/).

58. http://newsroom.cisco.com/dlls/corpinfo/factsheet.html.

Cisco is at the forefront of innovation in IP communications and services. In 2006 it invested more than $4 billion in research and development, with R&D facilities in San Jose, CA; Boxborough, MA; Richardson, TX; Lawrenceville, GA; Raleigh, NC; Bangalore, India; Shanghai, China; and Herzliya, Israel. Cisco has also incorporated leading technologies and innovation by acquiring over 108 companies since 1993. Its engineers are active contributors to the Internet standardization bodies.

Cisco perceives the network as being more than an infrastructure; the network is a secure platform that delivers a personalized and customized user experience. IP and its evolution are essential to Cisco's business and operation.

IT Profile

Cisco's global presence and highly mobile workforce require a robust and extensive IT infrastructure. Moreover, Cisco is promoting internally all the enabling features, services, and applications it advertises to its enterprise customers. Many of its operational activities are automated and virtualized over its internal IP infrastructure. All voice services are IP based and remote collaboration is facilitated through multicast services and Cisco Telepresence. These few examples indicate the fact that Cisco is implementing internally the next generation enterprise networks.

In the software, hardware development, and manufacturing market space, Cisco runs one of the largest IT infrastructures, with 400 worldwide sites. From an asset type and distribution perspective, Cisco's IT profile is summarized in Table 5-30.

Table 5-30 *Cisco Systems IT Profile—Assets*

Device Type	Number of Devices
Managed workstations and PCs	60,000
Servers	8000
IP phones	60,000
Routers and switches	5500
Unmanaged devices	15,000–20,000

The OSs currently deployed in the Cisco infrastructure and those it plans to use going forward are listed in Table 5-31.

Table 5-31   Cisco Systems IT Profile—Operating Systems

Device Type	Today	Future
PC and workstations	Windows 2003, Windows XP	Windows Vista (from 2007)
	Linux	Linux
	Solaris	
Servers	Windows Server 2003	Windows Server 2008
Routers and switches	Cisco IOS, CatOS	Cisco IOS, IOS-XE, and NX-OS

NOTE   Vista trials started in 2006 and the deployment is timed with the laptop refresh cycle because Vista has certain hardware requirements such as memory size and graphic cards.

Cisco's IT infrastructure supports a variety of web-based business applications that use Oracle 11i. Many of them have a thin client (web browser) like architecture and are internally developed. Even though most applications are developed to take advantage of a layer of abstraction from the IP network layer, currently there are no policies in place to explicitly enforce applications development in an IP version–agnostic manner. Many of the typical enterprise applications, such as Outlook, Exchange, Windows Media, SSH terminated access, PC backup applications, and so forth, are also deployed and managed by the IT department.

IP Infrastructure Characteristics

To support its operations and workforce, Cisco deploys a large Layer 2 switched and Layer 3 IP infrastructure. The network architecture implements recommended design guidelines for enterprise networks.

The IPv4 address management has the following characteristics:

- **Address lifetime:** Most endpoints are dynamically assigned temporary addresses. Network elements and devices in the data centers use fixed IP addresses. Endpoints with stationary, manually configured IP addresses are devices such as those used in building automation (badge access control, security cameras, sensors, and so on).

- **Address types:** Cisco IT is using both global IPv4 addresses and private (RFC 1918) IPv4 addresses.

- **Global IPv4 addresses management:** Very conservative address assignment policies are implemented in order to ensure very good utilization of the address space. Historically Cisco has been requesting public address space from the RIR every three to five years.

- **Addressing scheme:** The addressing scheme reflects geographical and topological boundaries. It enforces strong aggregation rules that lead to only 600 IP routes in the network backbone.

Figure 5-8 shows Cisco's global IPv4 address space consumption between 2000 and 2007.

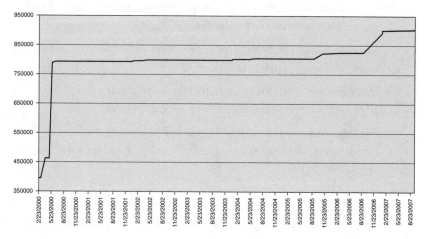

Figure 5-8   *Historical Data on Cisco's Global IPv4 Address Space Consumption*

NOTE	With the rapid proliferation of IP devices, Cisco's IT department expects to request global IPv4 address space more often, every 18 months.

Based on past experience, Cisco was able to avoid IPv4 address shortages and major renumbering events by designing and implementing a very good address plan. Integration of infrastructures from mergers and acquisitions is made easier to a certain extent by having the data center servers on prefixes that are easy to inject into the new networks. Moreover, as of late, companies that are acquired typically use RFC 1918 internally, so they can be renumbered and integrated in Cisco's addressing scheme.

Cisco's IT infrastructure is self-managed. A dedicated department provides security policies, manages incidents, and identifies requirements and configuration guidelines, which are implemented in partnership with the IT department.

In the opinion of Cisco's IT department, the primary challenge to the IPv4 infrastructure is posed by device proliferation:

- **Remote access:** More and more employees are accessing the corporate network and resources remotely, using multiple types of devices and maintaining sessions for long periods of time.

- **Wireless access:** With wireless access, mobile devices require twice as many addresses even when docked.

- **Voice devices:** VoIP led to a rapidly increasing number of voice devices. IP phones hold IP addresses for long periods of time.

- **Sensors:** Many of the sensors used in manufacturing, building management, and asset tracking are now using IP and they require fixed IP addresses.

The IT department also believes that even better summarization and an even cleaner architecture could be achieved for the IP addressing scheme if a larger address space were available.

Perspective on IPv6

Craig Huegen, in his role of managing Cisco's IT architecture, is interacting with peers in many other large IT organizations. His design and operational expertise is valued by Cisco's enterprise customers. Craig makes the following points with respect to IPv6 in the enterprise market:

- **Interest:** Over 70 percent of enterprises will ask about and investigate IPv6 in the 2007–2008 timeframe.

- **Drivers:** Government procurement and deployment of Windows Vista and Longhorn will push enterprises to deploy IPv6.

- **Deployment:** Over 70 percent of enterprises will have deployed IPv6 by 2010–2012.

So where does Cisco IT stand with respect to these three points?

Interest in IPv6 for the internal infrastructure was first expressed in 2003, while interest in IPv6 support for the development environment was expressed as early as 1996.

Figure 5-9 is a conceptual representation of the way the Cisco IT department provides internal IPv6 connectivity and access to the IPv6 Internet.

Cisco engineers had internal IPv6 connectivity, IPv6 Internet access, and IPv6 access from home over the corporate network since 1998.

By 2007, the motivation for deploying IPv6 became more diverse and it relates to the following aspects of the IP upgrade:

- **Device proliferation:** This is perceived as both a threat in the context of expected IPv4 address shortages and an opportunity in the context of a significantly larger IPv6 address space.

- **Simplicity of network operation:** The larger address space enables cleaner designs and easy management of all assets with a net benefit of reduced cost of operations.

- **Emergence of Windows Vista:** Several new features from Microsoft Windows Vista are still not yet fully evaluated by any IT department— for example, the Peer-to-Peer Networking framework that is leveraged by certain Microsoft applications. There is a stringent need for tools that will allow network managers to keep control of the traffic generated by Vista users.

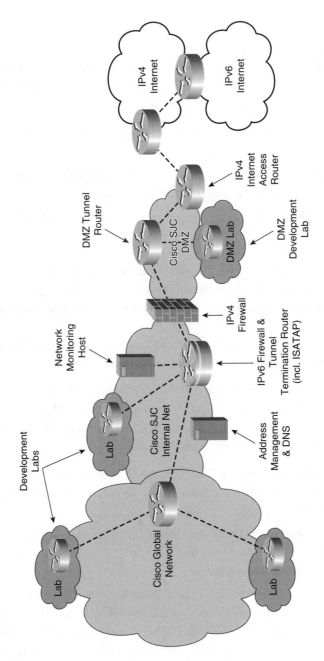

Figure 5-9 *Conceptual Depiction of Cisco's Internal IPv6 Infrastructure*

Drivers for IPv6 adoption in the IT infrastructure are both internal (engineering, customer support requiring connectivity, deployment of Vista) and external (Cisco customers are interested in its experience with the new protocol). Some of these drivers were met by Cisco's IT department providing IPv6 connectivity to employees since 1998. This was achieved by connecting Cisco to the 6bone and offering peering services to several other test sites.

The Case for IPv6

While Cisco made a clear business case for integrating IPv6 in its product line very early on, making a business case for its deployment in the internal, corporate network is a different matter. The early requests for IPv6 features in networking equipment were received from service providers in Asia-Pacific while interest from enterprises was nonexistent. Similar to any enterprise, the Cisco IT department could not justify the investment in an IPv6 deployment without a clear business need.

The general benefits of being an early planner or an early adopter of IPv6 were considered:

- **Staying competitive:** The IPv6 upgrade is a multiyear effort. If started late, it can put an organization behind its competition. An IPv6-ready infrastructure provides agility to an organization; it has the ability to support new applications as soon as they become available or of interest to users.

- **IPv6 access in regions with accelerated adoption:** Linking Cisco's network to regions where IPv6 is quickly becoming an incumbent technology will become a requirement to succeed in a Global Economy.

- **Reduced deployment costs:** Early planning reduces infrastructure investments by acquiring IPv6-capable equipment through the regular refresh cycle.

- **Stimulate innovation:** The extended and feature-rich infrastructure supports and stimulates innovations such as large-scale Cisco telepresence deployment.

In Cisco's case, besides the above list of generic benefits of IPv6 early adoption, there is a set of more compelling, strategic reasons for deploying IPv6 in the corporate network:

- **"Drink your own wine":** Even if the business case for IPv6 is not clear before the upgrade to Vista and before getting applications running over IPv6, one of the best ways to demonstrate seamless integration and support is to show it in your own network. Cisco has been doing this with many other enterprise features and services, such as VoIP.

- **Stimulate adoption by setting an example:** More and more customers are asking Cisco's IT architect about the IPv6 vision, plans, and experience for Cisco's IT infrastructure.

- **Maintain the role of trusted advisor:** Based on expertise and experience, the Cisco IT department takes an advisor role in many customer environments. This level of authority in the IT community must be maintained in the context of an IP upgrade.

The business case for IPv6 adoption revolves more around strategic, long-term targets, and this is reflected in the deployment timeline.

IPv6 Planning and Implementation

Defining a business case for IPv6 is just the first step in initiating the work on an IPv6 strategy. The deployment strategy is shaped by the perceived obstacles in integrating IPv6 in the existent infrastructure. In order of their priority, Cisco's IT department identifies the following challenges:

- **Training:** Bringing the staff up to speed on IPv6.

- **Lack of features widely used in IPv4:** The experience of running a stable IPv4 network for several years leads network designers and administrators to demand certain IPv4 features to be supported in IPv6 as well. Some of these features might not yet have been implemented or fully implemented in products.

- **Performance of the infrastructure:** IPv6 must coexist with IPv4; it should not impact any of the existent services and applications.

Cisco's strategy reflects its understanding of both IPv6's importance and the challenges it presents. It is a phased approach that in the short run addresses immediate connectivity needs while in the long run addresses the need for a dual-stack environment. The phases of this strategy are described in Table 5-32.

Table 5-32   *Cisco Systems' Strategy for Deploying IPv6 in the Corporate Network*

Phase 1 (1998–Present)	Phase 2 (2005–2007)	Phase 3 (2008 Onward)
Initial IPv6 connectivity through 6bone peering. Acquired IPv6 address space in early 2000. Renumber internal IPv6 users from 3FFE to 2001:420::. Provide IPv6 connectivity to users via ISATAP tunnels. Provide connectivity to the IPv6 Internet.	Upgrade the entire Layer 2 (Catalyst 6500, Sup720) and Layer 3 infrastructure, through the refresh cycle, to include support for IPv6. Network is ready for IPv6 deployment. Trial Windows Vista. Include IPv6 in Requests For Information to ISPs providing services to Cisco's IT department.	2008: Deploy Windows Vista. 2008: Provide native IPv6 internal access service, starting with labs, followed by users and data centers. 2008: Interim external services via IPv6 on separate hosting/ application infrastructure. 2009: Dual-stack presence for external services. Deploy IPv6 on a service-by-service basis.

NOTE   As early as June 14, 2000, Cisco acquired its provider independent global IPv6 address space from ARIN: 2001:420/32. Cisco's IT department engaged with its service providers regarding the availability of IPv6 services. The main concern identified is the fact that SPs did not guarantee the same level of operational support for the new dual-stack access as the one offered before for the IPv4-only access.

This phased approach enabled the IT department to minimize upgrade costs and to train its staff.

Lessons Learned

The large-scale deployment of IPv6 in the Cisco IT infrastructure is an ongoing project. This effort is carefully orchestrated to meet the enterprise IPv6 strategy and needs with minimal dedicated investment and minimal disruption to existent services.

The most important lessons learned from the Cisco IT experience are as follows:

- **The value of early planning:** The Cisco IT department monitored closely both the service provider and the enterprise market interest in IPv6 based on worldwide customer requests for IPv6 support in Cisco products and based on internal demand. Even prior to the emergence of a strong business case for internal deployment, IPv6 support was made a requirement in all infrastructure upgrades. The enterprise network became fully IPv6 ready in 2006 with no IPv6-specific investments.

- **The value of a phased approach:** The phased approach to offering IPv6 service addressed internal needs without jeopardizing the quality of existent services and without reactive, short-term investments. Tunneling was used to cater the initial sparse population of users, Internet access was added to internal connectivity, and the infrastructure was prepared for a dual-stack deployment.

- **The value of internal evaluations:** Each phase of the IPv6 service rollout has been used as an evaluation ground for various aspects of the protocol and its interaction with IPv4. IPv6 access to Cisco's web page was trialed internally to understand the operational and support implications. Windows Vista is trialed internally to fully understand the requirements for its smooth and secure integration in the IT network.

Cisco's leadership role in both developing the IPv6 protocol and supporting it in networking products matches its vision of the Internet and the needs of its customers. Cisco's IT department is a Cisco customer itself and, in accordance with the operational principles of any major enterprise, it systematically planned the infrastructure upgrade and took a pragmatic perspective to IPv6 adoption. Cisco's internal network is IPv6 ready and is in the process of migrating from a sparse IPv6 population to a dual-stack environment.

Global Engineering and Construction: Bechtel Corporation

> Bechtel is clearly a global corporate leader in enterprise IPv6 deployment. Our pragmatic approach has minimized cost and risk while concurrently developing a corporate competence in the new protocol. The start of our IPv6 deployment initiative in 2005 was timed right. While installing IPv6 has been successful, the real value is in positioning the company well to capitalize on the network-based applications and innovations of the future.
>
> —Fred Wettling, Bechtel Fellow

Company Profile

Headquartered in San Francisco, Bechtel is one of the world's premier engineering, construction, and project management companies. Since its founding in 1898, Bechtel has worked on more than 22,000 projects in 140 countries on all seven continents. Today Bechtel's 42,500 employees are teamed with customers, partners, and suppliers on hundreds of projects in nearly 50 countries.

The project-based nature of Bechtel's business demands a high level of agility not found in most companies. Many projects are started or completed each year. Complex projects require concurrent participation from multiple companies at many locations around the globe. Within this volatile environment, Bechtel relies on state-of-the-art technology to deliver engineering and construction projects to its customers. Technology drives its business—it speeds schedules, cuts costs, and ensures quality. Technology enables increasingly complex design work, brings Bechtel's global offices and personnel together, and maximizes productivity for a range of internal operations and external transactions with clients, suppliers, and contractors. To make the best use of cutting-edge technology, Bechtel is hard at work developing information systems and implementing e-business initiatives to support key priorities. Its corporate profile is summarized in Table 5-33.

Table 5-33 *Bechtel Corporate Profile Overview*

Profile Category	Status/Value
Organization	Bechtel Corporation
Industry	Engineering, construction, project management
Products	Roads and rail systems
	Airports and seaports
	Fossil and nuclear power plants
	Refineries and petrochemical facilities
	Mines and smelters
	Defense and aerospace facilities
	Environmental cleanup projects
	Communications
	Pipelines
	Oil and gas field development
Number of employees	42,500
Geography	Global
Revenue	$27 billion (2007)
New work booked	$34.1 billion (2007)

Maintaining industry leadership for generations requires constant attention to evolutions in business, project execution, labor force, technology, and other models within the context of the global economy and customer needs. Technology evolution applied to the business has become an increasingly significant ingredient in helping Bechtel maintain its industry leadership position in the services it provides to its customers.

Network and IT Profile

Dozens of projects with varying durations are executed concurrently around the globe with different customers, partners, and suppliers. Some projects are executed in a single location, while others have active engineering activities at multiple locations at once. Bechtel's project-centric business model with multiple global business units demands a high level of agility and intercompany collaboration in the company's Information Systems & Technology (IS&T) products and services.

Bechtel's IS&T organization provides orchestrated information systems, information technology, and business advocacy products and services to the company. Senior IT managers interface directly with executives of the company's global business units to ensure industry-specific needs are recognized and addressed. Corporate systems and infrastructure organizations provide applications and infrastructure that is used across business units. Project IT is responsible for delivery of IT products and services at Bechtel project sites. Continuous integration and collaboration occurs across the IS&T organization and with the business units and corporate services.

Bechtel's IPv6 initiative is sponsored out of the corporate information technology group responsible for enterprise infrastructure. Participants from other parts of IS&T and the company at large have been engaged throughout the life cycle of the effort.

This section highlights the infrastructure leveraged across business units and around the planet to serve the company's permanent and field operations. Table 5-34 summarizes Bechtel-owned assets at permanent Bechtel offices. Customer-owned assets at Bechtel-managed facilities are not included.

Table 5-34   *Bechtel Information Systems & Technology Profile—Assets*

Device Type	Number of Devices
Managed workstations and PCs	20,000
Servers	2000
IP phones	12,000
Routers and switches	1500
Wireless access points	400
Other managed devices	3000
Major global data centers	8
NOC/SOC	2
Applications	1000

Basic IPv6 features are available in today's OSs and have been noticeably improving with new major OS releases, such as Vista. Deploying IPv6 and capitalizing on new IPv6 features are throttled to some degree by lack of features in legacy products. For example, if an OS does not support address assignment through DHCPv6, an organization may need to use stateless address autoconfiguration for address assignment until DHCPv6-capable host OSs are widely deployed.

The OSs currently deployed in Bechtel's infrastructure and those it plans to use going forward are listed in Table 5-35 .

Table 5-35 *Bechtel IP Infrastructure Profile—Operating Systems*

Device Type	Today	Future
Desktops, laptops, and workstations	Windows XP, Windows Vista	Windows Vista, 64-bit processors
Mobile	Windows Mobile 2003, 5, and 6, Blackberry	Windows Mobile 6, Blackberry, others
Servers	Windows Server 2000, Windows Server 2003, HP-UX	Windows Server 2003, Windows Server 2008, increasing 64-bit
Routers and switches	Cisco IOS, Cisco CatOS	Cisco IOS

IP Infrastructure Characteristics

Bechtel's project-based business has prompted the company to look at addressing from the perspective of an ISP in its operations. IPv6 addressing makes the job much easier. Permanent offices naturally grow and shrink with project workload. In a growth mode, population increases sometimes require occupancy in new buildings in or near a campus, or even in another country. Bechtel projects have a life cycle in the field where communications are established, operated during field operations, and finally terminated. During these cycles, addresses are assigned, managed, and at the end of their use reclaimed for allocation to a future project or office. While some of Bechtel's projects last for years, others have a field lifespan measured in weeks or months. The constant flux in address allocations associated with project turnover and permanent office population growth and shrinkage is a challenge with IPv4, and has caused fragmentation (noncontiguous address blocks).

The use of IPv6 has eliminated the need for project or office fragmentation. Bechtel allocates a /48 block to each individual site that will be used by that location as long as it exists. The size is adequate for any foreseeable future site requirements without the need for additional allocations...very clean addressing.

Based on the ISP model in which Bechtel operates hundreds of concurrent projects, the company applied to ARIN for a provider-independent IPv6 address block. The request was approved in July 2005 and ARIN allocated 2001:4920::/32 to Bechtel.

IPv6 addressing introduces new opportunities, including improved efficiencies. However, the effective and efficient introduction of IPv6 into an enterprise requires thinking in new paradigms, starting with the actual address blocks that will be used. Bechtel uses a mix of public and private IPv4 addresses, as highlighted in Table 5-36.

Table 5-36   *Bechtel IP Addresses*

Type	IPv4	IPv6
Global range: direct assignment	147.1.0.0/16	2001:4920::/32
RIR assignment	ARIN: March 11, 1991	ARIN: July 21, 2005
Global range: carrier	Allocated from carrier IPv4 address space for some WAN traffic	Peering to advertise Bechtel global addresses
Other address ranges	Private addressing 10/8, 172.16/12, 192.168/16	Link-local, unique-local
Autonomous System Number (ASN)	2615 ARIN: April 29, 1993	2615

Bechtel's IP address allocation and management has the current and future characteristics shown in Table 5-37. The transition to the future state will occur over time, based in part on product availability.

Table 5-37 *Bechtel IP Address Allocation and Management*

Type/System	Timeframe	IPv4	IPv6
IP addresses	2007 and future	Mix of private and global IP addresses	System-generated IPv6 link-local addresses, global IP addresses
User devices (desktops, laptops, and workstations, IP phones, cell phones, PDAs, network cameras)	2007	DHCP	Stateless address autoconfiguration
	Future	DHCP	Stateless address autoconfiguration, DHCPv6 after 2008, MIPv6 for portable devices
Printer, FAX, scanner	2007	Static addresses	Stateless address autoconfiguration
	Future	Static addresses, possibly DHCP	Stateless address autoconfiguration, DHCPv6 after 2008
Servers	2007	Static addresses	Stateless address autoconfiguration
	Future	Static addresses	Stateless address autoconfiguration, DHCPv6 after 2008
Routers and switches	2007	Static addresses	Static addresses for fixed devices
	Future	Static addresses	Static addresses for fixed devices, stateless address autoconfiguration, NEMO/MIPv6 for mobile networking
DNS/DDNS	2007	Windows Server 2003 DNS using IPv4 transport	Windows Server 2003 DNS using IPv4 transport
	Future	Windows Server 2008 DNS using IPv4 transport	Windows Server 2008 DNS using IPv6 transport

Table 5-37 *Bechtel IP Address Allocation and Management (Continued)*

Type/System	Timeframe	IPv4	IPv6
Address management	2007	In-house systems for address allocation and mapping, including static IP address assignment	In-house systems for address allocation and mapping, including static IP address assignment
	Future	Commercial IP address management (IPAM) software integrated with Active Directory/DNS services	Commercial IPAM integrated with Active Directory/DNS services

Bechtel's IPv6 core team discussed and debated IPv6 addressing schemes for months, and finally contracted a consulting firm, Command Information (the subject of the final case study), to provide insight and help in finalizing the plan. The process highlighted a real need for a paradigm shift in how IPv6 addresses should be allocated. Bechtel's IPv6 address allocation guidelines are aligned with IETF standards, RIR policies, industry best practices, and the company's business needs. This approach helps ensure smooth deployment of IPv6-enabled products and services within the company and with its providers and business partners:

- Separate high-level blocks are used for permanent Bechtel offices, IPv6 labs, and project/customer sites.

- Bechtel defines a site as a physical location, delivery address, or contiguous campus, and each site can be related directly to a site in Microsoft Active Directory Sites and Services.

- Each site will receive a /48 assignment.

- Bechtel uses enterprise-wide aggregation-level patterns of /56 or larger for common functions such as general host assignments, DMZ, real-time traffic (voice and video), and network loopback addresses/link space.

- No subnets will use prefixes longer than /64.

- Each VLAN will be assigned one /64.

Having a structured approach to multioffice deployment of IPv6 improves manageability over IPv6 and provides a foundation for pattern-based administration of network services like security and QoS.

Perspective on IPv6

The company targeted the end of 2008 as the best time to complete the implementation of an enterprise IPv4/IPv6 dual-stack environment. Bechtel believes its early adoption of IPv6 to be a necessary, strategic technology change:

- **Industry leadership positioning:** For the past few years, IPv6 has started appearing directly in customer requests for proposals (RFP) from required installed components to warranty services. In addition, IPv6-enabled components are starting to appear in the market for control systems that are integral to the industrial infrastructure projects that are core to Bechtel's business. The company's understanding and effective use of new technologies is a significant contributor to Bechtel's leadership in the engineering, construction, and project management markets.

- **Business and project execution models:** Bechtel's infrastructure must constantly evolve in response to the ways it does work and runs its business. The technology and process foundation provides authorized users from all appropriate entities with seamless, secure, and interconnected access to information and resources required to maximize cost-effective business and project execution. Within this context, Bechtel sees IPv6 as being a key enabler in responding to emerging changes in four areas:

  - Changing project execution structures will require the computing environment and information to seamlessly integrate Bechtel with joint ventures, customers, business partners, and suppliers.

  - Infrastructure must be capable of meeting the rapid mobilization and demobilization requirements of Bechtel projects.

  - Infrastructure will be deployed in a manner to ensure projects can continue execution in the event of disruptions resulting from technological, natural, or human causes.

- End-user computing platforms will be smaller and more mobile with integrated voice/data/video and support business applications through wireless in an "always-on" environment.

- **Managing technology insertions:** Bechtel makes every effort to ensure that new technology insertions add value, with minimum risk and cost. The company has developed effective processes and governance around change management. IPv6 was perceived from the beginning as a technology with potential broad impact and a corresponding long implementation time. Based on these factors, Bechtel elected to employ a systemic change approach that touches systems and infrastructure in parallel. Use of new products, like Windows Vista Meeting Space, requires IPv6.

- **Foundation for innovation:** Legacy technologies often impose innovation limits and the development of fresh approaches to new challenges. Bechtel views IPv6 as a technology ripe for exploitation…as soon as the required infrastructure is in place.

NOTE   There was no real core-first or edge-first debate in Bechtel. Network, OS, and application work has been done in parallel with the understanding that all components are required for end-to-end IPv6 communications.

IPv6 will be adopted by the engineering and construction (E&C) industry over time in several areas. Bechtel's early enterprise adoption of IPv6 is developing a competence needed to capitalize on the new protocol in a very competitive global industry. The pace of adoption will vary, in part, based on the industry being served; power plants, refineries, bridges, rail systems, and so forth.

- **Industrial networking:** Building, plant, and process automation and control systems are moving from legacy protocols to IP-based communications. IPv6 is starting to be adopted by control systems suppliers, such as the industrial giant Matsushita. Engineering and construction companies capitalizing on IPv6 in the facilities they design will have a design, implementation, and operation advantage over those that are continuing with legacy control systems and protocols. The long life of control systems and the state of IPv6 industrial networking standards will make this a gradual transition of new systems over the next five years.

- **Meeting specific customer requirements:** The U.S. government relies on private industry to provide products and services, including the implementation of IPv6. Bechtel started seeing U.S. DoD contracts containing implicit and explicit IPv6 requirements in 2004. The pace has picked up as mandated IPv6 implementation dates for DoD and other U.S. federal agencies start their IPv6 planning and deployment. The demand for IPv6 products and services will grow rapidly over the next several years as global adoption of IPv6 increases with the focus moving up the stack from the network to applications and services.

- **Work process improvements:** Many innovative engineering and construction companies should start capitalizing on IPv6 within the next two to three years. Bechtel's use of IPv6-enabled work process changes for projects is starting in 2008 in parallel with the completion of its enterprise roll-out of IPv6 on its networks and hosts. Immediate areas of opportunity include collaboration, logistics, mobility, safety, security, rapid mobilization, and converged communications.

NOTE   IPv6 adoption by E&C companies will occur when available IPv6 products and the associated competencies to deploy them can be applied to customer requirements and internal work process improvements.

The Case for IPv6

Bechtel continually investigates ways to become more efficient and to provide superior services in a highly competitive industry. This includes the routine assessment and alignment of emerging technologies to support tactical and strategic business objectives. Risk, value, safety, cost, other priorities, and timing are key decision criteria for any significant IS&T initiatives or technology changes.

Web 2.0, virtualization, identity federation, SAAS, and other technologies go through the same scrutiny: Is there a fit within the company? If so, where, when, and how should it be deployed?

Bechtel's senior IS&T management decided to move forward with a phased enterprise adoption of IPv6 in late 2004. There were several business and technical drivers for the IPv6 deployment decision, including:

- **Customer requirements:** In 2003, Bechtel's DoD customers announced their intent to implement IPv6 to support Global Information Grid (GIG) and other initiatives requiring advanced communications. Bechtel started to see IPv6 products and services directly or indirectly required in DoD RFPs. Bechtel's Communications global business unit was also observing the wireless carriers starting to explore the use of IPv6 to deliver new quad-play (voice, data, video, and mobility) products and services based on the IMS specification. Bechtel sees clear and direct business necessity in having competence in technologies and processes that directly relate to project deliverables.

- **Partner adoption of IPv6:** Seamless and secure collaboration with customers, partners, and suppliers is a fundamental part of Bechtel's project execution strategy. As a result, Bechtel constantly adjusts to the changes in technologies adopted by itself and others. Bechtel's early adoption of IPv6 best positions the company to be able to collaborate with other organizations using the new protocol whenever they are ready.

- **Supplier-induced IPv6 insertion:** In 2004, Bechtel also saw IPv6 adoption in its regular dialogs with strategic technology partners, including Cisco and Microsoft. During these discussions with technology partners, it became clear that IPv6 was becoming part of their products that Bechtel is and will be purchasing, like it or not. These and other partners were also exploring new peer-to-peer, mobility, and location-based service paradigms that require IPv6. As IPv6 technology is becoming more common in products and services from Bechtel's providers, it was clear that the company had to deal with its inevitability.

- **Natural technology evolution:** Bechtel moved from DECnet SNA/SDLC and other communications protocols to TCP/IP more than 15 years ago. Within the TCP/IP timeframe, point-to-point circuits were replaced with Frame Relay and eventually the use of the Internet VPNs for WAN communications. 802.11 (Wi-Fi) is now broadly deployed throughout the enterprise, and the global transition to voice and video over IP is nearing completion. These changes have all been viewed as part of the natural evolution of network technology, including ubiquitous mobile converged communications. TCP/IP has served Bechtel well and has been the foundation for many services used throughout the company, from server farms for legacy client/server applications to extensive use of web technology for day-to-day work. With the growth in its usage, the shortcomings of IPv4 have introduced complexity and cost in two areas: NAT, and the elimination of secure any-to-any computing across company borders. Bechtel views the move to IPv6 to be both natural and an enabler for new innovations.

- **New capabilities for project execution:** Bechtel is constantly exploring how technology can be exploited to support revenue generation (executing projects) and running the business. Well over a decade ago, Bechtel introduced its first web servers. Innovation and ideas came from within and outside of the IS&T organization on creative and smart ways to use the technology. Since then the company has invested and benefited from the technology creativity of its employee, from Bechtel-hosted reverse auctions for purchase of materials for its projects to new ways of more closely collaborating with customers, partners, and suppliers. Bechtel views IPv6 as the next generation Internet enabler, providing a new foundation for future innovation.

- **Industrial automation convergence to IP:** Internet communication technology is usually viewed from the perspective of the office, end user, or consumer. Within Bechtel's business, there is a high level of focus on the building, plant, and process automation systems that are part of the industrial infrastructure projects that it builds and manages. A large refinery or other industrial plant contains tens of thousands of nodes used in the safe operation of the plant at optimal efficiency. There is an industry convergence in control systems and control networks, from legacy protocols to IP-based control systems. Industrial controls from some large, innovative suppliers are starting to come IPv6-enabled.

Beyond a common protocol for control systems, secure integration of industrial and business systems on a common communications protocol offers new opportunities.

Bechtel drew several conclusions from its assessment of the IPv6 drivers and past experience:

- **IPv6 is coming:** For Bechtel, the IPv6 debate was over and the IPv6 implementation decision process became one of technical positioning: how and at what pace.

- **Broad competence is needed:** A fundamental competence in IPv6 was seen as a requirement to bid and execute projects for Bechtel customers as well as for internal deployment. From its early assessment, the company became aware that the scope was well beyond a global network upgrade. It would touch applications, security, processes, quality assurance, and many other points in the organization.

- **Phased implementation:** In 2004 commercial products had less IPv6 maturity than they do today. Bechtel's implementation looked at a combination of customer requirements and technology maturity to develop its phased implementation strategy. Bechtel decided to engage people from internal IS&T groups to focus on first IPv6 production work in its offices of the government global business unit.

- **Planned vs. reactive transition:** Risk, cost, and timing evaluations are required for any IT project of significance in Bechtel. The company assessed the IPv6 deployment effort (networks, computers, applications, services, security, management, and so on) as well as the availability of IPv6 in commercial products. Bechtel decided to avoid the cost and risk of a forklift upgrade by taking a different approach: make IPv6 a required component for other activities. The project focus was placed on introducing IPv6 into existing proven practices for managing change in the global organization.

NOTE   Bechtel saw several parallels in the issues of DECnet/SNA vs. TCP/IP debated internally 20 years ago and its IPv4 vs. IPv6 discussions in 2004. The same questions came up: will the new protocol have broad adoption, where and when should Bechtel start, and what is the impact on the infrastructure and applications?

Bechtel uses a high-level Vision, Strategy, and Plan (VSP) process to solidify and communicate its strategic technology changes. The model, depicted in Figure 5-10, has been applied to the company's IPv6 initiative since 2005.

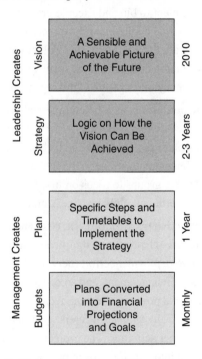

Figure 5-10   *Bechtel's Vision, Strategy, and Plan Process*

A brief look at the components of the vision and strategy shown in Figure 5-10 provides you with a context in which Bechtel is executing its IPv6 deployment initiative.

Bechtel IPv6 Vision

Bechtel's 2008 strategic IPv6 vision was developed early in 2005 and helped shaped the pace and approach for the enterprise effort:

- **IPv6 is broadly deployed:** Bechtel saw a ubiquitous IPv6 environment as a fundamental requirement for the future enterprise use of future IPv6 products and services. This vision addresses all touch points related to IPv6, including networks, applications, hosts, support, and security. A necessary byproduct of achieving this goal is the development of a broad and practical competence in IPv6.

- **IPv6 default in global dual-stack environment:** End-to-end IPv6 precedence over IPv4 is part of the design of the new protocol to assist in transition. Bechtel focused its early strategy on getting addressing, naming, and applications that would actually use IPv6 in end-to-end communications.

- **New products and services run IPv6 by default:** Bechtel has proven processes for managing technology evolution in the enterprise. The company's IS&T standards process classifies products and services in a time-relative form as part of its technology roadmap. Standards classifications are emerging, standard, restricted, and unsupported. The standards classifications guide acquisition, development, deployment, and support activities. Bechtel's position in 2007 going forward is that all new products and services will be acquired with IPv6 capabilities and deployed with IPv6 enabled.

- **Innovation foundation:** Progress requires change, and Bechtel views IPv6 as a technology ripe for expanding its network-centric environment for the execution of work. Like web technologies, many of the IPv6 innovations and thought leadership are expected from outside the IT organization.

- **Industry leadership:** As a premier global engineering and construction company, Bechtel is constantly focusing on the application of technical knowledge to improve on engineering, procurement, or construction tasks. This culture of innovation regularly turns new technologies into reliable tools that are of value to the company and its customers.

Bechtel IPv6 Strategy

Strategies and guiding principles throughout the deployment have been focused on contributing to achieving the vision while gradually developing a broad internal competence in the new protocol through internal deployment:

- **Foundation first:** Bechtel is taking a "building block" approach to its deployment, starting with the fundamentals such as addressing, naming, LAN transport, enabling hosts, and WAN connections. Because there are several paradigm differences between IPv4 and IPv6, it has been critical to get the fundamentals right first.

- **Keep IPv4 (for now) and add IPv6:** Bechtel will move to IPv6-only environments when IPv6 is supported by the products and services it uses. While that is clearly in the company's future, Bechtel has elected to go the dual-stack route used by many others by adding IPv6 to its existing IPv4 environment.

- **Minimize use of transition technology:** The company is focusing its efforts on broad deployment of IPv6 with minimum use of transition technologies, such as ISATAP, and address translation tools.

- **Broad deployment of expected successes:** Bechtel's strategy for getting *real* end-to-end IPv6 traffic on the network requires applications and services that will use IPv6. Bechtel's strategy includes regular assessment of its software and dialog with strategic suppliers to understand which products are IPv6-aware and which are not. Many products are still evolving in their IPv6 maturity. Bechtel has found value in enabling the new protocol on products that provide basic IPv6 services as a stepping-stone to future, more capable products. Although Windows Vista and Windows Server 2008 have more robust IPv6 features, Bechtel decided that the basic IPv6 functions work fine in Windows XP, Windows Server 2003, and IIS 6.0.

- **Ensure nothing breaks (in production):** Bechtel does not put its projects at risk by experimenting with new technology in a production environment. The company has controlled environments for development, QA, and production with managed transition processes between them. Bechtel established an isolated IPv6 lab environment at four sites to ensure potentially disruptive IPv6 work was contained. This has been very valuable in working out DNS, security, addressing, WAN routing, and other features that may be different with IPv6.

- **Maintain/improve security:** Bechtel is ISO 27001-certified with robust IT security techniques and information security management systems. All IPv6 deployment changes involve Bechtel's information security team as a matter of course.

- **Watch costs—use refresh cycles:** Bechtel is using an incremental and systemic approach to its IPv6 deployment, integrating the implementation with existing change processes wherever possible. This includes products that Bechtel purchases as well as internal changes, such as adding IPv6 to other development, configuration, and testing processes.

- **Actively engage key technology partners:** Bechtel realized that it needed help from others in developing required IPv6 skills and in its deployment of IPv6. Things are different with IPv6, and real external deployment experience is a needed perspective. Bechtel engaged some of its key technology partners, including Cisco, Microsoft, and Command Information, throughout its IPv6 deployment process. Some of the activities, such as training, were for a fee. Other work was done on a collaborative basis.

- **Use existing processes for introducing and managing change:** Bechtel's processes for managing change are well defined, are followed, and operate in a transparent mode. There is particular attention to the control points of transition from development to QA and finally into production environments. Bechtel has inserted IPv6 into transition points and provided guidelines for upstream activities. For example, QA testing, including user acceptance testing, is done in an environment with IPv6 enabled on all hosts and network segments. Developers have been instructed on what changes they are required to make to their software to pass the QA testing.

- **Address all touch points related to IPv6:** IPv6 is much more than a network upgrade. Bechtel's IPv6 deployment addresses many areas, including networks, applications, hosts, support, and security.

IPv6 Planning and Implementation

Bechtel's IPv6 deployment started with project planning and training in early 2005 with an enterprise deployment implementation targeted at two primary objectives:

- Enabling end-to-end IPv6 communications for existing applications and services

- Providing a foundation for future IPv6 applications, services, and innovations

The model in Figure 5-11 highlights the basic information flow in end-to-end connections. Security naming and other services are omitted for simplicity. This is a typical scenario that may represent a web browser (App 1) talking to a web server (Service 2) in another office. Bechtel's planning and implementation has been to address the hardware, software, and networks required to achieve end-to-end IPv6 communications.

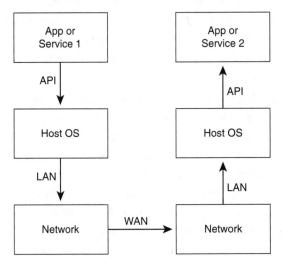

Figure 5-11 *Bechtel Application Communication*

This model brings to the surface many questions that Bechtel has to address within the context of its global operations, internally as well as with its partners, customers, and suppliers. These questions include:

- How are IPv6 addresses assigned and managed?

- How is routing different?

- How will host computers get routable addresses?

- Will applications fail if IPv6 is enabled on the OS and network?

- How will Bechtel manage the new environment?

- What are the dependencies and optimum sequencing of activities?

These and many other questions had to be addressed in a multiyear project plan that is used for the development and execution of tactical effort. Detailed plans have evolved with experience, but have maintained an overall structure. Basic decisions have been made step by step on the environment where the initial IPv6 work will occur.

Project Scope

Following is an extract from Bechtel's IPv6 Implementation Plan and Functional Spec:

> The goal of the project is to establish IPv6 as the protocol of choice on Bechtel's internal network and to accomplish a broad deployment across the enterprise. IPv6 has been designed with a view towards facilitating ease of transition from IPv4 and support for "dual-stack" configuration emerged as a key feature. A key aspect of Bechtel's implementation of IPv6 will be long term commitment to running in "dual stack" configuration. IPv4 and IPv6 will co-exist on our hosts/network. Connection services and applications which have an IPv4-only requirement will continue to function. It is expected that the prevalence of such IPv4-only applications will diminish over time as the functional solutions are updated (or replaced) to include compliance with IPv6.

The initial deployment strategy was to install IPv6 as a foundational building block in Bechtel's network architecture and to do so without dislodging the currently used IPv4 building block. This offers two specific advantages. In a network environment where both protocols are in place and functioning independently, IPv6 automatically becomes the default transport for upper layer services and applications. This triggers a transparent transition for all IPv6-ready services and applications. Secondly, the deployment of this underlying IPv6 foundational building block will meet the requirements of new IPv6-capable products and innovations.

The following network phases of the company's IPv6 project highlight the movement from lab to production networks and environments over time. We have included a sample of the major activities for each phase to provide an idea about the effort and scope involved. Each lab activity was targeted at developing the competence and documentation required to move to the production network environment. Note that the network phases listed include applications, services, and operating systems.

Phase I (Lab): IPv6 in "Local" Labs

Bechtel uses its isolate IPv6 lab environment to minimize risk to production users when the IPv6 technology being tested may be potentially disruptive or pose a security risk. Phase I established IPv6 labs at four locations. Each lab was equipped with at least one router, one switch, a domain controller, a file/web server, and two or more client computers.

The IPv6 isolated labs have been configured to support the following standard infrastructure services that are expected in a dual-stack environment. Not all services were implemented at each site. Below is a list of typical common infrastructure services enabled and tested in one or more labs.

- IPv6 stateless autoconfiguration
- DNS
- DHCP

- File and print
- Browsing (HTTP/HTTPS)
- Active Directory
- E-mail (Exchange) and Simple Mail Transfer Protocol (SMTP)
- Internet Information Services (IIS)
- Proxy (Microsoft ISA Server)
- System Management Server (SMS)
- Database servers
- Simple Network Management Protocol (SNMP)
- IDS/IPS
- VoIP
- Network Time Protocol (NTP) services
- FTP
- Certification authority (CA)
- Microsoft Internet Authentication Service (IAS)

Phase II (Lab): IPv6 and Intersite Connectivity

Bechtel connected the labs to each other through physically isolated WAN connections. VPN WAN connections and routing models were developed. The major components of Phase II included:

- Functional specs for setting up inter-site connectivity (lab)
- IPv6 OSPF authentication over IPv4 (protocol 41) WAN tunnels
- End-to-end WAN testing using IIS 6.0
- Address plan finalization

Phase III (Production): Pilot Deployment in Production LAN Environment (LAN/"IPv6 Islands")

IPv6 was enabled on production WANs at the sites hosting the four isolated IPv6 labs. Initial deployment was on selected VLANs within each office. This leveraged work done in Phase I, adding required production support and management components. Phase III activities focused on:

- Risk analysis and mitigation prior to pilot deployment in production LAN.

- Functional specs for pilot deployment in production environment (LAN).

- Using IEEE 802.1q VLAN standard to "overlay" IPv6 links.

- Incremental expansion of IPv6 "island."

- Application layer validation in production network environment (LAN).

- After the LAN pilot phase was complete, all future new LAN implementations include IPv6 on all VLANs. Other existing IPv4-only sites are being IPv6-enabled on a scheduled process.

Phase IV (Production): Pilot Deployment in Production Environment (WAN)

Production WAN connections were established between each of the sites hosting the isolated IPv6 labs. Separate WAN routers were deployed to minimize risk and allow any required configuration changes. The Phase IV tasks listed below positioned Bechtel for broader production deployment.

- Functional specs for pilot deployment on production network (WAN).

- Application layer validation in production network environment (WAN).

- After WAN pilot phase was complete, all future new WAN sites include IPv6 WAN connectivity.

- Other existing IPv4-only WAN links are being IPv6-enabled on a scheduled process, starting with large offices and major data centers.

Phase V (Lab): IPv6 and Connectivity to the Internet

Phases III and IV were completed "behind the firewall" to isolate Bechtel from any external IPv6 security risks. The major Phase V deliverables below positioned Bechtel for internal IPv6 interaction with IPv6 resources on the Internet.

- Functional specs for setting up IPv6-based connectivity to Internet (lab)
- Application layer validation (Internet-connected lab)
- IPv6 connections to the Internet with Bechtel's IPv6 address space
- Host firewalls
- IDS/IPS configuration and validation
- Security-related traffic logging
- Main connection scenarios are
    - Internal to DMZ
    - Internet to DMZ
    - Internal to Internet
    - Internet to internal

Phase VI (Lab): Wireless and Mobile Access

This phase expands connectivity to wireless and mobile users. The steps below were designed to ensure functionality and security for wireless users with IPv6-enabled 802.11 or cellular access.

- Functional specs
- Wireless access points and wireless router configurations including 802.1x authentication with user and machine certificates
- Wireless management servers for security, management, and configuration
- Application layer validation in the context of mobile access (lab)
- Cellular/802.11 phone pilots
- Mobile field trial, including MIPv6

Phase VII (Production): Pilot Deployment of IPv6-Based Internet Connectivity

This is the staged implementation of Phase V work. The following work was required to enable production access from Bechtel's protected network to IPv6 resources on the Internet.

- Functional specs
- Application layer validation (Internet-connected production network)
- Final compliance check for ISO 27001
- Added to standing agenda for regular global Information Security calls

Phase VIII (Production): Wireless and Mobile Access

This is the staged implementation of Phase VI work. Major steps for the final IPv6 802.11 production deployment are listed below.

- Application layer validation in the context of mobile access (production network).
- Production IPv6 deployment on wireless access points and wireless routers through wireless LAN servers.
- All future wireless implementations include IPv6.

Phase IX (Lab): Voice/Data/Video Convergence

Bechtel is a heavy user of VoIP and video over IP. This phase is addressing converged IP services across multiple platforms.

- Functional specs
- Application layer validation in context of VDV convergence

The implementation plan was originally designed to be executed in a relatively linear mode. However, in practice Bechtel has executed parts of some phases in parallel.

IPv6 Metrics

Bechtel uses targets and metrics to manage its activities throughout the implementation phases highlighted above. The targets shown in Table 5-38 were established in late 2005.

Table 5-38 *Bechtel IPv6 Implementation Goals (Late 2005)*

Milestones	2006	2007	2008
LAN/WAN	5	50%	95%
Windows clients	1000	10,000	95%
Websites	6 internal	25%	95%
Apps, dual-stack	50 major	90%	100%
Mobility	Wireless	Remote access	Always on
Management	Basic	Over IPv4	Over IPv6
Security	Internal	External IPv6	Borderless projects

The progress made in the IPv6 implementation was closely monitored, as shown in Table 5-39.

Table 5-39 *Bechtel 2008 IPv6 Implementation Progress Through 1Q-2008 and Planned for 4Q-2008*

Milestones	2006	2007	2008
LAN/WAN	5	40%	95%
Windows clients	1000	16,000 (93%)	100%
Websites	6 internal	25%	95%
Apps, dual-stack	50 major	90%	100%
Mobility	Wireless	Remote access	Always on
Management	Basic	Over IPv4	Over IPv6
Security	Internal	External IPv6	Borderless projects

Bechtel's IPv6 implementation was not always linear. Once scalable deployment models were successfully piloted, they could be rapidly deployed throughout the enterprise using standard tools through existing change management processes. Table 5-40 below shows some of the large incremental changes that occurred when using standard SMS scripts to enable IPv6 on Bechtel's desktop and laptop computers in 2007. Note the large jumps in cumulative IPv6 clients 2Q-2007 through 3Q-2007.

Table 5-40 *Bechtel 2008 IPv6 Implementation Progress Through 1Q-2008 and Planned for 4Q-2008*

Month Ending	IPv6 Clients	Percent Complete
Apr-07	2050	12.1%
May-07	2889	17.0%
Jul-07	4237	24.9%
Aug-07	9983	58.7%
Sep-07	14,229	83.7%
Oct-07	15,650	92.1%
Nov-07	16,100	94.7%
Mar-08	16,400	95.1%

Bechtel understood from the beginning that IPv6 would be a wide-reaching, multiyear project. The timeline shown in Table 5-41 highlights some of the milestones and high points since the initiative was approved in late 2004 through its expected conclusion in late 2008.

Table 5-41 *Bechtel Timeline for Enterprise Deployment of IPv6*

Period	Activity
Oct-2004	CIO/SVP approval to proceed with enterprise deployment within Bechtel's infrastructure. Bechtel's federal global business unit identified as first pilot company working closely with corporate IT.
1H-2005	Budget approved, teams formed, project scoped, and critical partners identified and engaged (Cisco, Command Information, and Microsoft). Enterprise-wide IPv6 Awareness campaign through a series of video "Tech Talks." First Bechtel IPv6 presentation at Cisco Technical Advisory Board. Network engineering training started. Started construction of IPv6 labs.

Table 5-41 *Bechtel Timeline for Enterprise Deployment of IPv6 (Continued)*

Period	Activity
2H-2005	Acquired provider independent IPv6 address space from ARIN: 2001:4920::/32. Four isolated IPv6 lab sites fully operational including wireless and tunneled WAN connections. Standard computing and infrastructure services tested and verified in dual-stack mode.
1H-2006	Command Information contracted to help with detailed production implementation planning, including IPv6 address allocation, more detailed project planning, and industry best practices. Instructions to developers issued on developing IP version–agnostic code. Testing criteria established. IPv6 included in base Windows XP image for computers used on federal projects. SMS scripts developed and piloted to deploy IPv6 to Windows XP and Server 2003 computers. SMS reporting developed to track progress. Cisco, Command Information, and Microsoft engaged in regular dialog to share ideas, challenges, and solutions.
2H-2006	IPv6 enabled on network and computers in Software QA (SQA) lab used for all application testing. SMS scripts used for enabling IPv6 on computers office by office.
1H-2007	IPv6 integral part of Office 2007 testing in Windows XP. All client-side applications verified to operate dual-stack without issue. IPv6 enabled at most major offices (LAN and WAN). IPv6-enabled IDS/IPS installed.
2H-2007	90 percent of Bechtel IPv6-capable desktop and laptop computers are dual-stack. Greater than 50 percent of network ports are dual-stack. Production intranet web servers are IPv6-enabled.
1H-2008	IPv6 enabled on all IPv6-capable wireless access points and wireless routers. IPv6 enabled on remaining enterprise infrastructure and web servers. Centrally hosted application servers IPv6-enabled.
2H-2008	IPv6 enabled on remaining application servers. Selected production deployment of Windows Server 2008.
End 2008	Bechtel enterprise deployment of IPv6 hosts and networks is substantially complete.

The IPv6 Team

IPv6 is not just a technology exercise. The work scope is broad, touching all aspects of IT in the enterprise. The success of Bechtel's IPv6 deployment can be mainly attributed to the people involved. Here are some of the primary team members in Bechtel's IPv6 deployment:

- **Senior IS&T management:** Bechtel's corporate IS&T leadership was involved in the discussion and decision about the company's IPv6 deployment from the beginning. They are involved in funding decisions and the priority of IPv6 in relationship to other initiatives.

- **Project sponsor:** Fred Wettling, one of Bechtel's senior IS&T leaders, proposed and sponsors the IPv6 initiative. His role in the project is overall coordination across the enterprise and allocation/management of the budget required for select IPv6-specific tasks.

- **Core team:** Fifteen seasoned professionals make up the IPv6 core team. They are from network, security, architecture, QA, and IT management disciplines. Brief coordination meetings are held weekly. These people also communicate IPv6 requirements, status, and actions to other teams in their disciplines.

- **Global Systems Engineering (GSE):** IPv6 change impact is greatest on the infrastructure. The GSE organization has gradually incorporated IPv6 in the products and services it supports as the product versions change, new products are introduced, or a modification is required to support IPv6 project objectives.

- **Global Infrastructure Operations (GIO):** The infrastructure that is installed in Bechtel's leveraged data centers around the globe is operated and supported by GIO. GIO works closely with GSE to ensure that technologies moved into production data centers are stable, manageable, and secure.

- **Information Security:** InfoSec participates in all security-related process, product, and service assessments and management. IPv6 compatibility and security mechanisms are integral in its daily work.

For example, IPv6 capabilities were a mandatory requirement in the selection and deployment of new IDS/IPS products recently placed into production.

- **Software Quality Assurance (SQA):** Applications go through Bechtel's SQA process and environment before being released for production usage. The SQA lab includes nearly 200 hosts and an IPv6-enabled subnet on Bechtel's production network. All applications going through SQA are verified to operate without error in a dual-stack environment. SQA is also responsible for management and enforcement of the company's software Development Methodology Framework that provides a structure for software development, testing, and validation. SQA instructions to developers in early 2006 provided details on the development and testing of applications to ensure they are IP version agnostic.

- **Software Engineering and Construction (SEC):** This organization is responsible for application development, including integration of Bechtel code with commercial products. Dual-stack compatibility is a required part of SEC process, verified by SQA. New platforms, such as Microsoft Office SharePoint Server (MOSS) 2007, are installed in development with IPv6 enabled. Bechtel created "Developer Guidelines for IPv6 Enabled Applications" and "IPv6 Application Checklist and Certification Steps" by and for developers to ensure IPv6-related consistency in applications. One of the byproducts is Bechtel's "IPv6 Ready" logo, as seen on the About page of Bechtel's internal website, BecWeb (see Figure 5-12).

- **Global Support Organization (GSO):** GSO has several functions, including the Help Desk. GSO became involved as production IPv6 deployment started. Basic IPv6 troubleshooting knowledge has been required to isolate and diagnose user support questions. For example, **ping** <*hostname*> will return an IPv6 address by default in an end-to-end IPv6-enabled environment.

Figure 5-12   *BecWeb Page with "IPv6 Ready" Logo*

Other organizations are involved in different ways with the IPv6 deployment based on their role in the organization and their customer base.

NOTE   Not one of the Bechtel participants is dedicated to the IPv6 project. IPv6 is just another part of their "day job," just like any other technology that is relevant to their work.

Lessons Learned

Over three years of planning, testing, deployment, and support have developed a solid IPv6 competence in Bechtel. The company's early investment has positioned Bechtel at least a couple of years ahead of others in the industry. During the process, Bechtel gained several insights. Most of them were associated with people and process, not the technology itself. Following are those insights:

- **Long term: strategic change:** In Bechtel's environment, IPv6 is viewed as a required strategic investment. IPv6 in itself does not resolve many current issues. However, the early systemic deployment will minimize future IPv6–related deployment efforts and better position Bechtel to serve its customers and explore new platforms for innovative work improvement. Bechtel's IPv6 experience will also help in exploiting IP-related convergence of enterprise and industrial systems as new control systems become IPv6-enabled.

- **Leadership:** A project of this nature requires leadership support at the most senior IT levels. IPv6 deployment will touch the entire IT organization. It also requires a sponsor with a broad visionary perspective that is well respected in most of the IT disciplines.

- **Broad involvement:** Do not underestimate the number of people and organizations that are involved in implementing IPv6. Engage the stakeholders early and keep them involved.

- **Persistence:** It takes time and continuous engagement to effect a broad change like IPv6.

- **Communications:** Dialog, project websites, regular meetings, and other methods of gaining and sustaining visibility have value. People need to be involved in or notified about changes that will impact them before the fact. A combination of the IPv6 core team and the regular communications within each of the IT disciplines has been effective.

- **IPv6 is a different type of IT project:** In one respect, IPv6 is like the Y2K effort the industry faced in the late 1990s, with all parts of the IT environment being inventoried, evaluated, and changed as required.

- **Fact-based decisions:** Bechtel manages complexity and understands that effective project management and communications need to be done based on facts. Inventory of hardware, software, network, and devices was required early to assess the scope of what had to be changed. Performance metrics, such as actual vs. planned, help identify areas that might need attention. Basic facts, such as percent of computers that are IPv6-enabled by site, can also be used as promotional communications material.

- **Capitalize on the newness:** While several people are resistant to change, many enjoy the challenge and satisfaction of learning something new. Getting a large percentage of people with the right frame of mind on the core team can help sustain momentum over the duration of the project.

- **Fear, uncertainty, and doubt (FUD) and naysayers:** A change of this type still has a few pockets of resistance in the company. What may be perceived as negative comments should be explored as potential implementation roadblocks. If you can ease fears and resolve perceived issues, the project will go much smoother.

- **Technology and paradigm shifts:** Many things with IPv6 are not the same as with IPv4. Project participants need to be encouraged and challenged to look at things differently in order to get the most value out of the new protocol. For example, Bechtel uses stateless address autoconfiguration for the IPv6 addresses on its servers, where static IPv4 addresses have been the norm. There are operational advantages to our IPv6 approach. Discussing the pros and cons of each option was educational and a necessary step to the development of a deeper understanding of IPv6.

- **Integrate IPv6 systemically into change management:** Bechtel has made very effective use of the existing change management mechanisms in its IPv6 deployment in two primary areas. Bechtel's approach has been to include IPv6 as a required review/update component for all changes. The first point is where life cycle state changes occur; moving from development and engineering to QA and from QA into production. Enabling IPv6 at the transition points has ensured that all IT components are tested in an IPv6 environment prior to production release. The second point is upstream from the gatekeepers at the source where changes are initiated, such as standard server build documents. The use of standards revision methods to existing applications and infrastructure components of the environments is well understood.

- **Minimize transition technologies:** Bechtel's IPv6 project has been focused on developing broad IPv6 competence through a natural transition to a dual-stack environment. The production deployment started with large offices first gaining the required critical mass of IPv6-enabled components quickly. With this in mind, the company did not deploy ISATAP, protocol translation gateways, or transition technologies. Although this has delayed end-to-end IPv6 communications for several sites, it has avoided the expense and effort associated with deploying temporary infrastructure. The exception has been WAN connections where IPv6 is not yet supported by the carriers. In this case, Bechtel is using protocol 41 tunneling to move IPv6 over IPv4 VPN tunnels.

- **Learn from others:** Bechtel had excellent results working with some of its key technology partners from the beginning, most significantly Cisco, Command Information, and Microsoft. The interaction has been beneficial to all participants.

- **Cost:** Bechtel's funding for its IPv6 implementation has averaged less than $150,000 per year and the number is declining. This has been possible by treating IPv6 as a new part of the way the company executes its work.

- **Training:** Early, in-depth, high-quality training was critical for an effective project start. Bechtel contracted Native6, now part of Command Information, to provide week-long, hands-on training of key project members from around the globe. Basic skills in IPv6 were developed, including an understanding of the difference between IPv4 and IPv6. Bechtel also viewed this as a train-the-trainer investment.

- **Learning:** Training is a start, but the real competence has been achieved by hands-on learning developed by working through the issues in Bechtel's environment. The company contracted Command Information to assist in several areas where Bechtel lacked skills or knowledge, such as finalizing Bechtel's IPv6 address plan. Cisco and Microsoft were also critical in helping Bechtel understand the technology and best practices from their perspectives. In-depth training is not required for all of the staff.

- **Things will fail:** Bechtel did its preproduction in isolated or controlled environments to minimize risk. During the learning process, things failed. Initial configuration for wireless routers did not work, tunneling protocols were changed based on experience, and a couple of applications failed when IPv6 was enabled from end to end. This was natural and expected when dealing with a new technology. The causes of failures were actively discussed and documentation was changed to reflect what works. This was also a learning experience.

- **IPv6 products may not be available when needed:** Bechtel ran into a few very frustrating cases where the lack of required IPv6 products and services caused the company to implement alternative solutions or postpone a part of its implementation. The initial lack of IPv6 services to the premises from Bechtel's major U.S.-based carriers caused the company to resort to tunneled WAN connections between sites. This was additional work that would not have been needed if native IPv6 services could be delivered to Bechtel's offices. In this and the few other cases, Bechtel has tried to work with the providers to get the needed IPv6 services, sometimes without success within the company's needed timeframe. In the cases where IPv6 services were not available, but on a critical path, Bechtel has selected products and services from alternate providers.

- **Competing priorities—complementary approach:** Bechtel makes efficient use of its resources. Its IPv6 deployment was structured in such a way that it would not be competing with other priority projects. By making IPv6 a natural part of the way Bechtel does work, IPv6 is just another part of other priority projects…along for the ride.

Networked Sensor Technology: Arch Rock

The next step for the Internet is for it to be embedded into the physical world, allowing users to remotely interact with things, spaces, assets, and the environment at large.

—Roland Acra, President and CEO of Arch Rock

In its simplest, most basic form, the title of this section, "Networked Sensor Technology," encompasses a huge field of technology and product developments with significant implications for both economic and quality-of-life improvements. The technology's impact is felt in areas that range from personal health, safety, security to the environment (for example, energy awareness and ecological preservation), to business and manufacturing (for example, asset monitoring and maintenance, machine control). It is not only a rich, multifaceted technology, but one with a long history. Sensors of various types and forms have been used in daily life, from home thermostats and smoke detectors to biological monitoring, structural engineering, and streamlining industrial processes.

Sensors themselves have evolved along with the technology and their applications, but the most interesting, and potentially most important, dimension of their evolution lies in their ability to communicate and transfer the data they gather. Sensors once were standalone devices requiring a manual collection process to retrieve data (for example, field meteorological probes). Today they can be devices wired to a central controller, such as a home alarm system or thermostat, more autonomous battery-powered devices communicating wirelessly on low power, or even devices such as water meters that can be read simply by driving nearby.

Until recently, sensors have been operated and managed using proprietary protocols tailored for specific functions. The newest sensors, however, leverage the IP infrastructure as well as modern, standards-based wireless radio technologies to communicate among themselves in a meshed topology with the much wider variety of devices and resources available in the IP world.

A major market shift is currently occurring that combines the deployment flexibility, reach, and autonomous long life of sensing devices (including hard-to-reach locations and mobile environments) with standards-based, interoperable protocols running over IP.

Sensors are designed and developed in the context of very stringent constraints, often related not only to specific physical deployment requirements but also to safety, simplicity, cost, and availability of power sources or communication links. Generally, sensors should play a nonintrusive role in their environment without becoming a management burden (which could counter the value of their use). Although more functions per sensor means higher return on investment, sensor design must balance complexity with resource availability in the targeted environment. Advances in science and technology are continuously leading to smaller, more-capable, and more-specialized sensors as well as more-powerful and power-efficient microcontroller and radio semiconductors. Improvements in battery technologies are likewise leading to the increased autonomy of these devices.

The true evolutionary leap in sensor technologies, however, resulted from enabling active sensors to work collectively rather than as individual entities. Inseparable from this evolution has been the development of distributed applications and multihop mesh networking that increased sensors' reach beyond the range of single radio hops.[59]

With an operational model based on a flexible, open-standards communication mechanism, active sensors can optimize the use of their resources and leverage external, dedicated computational resources, bringing a great deal of flexibility to different sensing applications. Networking enables sensors to gain global accessibility with minimal use of power by leveraging neighboring sensors. It also lets the sensors offload processing to more powerful, dedicated devices with fewer resource constraints, such as AC-powered computers with more memory or processing power.

At the physical and media layers, wireless technologies provide the most flexibility and autonomy to the deployment of sensors. Although dedicated or proprietary communications protocols can be used to build sensor networks, IP clearly represents a better option. Not only are today's communications infrastructures converging on IP, with most devices relevant to sensor networks already IP-enabled, but IP has already been augmented with ad hoc networking capabilities as well as adaptation to low-power and low-resource environments. All of this facilitates the deployment of sensors. The IETF is actively working on further enhancements of the protocol that would make it a natural choice in this type of environment and in classes of devices with severe resource constraints. A first step in that direction is the recently completed development of RFC 4944 (known as "6LoWPAN," for IPv6 over Low power WPAN) within the IETF.

NOTE   For a long time it has been argued that using IP to communicate with or between sensor devices adds overhead that is expensive in terms of precious power resources. This is the reason there are still many sensor environments that use specialized communications protocols that are optimized from a power consumption perspective. While this is an important constraint in designing sensor communication, optimal power consumption cannot come at the cost of significantly reduced capabilities. There are two general approaches to the optimization problem:

---

59. David Culler, Deborah Estrin, and Mani Srivastava, "Overview of Sensor Networks," *IEEE Computer* 37, no. 8 (August 2004): 41–49, http://www.archrock.com/downloads/resources/IEEE-overview-2004.pdf.

- **High optimization plus use of IP:** This combination offers a highly optimal implementation with the benefit of global networking and the ability for easy and dynamic remote interaction.

- **Extreme optimization and no use of IP:** This combination offers an extremely optimal implementation but with no benefit of global networking or ability for remote interaction.

The evolution of networking and IP's role in the rapid buildout of the public Internet has taught us that the first choice is the most compelling. Furthermore, the recent developments at IETF have removed the "excuse" that IP is too chatty or has headers too large to be a viable candidate for very long-lived sensor applications. It has now been shown that embedded IP can be made to be very efficient, even in the context of highly resource-constrained sensor networks, in terms of bandwidth utilization, computation processing, and memory utilization.

Technology advances push even more strongly in favor of making this choice. Their bias in favor of the IP approach is due to the points made earlier, such as advancements in battery technology, power-efficient radio chips and microcontrollers, and so forth.

With an expected explosion in the number of sensor nodes deployed, the natural extension of the IP infrastructure to integrate them will lead to an increased demand of IP address resources. In principle, sensor networks could use the private address space over and over again within enclosed domains. This approach, however, will limit the size of these domains, a potentially significant constraint when a high density of sensors of various types is deployed. Sensor nodes with globally unique addresses would also have more flexibility in building ad hoc networks and in communicating with global resources. This perspective on its own makes the case for using IPv6 in sensor communications. In reality, as detailed later in this case study, there are other potential benefits that make IPv6 a good fit for sensor networks. Nevertheless, as an emerging technology and associated market intent on leveraging the IP infrastructure, and in a world heading inevitably toward an upgrade to the next generation of IP, it makes practical sense for sensor technologies to leverage and integrate IPv6.

This case study covers a leading and pioneering systems and software company that builds innovative products and technology for wireless sensor networks: Arch Rock Corporation. It was developed with the assistance of Roland Acra, President and CEO of Arch Rock.

Company Profile

According to its corporate information page:

> Arch Rock Corporation is a systems and software company that builds innovative products and technology for wireless sensor networks. The Company's mission is to bridge the physical and digital worlds by bringing data gathered by wireless sensor networks into the enterprise IT infrastructure, where it can be easily viewed, analyzed and managed.[60]

Arch Rock realizes the vision of its founders, Dr. David Culler and Dr. Wei Hong, while building on their extensive research efforts in the field of sensor networks. According to the company history, Arch Rock was established to provide "a high quality, seamless integration of the physical and virtual worlds that would enhance the information awareness of the individual and the enterprise."[61] In the mid-1990s Dr. Culler and a small team of researchers at the University of California, Berkeley, and Intel Research developed TinyOS, an open source OS for small, wirelessly connected devices that form large embedded networks. In 2001, Culler and his team built the Open Experimental Platform for DARPA's Network Embedded Systems Technology program. Together with Hong, a member of his team at the Intel Research Berkeley lab, Culler developed a strategy to make the technology commercially viable and useful. They continued to pursue its development through various standards and research projects, and in mid-2005 they brought together technologists, investors, and business people to establish Arch Rock.

60. http://www.archrock.com/company/index.php.

61. http://www.archrock.com/company/history.php.

Today, Arch Rock is a partner in multiple projects and solutions that extend the capabilities of services and applications by providing immediate and open access to a vast world of sensory information. Projects such as Advanced Incident Response System (AIRS)[62], developed in collaboration with Cisco Systems and Command Information to improve resource integration, operating environment safety, and timely access to information in critical situations, is an example of the value provided by the sensor networks made possible by Arch Rock technology.

IP and Sensor Networks

Arch Rock is focusing not only on sensor technologies but also on their integration into the larger ecosystem of Internet technologies:

> Wireless sensor networking is critical for broad and immediate access to sensory information. The technology removes the physical boundaries that shackle instruments, bringing sensing to places and things previously unobservable and creating networks to make that information readily accessible. Equally important are leading-edge Internet and Web technologies which provide an architecture for highly scalable networks and efficient integration of diverse information sources.[63]

This perspective indicates a clear commitment to IP. That commitment, however, is supported by multiple other practical and technological arguments:[64]

- **Extensive interoperability:** Because IP has extensive interoperability with wireless embedded 802.15.4 data link layer and devices on any other IP network link (Wi-Fi, Ethernet, GPRS, WiMAX, serial lines, and so on), building an architectural framework on top of IP guarantees the model will be able to cope with any new wired and wireless technologies developed in the future.

62. http://www.commandinformation.com/labs/research/airs.php.

63. See note 60 above.

64. David E. Culler and Jonathan Hui, "6LoWPAN Tutorial: IP on IEEE 802.15.4 Low-Power Wireless Networks," May 2007, http://www.archrock.com/downloads/resources/6LoWPAN-tutorial.pdf.

- **Established security:** IP has established security through leverage of existing authentication, access control, and firewall mechanisms. The network design and policies, not the technology, determine access.

- **Established naming, addressing, translation, lookup, and discovery:** Deployment is similar to what has been done for years in IP.

- **Established proxy architectures for higher-level services:** IP can use available proxy, load balancing, caching, and mobility functions and features.

- **Established application-level data models and services:** Use of common IP APIs and profiles with HTTP/HTML/XML/SOAP/REST (often referred to as the Service Oriented Architecture, or SOA), now very familiar in distributed systems and open computing architectures, eases the open development of back-end applications.

- **Established network management tools:** Familiar management tools (such as ping, traceroute, and SNMP) and environments (such as OpenView, NetManager, and Ganglia) can be leveraged.

- **Transport protocols:** Transport protocols provide the end-to-end reliability of IP in addition to the link reliability inherent in the media.

Arch Rock has pioneered the development of IP sensor networks, yielding great benefits from the convergence of technologies and the "all IP" trend. The level of IP integration gives Arch Rock customers the ability to access and manage their sensor networks and sensor nodes using the familiar paradigms of TCP/IP networking and the Internet. This has the effect of dramatically reducing the cost of operating sensor networks and increasing their reliability, through reduced learning curves and the ability to leverage an immense range of existing IP methods, services, and management tools.

Arch Rock's technology provides direct access to the wireless sensor network as well as to individual sensor nodes using IP methods, services, and tools. Each Arch Rock sensor node can be configured with an IP address and a DNS name. It can be accessed via a node-specific web page using standard HTTP over TCP/IP protocols, and can also be reached via tools and services such as ping, traceroute, and Telnet.

Additionally, embedded sensor network parameters are represented as Management Information Bases (MIB) for access via standard SNMP and integration into pervasive enterprise management platforms such as HP OpenView. Arch Rock technology also enables monitoring of sensor networks using the widely deployed Ganglia resource monitoring infrastructure and tools (http://ganglia.sourceforge.net/).

Arch Rock's sensors are used in a wide range of industries and environments:

- **Environmental monitoring:** Energy and utility management, building commissioning, HVAC optimization, data center monitoring, cold chain monitoring

- **Industrial automation:** Machine monitoring, process control, predictive maintenance, regulatory compliance, automotive field testing

- **Location and proximity:** Asset tracking and monitoring, worker safety, QoS, hazardous material management, regulatory compliance

- **Action and control:** Lighting control, machine automation

Arch Rock demonstrated the practical use of these sensors through several solutions developed in collaboration with various integrators and technology partners.

The Case for IPv6

Arch Rock went beyond its technology commitment to IP and focused on IP's next generation. With little existing legacy in IP-based sensor networks or applications, there was an opportunity to pick the most efficient and future-proof IP technology for such an emerging field. Thus, enabling these devices to communicate using IPv6 makes sense considering that they are all part of the next generation networks and that they have rigid requirements for power, memory, processing, and bandwidth efficiency. Arch Rock's focus on IPv6, however, stems from several technological arguments:

- **End-to-end communications:** IPv6 facilitates end-to-end communications for sensor network applications deployed rapidly or "on the fly," which makes management of two-way communications easier.

- **Large address space:** IPv6 has the resources to accommodate millions of sensors that will be implemented in all market sectors whatever the selected addressing scheme, public or private.

- **Plug-and-play capabilities:** The number of sensor nodes will soon far exceed the number of networked PCs. IPv6 provides simple provisioning mechanisms suitable to low-power devices, thus facilitating easy deployment from the end-user perspective.

- **Energy efficiency and simplified protocol processing:** IETF developments offer an open environment to enhance IPv6 capabilities and their mapping into low-power communications media, leading to energy savings and longer life on limited power for autonomous devices. More specifically, the streamlined header structure of IPv6 was extended to the low-power and resource-constrained context. A "pay only for what you need" scheme dictates that in the simplest (and most frequent) cases, very little overhead is incurred. More demanding (and typically less frequent) cases incur additional overhead but are confined to the minimum required number of nodes, using the "header stacking/chaining" technique that is one of IPv6's signature features for option processing in packets.

- **Future growth potential:** IPv6 benefits from all standardization activities in various areas such as mobility, multicast, security, and "any to any" communication between sensor nodes and mobile and handheld devices, and so forth.

Extensive work has been done to map and optimize IPv6 for use over IEEE 802.15.4, a low-power wireless technology. The IPv6-based 6LoWPAN IETF working group[65] has standardized the use of IPv6 over this media, as specified in RFC 4944. The minimal Layer 2 dependency of an IPv6-based framework can be seen as a key benefit of the model, making any future evolution of wireless technology a candidate for support.

65. http://www.ietf.org/html.charters/6lowpan-charter.html.

NOTE   The IEEE 802.15 WPAN Task Group 4 "was chartered to investigate a low data rate solution with multi-month to multi-year battery life and very low complexity. It is operating in an unlicensed, international frequency band. Potential applications are sensors, interactive toys, smart badges, remote controls, and home automation."[66] The IEEE 802.15.4-2003 standards offer wireless technologies that require less than 1 percent of the power used by the commonly deployed IEEE 802.11 Wi-Fi technology.

Arch Rock offers low-power wireless sensor nodes, gateways, and data and management servers based on IPv6 standards developed by the IETF 6LoWPAN Working Group for the IEEE 802.15.4 low-power radio standard. Through its focus on standards-based IPv6 in low-power wireless meshed sensor networks, its standards-based embedded web services in sensor nodes, and its highly manageable and easy-to-integrate solutions, Arch Rock has taken a position of architectural leadership in this fast-growth marketplace.

NOTE   A 6LoWPAN Tutorial by David Culler and Jonathan Hui can be found at Arch Rock's website: http://www.archrock.com/ downloads/resources/6LoWPAN-tutorial.pdf. Additional references and research results can be found at http://6lowpan.net/.

Arch Rock combines its innovative technology with its extensive experience in deploying sensor networks in a variety of challenging environments and applications (in open field environmental monitoring, energy awareness, personnel safety, engineering structures, mobile high-value items, factory floors, office buildings, defense, and so on) to deliver rapidly deployable and highly extensible solutions to its customers. Arch Rock is also a key partner in multiple proofs of concept for IPv6-based solutions that integrate sensor networks and is now an IPv6 Forum member.

---

66. http://www.ieee802.org/15/pub/TG4.html.

Lessons Learned

The Arch Rock case study is unique among the others in this section because it reveals several technical and business reasons for adopting IPv6 in an emerging market. In this example, the focus is not on integrating IPv6 in an existing environment and into existing products, but rather on using it as a foundation for building new products, new applications, and a new communications environment. Through its contributions to the technology and standards and through its products and demonstrated solutions, Arch Rock provides an example of how the next generation of networked devices can be built to use the next generation of IP.

Arch Rock's progress to date offers several valuable lessons for both existing companies and startups focused on building products and applications leveraging IP communications:

- **Open IP model adoption:** The field of networked sensors may be considered new ground to many established and traditional industry segments. The proposed solutions have to minimize the cost of application development and user training. No technology is better adapted than IP, with its open model and a vibrant ecosystem of tools, products, and services, to achieve those objectives. Looking at similar transformations of long-established industries through the introduction of open IP-based frameworks gives us great examples such as IP telephony and VoIP and, more recently, IP-based video and television.

- **Low risk to initially adopt IPv6:** As a startup, Arch Rock carefully evaluated the risk and trade-offs involved with going with an IPv6-based protocol suite versus an embedded IPv4-based approach in the sensor networking solutions. A close analysis of IT industry readiness, combined with the efficiency arguments of embedded IPv6, led to IPv6 as the right architectural choice. To further facilitate sensor network integration, Arch Rock solutions offer standard "6-to-4" internetworking technology, allowing IPv6-based sensors to communicate with IPv4-based devices on enterprise networks. Also minimizing the risk were stable core IETF specifications, full dual-stack support from most OSs and development tools, mandates from U.S. and other governments, and the IPv4 address space exhaustion forecast. Although the choice of IPv6 may be seen as a bold bet on the future, the initial support and the warm reception by Arch Rock customers and partners are clear signs of technology leadership.

- **Needs for standards innovations:** Networked sensors have challenges not seen in traditional IT. Battery consumption, low-speed radio links, limited memory or processing resources, and on-the-fly ad hoc networking deployments were not prominent considerations in earlier standards efforts. Arch Rock engineers are committed to remaining involved in the IETF 6LoWPAN WG and other relevant IETF activities, helping to ensure that new standards are geared toward building a viable architecture that fulfills the vision of an Internet that is, in the words of Roland Acra, "embedded into the physical world around us, allowing users to remotely interact with things, spaces, assets, and the environment at large."

IPv6 and wireless sensor networks represent two prominent facets of the future of networking. As the number of sensor nodes deployed reaches the billions of devices (in homes, offices, streets, cars, fields, and so forth), they will benefit greatly from the scaling potential, the operational ease, and the rich feature set of IPv6 such as the larger address space, streamlined header processing, and stateless autoconfiguration support, to name a few. The combination of the two technologies provides a realization of the vision of an expanded Internet whose scope is to improve ever-larger aspects of our daily lives, beyond today's traditional computing.

Professional Services: Command Information

IPv6 represents one of the greatest advancements to the Internet in the past 20 years. It will allow us to realize a potential from the network we've been unable to access due to the limitations of the current version of Internet Protocol. While organizations need to integrate IPv6 in an economically sensible fashion, failure to begin that integration process today will only yield higher integration costs in the future, as well as loss of market leadership and missed opportunities to be an organization of innovation.

—Yurie Rich, Director IPv6 Services

One of the IPv6 deployment challenges most commonly cited by early planners and early adopters is the shortage of IPv6 expertise, IPv6 knowledge, and practical experience. Assistance is typically needed in all aspects of IPv6 planning: from running and assessing the IPv6 capabilities of the infrastructure to designing the IPv6 deployment; from translating the results of the inventory, in the context of the future design, into purchasing policies to planning the resources necessary for operations; from training the staff to developing new, IPv6-enabled services. Clearly, the IP-enabled organizations—in other words, most organizations—are and will be investing significantly in IPv6-related competency and IPv6 consulting services.

This reality creates a business case for IPv6 professional services with demand rapidly growing as the IPv4 global address space exhaustion approaches. IPv6 expertise is becoming an asset that can help grow business. Although specialized IPv6 consultancy and training firms have been operating in the market for some time, until recently they were typically small in size, a reflection of demand. As IPv6 became important to large organizations such as the U.S. government, a need emerged for professional services and consulting companies large enough to support lengthy and complex IPv6 deployment projects. Large integrators have to develop IPv6 expertise. In some cases, this goal has been achieved through market consolidation where IPv6-specialized consulting companies were acquired for their extensive experience in the protocol and the related training. IPv6 is becoming one of the specialties, one of the services offered by many leading professional services companies.

Understanding the perspective developed by these companies toward IPv6 is insightful in all its aspects, including:

- **Business model:** Their business model, the level of investment, and the services developed reflect not only the current market demand but also the anticipated market demand. Through existing customer engagements and through partnerships, professional services companies have a unique, first-hand view of what are the market priorities.

- **Technology focus:** Based on current and previous engagements covering a wide range of communications technologies, professional services companies are very well positioned to understand the challenges faced by the market in integrating IPv6. This exposure enables them to focus on identifying solutions or innovating for important aspects of the technology that have high impact for customers.

- **Training:** A comprehensive, in-depth training curriculum represents not only an important source of revenue, but also an important strategy for promoting and showcasing expertise. The training offerings must be constantly updated to ensure relevance within existing markets and to address emerging IPv6 interest in new markets. In this sense, the training plans of these companies are a good reflection of market interest and the technical depth of current adoption plans.

- **Leadership:** Professional services companies have a unique opportunity to distinguish themselves from the competition by becoming early adopters of the technologies they offer expertise in. The same applies to IPv6, making their IPv6 integration plans and strategy a valuable case study in itself. They can take a leadership and active role in standards and the development of the protocol and of applications using it. As an infrastructure technology, IPv6 has fewer champions than technologies such as Bluetooth. Professional services companies have the opportunity to step into this role.

Each of these points provides a measure of perceived and anticipated interest in IPv6 as well as a set of enterprise-level strategies on IPv6. Professional services companies with focus on IPv6 are natural leaders and promoters of adoption within the realistic conditions of businesses.

This case study covers the leading provider of next generation Internet services: Command Information. Through its IPv6 expertise, training offerings, research and development, and active participation in IPv6 standardization and promotion bodies, Command Information established a leadership position in delivering IPv6-related services. This case study was developed with the assistance of Yurie Rich, Director IPv6 Services at Command Information.

Company Profile

According to its corporate information page:

> Command Information is the leading provider of next generation internet services, and has been the trusted partner of global customers for more than 15 years. Committed to delivering the finest solutions and customer service, Command was built from the ground up to help federal and commercial clients solve today's challenges with the technologies of tomorrow.[67]

Command Information offers a wide portfolio of professional services: consulting services (Envision Services, IT Strategy, Business Intelligence, Netcentric Consulting), application services (Application Development, Solutions Planning and Design, SOA Strategy and Development, Systems Integration, Migration Services), network services (Network Engineering, Network Convergence, Network Migration, Database/Information Engineering), and dedicated IPv6 services (Technical Training, IPv6 Executive Briefings and Seminars, Courseware Development, Training Program Development, Certification Program Development). Yurie Rich states, "Command Information is fully committed to helping organizations make the transition from an IPv4-dominant world to an IPv6-dominant world."

Command Information's corporate profile is summarized in Table 5-42.

Table 5-42 *Command Information Corporate Profile Overview*

Profile Category	Status/Value
Organization	Command Information
Industry	Professional services
Number of employees	400
Geography	U.S. and global
Revenue	$50 million

---

67. http://www.commandinformation.com/.

Command Information focuses on two major business practices:

- **Federal:** "Command Federal has supported the missions of government agencies for more than 15 years. Today we continue this effort with the most complete suite of next generation technology solutions."[68] Its major clients are: Defense Information Systems Agency, Defense Business Transformation Agency, Defense Threat Reduction Agency, Surface Deployment and Distribution Command, Secretary of Defense, Department of Transportation, Army, Air Force, Navy, Marine Corps, and Federal Aviation Administration.

- **Commercial:** "As the leading provider of next generation internet services, Command combines proven agile methods with IPv6 expertise to offer a robust set of IT services and solutions to Fortune 1000 clients."[69] Its major clients are: AOL, Abritron, Bechtel, British Telecom, Cisco, CSX, Enterasys, EMC, Ericsson, GMAC Bank, HP, Intel, Lafarge, McKesson, OnStar, Sallie Mae, Symantec, VeriSign, and Verizon.

This wide spectrum of customers and leaders within their respective markets provides Command Information with a good perspective on the IPv6 adoption trends and challenges. Another important aspect of its business is its R&D arm, Command Labs, which focuses on proving IPv6-based technologies, integrating them in production, and developing new applications and services over IPv6. "Command Labs is a resource for organizations of all shapes and sizes to learn how IPv6 can improve the way business is done," said Tom Patterson, past CEO of Command Information, at the Command Labs ribbon cutting ceremony on September 13, 2006. While transferring the extensive IPv6 expertise into training material development, Command Labs pursues detailed evaluations of OSs such as Microsoft Vista and the development of IPv6-enabled environments such as the Advanced Incident Response System (AIRS), which is dedicated to integrating EMS resources, and Veesix, an IPv6-instrumented car.

68. http://www.commandinformation.com/federal/.

69. http://www.commandinformation.com/commercial/.

Command Information fosters partnerships with leading ICT manufacturers in order to expand its expertise and to help them with their IPv6 training needs. Its subject matter experts have a wide range of industry certifications and are actively involved in many standardization and promotion organizations.

IT Profile

This case study focuses on all aspects of Command Information's IPv6 strategy, including its internal adoption of IPv6. In this context, it is important to review the main elements of its current IT infrastructure, the elements that shape its deployment plans.

The OSs currently deployed in Command Information's infrastructure and those it plans to use going forward are listed in Table 5-43.

Table 5-43 *Command Information IT Profile—Operating Systems*

Device Type	Today	Future
PC and workstations	Windows 2003, Windows XP	Windows Vista
	Linux Redhat Enterprise	Linux Redhat Enterprise
	Sun Solaris 8	Sun Solaris 10
Servers	Windows Server 2003	Windows Server 2008
Routers and switches	Cisco IOS, CatOS	Cisco IOS

NOTE   Vista trials started in 2006 with the IPv6 Services Group being part of the Vista beta program. Command Information subject matter experts are actively sharing their Vista experience with the IPv6 community through various forums.

Command Information's networking infrastructure is based on Cisco equipment and is IPv6 ready.

This IT environment supports a set of typical applications for a medium-sized enterprise. These applications are summarized in Table 5-44.

Table 5-44   *Command Information IT Profile—Applications*

Application Type	Facility
E-mail	Microsoft Exchange/MAPI, RPC, HTTPS, POP3, and LDAP
Accounting	Deltek Vision, HTTP
File/print sharing	CIFS
Web-based tools	HTTP
VoIP	Cisco Unified Communications Manager

NOTE   Around 95 percent of all applications are commercial products, but many, such as Apache and FitNesse, represent frameworks for internally developed content and interfaces.

The previous review of the major applications used by Command Information is important because their availability over IPv6 has been identified as important criteria for IPv6 internal adoption. Due to a limited number of in-house-developed applications, no relevant IPv4 dependencies are introduced internally. The new systems and applications developed within Command Labs are designed and developed around IPv6.

IP Infrastructure Characteristics

Command Information's IT infrastructure is typical for a medium-sized enterprise. The network and the security of the IT environment are fully managed internally even though some stationary devices such DNS secondaries are outsourced.

The IPv4 address management approach is typical for an enterprise of this size:

- **Address lifetime:** Most endpoints are dynamically assigned temporary addresses. Network elements and devices in the data centers use fixed IP addresses.

- **Address types:** Command Information is using private (RFC 1918) IPv4 addresses for almost all internal devices. The private addresses are translated via NAT to global IPv4 addresses.

- **Global IPv4 addresses management:** The global addresses used with NAT and the global addresses used for devices in the demilitarized zones (DMZ) are acquired from their ISP.

Based on the size of the infrastructure and the number of devices, the private IPv4 address space is sufficient for Command Information's current and future needs. Whether in terms of number of addresses or in terms of address scheme design, addressing is generally not challenging in this type of environment. Moreover, Command Information's acquisitions were small in size, so their infrastructures could be easily renumbered with no significant productivity impact. In other words, for a business of Command Information's size, there are no evident IPv4 addressing constraints to drive IPv6 adoption.

Perspective on IPv6

From the internal deployment point of view, Command Information's perspective on IPv6 is interesting as an early adopter, midsize enterprise. More interesting, however, is its perspective on IPv6 as a provider of IPv6-related professional services. The decision to focus a significant part of its service offering on IPv6, and to invest in it, required a close and detailed analysis of the market demand and trends. The perspectives follow:

- **Internal adoption perspective:** From a business operations perspective, Command Information is continuously searching for ways to leverage IPv6 to enhance operations. With a geographically distributed and mobile workforce, Command Information is looking to leverage its IPv6 network in conjunction with a Microsoft Vista rollout to take advantage of the collaboration tools built into Vista. While other technologies have been utilized in the past to achieve these capabilities, IPv6 offers a cleaner and more cost-effective option. This is merely one example of the ways in which Command Information is envisioning its adoption of IPv6.

- **Service offering perspective:** From a revenue perspective, there is tremendous advantage to taking an early adopter position in this market. Command Information believes that its commitment to IPv6 over the past five years provides a level of insight into the protocol that most companies will not be able to achieve. IPv6 is one of its core competencies. This fact is, in part, one of the drivers for Command Information's increasing customer base. The years invested in gaining protocol experience provide Command Information with a clear competitive advantage over its competition and serve as a market entry barrier for other organizations. With a rapidly increasing interest in IPv6, time is of the essence, competitors will not be able to achieve similar levels of expertise to successfully bid on emerging, large-scale contracts.

Clearly an important factor in the success of the business model pursued by Command Information is the overall market perspective on IPv6. We asked Yurie Rich of Command Information when he expects that at least 70 percent of the market will start investigating IPv6. Following is his response:

> Command Information has two major business practices—
> Commercial and Federal. Command Federal (CF), the federal arm
> of Command, has a 15-year history of servicing the federal govern-
> ment—both Department of Defense (DoD) and Civilian federal
> agencies with IT support and the integration of new, advanced tech-
> nologies. For this division, the federal and DoD mandates for IPv6
> adoption by 2008 would imply that in 2007, over 70% of this space
> will be focusing on IPv6. The term investigate is somewhat flexible.
> If we accept a loose definition of "investigate" such as: "looking
> into the impacts of integrating IPv6 into their network environ-
> ments" then the Federal agencies have already reached this point.
> However, if "investigate" means some level of financial commit-
> ment into testing, education, and research on the impacts of inte-
> grating IPv6, then we believe 2008–2009 is the timeframe when
> 70% or more of Command Federal's market segments will be inves-
> tigating IPv6.

On the commercial side, the answer is different. Unlike the federal space, driven by mandates, the corporate commercial sector is driven exclusively by three simple rules that influence technology uptake rates:

It increases revenue

It reduces costs

It provides competitive edge

In the context of these rules, the commercial sector is looking for links between the technical capabilities of IPv6 and clear business drivers. Unfortunately, these links, while available, are not being well communicated to the business sector. Companies like Command Information—and Cisco for that matter—continuously provide insight into the business values generated by using IPv6 as a foundation for innovation. However, it is likely that it will be 2010–2012 before there is enough momentum behind IPv6 business-related messaging for 70% or more of the commercial sector to take a dedicated interest in investigating the IPv6 technology.

The subsequent question we asked Command Information, a question we asked all participants in the case studies, was: By when do you expect at least 70 percent of the market to start adopting IPv6? Command Information's perspective, as stated by Yurie Rich, follows:

Command Information defines "adoption" as an organization physically incorporating IPv6 capability into its network environment and then leveraging that capability for actual "business" purposes. We would not consider a test bed, for example, as a measure or indicator of adoption. An organization must be utilizing IPv6 to drive some organizational value—be that business objective or mission critical service. In this sense Command Federal perceives adoption occurring sometime in the 2010–2014 timeframe.

The current federal mandates set relatively low bars for what IPv6 integration means (enabling the infrastructure). We are not minimizing the level of effort required to achieve the milestones set by the DoD and OMB mandates. Command Information has a full appreciation for the challenges related to this task. However, the mandates merely detail a level of technical achievement. They do not identify clear metrics for the benefits of an IPv6 integration into the network environments. With 2008 being set as the "line in the sand," many federal organizations invested the resources and effort necessary to successfully meet the requirements of the mandates. But the federal agencies will not be truly leveraging IPv6. It will take several more years of effort and investigation to begin benefiting from IPv6. This explains our estimate of a 2010–2014 timeframe for IPv6 adoption in the sense we define it.

For our commercial practice, the timeframe between investigation and adoption will be significantly shorter. Businesses must translate efforts and investments related to IT into quarterly earning benefits in relatively short order. Not surprisingly then, it is reasonable to assume that the commercial sector will also have an adoption timeframe of 2011–2014, overlapping the adoption timeframe anticipated for the federal space. It is important to note that this overlap is most likely a positive occurrence. Many federal organizations have IT requirements that mirror those of their corporate counterparts. Commercial adoption of IPv6 will drive the development of new applications and services that extract additional benefit from the network. The federal sector, with its continued efforts to work with Commercial Off-The-Shelf (COTS) products, will benefit from the commercial success of IPv6.

This of course reflects primarily the U.S. market perspective; however, some of its aspects can be extended on a global scale. Command Information's expertise is gaining international recognition and its services are requested by organizations outside the United States.

The Case for IPv6

Based on its IPv6 perspective detailed earlier, Command Information clearly sees IPv6 as a unique opportunity to gain leadership in the professional services market. This position represents the foundation of both a business case for developing an IPv6-focused service portfolio and a business case for early planning and adoption of IPv6 in its internal infrastructure.

The perceived drivers for an early development and introduction of IPv6-centric services portfolio are as follows:

- **Capturing mindshare early:** Command Information plans to capitalize on the surging interest in IPv6 and the following demand for IPv6 expertise and experience. Making IPv6 services available early and working closely and publicly with early adopters positions Command Information as a recognized leader in the market.

- **Distancing from future competition:** The acquisition of IPv6 expertise and experience, both theoretical and hands-on, requires commitment of resources and time. Although Command Information assumes a risk in terms of when it will see the ROI of its strategy, its early start can significantly distance Command Information from competition. This distance might become irrecoverable as the IPv6 project timelines shorten with a rapid increase in interest and adoption.

- **Take advantage of the market's knowledge preceding focus on deployment:** A relevant, comprehensive, and practical IPv6 training curriculum is seeing significant demand from various organizations. As repeatedly highlighted in other case studies, training represents one of the challenging and costly elements of an IPv6 strategy. In the short run, training combined with certification programs represents a significant source of revenue ahead of true adoption. In the long run, training represents a mechanism to showcase Command Information's expertise and capabilities, thereby preparing its future customer base.

- **Stimulate innovation:** Early development of IPv6 services provides a unique environment that fosters innovation in applications and services operating over IPv6. Interactions with early adopters and industry visionaries highlight problems that could benefit from an IPv6-based solution. With the help of a research facility such as Command Labs, revenue can be generated through customized solutions. More-general solutions can also be pursued collaboratively with IT industry partners. Such solutions made available by Command Information can significantly expand its market and offering.

This business case can be implemented through funding dedicated to developing expertise and through acquisition of consultancy firms with extensive expertise in IPv6. It is important, however, to remember that IPv6 is not the only area of expertise for Command Information; the rest of its portfolio remains IP version independent. IPv6 services address existing and emerging market needs and at the same time help expand the market for Command Information's other services.

NOTE	In 2006, Command Information acquired a small IPv6 consultancy firm, Native6 (http://www.native6.com/). Native6 was well known in the IPv6 community for its technical expertise, its excellent training material, and its major contributions to the promotion of IPv6. This acquisition, along with the recruitment of leading industry experts, provided Command Information with a core of well-known and experienced subject matter experts (SME).

The business case pursued by Command Information automatically qualifies it, to a certain extent, as an IPv6 promoter and supporter. Along with this image, Command Information must embrace an early adopter position as well, so it must develop a business case for the internal adoption of IPv6. The leading arguments in favor of IPv6 adoption are as follows:

- **Showcase deployment and operations expertise:** Along with the extensive IPv6 expertise developed and demonstrated through the work of Command Labs, an internal, production deployment of IPv6 would demonstrate system-level planning, implementation, and operational expertise.

- **Stimulate innovation:** Command Information's pursuit of new applications and services delivered over IPv6 can benefit from the extension of its IPv6 environment outside Command Labs. A corporate-wide IPv6 network with IPv6-enabled users can be used to trial the migration of services and applications from IPv4 to IPv6 or the introduction of new, IPv6-centric ones.

- **Interface with customers and partners over IPv6:** Whether Command Information establishes direct links with partners over IPv6, performs integration or maintenance on a customer's IPv6 environment, or delivers IPv6 training leveraging material or lab resources over IPv6, Command Information benefits now and will soon need to have the ability to interface with other organizations over IPv6.

With a relatively new infrastructure, Command Information's Cisco-powered network is IPv6 ready. Parts of the network were built from the ground up with focus on IPv6. This minimizes the costs of IPv6 integration.

NOTE   As an example of using its own infrastructure to stimulate innovation, Command Information used an IPv6 readiness assessment tool developed in collaboration with Cisco to evaluate and monitor the IPv6 readiness of its network.

As explained in the "Perspective on IPv6" section, Command Information's definition of adoption is more demanding; it does not stop at mere enablement of the infrastructure or integration and migration of some applications, but also requires drawing business benefits from the IPv6 deployment. In this context, despite its internal use of IPv6, Command Information would qualify the internal adoption a success when some of the above arguments materialize and generate value.

IPv6 Planning and Implementation

Similar to the preceding case studies, Command Information's IPv6 strategy includes both planning and implementation. However, unlike the other case studies, Command Information's business model requires not only planning and implementation of its internal use of IPv6 but also the planning and implementation of its IPv6 services offered to others.

The strategy of IPv6 services development reflects market realities and Command Information's commitment to take an early leadership role as a professional services provider. Three major focus areas have been identified:

- **Training:** Develop comprehensive IPv6 training for the general industry at both the technical and executive level. Customize training for large organizations based on their needs, their products, and the requirements of various internal groups.

- **Consultancy:** Engage initially with leading early adopters and assist with the design, planning, and implementation of their IPv6 strategies. As market focus is moving from investigating and understanding IPv6 toward actual adoption, so will Command Information's focus move from its established training program to assisting customers with their IPv6 integration.

- **Research and development:** Develop and prove IPv6-based solutions and services in collaboration with industry partners.

The timeline for implementing these focus areas is summarized in Table 5-45.

Table 5-45 *Command Information IPv6 Service Development Strategy*

Phase 1 (2001–2006)	Phase 2 (2006–2007)	Phase 3 (2008 Onward)
Develop experience through customer interaction, partnerships with IT companies, and involvement in industry activities such as the beta evaluation program for Vista.	Develop IPv6 training customized to large organizations.	Move emphasis toward consultancy services and application development.
Develop training material for the general market.	Develop tools supporting professional services around IPv6 integration, both for network integration and for vendor equipment and software.	Identify and promote best practices in IPv6 deployment and adoption.
Provide consulting services on IPv6 integration to early adopters. Activities include network design, infrastructure, inventory, and so on.	Initiate research and development projects to deliver IPv6-based solutions to pressing industry problems.	Market and support the results of R&D projects. Commercialize advanced networking technology solutions.
Stay actively involved in IPv6 promotion bodies such as IPv6 Forum and North America IPv6 Forum.		

Command Information's commitment to this IPv6 strategy generated significant contributions to the three focus areas identified above:

- **Training:** Command Information has the most comprehensive and practical training materials in the market.[70] It also developed and continues to develop customized training for large organizations such as Cisco Systems.

- **Consultancy:** Command Information has an extensive list of customers with whom it works on their early adoption of IPv6: Bechtel, Cisco Systems, HP, Symantec, DISA, U.S. Army, U.S. Navy, U.S. Air Force, U.S. Marine Corps, JITC, VA, and Space & Missile Defense Command.

70. http://www.commandinformation.com/labs/catalogue/index.php.

- **Research and development:** Command Information initiated several development projects with an IPv6 focus. These are a few examples:

  - In support of its professional services and to help customers, Command Information in collaboration with Cisco developed a network assessment tool that automatically evaluates IPv6 readiness of network elements.

  - It is one of the four partners involved in the Advanced Incident Response System (AIRS)[71], which, in a context similar to projects such as Metronet6 and U-2010, provides practical solutions for integrated communications between emergency response resources and assets.

  - It launched other projects, which are focused on networked sensors and communications systems networked over IPv6.[72]

Command Information is recognized in the U.S. market as a leading provider of IPv6 training and professional services. Demand for its services continues to grow outside the United States as well, reflecting an increasing global demand for IPv6 professional services.

From an internal adoption perspective, as well as based on the IPv6 integration experience of its clients, Command Information sees the lack of IPv6-enabled enterprise services as the biggest obstacle to full IPv6 migration. The IPv6 upgrade should not lead to the loss of any fundamental enterprise services currently in use. While recognizing the potential benefits of an IPv6 environment, similar to most enterprises, Command Information relies on basic services to operate (e-mail, network file services, security tools, web services, network management, and so forth), and in its opinion the only way to maintain existent functionality with the current level of IPv6 support by the applications is to operate a dual-stack environment.

71. http://www.commandinformation.com/labs/research/airs.php.

72. http://www.commandinformation.com/labs/research/.

NOTE	Command Information believes a dual-stack environment is an acceptable intermediate solution, but it is more expensive to operate than an IPv6-only network, Command Information's long-term goal. On the other hand, a one-step migration to an IPv6-only environment is more expensive in the near term than a gradual transition through an integration phase when the environment is dual-stack.

Command Information's strategy toward internal adoption of IPv6 reflects its continued efforts to couple technology and business benefits of IPv6 within the enterprise environment. It also evaluates in great detail various IPv6-enabled OSs, applications, and tools, as the result of this work will be leveraged in helping its customers integrate IPv6 more successfully.

The phased approach to IPv6 integration is described in Table 5-46.

Table 5-46   *Command Information Internal IPv6 Deployment*

Phase 1 (2005–2006)	Phase 2 (2007–2008)	Phase 3 (2008 Onward)
Build the new networking infrastructures with IPv6 support. Existing infrastructure assessment for IPv6 capabilities. Vista trials on application-by-application basis for migration of current IPv4-based enterprise services. Review of security policies in the context of IPv4-IPv6 coexistence. In most cases, IPv6 security policies are aimed at maintaining the same functional level of security as for IPv4, while taking into account IPv6's unique strengths and operational requirements.	Select an ISP that provides native IPv6 transport and Internet access services. Acquire IPv6 address space. Perform trials for Windows Vista SP1. Develop interim solutions for network services with no production IPv6 support. Trials of the Advanced Incident Response System (AIRS) and Message Caster solutions. Provide IPv6-based services such as: IPv6-only website Internal IPv6 e-learning VoIPv6 trials IPv6 IM trials	Deployment of Windows Server 2008. Migrate internal infrastructure to IPv6-dominant framework. Begin the migration of IPv4-only services to IPv6-only.

NOTE	Command Information acquired its provider independent global IPv6 address space from ARIN in 2006: 2610:00F8::/32.

NOTE	As an IPv6-centric company, it was critical that ISP services not only provide support for IPv6, but also provide native IPv6 transport services as well as support Command Information's presence on the IPv6 Internet with a presence in the default-free zone (DFZ) and pointers to its authoritative DNS servers. Command Information hosts its own services and wanted to ensure that it could do so on both IPv4 and IPv6 protocols. For this reason, it retained the services of an ISP who could facilitate these requirements across the U.S. geography.

Wherever possible, Command Information strives to use IPv6, including in its own corporate environment. Its strategy matches its messaging toward enterprise customers: "We are still leveraging our existing IPv4 infrastructure for most of our daily IT activities simply because the level of support for IPv6 is still nascent." However, Command Information strives to clearly be at the leading edge of the curve for adopting IPv6-capable products and services as they become available.

Lessons Learned

Since Command Information opened its doors in early 2006, it has had a number of successful IPv6-related projects that have provided critical insights with regard to IPv6:

- **IPv6 drivers:** Organizations have little interest in IPv6 as a standalone technology, an observation that applies to U.S. government agencies being driven by mandated adoption. The key to successful integration is a clear mapping of IPv6 to organizational IT initiatives. By identifying how IPv6 may improve or enhance general IT initiatives, organizations are able to create ROI models around their integration efforts.

- **IPv6 differentiators:** The uniform support for security and MIPv6 have proved to be fundamental in architecting and developing of network-centric solutions from Command Labs. The AIRS solution, developed in collaboration with Cisco and Arch Rock, heavily leveraged IPv6 to create a resilient first-responders solution that would have been technically unscalable using IPv4.

- **Address space size matters:** Although the volume of IPv6 addresses has never been considered a "sexy" driver for IPv6 integration, it has proven to be foundational in sustaining interest in adoption. With the notice from ARIN in mid-2007, the world was put on notice that IPv4 address exhaustion was no longer an "if" but a definitive "when," with real impacts on the growth of the Internet and the costs of maintaining a legacy infrastructure.

- **IPv6 skill sets:** One of the greatest challenges Command Information has faced is scaling its technical workforce. IPv6 SMEs are in short supply. Command acquired a fair amount of talent initially, but quickly exhausted the marketplace. To overcome the challenge, it turned its training program inward, developing IPv6 SMEs by taking seasoned IT engineers and putting them through an exhaustive sequence of training and consulting exercises. Command Information overcome the timing in service issue by ensuring that these trainees focus exclusively on IPv6 for at least a year.

Command Information views IPv6 as a disruptive technology, requiring new and innovative ways of deploying and leveraging IT. At the same time, it must also provide value and help drive the total cost of ownership for technology initiatives downward. Currently the world works largely on a client/server model. This model leads to solution complexity and costly infrastructure to mitigate single points of failure. IPv6 provides a resilient and scalable framework for P2P applications that reduces the need for middleware and intermediate infrastructure. It is Command Information's belief that one of the most challenging obstacles will be to overcome the client/server mentality and build applications and services that use the computing power of end nodes and the reliability of the IPv6 and basic network infrastructure.

Summary

Although not always commonly known, large IPv6 deployments do exist today and detailed IPv6 adoption strategies are in place awaiting implementation. It is true, however, that the maturity level of the IPv6 strategies and related business cases varies across market segments. This chapter highlighted several examples of the many worldwide organizations that developed IPv6 strategies with various implementation timelines. More importantly, the case studies reveal aspects of the process that led these organizations to early planning, early adoption, or even the decision that IPv6 is not yet a high priority. It shows the fact that, as an infrastructure technology, making the case for IPv6 is not straightforward and, even when the case is made, the implementation of an IPv6 strategy depends on many other factors. When, however, the IPv6 planning is integrated seamlessly in the overall IT planning, an IP version–agnostic planning process, implementations are simplified and costs are reduced. Besides this general rule of thumb, each case study reveled a few specific lessons learned, some of which are specific to a market segment whereas others are common to most case studies. The following are the three most common lessons learned:

- **Early planning means reduced costs:** Organizations invariably experienced the cost benefits of early planning. Early planning has multiple facets, each contributing to a smoother and less expensive deployment of IPv6.

- **IPv6 technology is mature, but some challenges remain:** Overall the technology was found to be mature for deployment and revenue-generating service offerings. Nevertheless, challenges are still identified in various aspects of its operation. Increased adoption highlights some of these challenges but also leads to the development of solutions for them.

- **Product availability remains an important gating factor and can be mitigated through close vendor relationships:** The integration of IPv6 in products is market driven, and current gaps reflect the inconsistent past interest in the technology across the industry. Even as we approach parity between IPv4 and IPv6 support across products, close relationships with vendors is important in driving priorities and working on developing new, innovative IPv6 capabilities.

Without a doubt, the lessons shared by the organizations featured in these case studies will be, to a certain extent, practically relevant to the reader in their pursuit of an IPv6 strategy or its implementation. One of the messages carried over and over again by these case studies is the importance of planning for IPv6 and starting that process as soon as possible regardless of when an actual deployment is envisioned. To further assist your planning efforts, we collected their experiences on the topic and provide concrete steps and processes in Chapter 6, "Planning Your IPv6 Migration."

Planning Your IPv6 Migration

To this point, the goal of this book has been to help you understand the trends and strategies for adopting and leveraging IPv6 as part of natural technology evolution to sustain growth and specific business and competitive differentiators. The market overviews and the concrete examples presented in the case studies should enable decision makers to see the opportunities offered by IPv6 and to become familiar with the adoption experience of businesses in their market segments. Regardless of the conclusions drawn from an accelerated adoption or a continual monitoring of the technology, planning for IPv6 is essential to all businesses. The potential disruptive effects of not implementing IPv6 make an old saying applicable to this technological evolution: "There is absolutely no substitute for genuine lack of preparation."

Plan for IPv6 in the IT Environment

Planning for IPv6 takes a multidimensional effort, and a comprehensive approach to this undertaking is essential to its success. As a foundational technology, IPv6 touches all aspects of the IT ecosystem, as shown in Figure 6-1. The network is the platform that ties together people, services, devices, and information resources. The network facilitates communication among people, people's use of services and devices, and their access to information. The network also enables devices to communicate with each other and with services to leverage information. Figure 6-1 represents just a few of these interactions among the elements of the IT environment. IPv6 is not just about the IP network infrastructure, which in fact might be the simplest problem to solve; it is also about all these components and their interactions.

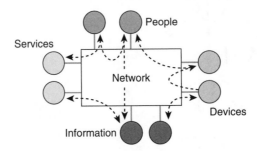

Figure 6-1   *Interactions in the IT Environment*

There is also the important temporal dimension of IPv6 planning. The title of this chapter, without a time scale attached to it, might lead to visions of daunting tasks with flag-day migrations that lead to dramatic disruptions. Because nobody really knows when the last IPv4 packet would be sent through a network, the full migration to IPv6 is a long string of protocol integration steps. Planning for IPv6 migration has to focus on the protocol integration and its co-existence with IPv4 as well.

A complete and global perspective of the IT environment reveals the multiple facets of an IPv6 integration planning effort. Figure 6-2 translates the generic concepts presented in Figure 6-1 into the following building layers of the IT environment:

- **Infrastructure:** Assets that support IT services and communications in an organization. Multiple infrastructure changes are needed with the implementation of IPv6; these changes go beyond apparent network transport upgrades. Individual, self-contained computing units must be IPv6-addressable and communicate using IPv6 as the preferred protocol over IPv4 from the operating system and through other local software such as browser and office automation (OA) applications. Attention also needs to be paid to infrastructure services used throughout the organization, starting with basic naming services, such as DNS and DHCP (v6). Common shared infrastructure services such as file, print, database, and web services are part of the IPv6 transformation.

- **Information:** Data essential for performing and supporting business functions. Information itself will generally not be changed when IPv6 is turned on. However, IPv6 does offer new alternatives in information access and sharing. Secure end-to-end IPv6 communications should be explored in the context of different information assurance (IA) and intellectual property paradigms.

- **Applications:** Software tools that enable users to perform business functions. Application development and certification processes ensure that IPv6 is used as the preferred communications protocol. This may not be possible with legacy third-party applications. Beyond qualifying existing applications to use IPv6, new applications are now possible that could not be achieved or easily developed with IPv4. Development environments, service-oriented architecture (SOA), web services, and maintenance routines should be updated to include IPv6.

- **Business functions:** The tasks that individually or in various combinations achieve the objectives of a business. Changes to core business functions can sometimes be supported by new capabilities offered by IPv6. Perhaps new ways to meet and interact with customers, develop products, or execute a task with IPv6 would be applicable. Readers should consider the way in which telephones or the Internet changed their organizational business functions as an example of infrastructure-enabled business function transformations.

These layers are bordered by two overarching structures, as indicated in Figure 6-2:

- **Processes:** Governance and methodologies that are used for the integrated management of the environment. IPv6 should be quickly integrated into existing IT processes and architectures such as development methodologies, certification processes, purchasing, and enterprise portfolio management. Enforcement of IPv6 requirements should be accomplished through IPv6 changes to quality assurance (QA), configuration management, and production deployment processes.

- **Standards:** Architectures and technical standards that provide the structure for integrating components at all levels. Standards interrelationships should be examined. We discussed earlier that IPv6 support is required for other standards such as 3GPP IMS (IP Multimedia Subsystem) and CableLabs DOCSIS. Organizations should carefully explore the current standards they are using, the emerging version of the standards, and any dependencies on IPv6.

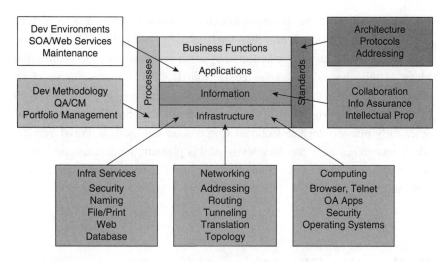

Figure 6-2 *High-level Reference Model for the IT Environment*

The IPv6 integration plans must be detailed for each IT environment element highlighted in Figure 6-2. These considerations are integrated in the major planning steps identified in this chapter:

- **Define the objectives:** Identify the scope of the project, its timeline, and the phases of implementation.

- **Assess the IT environment:** Inventory the IT assets to assess the changes required for IPv6 capabilities in the context of the identified integration objectives.

- **Review the operational and governance policies:** Tie the integration plans into the business and organizational structures to ensure the success of all aspects of adoption at all levels of the organization.

- **Initiate and support technology education:** Provide the individuals in the organization with the appropriate level of IPv6 knowledge and awareness.

- **Leverage the IPv6 industry experience:** Learn from the IPv6 experience of others in order to streamline the integration process and increase its chances of success.

We provide recommendations in this chapter for each of the previous steps of the IPv6 planning effort and how they can be used by both early and late adopters. Each recommendation is complemented by a concrete example of its application. Many of this chapter's examples come from Bechtel, a representative of an emerging category in the theory of technology adoption: an early planner (detailed in Chapter 5, "Analysis of Business Cases for IPv6—Case Studies"). Examples of other early planners include Comcast Corporation and the U.S. Postal Service, which recognized early the complexity of this planning process and initiated it well in advance of the actual technology deployment. Early planners often become early adopters.

Define the Objectives

The ramifications of IPv6 adoption depend on the scope of its integration. Although IPv6 will ultimately become ubiquitous throughout the organization, the initial steps in its integration might vary in terms of depth and coverage. Some organizations might decide that IPv6 deployment is not a priority at this time and choose to update only their security policies and monitoring/management capabilities to deal with potential IPv6 threats. Other organizations might fully commit to IPv6 and plan a complete strategy for its integration in all aspects of the IT environment.

There are four major aspects to defining the scope of an IPv6 integration project and its planning:

- **Alignment with strategic objectives:** Identify strategic value of the change.
- **Project goals:** Define what will be achieved.
- **Project scope:** Identify the areas of the IT environment that will be affected.
- **Project timeline:** Identify the time scale, metrics, and milestones for the project and its financial impacts.

The textbook project management elements are described in the following sections to provide IPv6 examples for them using companies included in Chapter 5.

Alignment with Strategic Objectives

Organizations should ensure that the implementation of a new technology has strategic value to an organization. This alignment requires an understanding of the business and the capabilities of the new technology. The change may not have immediate and direct short-term ROI, but may be the foundation for other more significant changes over time. The alignment discussed below is applicable within the Bechtel context. Each organization should make its own assessment based on its strategic business and technology objectives.

Bechtel is a global leader in the development, support, and management of industrial infrastructure. As with any significant technology transformation, Bechtel is approaching IPv6 in the context of its strategic applicability. Its constantly evolving project-based environment has several implications. They see IPv6 as one of the technology enablers to address its changing business. Bechtel established IPv6 project goals to address the combination of changes in its business and evolution of technology, including the following:

- **Volatile infrastructure:** Bechtel works on scores of concurrent large projects annually, each with an average life of 30 months. Some of the more complex projects are served by several global locations concurrently. The process of creating, tearing down, and moving populations and networks on a regular basis has created an increased demand for infrastructure agility, especially in the area of rapid project deployment. IPv6 can aid in rapid project mobilization and demobilization.

- **Highly mobile workforce:** People are moved and hired to support project execution. Getting the right people engaged at the right time involves a mix of global information access combined with travel. Reducing travel dependencies improves performance. IPv6 capabilities support improved and more secure communications to project participants, anytime and anywhere.

- **On-demand collaboration:** Many of organizations have an increasing degree of integration with customers, business/joint-venture partners, suppliers, and other external people. The transition to "snap-your-fingers quick" secure collaboration requires changes in network and security paradigms that can be improved or enabled with IPv6.

- **Dynamic intellectual property and IA needs:** Collaboration with multiple constituents requires an increasing reliance on securely sharing intellectual property and providing a high level if IA. In this more collaborative environment, information used in project execution may be controlled by Bechtel or some of its business partners. The dynamic management of sensitive information requires information security while fixed or in transit. Complexity and agility are both increased with the introduction of new paradigms, such as peer-to-peer computing.

- **Constant tech evolution:** Developing and maintaining industry leadership requires ongoing assessment, exploitation, and deployment of technologies that improve business operations. Like many other dynamic companies, Bechtel sees IPv6 as an enabler for transformation, just as web, database, and other technologies have been in the past.

- **Engineering systems convergence to IP:** IT is becoming more involved in areas outside of the traditional comfort zone. This is particularly apparent in industrial automation as building, plant, and process automation systems transition to IP-based communications. The IPv4 address shortage becomes a much more relevant and urgent issue when considering everything from building badge readers to motor-operated valves in an industrial plant.

- **IPv6 insertion from others:** Bechtel has selected the option to plan for change rather than being forced to react to it. Linux, Windows Vista, and other core computing technologies are now shipping with IPv6 turned on by default, generating IPv6 traffic that has to be under control. Bechtel's IPv6 project plans are designed to ensure that new technologies inserted into its environment work securely and effectively when production deployment starts.

Project Goals

The goals of the IPv6 project are essential in defining the resources necessary for its planning and later for its implementation. There are multiple options and they are often organization- or business-specific. The following list provides several examples of IPv6 project goals of varying complexities:

- Launch of a targeted, tactical project for which IPv6 is not yet important but for which security policies and monitoring capabilities must be updated to address the presence of IPv6-capable devices.

- Establish a test environment for protocol, application, security, and equipment evaluation.

- Deploy a single application running over IPv6 or take advantage of the Microsoft Windows Peer-to-Peer Networking framework (http://www.microsoft.com/p2p).

- Insert Linux, Microsoft Vista, and Microsoft Longhorn products with IPv6 enabled by default.

- Integrate new devices such as sensors or new services such as video content distribution over IPv6.

- Get IPv6 connectivity in a part of the world that is rapidly adopting IPv6.

- Deploy the next generation of services using IPv6.

The clear definition of project goals leads to well-defined success criteria and the means for tracking the progress of the project toward achieving them.

Bechtel views IPv6 as a critical component of its next generation infrastructure that must work in harmony with other fundamental changes that support strategic business objectives. IPv6 is not the "silver bullet" but it is clearly a strategic, foundational requirement for the future, with immediate near-term benefits. Within this business context, Bechtel established an IPv6 vision for 2008 that has these goals:

- IPv6 is broadly deployed.

- IPv6 is the default in a global dual-stack environment.

- New products and services run IPv6 by default.

- Bechtel is an IPv6 industry leader.
- IPv6 is the foundation for innovation.
- Bechtel is well positioned for rapid deployment of new IPv6 products and services.

Achieving these objectives will develop sustainable IPv6 competence in Bechtel through practical experience.

Project Scope

The goals of the project identify the IT environment elements that would be involved in its implementation. Nevertheless, the nature of the project influences its coverage. For example, an enterprise that is ready to interface with regional IPv6 ISPs requires localized coverage, whereas an ISP that delivers video content in accordance with national regulation that requires the service to be available to a service provider's entire subscriber base needs global coverage. The project coverage can be defined in terms of geography (specific markets or theaters), network architecture elements (campus or data center, branch offices, core), infrastructure elements (public wireless infrastructure, broadband, cars, planes, ships, trains), services (content delivery, VoIP), and policies or standards.

The opportunities for significant transformations are great, the impact footprint is broad, and the transition to an IPv6-dominant environment will take several years. Bechtel defined a governing strategy to guide its enterprise IPv6 transformation that addresses all major aspects of its enterprise architecture related to its comprehensive IPv6 deployment highlighted in Figure 6-2:

- Applications
- Information
- Computing platforms
- Networking
- Infrastructure services
- Processes
- Standards
- Governance

In the context of the "foundation first" principle, technology/product maturity, external influences, and dependencies should be used to determine the sequence and possible degree of parallel effort that could be achieved. A basic IPv6-enabled environment is required before advanced IPv6 products and services can be successfully deployed. The logical deployment sequence selected by Bechtel was as follows:

- Client computing platforms

- Network services (DNS, DHCP, NTP, and so on)

- LAN (intra-site) and WAN (between sites)

- Server computing platforms, early applications, and basic infrastructure services

- External IPv6 network connections

Bechtel elected to start its client site of IPv6 deployment with Windows XP SP2 rather than wait for the more comprehensive features of Windows Vista. Bechtel deployed stateless address autoconfiguration (routers), network switches, DNS, web services, and similar functions on IPv6-enabled computing platforms first. In parallel, Bechtel enabled IPv6 in all application and infrastructure development and engineering environments. This broad multidiscipline approach has been successful.

Maintaining and improving security is essential to the success of the deployment. IPv6 offers new security paradigms and potential disruption to existing practices. Bechtel approached security from the perspective of meeting current and emerging requirements, not from the view of just replicating the security systems of today. Typical requirements include border/firewall rules, logging criteria, and remote access. However, Bechtel's vision of the next generation infrastructure has to meet new demands that can be enabled by IPv6, such as on-demand collaboration with others, projects without borders, and dynamic transport security in an always-on environment. Bechtel information security professionals are an integral part of its IPv6 design and verification.

Maintaining and improving management represents another important operational aspect of the deployment. Several major vendors have enabled IPv6 features on their products before fully enabling IPv6 component management over IPv6 transport. This is not always a problem. However, in some cases, Bechtel has had to make tactical changes in management tools and process approach to get around product shortcomings.

Project Timeline

The overall migration to an IPv6-only network will probably take a long time and is likely to be achieved through either multiple projects or a single multiphase project. Similar to any technology integration, planning of each step has to meet the delivery dates while taking into consideration multiple timelines, some under the control of the organization and some not:

- Budget cycle
- Equipment refresh schedules
- Equipment and software certification cycle
- Timelines of related projects
- Manufacturer product and feature delivery schedules
- Technology standards development and adoption

NOTE   New hardware or software certification by the major service providers takes an average of 24 months. To be ready to offer services to U.S. federal agencies that need their infrastructures to be IPv6 ready by 2008, U.S. service providers had to start the IPv6 certification process by 2006.

When they decided to deploy IPv6 in their networks, the U.S. cable operators had to adjust their project schedules to two timelines: the development of the DOCSIS standard that supports IPv6 and the availability of products that would implement the new standards.

Systems integrators that cater to the federal market and were ready to support IPv6 by 2006 leapfrogged their unprepared competition ahead of the 2008 deadline for the defense and civilian government agencies.

The importance of these timelines should not be underestimated, because they can significantly impact an organization's ability to implement the IPv6 project in time to meet business needs.

Most aspects of today's IT environment relate to IP, so understanding all dependencies is important in defining the pace of the IPv6 integration. Foundational elements should be addressed first to provide an infrastructure that can be leveraged to insert IPv6 anytime a window of opportunity opens in the context of these dependencies. At the same time, longer timelines enable an IPv6 integration project to leverage dependencies to its advantage. The cost of deployment can be significantly reduced if the equipment and software are upgraded to IPv6 through a regular refresh cycle.

Metrics and Milestones

Effective project management requires the ability to objectively measure progress. Use of existing IT management tools can help in many cases. Bechtel defined a clear timeline for all aspects related to the IPv6 integration. Table 6-1 lists the major milestones of IT environment elements that were ready or enabled for IPv6. For example, in 2006, five production LANs and WANs were IPv6-enabled. The target number for 2007 was 100 network segments, and the goal for 2008 is for 95 percent of all network segments to be IPv6 enabled. In 2006, there were 1000 Windows clients enabled for IPv6 (XP or EFT Vista), and by early 2008, over 16,000 (95 percent) of all Windows clients were IPv6-enabled.

During planning, Bechtel, which is a project-oriented company, had to take into consideration the timelines of individual projects. Project managers would consider any significant technology insertion in the middle of a project to be a high risk.

Detailing the timeline for several key aspects of the IPv6 integration project provided Bechtel with the ability to track progress in a realistic manner. Saying that my network is 95 percent ready might not mean too much if the missing 5 percent makes it inoperable.

Table 6-1 *IPv6 Integration Milestones at Bechtel (1Q-2006)*

Milestone	2006	2007	2008
Global IPv6 labs	4	5	5
LAN/WAN	5	100	95%
Windows clients	1000	10,000	95%
Websites	6 internal	25%	95%
Applications: dual-stack	30 major	90%	95%
Mobility	Wireless	Remote access	Always on
Management	Basic	Over IPv4	Over IPv6
Security	Internal only	External IPv6	Borderless projects

You may find deployment pace being constrained, to some degree, by commercial product maturity. This can be at least partially mitigated by working closely with key technology suppliers to determine in which products IPv6 is enabled and to what extent. Consider a focus on ensuring that network, computing, application, and service components are enabled in a sequence that will generate the maximum amount of meaningful end-to-end IPv6 activity. Sometimes an immediate incremental change has advantages over waiting for all IPv6 features to be available in the next version of a product.

Project Plan Development

From this point on, the planning discussion focuses on projects with a larger scope, projects that pursue the integration of IPv6 in an existent infrastructure. The process is in great measure incremental and evolutionary, similar to the experience of adopting the web. The following steps are to be expected:

- Assess the current state.
- Define the future state.
- Perform a gap analysis.
- Develop a strategy to achieve the future state.
- Prioritize activities while considering dependencies.

Assess the IT Environment

After the strategic perspective on IPv6 is established at the business level and the scope of the IPv6 project is defined, the next step is to understand the environment in which the new protocol is integrated. This exploration of your IT environment landscape should take place in the context of the reference architecture described in Figure 6-2. Review the high-level reference models and planned technology initiatives for each layer that will be touched by a change in network protocols. You will find that many aspects of the IPv6 integration can be covered through minor changes in existing standards and processes. Established processes and procedures for technology changes should be used to the extent possible.

The assessment process corresponds to a deep analysis of the "Internet penetration" in your organization. Often, this is seen as an inventory of the network devices to evaluate their readiness to support necessary IPv6 features. In reality, this process is far more complex than that, and the transport infrastructure assessment is sometimes the least complex aspect of it. IPv6 is not a feature; it is an update of the TCP/IP network layer, so any device, service, or application that uses this protocol stack is in the scope of the assessment. All these elements of the IT infrastructure and the policies governing them must be inventoried in order to understand what they need to support IPv6. The IT environment elements can be categorized into three classes:

- **Hosts:** For hosts, the OS must include an IPv6 stack or, more generally a dual stack (IPv4 and IPv6). The hardware configuration for a given host must comply with the OS release requirements.

- **Networking devices:** Devices must support an IPv6 feature set that matches the deployment requirements.

- **Applications:** The inventory of the applications portfolio should deliver a matrix that provides the upgrade options.

The components of each of these three categories are listed in Table 6-2.

Table 6-2 *Classification of IT Environment Elements*

Hosts	Applications	Networking Devices
Computers (mainframe, workstation, desktop, laptop, and so on).	Mandatory services such as DNS server, NTP server, network management, and so on. The IPv6 support is a *must* because these services are crucial elements to any deployment.	Routers (software forwarding and hardware forwarding based platforms).
Mobile devices (PDA, smartphone, UMPC, and so on).	Off-the-shelf applications. These are dependent on the software vendors who have to integrate IPv6 in their roadmap (for example, Microsoft Exchange 12).	Layer 3 switches (hardware forwarding and service line cards).
VoIP devices (IP phone, conference bridge, and so on).	Homemade applications (applications developed internally that would have to be upgraded for future use).	Layer 2 switches (support for device management and other L3-related features such as Multicast Listener Discovery snooping).
Video over IP devices (IP camera, video server, and so on).	New applications. These are the best candidates to deploy over IPv6.	Security appliances (firewall, IDS, VPN concentrator, hardware encryptor).
IP-enabled industrial devices (sensors, readers, and so on).	Old applications (applications that will never be upgraded to IPv6). Similar to what happened when transitioning from X.25, SNA, or DECnet to TCP/IP, there is no need to focus on applications that will get phased out in the future.	Data center networking (storage networking, load balancers, and so on).
		Network management appliances (Network Analyzer Module, testers, probes, and so on).
		Wireless infrastructure devices (Wi-Fi access point, GGSN, Packet Data Serving Node (PDSN), and so on).

The assessment process can be simplified to a certain extent. Automated tools have been developed to determine the capabilities of subsets of elements within the IT environment, such as networking devices.[1] Such tools can provide a quick, high-level inventory. However, for a complete evaluation, today's complex IP equipment typically requires lengthier and more resource-demanding assessment efforts. In a "per-application" or "per-service" integration approach, the assessment process can be simplified by reducing its scope to a subset of IPv6 features and capabilities that are necessary to support well-defined services and applications.

NOTE   Identifying the OS running on a high-end router and Layer 3 switch is sufficient to indicate support for IPv6 control plane features. But to understand its full hardware capabilities for IPv6, an important detail for a deployment, the revision of each line card must also be determined.

Assessment is more than just a software/hardware inventory. It has to also include a review of the design principles and decisions applied to the existent environment. This review identifies the constraints for the IPv6 integration and highlights the opportunities where optimizations can be made based on past experience.

Product Assessment

Bechtel continues to work closely with its technology partners to understand and communicate IPv6 capabilities in ways that can be used throughout the lifecycle of each product and service that is in use or planned. They have found that a platform-based approach is very effective. Table 6-3 is an example of this approach, with platforms listed on the vertical axis and IPv6 capabilities and applications listed on the horizontal axis. Bechtel tracked vendor-reported IPv6-supportable services and devices by indicating "Y" in the IPv6 columns. This is

---

1. "IPv6 Capability Assessment," Cisco Systems data sheet, http://www.cisco.com/web/strategy/docs/gov/IPv6CapabilityAssessment_DS.pdf.

the first indication of areas to be assessed. The platforms are then evaluated to ensure that they have the correct hardware and software versions to support the desired features. Using a mix of vendor-supplied assessment tools and extensions to existing discovery and inventory tools will help complete the base assessment.

Configuration instructions and feature references are links under the "Doc" column. After an organization determines that a platform and feature combination is capable of supporting IPv6, it can use vendor input to document the standard configurations. This is the bridge between what can be done and how to do it.

Table 6-3   *Example of a Feature/Product Support Matrix*

	Desktop XP		Desktop-Vista		Server 2003		Server 2008		Network_IOS	
Hosts	IPv6	Doc	IPv6	Doc	IPv6	Doc	IPv6	Doc	IPv6	Doc
IPv6 address types: Unicast	Y		Y		Y	R[a]	Y	R[a]	Y	C[b]
IPv6: ICMP	N		Y	R[a]	N				Y	C[b]
—	—	—	—	—	—	—	—	—	—	—
SNMP Client			Y	R[a]	Y	R[a]	Y	R[a]	Y	C[b]
DHCP Server					N		Y	C[b]	Y	
SharePoint Server					Y	C[b]	Y	C[b]		

a. R = Reference
b. C = Config

It may not be productive to attempt to configure or deploy IPv6 on products and services for which suppliers have clearly stated there is no IPv6 support. You may find that vendors are not always clear on the extent of IPv6 support in their products.

Actions Based on Product Assessment

The outcome of the assessment should be a matrix that lists the following information:

- **IPv6 requirements for each element:** This information comes from the targeted goal of the deployment.

- **What it takes to make the element IPv6 compliant:** The added capabilities required by each element.

- **How to make each element IPv6 compliant:** Points to the procedures for making the element IPv6 ready. Documenting this information at this time is helpful during the implementation phases of the project.

- **Cost implications for making the element IPv6 compliant:** Vendors or consulting firms can provide the roadmap information for a given product and the processes already validated by others to upgrade at minimum costs.

Operational and Governance Policies

The integration of IPv6 in the IT environment, whether in the near or distant future, has wide-ranging implications. As a foundational technology, its immediate integration benefits might be less apparent to most users. This challenge, combined with the natural challenges related to its integration, can lead to adoption resistance or a tendency to marginalize it.

NOTE	Often, organizations facing calls to integrate IPv6 in their network try at first to achieve the goal by mapping outdated IPv4 designs at minimal costs. Invariably, after a while, the same organizations recognize the opportunity they have to explore new options and new architectures with IPv6 and they adjust their planning efforts accordingly.

It is important to take an organization-wide, complete perspective on the IPv6 project. The commitment to the project must come from all levels of management and must be clearly represented through messaging, assignment of responsibilities, and tracking of progress. Operational and governance policies must be updated or implemented in order to reflect this commitment and to support the execution of the project. It is also important to remember that the integration of this new protocol offers an opportunity to redefine old policies in accordance with the current business realities of the organization and its future goals.

Governance Considerations

Regardless of its implementation pace, IPv6 integration is not a single, isolated, network-centric project. It is an evolution of the IT environment that gives it a strategic dimension. The success of a strategic project depends on supporting guidelines and rules that span the entire organization at all its levels:

- **Senior management visibility and support:** A clear and consistent message of commitment from the senior management is essential to making sure that each group within the organization is prioritizing appropriately the IPv6-related activities.

- **Enforcement:** Adherence to the IPv6 strategy and meeting the project goals should be a measure of the organizational, group, and individual performance.

- **Cross-functional coordination:** All groups within the organization must collaborate in addressing mutual dependencies with respect to IPv6 integration.

- **Communicate frequently at all levels:** Continued communication on the IPv6 adoption topic reinforces the expressed importance placed on the project and enables its progress to be tracked closely.

- **Make IPv6 a natural part of other activities:** Raise awareness about IPv6. Reward IPv6-related achievements and innovation.

Organizational Leadership

Effective governance requires a mix of actively engaged senior leadership, champions, early adopters, and policy enforcers. IPv6 champions must be identified throughout the organization in each of these areas.

NOTE	Bechtel discussed IPv6 internally for a few years before making the transition commitment in late 2004 at the senior management level. At that point, senior managers felt that there were sufficient business drivers and that IPv6 technology and supported products had reached the required level of maturity and global industry adoption. Bechtel's federal global business unit was identified as the organization with the highest immediate need, based in part on the 2003 DoD mandate. Over the following two years, Bechtel has identified additional IPv6 opportunities. Through this process, Bechtel tied the need and pace of IPv6 adoption to its business-related IT strategic planning. The approach is parallel in several ways to the introduction and development of web technologies over the last 13+ years. IPv6 continues to be part of the IT planning process. Senior management buy-in and support, senior IT leadership oversight, and the other critical success factors identified previously made a significant difference in the progress of the IPv6 adoption project.

Enforcing the governance and guidelines is essential with the many interdependencies that characterize the IT environment. Thus, it is important to highlight the role of gatekeepers in ensuring the proper and complete implementation of IPv6-related requirements.

As shown in Figure 6-3, gatekeepers play a significant role in enforcing the implementation of the IPv6 policies in the functional groups (Development and Engineering, Quality Assurance and Configuration Management, Production) by tracking the handover process between these groups.

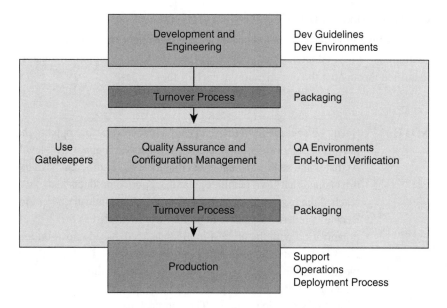

Figure 6-3 *Role of Gatekeepers in the Consistent and Optimal Integration of IPv6*

Well-defined IPv6 entrance and delivery criteria help its organic integration throughout the IT environment.

Policy Considerations

IPv6 adoption requires the implementation of specific policies that facilitate its integration and reduce the deployment costs and the operational risks. At the same time, IPv6 offers an opportunity to revisit existent policies and improve them in the light of past experiences and the future goals of the business.

There are multiple areas of the IT environment in which IPv6-specific policies will be required, and they should be identified during the assessment process. Some of the larger-scope policies that apply to any business are the following:

- **Update purchasing policies:** Regardless of whether the IPv6 deployment is a short-term or long-term project, the best way to reduce the potential cost of integration is to add IPv6 requirements to every purchasing policy in an organization. When IPv6 standardization was in its infancy, it was more difficult to request features that were still evolving. Today, the core IPv6 specifications are stable and a base feature set can be expected from most vendors. The requirements are identified through the design process and are related to concrete IT environment elements through the assessment process. This enables the organization to acquire products with the current IPv6 capabilities through the regular refresh cycle and to request vendors to implement new features as necessary for the envisioned deployment.

Real-Life Case of Updating Purchasing Policies

Let's evaluate a real-life case of updating purchasing policies. At the beginning of 2005, a service provider was running an IP network based on Cisco 12000 series routers equipped with Engine 0, 2, 3, and 4 based line cards. Under pressure from a couple of its customers who requested IPv6 connectivity, the service provider did a network assessment, which clearly identified the need to upgrade all line cards to Engine 5 in order to offer IPv6 services at production level and on a large scale. Eighty line cards were identified for the update. An immediate upgrade (considering an average price of $200,000 per line card) would have cost: $80 \times \$200,000 = \$16$ million.

When tying into the refresh cycle of 3 to 5 years, the service provider evaluated that the upgrade could be done over the next 24 months, making the integration of IPv6 transparent and removing the cost of an immediate upgrade. To meet immediate needs, Engine 3 line cards that support IPv6 in hardware as well were redeployed where required. In conjunction with features such as IPv6 over MPLS—also known as 6PE (RFC 4798) and 6VPE (RFC 4659)—the service provider can deliver the services where and when needed with minimal costs. By mid-2007, the network was fully upgraded and ready to offer IPv6 services to any customer.

- **Update development policies:** IPv6 must become an integral part of all internal development efforts. Even if the IPv6 deployment is not imminent, it is important to institute as early as possible rules requiring internally developed applications to be IP version agnostic. The IPv6 requirements across products must be clearly defined and adherence to them must be enforced.

  The development policies should also encourage the exploration of new implementation approaches that leverage capabilities that are specific to the IPv6 protocol (self configuration) or the IPv6 environment (sufficient addresses to support peer-to-peer computing).

NOTE   From a product development perspective, Cisco defined and maintains an internal IPv6 Architecture Baseline document to which all products must adhere.

- **Update security policies:** Current IT security policies will have to be modified to account for IPv6-related vulnerabilities and the coexistence of the two protocols. The review and update of the security policies must start well in advance of the actual IPv6 deployment. Devices might establish, without the express knowledge of the user, dynamic tunnels for IPv6 traffic and open security holes.

NOTE   The new Microsoft Windows Vista operating system establishes dynamic IPv6 over IPv4 tunnels for certain applications if it does not detect native IPv6 connectivity. At a minimum, organizations must enhance their monitoring capabilities to keep control of this traffic.

- **Redefine entrance and acceptance policies:** Entrance and acceptance criteria for IT environment elements must be updated to include IPv6 requirements as defined by the integration projects. Observing and evaluating product compliancy with IPv6 standards are significant parts of the entrance and acceptance policies. This is especially important in the early phases of product acquisition, because manufacturers might take a more liberal perspective on protocol implementation or might have to deal with non-IPv6-ready designs of their products. A more interesting perspective on this topic is that of reevaluating the existing entrance and acceptance policies and adapting them (IP version agnostic) based on past experience.

NOTE	As part of its IPv6 integration plans, Comcast Corporation restructured and tightened its requirements related to IP product acceptance.

- **Define content availability policies:** Content should be made available over IPv6 and not only over IPv4. All absolute URLs on a corporate website should be banned; only relative URLs that support IP version–agnostic access should be used. Content accessibility can be updated for IPv6 support during periodic content review and maintenance.

The identified policies must be paired with appropriate owners within functional groups and with gatekeepers for the interface between the functional groups. Compliance should be constantly monitored and reported.

Project Execution Policies

Bechtel used governance oversight to change relevant IT policies to make IPv6 "part of doing business." These are some of the policies changed or introduced in the context of the IPv6 adoption project:

- **Stop the bleeding:** Bechtel determined that it was important to stop perpetuating IPv4 dependencies. It installed cost-avoidance changes in purchasing policies and development activities to avoid buying, developing, and deploying technologies that would have to change.

- **Ensure nothing breaks in production:** IPv6 is new territory for most IT people. Bechtel has modified testing procedures, release notices, change management work orders, and related processes to ensure IPv6 compliance and minimize risk of adverse impact with production deployment. Enabling the "gatekeepers" with IPv6 tools and conformance authority is critical to success.

Figure 6-4 presents schematically Bechtel's developed approach to building scalable components that can be broadly deployed to multiple sites. Potential risks are contained in an isolated multisite lab environment until that environment is determined to be stable, secure, and manageable. From there Bechtel uses standard procedures for moving new or modified technology into production. This includes formal turnover from development to QA followed by controlled change management when moving into production. At each state transition point, controls have been inserted to ensure IPv6 compliance. The basic process applies to all hardware, software, and network changes.

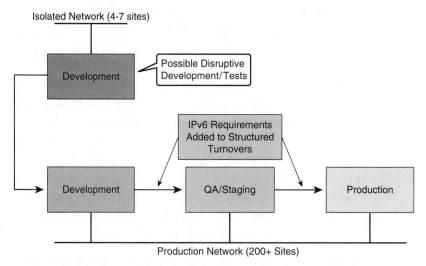

Figure 6-4 *Technology Insertion Process at Bechtel*

- **Use natural change mechanisms when possible:** Bechtel is capitalizing on proven technology change processes for its IPv6 transformation to the extent possible. For example, when upgrading an OS on a computing or network platform, Bechtel will ensure that all IPv6 features are included and enabled as part of the change. The same approach is being used for all software and hardware. The incremental approach has helped Bechtel develop a broad competence and deploy IPv6 in several IP areas in parallel.

- **Actively engage key technology partners:** Bechtel maintains regular active dialogs with key technology product and service providers, partners, customers, and industry consortia. The information and experience sharing has been mutually beneficial.

As the newness wears off, IPv6 becomes an understood and respected technology that is often just another check box on a configuration or test plan.

Initiate and Support Technology Education

The proper planning of the IPv6 integration project, the development and implementation of complete related policies, and the seamless deployment of the technology depend on the staff's familiarity with IPv6. All planning steps presented so far in this chapter cannot be successfully implemented without a good understanding of the various aspects of the technology. The scope of the project cannot be clearly defined without the strategy team understanding the protocol characteristics and its potential. Assessment cannot be effectively performed without understanding the IPv6 features that must be supported by various elements of the environment. Entrance/acceptance and security policies cannot be updated without an understanding of the standardization state of the protocol and its features. The successful deployment of the protocol requires an operations team that is familiar with managing and troubleshooting IPv6. For these reasons, initiating IPv6 training very early and scaling it to match the project evolution is essential to its success.

NOTE   Many businesses that are planning IPv6 integration report that training is one of the most expensive aspects of the project. Initiating the process early allows time for internal dissemination of information. "Train the trainer" strategies can help reduce costs.

Training Domains

The diverse population involved in the various aspects of the IPv6 integration requires diverse forms of targeted training. The right amount and level of education needed for each technical or business function must be delivered in a timely and cost-effective way:

- **IPv6 technology:** The most common form of training available today focuses on describing the protocol operation through a side-by-side comparison with IPv4.

- **IPv6 deployment:** This type of training focuses less on the protocol description and more on its integration in real networks. It has to address the specific interests of each environment: enterprise (branch office, campus, data center) versus service provider (core, broadband, wireless). It also focuses on the operational aspects of IPv6 infrastructures.

- **IPv6 security:** The unique aspects of IPv6 security must be well understood by the IT operations staff well in advance of a deployment. The security policies must be adjusted to deal with the new protocol and its use by various user and device types. New security paradigms might emerge with IPv6.

- **Networking equipment:** These are traditional vendor classes that describe the specifics of equipment configuration and operation.

- **Operating system and applications:** New versions of OSs or applications that include IPv6 require additional training for system managers and software developers.

- **Software development:** This type of training focuses on the IPv6 features that can be leveraged when developing new applications.

- **End users:** Although this type of training is for the most part IP version agnostic, it familiarizes users with new applications that run over IPv6. This training is important in ensuring the smooth adoption of applications and services deployed over IPv6.

Educational and Information Resources

There are multiple sources of information regarding IPv6, each catering to one of the categories mentioned above. Some resources are free to those who are interested in a self-study approach or are just starting to get familiar with IPv6. An example of such a source of information is the European 6DISS project (http://www.6diss.org). 6DISS is a Specific Support Action in the 6th Framework Program of the European Union. The project aims to promote widespread adoption of IPv6 by providing IPv6 training and knowledge transfer in developing regions. 6DEPLOY project (http://www.6deploy.org) is another example. The European-funded project began in March 2008; its purpose is to support the deployment of IPv6 in (i) e-Infrastructure environments, (ii) FP7 projects, (iii) developing countries (Africa, Latin America, Asia, and Eastern Europe), and (iv) industrial environments in Europe. Partners offer basic training to organizations in Europe and developing countries, and support real IPv6 deployments.

Integrators or consulting groups, such as Command Information cited in Chapter 5, often have IPv6 training, consulting practices, and "jump-start" services that can be very valuable in helping an organization achieve a solid level of competence in IPv6.

Vendors are another source of IPv6 training that is both generic and specific to its implementation in their product line.

NOTE   An example training course is Cisco Networkers.[2] At Europe 2008 in Barcelona, Spain, there were several IPv6 sessions, including:

- IPv6 basics

- IPv6 advanced

- IPv6 deployment

- IPv6 security

- IPv6 Birds of a Feather (BoF)

Similar coverage is available in the Networkers sessions that cover the other theaters as well.

Several vendors include IPv6 as a separate part of their certification programs. For example, IPv6 has been included in the Cisco Academy training material and is part of all Cisco certification tests.

Only a limited number of academic institutions developed curriculums with comprehensive coverage of IPv6; hence, we will have to wait several more years for large numbers of new graduates who are IPv6 knowledgeable.

Training Assessment

Everyone does not need the same skill set or training at the same time. Just-in-time training is based on technology being a required skill set, technology being developed/deployed, and location (some sites are first). The simplified matrix example shown in Table 6-4 can be completed with the appropriate training dates for each location. The tiers refer to the level of competence required, from Tier 1 (limited basic education) to Tier 4 (the highest level of technical skill needed). The focus of the assessment should be to enable people for success at the right time.

2. http://www.cisco.com/web/learning/le21/le34/learning_networkers_home.html.

Table 6-4 *Training Matrix Example*

Function	Tier 1	Tier 2	Tier 3	Tier 4
App Development				
Architect				
Help Desk				
Information Security				
Infrastructure Engineer				
Network Engineer				
NOC				
SOC				

IPv6 Address Planning

One critical technical aspect of the IPv6 integration project is that of planning the IPv6 addressing scheme. This process must be initiated well in advance of deployment and cannot be properly executed without extensive training in the following:

- IPv6 address architecture (RFC 4291)

- IPv6 allocation policies defined by each regional registry: AFRINIC (http://www.afrinic.net/policy.htm), APNIC (http://www.apnic.net/policy/index.html), ARIN (http://www.arin.net/policy/nrpm.html#ipv6), LACNIC (http://lacnic.net/en/politicas/ipv6.html), and RIPE (http://www.ripe.net/rs/ipv6/index.html)

- IPv6 address scheme design considerations (http://tools.ietf.org/wg/v6ops/draft-ietf-v6ops-addcon/)

- IPv6 address assignment mechanisms

External input to developing competence in IPv6 addressing is very important, especially in the area of best practices. With this knowledge, the IT staff is able to select and implement the best IPv6 address space and model suited for the organization. The address space can then be acquired and the addressing plan design options can be explored.

Leverage the IPv6 Industry Experience

Most of the IPv6 deployment will occur far after the early IPv6 adopters begin to master the technology. There is no reason for newcomers not to leverage the experiences that have been documented by different organizations. Over 11 years' worth of experience with the next generation Internet Protocol produced a wealth of information that can help others understand the aspects related to IPv6 adoption, such as the protocol idiosyncrasies and deployment impact. Some of the topics that will interest organizations that haven't adopted IPv6 yet include:

- Business and technology news
- Standards compliancy and interoperability information
- Vendor and application references
- Research efforts
- Documented deployments
- IPv6 in other standards

Business and Technology News

The need for IPv6 business cases led to the creation of forums and task forces that are promoting the technology and helping with its understanding. The most active of such organizations are the following:

- **IPv6 Forum (http://www.ipv6forum.com):** The IPv6 Forum is a world-wide consortium of leading Internet vendors, Industry Subject Matter Experts, Research & Education Networks, with a clear mission to advocate IPv6 by dramatically improving technology, market, and deployment user and industry awareness of IPv6, creating a quality and secure new Generation Internet and allowing worldwide equitable access to knowledge and technology, embracing a moral responsibility to the world.

- **IPv6 Task Force (http://www.ipv6tf.org):** Regional and national IPv6 Task Force chapters have been established all over the world. They offer an opportunity for local industries, educational institutions, and government agencies to shape the adoption of IPv6 in their region. Regional task forces and business councils have established their own sites:

  - North American IPv6 Task Force (NAv6TF): http://www.nav6tf.org

  - European IPv6 Task Force: http://www.ipv6tf.org/meet/tf/eutf.php

  - IPv6 Promotion Council (Japan): http://www.v6pc.jp/en/index.html

Several websites are specialized in tracking the latest IPv6 news and information. They help readers learn about vendor announcements and public deployments. Examples of such informative sites are

- **IPv6 Style (http://www.ipv6style.jp/en/index.shtml):** Japanese site that delivers interesting news about the IPv6 adoption in Japan

- **Go6 (http://www.go6.net):** An online meeting point where members of the Internet community share their experiences with IPv6 implementations and applications, and are provided with access to the latest IPv6 tools and information

- **6journal (http://www.6journal.org):** An IPv6 publications database, maintained at the University of Southampton as part of the 6DISS project

Standards Compliancy and Interoperability Information

As with any new protocol suite, the industry needs to define and ensure standards compliancy and full interoperability among products from various vendors. Over the past ten years, it was an objective of several test environments to validate the IPv6 implementations. Official agencies and events also work on testing and publishing reports on the topic. Table 6-5 provides a non-exhaustive list of organizations involved in the IPv6 certification process. Keep in mind that IPv6 is not a feature; it is the network layer of the TCP/IP protocol stack. This means that standards compliancy is only one of the multiple aspects of an implementation. Many features are vendor-specific and are not standardized. For example, a platform might conform to the IPv6 standards, but its performance in handling specific aspects of IPv6 might be poor due to hardware designs that do not have IPv6 in mind.

Table 6-5 *IPv6 Standard Compliancy Testing*

Organization or Program	Website
IPv6 Forum IPv6 Ready Logo	http://www.ipv6ready.org
U.S. DoD Joint Interoperability Test Command (JITC)	http://jitc.fhu.disa.mil/apl/ipv6.html
Moonv6	http://www.moonv6.org/
IPv6 Promotion Council (Japan) Certification WG	http://www.v6pc.jp/en/wg/ certificationWG/index.phtml
Indian Government Telecommunication Engineering Center (TEC)	http://www.tec.gov.in/act-it.html
ETSI Plugtests	http://www.etsi.org/Website/OurServices/ Plugtests/home.aspx

IPv6-specific benchmarking methodologies are still emerging in an attempt to provide consistency in evaluating the IPv6 capabilities of networking devices, appliances, and hosts.[3]

Vendor and Application References

Over the years, most vendors have developed or enhanced their IPv6 implementations and published product information, technology-related white papers, and other documents related to their existent and planned IPv6 support. As examples, refer to

- Cisco: http://www.cisco.com/ipv6
- Linux IPv6: http://www.bieringer.de/linux/IPv6/

3. IETF Benchmarking Methodology WG Status Pages, http://tools.ietf.org/wg/bmwg/draft-ietf-bmwg-ipv6-meth/.

- Microsoft: http://www.microsoft.com/ipv6

- Global Crossing: http://www.globalcrossing.com/ipkc/ipkc_ipv6.aspx

- 3G Americas: http://3gamericas.com/pdfs/2008_Ipv6_transition_3GA_Mar2008.pdf

It is nearly impossible to publish a full list of vendors in a book. This is dynamic information that is best maintained and comprehensively covered on websites that list the vendors along with the IPv6 status of their products. Refer to some of the well-known sites at

- http://www.ipv6-to-standard.org/

- http://6net.iif.hu/ipv6_apps

- http://www.deepspace6.net/docs/ipv6_status_page_apps.html

- http://applications.6pack.org/

Research Efforts

As mentioned repeatedly throughout this book, IPv6 is an opportunity for innovation, because the Internet can now be expanded in market places that were out of reach in the past. These opportunities range from research projects investigating new architectures and services to OS frameworks that give software developers the opportunity to create the next generation of applications. Examples of such research projects follow:

- The European U-2010 (http://www.u2010.org) and U.S. MetroNet6 (http://www.metronet6.org/) projects focus on the use of Internet technologies for public safety.

- The European RUNES (http://www.ist-runes.org) project evaluated embedded Internet applications in a diverse range of appliances, from mobile phones to smoke alarms, from refrigerators to trucks.

- The Globus Toolkit (http://www.globus.org) is an open source software toolkit used for building grids that was enhanced to support IPv6 starting with GT3.

- The Microsoft Windows Peer-to-Peer Networking framework (http://www.microsoft.com/p2p) enables software developers to make their application "peer-to-peer capable."

Documented Deployments

Despite much skepticism, many IPv6 deployments around the world followed the initial definition, prototyping, and implementation of the IPv6 protocol suite. More interestingly, several of these deployments have fully documented their work to be used as references for other deployments. Some of the well-known references follow:

- **6bone (http://go6.net/ipv6-6bone/):** The 6bone was the initial IPv6 infrastructure deployed to test the standard and its implementation. Created in the middle of the 1990s, it ended on June 6, 2006, (RFC 3701) after validating the operational procedures to integrate IPv6.

- **6NET (http://www.6net.org), 6DISS (http://www.6diss.org), and 6Deploy (http://www.6deploy.org):** 6NET, a three-and-a-half-year European project, was run from 2001 to June 30, 2005, by the research and academic community to validate the deployment of native IPv6 networks. Research labs and universities from 16 countries participated in the project, publishing a wealth of material that is widely referenced today by the IPv6 community. The direct result of this project is the IPv6 production services available today to the European research community. Upon completing its mission to disseminate the lessons learned through 6NET, the 6DISS project closed at the end of 2007, delivering countless instructor-led classes and e-Learning materials. 6Deploy, another project sponsored by the European Commission, was launched in March 2008 with the goal of speeding up IPv6 deployment across Europe.

- **Moonv6 (http://www.moonv6.org):** The Moonv6 project is a global effort led by NAv6TF that involves the University of New Hampshire–InterOperability Laboratory (UNH-IOL), Internet2, vendors, service providers, and regional IPv6 Forum Task Force network pilots worldwide. It is taking place across the United States at multiple locations and is a large, permanently deployed, multivendor IPv6 network.

- **Japan IPv6 Promotion Council Transition Working Group (http://www.v6pc.jp/en/wg/transWG/index.phtml:** This Working Group evaluates specific innovative deployment models (scenario, cost, architecture, and so on) and shares the results of its studies with the IPv6 community.

IPv6 deployment and operational experience and expertise continue to grow as the protocol is integrated in more and more large-scale networks. No all-inclusive recipes for IPv6 deployments have emerged, so it is important for IPv6 planners to monitor the IPv6 community resources for new ideas and experiences.

IPv6 in Other Standards

In addition to products and services, IPv6 is being adopted in standards that enterprises are implementing. Table 6-6 lists some of these standards.

Table 6-6   *IPv6 in Other Standards*

Organization	Standard	Website
WiMAX Forum	802.16	http://www.wimaxforum.org
3GPP (3rd Generation Partnership Project)	IMS (IP Multimedia Subsystem)	http://www.3gpp.org/
SNIA (Storage Networking Industry Association)	SMI-S (Storage Management Initiative Specification)	http://www.snia.org
DMTF (Distributed Management Task Force)	CIM (Common Information Model)	http://www.dmtf.org
OASIS (Organization for the Advancement of Structured Information Standards)	Several XML standards	http://www.oasis-open.org

continues

Table 6-6 *IPv6 in Other Standards (Continued)*

Organization	Standard	Website
IEEE	Several standards and specifications	http://www.ieee.org
W3C (World Wide Web Consortium)	URL, URI, and several other specifications	http://www.w3.org
DSL Forum	Several standards and specifications	http://www.dslforum.org
CableLabs	DOCSIS 3.0 and other specifications	http://www.cablelabs.org/

Summary

There are many documents, training modules, and books that present the technical aspects of IPv6 integration and its planning in great detail. Two of the resources we recommend are

- *Deploying IPv6 Networks*, by Ciprian Popoviciu, Eric Levy-Abegnoli, and Patrick Grossetete (Cisco Press, 2006)

- *6NET: An IPv6 Deployment Guide*, edited by Martin Dunmore (Lancaster University, 2005), available at http://www.6net.org/book/deployment-guide.pdf

Because this book is intended for decision makers, not technicians, this chapter focused on the nontechnical aspects of IPv6 planning, which are just as important to the success of a deployment as are the technical aspects. Table 6-7 concludes the chapter with a checklist that will help you start the planning process, organize it, and track it to its completion.

The integration of IPv6 is a multifaceted, strategic project requiring commitment at all levels of an organization. The early, comprehensive planning of the project is essential in the cost-effective delivery of IPv6 capabilities in time to meet the market needs. Regardless of whether the IPv6 deployment is imminent or not yet under consideration, it is never too soon to start planning for it.

Table 6-7 *IPv6 Planning Process Checklist (to be completed by reader)*

Action	Owner	Milestones	Status
IPv6 strategy definition			
Project scope definition			
Stakeholders, gatekeepers, and messaging			
IT environment assessment			
Policy updates			
Purchasing			
Development			
Security			
Entrance/acceptance			
Training			
Deployment planning			

Conclusion

At the start of this project in 2006, the exhaustion date for the global IPv4 address space was hotly debated, with some studies identifying a 2009 date and others a 2035 date or even later. By the time we completed writing the book in early 2008, the two principal estimates converged, and we arrived at an exhaustion time frame of 2010 to 2012. That assumes, of course, that the industry "behaves nicely" and there is no market rush to subscribe the latest pieces of the IPv4 address space. If you are involved in IT communications, you must appreciate the fact that, regardless of the precise exhaustion date, two to three years represents a short time when it comes to planning and rolling out a new networking protocol. The last thing you want is to have to rapidly deploy a costly IPv6 infrastructure to sustain growth and communicate with customers, suppliers, and partners. The worldwide demand for IP is not tied to an Internet Protocol version but rather to applications and services.

So what can we conclude at the end of this book that captures the industry's struggle to deal with the address limitations of IPv4 and with making the decision to engage in the upgrade process? One statement sums it up well: *The IPv6 integration is happening now and no other alternative has been proposed or developed!* We know there are people who flip straight to the conclusions. To those who already work on IPv6, this conclusion makes perfect sense. The ones who still have strong reservations about IPv6 may not resonate with this one-line conclusion. The statement would not change their view. For those who doubt, we want to take here one final, condensed look at IP that considers the evolutionary, adoption, and future perspectives.

Evolutionary Perspective

One of the best perspectives on the evolution of IP and the implications of IPv6 comes from the architect of the next generation of the Internet Protocol. In a brilliant presentation delivered on August 30, 2001, at IETF 51 in London, Dr. Steve Deering made the analogy between the protocol stack and an hourglass, as shown in Figure Conclusion-1.[1]

1. Steve Deering, "Watching the Waist of the Protocol Hourglass," "http://www.ietf.org/proceedings/01aug/slides/plenary-1/index.html.

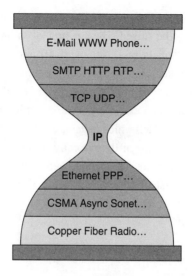

Figure Conclusion-1   *Protocol Stack as an Hourglass*

Deering placed the IP layer at the waist of the hourglass, justifying its "narrowness" by the fact that we needed a simple protocol that could maximize the number of useable networks. New requirements led IP to put on some "weight" as it had to support multicast, QoS, and mobility functions. This trend is likely to continue, leading to more complexities. A life-changing event happened, however, when solutions based on Network Address Translation (NAT) and Application Layer Gateway (ALG) were adopted to alleviate the IPv4 address limitation constraints. These tools broke the hourglass and today we have to deal with the consequences. We lost many Internet features and spent too much energy solving traversal problems.

IPv6 can mend the protocol stack hourglass and shed some of the weight accumulated by IPv4. All of this can be done by the mere increase in the address space. Deering rightfully called the IPv4-IPv6 coexistence period a midlife crisis; this book is a testament to the validity of the analogy. Nevertheless, IPv6 represents an opportunity to streamline the IP layer again and reduce the entropy accumulated over the decades by IPv4.

Not everyone agrees with this vision. Some believe a mere evolution of IP implemented through larger addresses and a few small tweaks is not sufficient to heal the Internet. Routing, ubiquitous mobility, and scalable DNS are just a few of the problems that have to be solved. The position taken on solving the Internet's problems vary from a "tabula rasa" (blank slate) approach, led by the GENI project (http://www.geni.net/), to attempts to solve some of the problems at upper layers. Stream Control Transmission Protocol (SCTP) and Peer Naming Resolution Protocol (PNRP) are such examples of the evolution of layers above the IP network layer. Only time will tell which path we end up on, but the success of IPv4 might have delayed our pursuit of dramatically different solutions to the point where such solutions might not be available before the exhaustion of the IPv4 address space. So, at the time of this writing, Deering's wineglass (resembling the hourglass with the thin, long IPv6 waist) seems to be our best bet. So you might as well enjoy it: Cheers!

Adoption Perspective

Enabling IPv6 in the environment is not the end game. However, it is a critical requirement for many network-based products and services of the Internet going forward.

Regardless of how good the wine, the company of people will always enhance its enjoyment. So do we have an IPv6 party yet? We shared with you through market overviews and through concrete examples how IPv6 adoption is starting to gather steam. At the time of this writing, the mixture of clear business cases, environmental pressures, and resource exhaustion has not pushed the industry to the adoption tipping point but we are close to it. Several events are likely to precipitate the process:

- **IPv4 Internet address depletion:** IPv4 address exhaustion will be a strong incentive for IPv6 adoption where IPv4 addresses are most limited and there is rapid growth in Internet usage for large populations. However, the industry may also have to handle multiple NAT layers as workaround in some regions or market segments.

- **Operating systems and applications:** Increasing support for IPv6 in operating systems and new applications will drive adoption both for consumers and enterprises. A particular example is that of Microsoft

Vista and Microsoft Server 2008, which have IPv6 "on" and "preferred" by default, introducing new capabilities such as the Layer 3 clustering and a Peer-to-Peer framework. In addition, applications such as Meeting Space, Remote Assistance, EchoMyPlace, and others, designed to only run over IPv6, may represent a major catalyst for adoption.

- **Government mandates and national IT strategies:** Government mandates and national IT strategies worldwide will stimulate adoption at the national level. Their implementation, as in the case of the United States, Japan, China, Korea, and the European Union, will jump-start the adoption of IPv6, and in many cases they already have helped to highlight the need for an IPv6 strategy.

- **New standards that leverage IPv6:** The deployment of new standards that support and leverage IPv6 leads to networking environments primed for IPv6 deployment. For example, the adoption of DOCSIS 3.0 and 3G IP Multimedia Subsystem (IMS) architectures will bring along IPv6 in the cable and mobile environments.

- **Financial opportunities:** IPv6 will be used by many organizations to generate new revenue streams or reduce costs by exploiting the new protocol in innovative ways. Natural economic competition will drive broader adoption. Consumers are starting to see IPTV, cellular, gaming, and broadband access products and services based on IPv6. Mobility enhancements are being leveraged for commercial and consumer customers. Industrial control systems are adopting IPv6. Enterprises are discovering new efficiencies in their daily operations, including those required to run the business as well as areas supporting more efficient revenue generation.

- **IPv6 product maturity:** Stable standards will help mature the products necessary to deploy IPv6. Product and service suppliers will select the timing to introduce new IPv6 features based on various factors, including perceived demand and natural product life cycles. Product maturity will support an accelerated pace of IPv6 adoption in many organizations and industries.

These four major catalysts are likely to bring the IPv6 adoption to the tipping point sometime in 2008. There are, however, much bigger forces that drive the adoption. The IP challenges must not be looked at in isolation; they have repercussions throughout the protocol stack. The continued evolution of the data link layer protocols and their adoption is highly dependent on IP's ability to deliver services to their users. At the same time, new IP services such as those requiring symmetrical bandwidth at the access layer continue to stimulate the development of the Layer 2 technologies. The application layer is seeing an explosion in the number of new types of applications, such as collaboration, Web 2.0/3.0, peer-to-peer, and quad play services with migration from analog TV to digital TV to HDTV. These applications demand more from the IP infrastructure, and their evolution and growth depends on the flexibility of IP and the availability of IP resources. All the innovation happening at the layers above and below IP represents a major driver for IPv6 adoption.

Whether publicized, overpublicized, or not mentioned at all in the press, IPv6 planning and deployment activities are in progress throughout the world. In 2007, there were already service providers that individually claimed over 2,000,000 IPv6 subscribers.

Futuristic Perspective

From the start, our goal was to provide a balanced view about the value of IPv6, in spite of our passion for the subject of IPv6 adoption. The market analysis stayed focused on the opportunities that have been implemented and, as the case studies show, the stage was offered to both early adopters and to those who expect several more years to pass before they will deploy IPv6. It is, however, tempting to try to look further into the future, so we will take this last opportunity to do so.

In his 1957 book *The Naked Sun*, Isaac Asimov speculated that in a distant future people would not meet in person anymore but would instead communicate via "holographic telepresence." The Internet Protocol helped partially materialize that prediction three millennia earlier here on Earth instead of on Asimov's planet of Solaria, by supporting the telepresence applications that give video communication a "human feel." This is just the beginning, because, despite being the narrow portion of Deering's hourglass, IP will continue to support a rich, fast-paced, and innovative environment for implementing new services and applications.

This is particularly the case in an environment free of NAT. How many more of the applications used in Asimov's futuristic cities became or will become reality because of IP? In a not distant future, our environment and our health will be monitored through networked sensors and our vehicles will be true networks in motion. Web 2.0 will take the Internet past the threshold of a massively adopted technology worldwide. The communication among all devices will take place over converged IP networks that will facilitate virtualization of resources and devices. And for all these things to happen at the envisioned scale, here on Earth or over there on Solaria, we need more IP addresses. We need IPv6.

There are many problems that need to be resolved in order to scale up and to increase the capabilities of an all-IP world. For now, the most-pressing, most-limiting factor is the lack of IPv4 address resources, and the solution is available with IPv6. With plenty of addresses available to sustain the growth of the IP world, the engineers can start to focus on solving the other technical challenges such as routing, QoS, and security. This is a natural process for any protocol that is still alive and still evolving. At the same time, sociologists can and should start to focus on making sure that all these advancements in communications and applications do not push us too close to the habits of Asimov's Solarian society.

Index

Numerics

A

D

Q

U